Passionate Views

Passionate Views

FILM, COGNITION, AND EMOTION

EDITED BY

Carl Plantinga and Greg M. Smith

THE JOHNS HOPKINS UNIVERSITY PRESS   BALTIMORE & LONDON

© 1999 The Johns Hopkins University Press
All rights reserved. Published 1999
Printed in the United States of America on acid-free paper
9 8 7 6 5 4 3 2 1

The Johns Hopkins University Press
2715 North Charles Street
Baltimore, Maryland 21218-4363
www.press.jhu.edu

Library of Congress Cataloging-in-Publication Data will be found at the end of
this book.
A catalog record for this book is available from the British Library.

ISBN 0-8018-6010-5
ISBN 0-8018-6011-3 (pbk.)

CONTENTS

Passionate Views

Introduction

CARL PLANTINGA AND GREG M. SMITH

In the emotional landscape of the modern world, the movie theater occupies a central place, as one of the predominant spaces where societies gather to express and experience feelings. The cinema offers complex and varied experiences; for most people, however, it is a place to feel something. The dependability of movies to provide emotional experiences for diverse audiences lies at the center of the medium's appeal and power, yet the nature of these filmic emotions is one of the least-explored topics in film studies. Emotions are carefully packaged and sold, but they are rarely analyzed with much specificity.

This anthology is devoted to discussing some of the ways films cue emotional responses, and these discussions are from an explicitly cognitive perspective. On first impression, a cognitive approach seems an unlikely choice to provide insight into emotional processes. After all, its theories deal with cognitions, and thinking is clearly separated from feeling according to the Cartesian coordinates that govern much of Western debate. An emotional state can potentially interfere with rational thought; therefore emotion has often been seen as the enemy of thinking. From the 1950s to the 1980s, it would seem easy for scholars studying the processes of thought to dismiss such irrational phenomena.

Many academic fields once neglected the emotions. Cultural anthropologists using traditional methods of observation had difficulty reporting such highly "subjective" states of mind in other cultures. Instead they focused on more externally observable differences, such as those in language and ritual performances. The agenda of sociology led academics to areas in which socialization was most clearly at work. These thinkers recognized that emotions were manipulated by society, and so they tended to view emotions in a purely instrumental fashion, as a means of socialization. Socializing processes relied upon fear or love to create prejudice or empathy, but few sociologists examined the basic nature of these emotions. Emotions existed as bodily states that could be "managed" socially, but the social nature of their origins remained virtually unexplored. In psychology, the influence of behaviorism led theorists away from such subjective states within the "black box" of the human mind. Similarly, the emphasis on reason within the philosophy of mind kept many philosophers away from such "messy" states as emotions.

At first, cognitive research also ignored emotion. When cognitive psychology emerged, it emphasized human functions that could be modeled after the logical linear processing of a computer. Subjective states such as the emotions were not on the early research agenda for cognitive research, since they were thought to be too unpredictable to be modeled using classical logic. It was conceivable to think of computers as being able to model memory, but it was more difficult to conceptualize a computer-based model of emotions. When modern cognitive theory emerged with the development of the computer, it considered the emotions to be a source of interference.

More recently, however, cognitive researchers are discovering the inadequacies of a strong Cartesian division between the mind and the body. As neurophysiological research becomes increasingly more sophisticated, the mind and the brain become more closely linked. Also, researchers are discovering the complex interrelationship between bodily states (such as stress and mood) and thought processes. As the study of cognition begins to consider more and more bodily processes, it no longer seems strange to discuss emotions from a cognitive perspective.

A key assumption for the authors in this volume is that emotions and cognition are not necessarily enemies. A cognitive understanding of emotions asserts exactly the opposite: that emotions and cognitions tend to work together. Putting Western prejudices against the messy emotions aside, cognitivists emphasize the way that emotions and cognitions cooperate to orient us in our environment and to make certain objects more salient. Emotions help us to evaluate our world and react to it more quickly. Fear or love provides a motive force that more often than not works in tandem with thought processes.

The cognitive perspective, therefore, tends to depict emotions not as formless, chaotic feelings but as structured states. The assumption that emotions are structured is another key one for cognitivists. Cognitivists tend to describe emotion as a combination of feelings, physiological changes, and cognitions. Emotions direct both mind and body toward an object and tend to provoke action toward that object. Love drives me toward the loved one, fear moves me away from the fearful object. Understanding how we conceptualize an object goes a long way toward understanding how we feel about that object. Cognitive scholars emphasize how certain salient characteristics in an object lead us toward certain emotions. When we cognitively evaluate objects to determine their significance for us, we assign characteristics to them, and this evaluation leads us toward particular emotions. What characteristics of monsters make us respond with fear and disgust? What qualities are most salient in a comic situation, and why do these qualities encourage us to laugh? A cognitive understanding of the emotions helps us to pay close attention to the stimuli that evoke an emotional response.

Cognitive scholars tend to discuss emotion states in terms of goals, objects, characteristics, behaviors, judgments, and motivations. Necessarily this means that these scholars tend to break down emotions into component processes, and this process of dissection is central to a cognitive perspective on emotion. Emotions are commonly conceptualized as gestalts; I can feel them, but these feelings cannot be dissected without doing violence to the emotional experience, according to such common usage. But the cognitive perspective believes that there is much insight to be gained by breaking down processes into subprocesses. Even processes as seemingly simple as visually recognizing an object can be usefully understood as a series of component processes. A cognitive scholar believes that complex processes can be modeled. Although such scholars understand that not all processes can be modeled using the rational logic of a computer, we still share a faith in using conceptual models to dissect complex processing. The authors in this volume posit explicit models for how we process films and experience emotions, and we believe that such specific attention to film emotion gives a richer and more detailed understanding of audiences' emotions in the theater.

With this emphasis on modeling and subprocesses comes an added benefit of a cognitive approach: its specificity. Cognitive scholars tend to examine phenomena in quite precise detail. We believe that this specificity will help give a clearer understanding of the emotional process of watching a film. Instead of dealing with broad emotional concepts such as pleasure, the authors in this volume tend to discuss particular kinds of emotion cuing. These authors tend toward examining specific emotion phenomena such as sentimentality or comedy. They examine narrational and stylistic devices designed to elicit emotion, such as film music and facial expression. Some authors in this volume do articulate broad frameworks for explaining, say, the way narrative films are constructed to cue emotions. However, they do so by specifying distinct subprocesses that interact to shape more global experiences. A cognitive approach, whether describing a global system or a specific phenomenon, never strays very far from specific attention to subprocesses.

In summary, a cognitive perspective on emotions asserts that cognitions and emotions work together. Instead of conceptualizing emotions as formless, a cognitive scholar emphasizes the structure of emotions. They are processes that may be broken down into component processes, thus revealing their underlying structures. These structures might include scripts or a set of distinguishing characteristics or descriptions of typical goals and behaviors. This close analysis, we believe, will be invaluable in gaining a more precise understanding of how films cue emotions.

Finally, a cognitive perspective is an interdisciplinary one. Cognitivism is not a field or a discipline; it is a set of assumptions held by researchers across several fields and disciplines. Linguistics, artificial intelligence, anthropology, neurology, psychology, and philosophy all contribute insights from their particular fields toward cognitive research, and the perspective encourages such cross-fertilization. It is in the spirit of this interdisciplinary work that this volume exists. The work in this volume is rooted primarily in two of the dominant areas in cognitive study: cognitive philosophy and psychology.

Emotion and the Arts in Philosophy

Throughout the long history of Western aesthetics, the arts have been consistently linked with the expression or elicitation of emotion. Such a linkage dates back at least to Plato, who thought that the emotions elicited by the arts could weaken or mislead the young citizens of his republic, and to Aristotle, who described tragedy as arousing beneficial and pleasurable emotions. Philosophers of art have long been concerned with the functions of the emotions in the arts. In literature, theorists and philosophers have attempted to understand the means by which certain genres elicit specific emotional responses. Aristotle claims that tragedy arouses pity and fear, clarifying and purifying those reactions in such a way that it brings us pleasure and understanding. While Aristotle's work on tragedy is most famous, philosophers have also explored the emotions associated with other genres of literature (e.g., the sublime, humor) and the other arts.

Although it has long been recognized that the emotions have a central function in the experience of arts and artists, evaluation of the purposes and importance of the emotions has been a controversial activity. During the Romantic period, the enjoyment of feeling and emotion was promoted as the chief pleasure of art. Romanticism brought a more intense awareness of the felt qualities of the hearing or viewing experience. In fact, one prominent way to define art, often allied with Romanticism, has been to find its essence in the expression or embodiment of feeling; such theories were held by prominent thinkers, for example, Leo Tolstoy, R. G. Collingwood, Benedetto Croce, Susanne Langer, and John Dewey. For expression theorists (broadly speaking), the purpose of art is to express emotions, and especially those emotions that through their nobility, novelty, suggestiveness, and/or intensity had something to teach us.

The New Critics were some of the most vehement in denouncing the Romantic attachment to feeling. Prominent New Critics W. K. Wimsatt and

Monroe Beardsley tell a story to support an opposing position on the place of emotion in art. The German novelist Thomas Mann and a friend emerged from a movie theater "weeping copiously." Mann recounted this (probably apocryphal) incident to support his view that, whatever they are, movies are not art, since art is "a cold sphere."[1] For one thing, the Romantics decreased the value of the objective work of art by emphasizing the emotions of both artist and spectator. The New Critics sought to direct attention from the emotions of the artist and the reader back onto the text itself, and onto the tradition out of which it emerges. T. S. Eliot sounds something like a cognitivist when he claims that we express emotion in art "by finding an 'objective correlative'; in other words, a set of objects, a situation, a chain of events, which shall be the formula of that *particular* emotion."[2] However, Eliot made this intriguing observation not to suggest a means to study the emotions elicited by literature but to dissolve such emotions into the study of meaning, structure, and style. Since emotions have reasons, or in more modern parlance, "objects" or "causes" embodied in the text, why not focus on *these* rather than on the subjectivity of the viewer or artist? As Eliot says, "Poetry is not a turning loose of emotion, but an escape from emotion."[3]

In aesthetics, another topic of debate revolved around the "aesthetic attitude," the stance or perspective necessary to attend to the aesthetic qualities of objects. Such a stance, it was sometimes said, requires a psychical or emotional distance that blocks impulses to action and "practical" thoughts. The concept of aesthetic distance, with its implication that art occupies a realm hermetically sealed from "real life," has been controversial.[4]

Another strand of thought attempted to identify an "aesthetic emotion," that is, an emotion or emotional experience qualitatively different from those of everyday life and peculiar to the contemplation of great works of art. Such theories stemmed from the "art for art's sake movement" and thus attempted to locate aesthetic experience outside the realm of the practical world. As Clive Bell claims, one who contemplates a work of art inhabits "a world with an intense and peculiar significance of its own; that significance is unrelated to the significance of life." "In this world," Bell goes on, "the emotions of life find no place."[5] However, aesthetic emotion theorists failed to satisfactorily identify either the causes or the nature of such aesthetic emotions. For Bell, it was almost a case of "you'll know it when you see it." Bell claimed that these profound emotions resulted from the contemplation of "significant form" (significant because it elicits aesthetic emotion) and that the aesthetic emotion was difficult to describe, but once experienced it would never be forgotten and could never be confused with the "warm tilth and quaint nooks of romance."[6]

The more contemporary cognitive approach, characteristic of all of the essays in this volume, begins with the opposite assumption, that the emotions that fiction films (and other fictional texts) elicit have their roots in the same kinds of processes that generate real-world emotions. Emotions consist of (at least) physiological changes, feelings, and thinking. The cognitive philosopher emphasizes the thinking part of an emotion, with thinking consisting of the emoter's evaluation or judgment about the object of the emotion. We should not let the concreteness of the term "object" mislead us. Cognitive philosophers of emotion hold that an object of an emotion need not be physical. It can be a false belief, or it can be something with regard to oneself. Most cognitive philosophers agree, however, that whatever form it takes, an emotion always has a particular object—a thing, person, animal, the content of one's own beliefs or imaginings, and so on—that is the focus or target of an emotional state.[7]

The most recent developments in philosophical thought about emotions in fiction arise directly from this cognitive perspective. One preoccupation of late has been with the nature and possibility of our emotional responses to fictional characters and events. Colin Radford originally raised the issue with his claim that emotional responses to fiction are irrational and incoherent. His argument is as follows. Having an emotion depends on our having a belief of a certain sort. I believe that the rabid dog chasing me is trying to bite me, so I experience fear. When we read or view fictions, Radford assumes, we do not believe that either the fictional characters or situations exist. Thus we either do not have the requisite beliefs, and thus have no emotions, or we experience irrational beliefs (believing that what we see is real) and thus irrational emotions.[8] This issue has attracted significant attention, and various solutions to this seeming paradox have been offered. Among them is the claim that we can respond emotionally to mere unasserted thoughts such as imaginations.[9] Alternatively, Kendall Walton makes the argument that emotions at the movie theater are quasi-emotions, and that when Charles feels fear when he sees the green slime, he could not have been actually terrified. He felt something, but it was not actual fear.[10]

One promising development has been the interest in mental simulation as it relates to our experience of fictions. Philosopher Gregory Currie's formulation of the "Simulation Hypothesis" is particularly useful for our purposes because it is developed within an overall psychology of film viewing. Currie says that our basic access to the minds of others comes from a form of imagination we may call mental simulation. When we see someone in a situation and attend to what is occurring, we take on the beliefs and desires we imagine they must have. Unlike our own beliefs and desires, however, these are run "off-line." As Currie writes, they are "disconnected from their normal perceptual inputs and behavioural outputs."[11]

When we experience fictions, then, we engage in a similar process. We have imaginings that simulate belief, and our mental processes are engaged "off-line." Yet such simulations retain belief-like connections to other mental states and to the body, in part accounting for the emotional power of movies despite our knowledge that they represent fictional characters and situations. This can also account for the benefits of fiction; fictions allow us to exercise our capacities for mental simulation, and thus have adaptive significance. Currie also suggests the possible destructive and moral dangers of mental simulation in film viewing, a warning that he develops more fully in his essay in this volume.

The interest in the arousal or expression of emotion in film and the other arts has recently attracted growing attention in the field of philosophy. In part this resurgence of interest can be attributed to the cognitive theory of emotion, an approach that offers intriguing new ways to think about age-old problems.

The Psychology of Emotion

Unlike the philosophers surveyed above, psychologists do not have a long tradition of examining aesthetic experience. Questions about the aesthetic experience are less central to psychology than they are to philosophy. A few psychologists have attempted a comprehensive discussion of the arts,[12] although researchers in related subfields (such as musicology) explore their specialties using the empirical methodologies that dominate psychology. Psychologists are concerned with the mechanisms important in aesthetic experience, such as empathy, identification, visual recognition, and the emotions. However, they tend to emphasize these mechanisms either as self-contained processes within the human being or as interactions with other humans, instead of emphasizing interactions with fictional film characters. If one believes that there are continuities between the real-world experiences studied by psychologists and the spectatorial experiences examined by film scholars, this body of empirical evidence can provide rich insight. The cognitive approach stresses the continuities between typical emotions and those experienced in relation to fictions, and this makes available the broad range of psychological research concerning how emotions function.

Psychologists studying the emotions tend toward one of four broad theoretical emphases in their researches. The oldest approach is to emphasize how important the peripheral nervous system (the nerves connected to the muscles and the visceral organs, such as the heart, lungs, and stomach) is to emotions. This research agenda began with William James, who believed that emotion is the perception of bodily changes. James argued that although the bodily expression of emotion seems to be caused by a mental state (we cry because we are sad), this causal sequence is actually reversed. We are sad, according to James, because we cry.[13]

Peripheral theorists, following James, emphasize the feedback that we get from various peripheral systems. In particular, many of these theorists have recognized the unique contribution played by the face. "Facial feedback" theorists, noting the high concentration of nerves in the face and the importance of the face in emotional displays, argue that the information provided by the face is particularly important in determining emotional experience. Elaborating on the folk wisdom that smiling will make you feel happier, these theorists believe that information from facial muscles and nerves can either determine emotions, distinguish among various emotions, or modify an emotional state.[14]

Not long after James proposed his theory emphasizing the importance of the periphery to emotion, another psychologist proposed an alternative: that the emotions are based in the central nervous system. Walter Cannon challenged what came to be known as the James-Lange theory, stating that the seat of the emotions was in the thalamic region of the brain. Cannon noted that the emotions underwent much more rapid changes than did the viscera (the periphery). Emotions can change more quickly than heart rates or breathing patterns, and so the peripheral areas such as the heart and the lungs could not be responsible (as James hypothesized) for the emotions.[15] Cannon's attention to the central nervous system has been elaborated by several researchers who take advantage of neuropsychology's increasingly sophisticated understanding of the brain's chemistry.[16]

A third psychological approach emerged as a theoretical outgrowth of Magda Arnold's appraisal theory and an experimental outgrowth of Stanley Schachter's and Jerome Singer's 1962 study.[17] Schachter and Singer gave subjects an injection of adrenaline, telling them that they were involved in an experiment on the effects of vitamin supplements on vision. The injections caused the subjects to have bodily arousal that they could not explain, and the subjects labeled their feeling states according to the emotional cues provided by their environment. This experiment reinserted the importance of cognitive appraisal of the situation into the psychological study of emotion, and a large body of work followed. Such appraisal theorists have produced elaborate models of how we process situational cues and respond emotionally based on our assessment of these situations. Arnold examined how we appraise our situation and determine if objects may harm or benefit us, and this appraisal urges us to approach or avoid these objects. Richard Lazarus's understanding of emotional appraisal asserts that cognition is both necessary and sufficient for emotion. Cognitions that he calls "core relational themes" help distinguish emotions from each other. Anger, for instance, is a matter of believing that a "demeaning offense"[18] has been committed against you or those close to you. Nico Frijda posits a series of "laws" which govern the appraisal of stimuli and which produce action-oriented responses.[19] For a cognitive appraisal theorist, emotion depends on how people characterize objects and how they assess their relationships with those objects.

A fourth psychological perspective accentuates the social nature of the emotions. Social constructivists assert that cultural forces are not merely overlaid onto more essential biological foundations of the emotions, as a modifier might inflect a noun. Instead, they argue that emotions cannot be understood outside of culture and the shaping forces of society. The rules of emotion are learned through socialization, which guides us toward a preferred set of responses. Emotions serve social functions; they help us occupy roles within society overall. For Averill emotions *are* a special kind of role we inhabit briefly. We are socialized to know what the experience of sadness is like and when we should inhabit this "role."[20] Emotional experience cannot be examined independently of the way a society constructs the emotion. This emphasis on social construction helps this perspective privilege cultural differences in emotion.[21] Language has an important socializing function in shaping how we conceptualize our experiences, and social constructivists study the way language parses our world into different configurations. Social constructivism reverses the individualistic emphasis of the other three perspectives and situates the emotions within a broader context.

Although certain psychologists have created integrative approaches which attempt to synthesize a range of perspectives,[22] most research occurs within one of these perspectives: the peripheral (Jamesian) theories, the central neurophysiological theories, the cognitive appraisal theories, and the social constructivist theories. In addition to choosing a theoretical perspective, most researchers must choose what portion of the emotional spectrum they will study.

Psychologists choose an object of study from the spectrum of emotion phenomena. Most emotion research emphasizes either emotion experience or emotion expression. Emotion experience is the subjective-feeling state consciously perceived by the individual, which is often studied using self-report measures. Researchers concerned with more complex levels of cognition tend to emphasize this facet of emotion. A social constructivist, for instance, tends to study emotion experience and the cognitions required to guide that experience. For those who study emotion experience, there can be no emotion without conscious awareness of the subjective state. By their definition consciousness is necessary for emotion experience, and so emotional experience is always subjective. Using more complex processing, emotion experience involves an object of the emotion, a cognitive appraisal of that object, and a desired goal.

Those concerned with less complex structures emphasize emotion expression, the physiological or behavioral response to an emotion stimulus.

Emotion-expression researchers concerned with responses from the autonomic or central nervous systems need not be concerned with conscious processing. They can examine emotion by studying these physiological responses, and so for them the issue of conscious experience is not crucial for their understanding of emotion. In such research, emotion states need not have objects, cognitive appraisals, or goal concepts.

Choosing one object of study over another necessarily lends certain advantages and disadvantages to research. Researchers studying emotion experience find it difficult to study emotion in subjects who cannot communicate verbally (animals and infants, for instance). Researchers studying emotion expression may be unable to study the "subtler" emotions whose physical expressions may not be so clear without consulting conscious thought processes. However, most ordinary emotions involve both expression and experience, and so both kinds of research have value.

The breadth of this work in psychology, in conjunction with the philosophical inquiries discussed earlier, provides a rich source of insight for the study of film. This breadth is not purchased at the price of specificity, however. Psychologists and philosophers have labored long to make their understandings of emotion precise and clear. We believe that these advantages provide a much sounder foundation for studying filmic emotion than the current leading model within film studies.

Film Studies and Psychoanalysis

By following the perspectives provided by cognitive psychology and philosophy, we differentiate our approach from the dominant understanding of cinematic affect in film studies. Like most academic pursuits, film studies has tended to avoid direct contemplation of the potentially messy concept of the emotions. Contemporary film theory of the 1970s concentrated on issues of meaning and representation and their ideological implications. When contemporary film studies did examine the affective experiences of spectators, it tended to frame its discussion in terms of "pleasure" or "desire." What pleasure does the cinema afford, and what desire motivates our viewing? Beginning with Christian Metz and Laura Mulvey,[23] film studies has asserted that cinematic pleasure and desire can best be explained by a Freudian/Lacanian psychoanalytic approach.

Linking Althusserian theories of ideology with theories of Freudian/Lacanian subject formation, Metz foregrounded identification as the principal emotive effect of film. Identifying with the camera positions viewers as cohesive subjects, reminding us of our earliest experiences of wholeness. Luring spectators with the pleasure of visual mastery over a world, mainstream films ask us temporarily to reconstitute our identities by taking up the cohesive all-seeing position offered to us.

This is not the only pleasure that the cinema yields, Metz argued. Film also gives us the possibility of secondary identifications with onscreen characters. Mulvey emphasized the way that these two identifications frequently coincide to give subject positioning in the Hollywood cinema a particular ideological force. Mulvey noted that the two "looks" of the cinema (the camera's and the character's) frequently join forces to ally us with certain characters, paralleling our desires with theirs. According to Mulvey, one cannot isolate the narrative structures of classical cinema from their history of ideological usage, making the desire for Hollywood pleasures complicit in structures of domination.

An enormous body of film feminism has emerged from the Freudian/Lacanian tradition pioneered by Metz and Mulvey. Feminist film theory has pursued questions of how men and women might desire differently, how the film apparatus structures those desires, and if spectators might possibly gain pleasure without reiterating the structures of patriarchy.[24] In all this discussion of pleasure and desire, however, there is a conspicuous absence of the word *emotion*. Psychoanalytic scholarship rarely talks about the particulars of filmic emotion, and instead concentrates on articulating the filmic mechanisms of subject positioning and on labeling the mechanisms of desire. Psychoanalytic film theory, with its joint emphasis on identification and ideology, has tended to discuss the politics of identity in much more detail than it does the nuances of a film's emotional appeal.

The distinctions among pleasure, desire, and emotion are not purely terminological. The choice of pleasure and desire over emotion is symptomatic (to use a Freudian term) of a larger theoretical neglect of the emotions. E. Ann Kaplan recognizes that psychoanalytic film theory's reticence about emotion has deep roots: "It was largely our anti-realism theory that made it difficult to use the word 'emotional' in recent feminist film theory: we have been comfortable with the 'cool,' theoretical sound of 'desire.' . . . We were led to advocate a cerebral, non-emotional kind of text and corresponding spectator response."[25] While discussing "desire" and "pleasure," psychoanalytic film theory could appear to be dealing with questions of emotion without having to pay closer attention to the specifics of emotional experience.

The concepts of pleasure, displeasure, and desire used in film studies are too broad to provide specific insight into how a particular film makes its emotional appeal at any given moment. If the range of emotion in the film theater is reduced to some point on the continuum between pleasure and displeasure, we lose the flavor of individual texts. Similarly, if we claim that all mainstream film viewing emerges from the same scenario of desire, we ignore the diverse motivations driving the spectator's interest and emotion. The ambiguity and spaciousness of these concepts, as currently used, compromise their usefulness. A significant difficulty with psychoanalytic concepts of desire and pleasure is that they do not encourage close attention to the means by which individual films elicit emotion.

Recent psychoanalytic theory has attempted revisions to correct its reductive, overly broad approach. It has posited various positions of desire, rather than the former one or two positions. It has also articulated contradictory pleasures in an effort to make discussions of emotion more nuanced and specific.[26] Current psychoanalytic theory situates spectator desire within history as an interaction between the social and cinematic structures of the day.[27] One could argue that the best of recent psychoanalytic theory is attempting to elaborate and enumerate pleasures instead of "pleasure," desires instead of "desire."

However, when psychoanalytic film theory inherited these concepts from Freud, it also inherited many of Freud's assumptions about emotions, and these assumptions contribute to the continued lack of specific attention to the emotions. Although film scholars have treated Freud as a primary source of insight into emotional experience, psychologists generally agree that Freud's writings do not contain a well-developed theory of the emotions. Freud provides a comprehensive theory of the instincts and sexuality, but there is no correspondingly rigorous body of Freudian theory dealing with emotion,[28] creating an absence that Jerome Wakefield calls the "Achilles' heel of theoretical psychoanalysis."[29]

For Freud the emotions are a discharge phenomenon. In his economy of psychic energy, emotional actions and expressions were ways to release and dissipate this energy. Psychic dysfunction occurred when Victorian morality encouraged an unhealthy restriction of emotional expression, thus bottling up the emotions. If the emotions were improperly discharged, they could cause physical symptoms and affective disorders.

For Freud, the foundation of human behavior is the instincts, particularly the sexual instincts. These instincts provide the energy that drives his psychic economy. Libido (sexual energy) is the motive force behind dreams, creative expression, and attachments to other people. Though he nuances his description of the instincts across his career (for instance, the conception of "life" and "death" instincts that emerges in his later work), throughout his writings Freud consistently maintains the centrality of the instincts as prime movers. His work can be seen as a longstanding defense of the importance of sexuality and the instincts as the key factors explaining human behavior.

With the instincts and sexuality at the core of the psyche, Freud finds little room for the emotions as another foundational concept, and so emotions become less central to his research agenda. They become symptoms of the more basic factors, which are the more important object of study. Wakefield argues that in the Freudian system, "affects do not seem in the end to be very important in themselves; they are only of interest as a side-effect of instinctual processes."[30] This orientation in his practice led Freud to confine himself to reporting the emotional details of the clinical data, neglecting them in his theories in favor of "deeper" explanations.

The difficulty of a theory of cinematic emotions based on instincts and drives is that it tells the same story over and over again, regardless of differences between particular examples. The differences in various stimuli eliciting this discharge are matters of detail, not of deep explanatory power. To understand a cinematic pleasure, in such a model, it is ultimately more important to understand the instincts and drives behind the emotion than the specifics of the emotional situation itself. By reducing cinematic emotional response to its drive component, Freud's followers in psychoanalytic film theory deemphasize the richness of that response.

Freud, therefore, is a poor choice for a theory of emotions. Since his emphasis is elsewhere, he tends to treat the emotions as a byproduct of more central behavioral determinants: the instincts. The important function of emotions for Freud is that they discharge energy from the psychic economy, and so it is not particularly important to study the specifics of how they discharge this energy. These assumptions lead to the broad concepts of "pleasure" and "desire" which psychoanalytic film theory has inherited. The problem with these concepts is not that film theorists have applied them too broadly. The Freudian concepts of "desire" and "pleasure" themselves lead theorists' attention away from the emotions.

In turning to cognitive philosophy and psychology, we choose an intellectual inheritance very different from psychoanalysis. Both cognitive philosophers and cognitive psychologists have focused their attention specifically on the study of emotions, and so we rely upon theories which, unlike psychoanalysis, are centrally concerned with emotions.

Film and Emotion

In film studies there have been precursors to the study of film and emotion from a broadly cognitive perspective. Hugo Munsterberg, for example, wrote in his still-important *The Film: A Psychological Study* that to "picture emotions must be the central aim of the photoplay." Munsterberg combined Kantian faculty psychology with the psychology of his Harvard colleague, William James. The sixth chapter of Munsterberg's interesting book deals with the expression of emotions and with the emotional experience of the spectator. His theory of identification, if not in accordance with contemporary thought in some respects, is nonetheless as sophisticated as many more current theories. He writes, for example, that spectator emotions are of two broad types—those identical with the emotions of the protagonist and those "which may be entirely different, perhaps exactly opposite to those which the figures in the play express," and which stem from the spectator's "independent affective life." For Munsterberg, the former, empathic type of emotional response is by far the most prevalent. The emotions a film elicits, he writes, are central because they bring "vividness and affective tone into our grasping of the [film's] action."[31]

V. F. Perkins, in his 1972 book *Film as Film: Understanding and Judging Movies,* argues for film criticism that takes account of and values the spectator's involvement and emotional experience. Perkins challenges critical theories that would disengage our emotional experience in favor of a film's abstract meaning. Perkins also offers insights into how to think about spectator experience. In particular, his chapter on identification deserves more attention than it has received. Here Perkins presages many current discussions of screen emotion. For example, he suggests that the term "identification" is too narrow because, strictly speaking, it "refers to a relationship which is impossible in the cinema—namely an unattainably complete projection of ourselves into the character on the screen." Perkins also has insights into the nature of our emotional reactions. He denies that emotional reactions submerge intellect and judgment. On the contrary, they often involve a kind of second-order, reflexive response even while we experience them. Perhaps most refreshing about Perkins is his refusal to denigrate the experience films offer. He argues that the experience we have in viewing films is not just an escape from our "real lives" but an addition to them. Film experiences are real experiences; moreover, they are often worthwhile and occasionally profound.[32]

To build on the insights of Munsterberg, Perkins, and others, however, film studies first required a challenge to the dominance of psychoanalytic theory. This challenge initially came in the form of cognitive approaches to film theory, first introduced by David Bordwell, Edward Branigan, and Noël Carroll. In the mid-1980s Bordwell and Branigan developed alternative ways to think about spectatorship, proposing constructivist approaches that emphasized the cognitive activities of the spectator. Then Carroll and Bordwell presented more straightforward critiques of "psychosemiotic" film theory and the conventional critical practices of the field.[33] In the meantime, the development of various cognitive approaches continues. A recent collection of essays edited by Bordwell and Carroll attempts to solidify an alternative and broadly cognitive perspective. The perspective is characterized not only by its cognitive orientation but also by a piecemeal approach to theorizing and its encouragement of vigorous debate.[34]

Within this context come cognitive approaches to film and emotion. When we initially decided to put together this collection, the only book-length study of the topic was Noël Carroll's work on the horror film, which dealt with the emotions elicited by that genre and also provided ways of thinking about film emotions in general. Since that time, however, general studies of filmic emotion have begun to appear with some regularity.[35] *Passionate Views: Film, Cognition, and Emotion* appears at a time when interdisciplinary interest in the emotions and affects elicited by films is growing rapidly. The interdisciplinary and international scope of this interest is reflected in the contributors, who hail from six countries and represent the disciplines of film and media studies, philosophy, and psychology. Needless to say, the perspectives here, though united by an overall cognitive approach, differ in many ways, and are not meant to represent a single theory of film and emotion. Thus we call the cognitive perspective an "approach" rather than a "theory." The cognitive approach does not presume to answer all pertinent questions; history, criticism, and other theoretical perspectives are vitally important. Neither does it offer a group of scholars who work in lockstep.

The essays of the first section, "Kinds of Films, Kinds of Emotions," examine the relationship among genre, emotion, and emotion types. Noël Carroll presents a general outline of the relationship between genres and the particular emotions they elicit. After a discussion of the nature of the emotion, Carroll goes on to argue that films are "criterially prefocused" to activate our subsumption of characters and events under categories appropriate to given emotion states. This, together with the encouragement of "pro attitudes" toward certain story developments, is apt to elicit specific emotional responses from the audience. Carroll goes on to demonstrate how such processes function in relation to the genres of melodrama, horror, and suspense.

The dominant "feeling tone" of a genre frequently defines the corpus and gives it its name (e.g., suspense, horror). The three other essays in this section each take a particular genre or kind of response and identify the conditions that make particular responses possible. Ed Tan and Nico Frijda investigate the arousal of sentiment in film viewing, approaching the subject from the standpoint of Frijda's well-known theory of the emotions and Tan's systematic analysis of film and emotion. Cynthia Freeland provides a new theory of the grounds of the sublime, shows how specific films elicit such a response, and examines the very possibility of a cognitive approach dealing with the sublime. Dirk Eitzen approaches film comedy from a functionalist/evolutionary perspective, arguing that film comedy has become widespread because it serves human adaptation in varied and significant respects.

The second section concentrates on film narration and style, examining how different film devices elicit affective response. Cinematic narration is usually thought of as communicating narrative information to an audience, but the essays by Greg Smith and Torben Grodal emphasize the narration's important role in guiding the audience through a sequence of emotional reactions. Smith proposes an approach to analyzing film structures which emphasizes stylistic emotion cues as much as character-oriented information. Relying on an associational model of the emotions, he discusses how film narration cues an overall emotional orientation to the film, a mood that is bolstered by brief bursts of emotion. Grodal's discussion of how narrative elicits emotion builds on the systematic treatment of film and emotion presented in his recent book *Moving Pictures: A New Theory of Film Genres, Feelings, and Cognition*. In the essay, Grodal begins with a general discussion of how film narratives in particular elicit affect and then goes on to describe some of the diverse means by which films manipulate or filter affective response through, for example, various kinds of "activations," "feelings of reality," or genre conventions. The essays by Jeff Smith and Susan Feagin shift focus from narrative to various uses of film style and technique. Smith argues that cognitive theories of film music are well equipped to deal with the expression and evocation of emotion. After a discussion of emotivist and cognitive theories of emotion and music, Smith elaborates on the functions of the film score in relation to emotion, and in addition describes two important functions of film music: "polarization" and "affective congruence." Film is a manifestly temporal art, one that, like music, binds the spectator to the rhythm and tempo of its presentation. Feagin explores how the temporal aspects of film, and more specifically, timing, affect emotional response.

The third and last section deals with issues that have been the province of psychoanalytic theory until recently—desire and identification. As Noël Carroll has argued, psychoanalytic film studies has tended to treat desire as a Platonic concept: "All different sorts of desire, such as a male viewer's sexual desire for a movie character and any viewer's desire that a movie be intelligible, are slotted under the abstract noun *Desire*." Carroll suggests that it would be more productive to think of specific desires for this or that, rather than "instances of some unified, univocally named force."[36] Gregory Currie recognizes that desires play an important role in our responses to film narrative, and offers a framework for thinking of the relationship between desires and narrative. His essay develops further his initial discussions of desire and emotion in his recent book *Image and Mind: Film, Philosophy, and Cognitive Science*.

The next three essays all deal, in some way, with the notion of "identification," that controversial term that denotes the spectator's response to film characters. Berys Gaut notes that in response to psychoanalytic accounts of identification thought to be vague and/or misconstrued, theorists such as Gregory Currie, Alex Neill, and Murray Smith have rejected the notion and supplanted it with other formulations of spectator response to film characters. Gaut argues that such a rejection is premature and goes on to revive "identification" by developing a more nuanced account of its processes. Murray Smith, in his *Engaging Characters: Fiction, Emotion, and the Cinema*, has proposed a promising alternative to notions of identification, advocating use of the term "engagement" to describe our response to and interaction with characters. In his essay here, Smith is interested in how spectators are invited to respond to "perverse" acts, in part through allegiances with characters. Smith's analysis extends to our response to "perversity" generally, and he ends by arguing that in accounting for our response to such representations, psychoanalytic explanations should not be the sole or even primary form of explanation. Finally, Carl Plantinga accounts for the use of the human face in what he calls the "scene of empathy." He argues that within such scenes the face is used in conjunction with other techniques to elicit spectator empathy. He describes empathy as consisting of both cognitive and feeling components, some based on involuntary responses stemming from emotional contagion and affective mimicry. Plantinga then goes on to describe the specific techniques filmmakers use in scenes of empathy.

We are not pretending to offer complete answers to the difficult and important questions each essayist asks. Our aim is rather to showcase the utility of a new approach to the cuing and elicitation of emotion in film and to provide a new way of talking about affect. Of course, much of this work is initiatory, part of the burgeoning interest in cognitive theories of emotion that gained momentum in the 1980s and the even more recent interest in the emotional power of films. As such, we hope that this work will contribute to a healthy debate and lead to continued research in this area.

Kinds of Films, Kinds of Emotions

ONE

Film, Emotion, and Genre

NOËL CARROLL

Film and Affect

A nasty, largish beast rushes at the camera, backed by a pounding score and crushing sound effects, and the audience flinches. The villain abuses the innocent heroine and our jaws clench in anger; our longing for revenge keeps us pinned to the screen, awaiting the moment when the loutish brute is dealt his due. The young lovers are separated by the callous vagaries of fate, or the child dies long before his time, and we weep. Or perhaps the camera pans over a vernal landscape of rolling gentle greenery and a feeling of serenity wells up in us. These are very common movie events. They bear testimony to the hardly controversial observation that, in large measure, affect is the glue that holds the audience's attention to the screen on a moment-to-moment basis.

I have said "affect" here rather than "emotion," even though it might be acceptable in ordinary language to label all the preceding examples as instances of emotional response. My reason for this way of speaking is that the ordinary notion of *emotion* can be exceedingly broad and elastic, sometimes ranging so widely as to encompass hard-wired reflex reactions (like the startle response), kinesthetic turbulence, moods, sexual arousal, pleasures and desires, as well as occurrent mental states like anger, fear and sorrow.

The everyday usage of *emotion* can be rather catch-all, referring to quite a lot of heterogeneous phenomena. It is not clear—indeed, it is very unlikely—that this conception of emotion, which can be found in everyday speech, captures a natural kind, like gold; therefore, using it in a discussion of film and something called "the emotions" is likely to be a barrier to the construction of precise, theoretical generalizations. As a result, in what follows I will use the notion of *affect* where everyday speech might talk of the emotions, reserving the term *emotion* to name a narrower subclass of affect, namely, what might be even more accurately called *cognitive emotions* (i.e., affects that include cognitive elements).

By subdividing the affective life—what might be called the "life of feeling"—in this way and putting to one side many of the phenomena that comprise it, I do not mean to privilege one sort of affect over others. I would not deny that many of the affects that I am ignoring are integral to the experience of film. Through the manipulation of sound and image, filmmakers often address audiences at a subcognitive, or cognitively impenetrable, level of response. Loud noises—either recorded effects or musical sounds—can elicit instinctual responses from spectators as can the appearance of sudden movement. The movie screen is a rich phenomenal field in terms of variables like size, altitude, and speed, which have the capacity to excite automatic reactions from viewers, while the display of certain phobic and sexual material may also call forth responses barely mediated by thought. Such transactions certainly need to be studied and analyzed.[1] By hiving these affects off from the category of the emotions, I do not mean that we can neglect the cognitively impenetrable affects. I only intend, for methodological purposes, to bracket consideration of them for the time being in order to focus upon the subclass of affect that I am calling the emotions.

Though I may be departing somewhat from certain ordinary usage in this matter, since I am not leaving everyday speech altogether behind me, I hesitate to say that I am *stipulating* what shall count as an emotion. For ordinary language has broader and narrower ideas of the emotions. I am certainly eschewing the broader usages in favor of the term *affect.* However, there are narrower senses of *emotion* in everyday speech and my account stays fairly close to those.

Certain phenomena, such as fear, anger, patriotism, horror, admiration, sorrow, indignation, pity, envy, jealousy, reverence, awe, hatred, love, anxiety, shame, embarrassment, humiliation, comic amusement, and so on, are paradigms of what counts as emotion in ordinary language, even if sometimes ordinary language also stretches farther afield.[2] These garden-variety emotions are the sorts of phenomena that I will regard as emotions proper in this essay. In this, I do not think that I am doing great violence to ordinary language.

Moreover, inasmuch as these garden-variety emotions are not only paradigmatic but also exhibit common structural features, I think that I am merely pushing ordinary language in a direction toward which it already inclines, rather than stipulating a brand-new concept of the emotions. That is, by treating certain states as paradigmatically emotional, ordinary usage perhaps already regards them as composing a core class of like phenomena. In this respect, my analysis may be regarded as a rational reconstruction of some already existing intuitions rather than as the invention of a new concept that, in fact, tracks a somewhat unified field of phenomena.

In this chapter, I attempt to develop some generalizations about film and what might be called "emotions proper" or "core emotions" or "garden-variety emotions." This requires that I provide a characterization of the emotions that I have in mind as well as suggesting their relevance to film analysis. In the concluding section, I discuss the applicability of my approach to film and the emotions to certain genres, including melodrama, horror, and suspense.

Film and the Emotions

Though I do not consider film in relation to every kind of affective state, it should be clear that the affective states I intend to look at—garden-variety emotions, like anger, fear, hatred, sorrow, and so on—are central constituents of the film experience as we know it. Often it is our hatred of certain characters, like the redneck boyfriend in *Sling Blade* (1996), that keeps us riveted to the screen. Our mounting anger at his treatment of his lover and her son, along with the way he continually insults and torments the gay store manager and the retarded giant, stoke our indignation and encourage us to anticipate hopefully and vindictively his downfall and even his death. A primitive feeling for retributive justice shapes the way that we attend to *Sling Blade*, along with so many other films. That is probably why most of the time astute filmmakers wait until near the end of the film to kill their villains off. If the characters that we love to hate die too soon, there may be little left on-screen to hold our interest.

It is surprising to what extent darker emotions like anger, hatred, and revenge provide the cement that holds our attention on the popular movies we consume. But more socially acceptable emotions can do the job as well. A certain *tristesse* pervades our experience of *Letter from an Unknown Woman* (1948). And, of course, most movies elicit a gamut of garden-variety emotions over the duration of the narrative. *God Is My Witness* (1992) engenders, among other emotions, both feelings of revenge toward figures like the bandit chief, and sadness for those other central characters who have been separated from their loved ones. The pleasure that attends the conclusion of the film is a function of the desires that subtend these different emotions being finally satisfied.

The garden-variety emotions underwrite our experience of most films, especially popular movies. Undoubtedly, the degree to which our experience of movies is emotional is so extensive that we may lose sight of it. Emotion supplies such a pervasive coloration to our movie experience that it may, so to speak, fly in under the radar screen. But a little apperceptive introspection quickly reveals that throughout our viewing of a film we are generally in some emotional state or other, typically one prompted and modulated by what is on screen.

Nor is it only the case that a great deal of our experience of films is saturated with emotion; it is also that our emotional engagement constitutes, in many instances, the most intense, vivid, and sought-after qualities available in the film experience. Perhaps that is why the Dutch film psychologist Ed S. Tan subtitles his recent important book *Film as an Emotion Machine*.³

Clearly, then, it is crucial for a theoretical understanding of film that we attempt to analyze its relation to the emotions. But in order to do that we first need a clearer sense of what constitutes an emotion proper.

If one reflects on the states that we paradigmatically think of as emotional, one is first struck by the fact that they involve feelings—sensations of bodily changes, like muscle contractions, often attended by phenomenological qualities, such as being "uptight." Such states are very apparent with respect to violent emotional states like fear, but they can also be detected in what Hume called the calm emotions. Thus, a first, albeit reductivist conception of the emotions is that they are nothing more than bodily feelings. Moreover, this position might be bolstered by noting that in English the term *emotion* is interchangeable with the term *feeling*.

In fact, a theory very close to this was quite popular in psychology for some time. William James claimed that an emotional state was just a perception of a bodily state.⁴ For James, I notice myself crying and then label the state sadness. Since C. G. Lange proposed a similar theory at roughly the same time, the view is often called the James-Lange theory of the emotions.⁵

But neither of these views—the emotion-as-bodily-feeling view nor the emotion-as-bodily-feeling-plus-perception view (the James-Lange theory)—is adequate. The problem with the first view is that it excludes cognition from the emotional complex and the problem with the James-Lange view is that, in a manner of speaking, it puts the relevant cognitive states in the wrong place. In order to explain these objections, let's indulge in a little science fiction.⁶

First, if an emotion were simply a bodily feeling, marked by certain sensations, then if a person were presently in a bodily state that resembled exactly the bodily state she was in the last time she was angry, then we should be prepared to say that she is angry now. But that doesn't sound quite right. For imagine that we have enough pharmacology at our disposal that we can induce any bodily state along with any phenomenological quality in anyone we wish. The last time our subject was angry was when she discovered that her lover was cheating on her. We can provoke the same bodily state and the same phenomenological qualia in her now that she felt back then. Suppose we do it? Shall we say that she is angry?

I suspect not. Why not? Well, the last time that she experienced this bodily state and its attendant qualia, she was angry at her lover. But that was a while ago. She no longer has a lover, and if the truth be told, she's forgotten the old one. Thus, *ex hypothesi*, there is no one for her to be angry with now.

But if there is no one for her to be angry with—if there is no object to her emotional state—can she really be said to be in an emotional state?

She is in a bodily state, probably an uncomfortable and even confusing bodily state. But is she angry? No—because there is no one or no thing with whom or with which she is angry. You can't be angry, unless there is someone or something that serves as the object of your anger. Emotional states are directed. You hate Marvin or you are afraid of the smog. This is what it means to say that emotions take objects.[7]

But sheer bodily states do not take objects; they are not directed. They are internal events with no external reference. Thus, the subject of our science-fiction experiment is not in an emotional state. For her disturbed visceral state is not directed, nor does it have an object. Therefore, the view that emotions are simply bodily states cum some phenomenological qualia is wrong. Emotions may always involve bodily states and phenomenological qualia. However, something must be added to the mix if the state is to count as a full-fledged emotion.

What has to be added? Something that functions to connect the relevant bodily states and phenomenological qualia to some object. When I am angry at my lover for betraying me, I am racked by inner bodily turmoil. What is the bridge between that inner turmoil and my lover? Presumably, it is some cognition that I have about my lover. That is, I either believe or imagine that my lover has betrayed me. Of course, I can be mistaken in this. But in order to be angry with my lover in this case, I must believe or imagine that my lover has done me wrong *and* that cognitive state must be the cause of the inner consternation that buffets me. Together the cognitive state in causal conjunction with the bodily state and its phenomenological qualia comprise the emotional state of anger. This state can take objects and be directed—can have intentionality—because the cognitive states that are necessary constituents of the overall emotional states possess intentionality.

Emotions cannot simply be bodily feelings, since sheer bodily feelings lack intentionality. But if cognitions are necessary constituents of emotional states, this lacuna disappears. Thus, if adding cognition to bodily feeling is the right way to solve the preceding problem, then the reductivist theory that emotions are just bodily feelings is false, since emotions also require cognitive components (either beliefs or belief-like states such as thoughts and imaginings). This gets rid of the emotion-as-bodily-feeling view. But what about the James-Lange theory?

According to the James-Lange theory, emotions have a cognitive component. My brother is hit by a car; I choke up and I weep; I perceive these bodily changes and I interpret or cognize them as sadness. Here, the bodily state causes the relevant cognitive state. But the causal order seems backwards. The cognitive state appears epiphenomenal.

Undeniably, there are some occasions where a loud noise, say a fire-cracker, makes us frightened and where upon reflection we say, "I guess that really frightened me." But this is not paradigmatic of garden-variety emotional states. When I am jealous of a rival, that is *because* I believe that he is stealing affection that belongs to me; it is not because I observe myself over-whelmed by the phenomenology of the green-eyed monster and surmise that I must be jealous. To return to our science-fiction example once again, one can imagine pharmacologically counterfeiting the sensations of my last episode of jealous rage where it makes no sense to say that I am jealous now—perhaps because I have become a spiritual adept who has successfully renounced all earthly attachments.

Thus, our thought-experiment suggests that what we are calling emotions proper at least involve both cognitions and feeling states where the two are linked inasmuch as the former cause the latter.[8] In this account, certain affects—like the churning stomach sensations that viewers reported resulted from watching the car chases in *Bullitt*—are not examples of emotions proper. Emotions proper require a cognitive component. Admittedly, not all of the affects that are important to the analysis of cinema fall into this category. What might be called cognitively impenetrable affects—like the startle response—don't. Nevertheless, a great many of the affects experienced in response to film are of the nature of emotions proper. To get a handle on them, we must now say a little more about the way in which the cognitive component in these emotions operates.

I am angry at Leslie because he is telling everyone that I failed my first driving test. I told this to Leslie in strictest confidence, but Leslie has broadcast this all around the neighborhood. When I learn and come to believe that Leslie has divulged my secret, my blood pressure skyrockets and I feel hot under the collar. My cognitive state, in other words, causes a spate of bodily disruption. How does this come about?

Notice that though in this case my anger is caused by Leslie's indiscretion, indiscretion is not the only thing that can function to elicit an emotional response. If someone smashed my car or if someone ruined my print of *The General*, I might also find myself in an angry state, if I believed that these things were done to me wantonly or inexcusably. That is, I will be angry where I subsume the events in question under the rubric of wrongs done to me or mine and where that formation of that belief functions in provoking some bodily disturbance in me. Cognitions, in other words, play not only a causal role in emotions in that they figure in the etiology of bodily alterations; they also play a role in identifying what emotional state we are in when we are in one. My response to Leslie is anger because I have subsumed or assessed Leslie's indiscretion under the category of a wrong done to me or mine, and forming that belief has caused the pertinent bodily upset.

What this example suggests is that emotional states, like anger, are governed cognitively by criteria of appropriateness. Where the cognitions in a given emotional state come about through the subsumption of a person or event under the category of wrongs done to me or mine, the emotional response is apt to be anger. Moreover, other emotional states are also like this. The harmful or the dangerous is the criterion (or the category appropriate to) fear; thus when I subsume the object of my state under the category of the harmful, I am, other things being equal, apt to undergo fear. That is to say, for example: I cognize the scorpion next to my hand under the harmful, that cognition causes my blood to freeze, and the overall state is fear.

Similarly, in order for me to feel pity for x, I must believe that x has suffered some misfortune; the criterion for pity, in other words, is misfortune, just as in order to envy y I must believe that y has something that I have not. If y cannot move and I know this, then I cannot envy y's athletic prowess. For in order to envy y I must be able to form the belief that y possesses some advantage that I lack, or some degree of advantage over and above what I take myself to command. Envying y signals that I have subsumed y under the category of someone who possesses more than I do.

Emotions require cognitions as causes and bodily states as effects. Moreover, among the cognitions that are essential for the formation of emotional states are those that subsume the objects of the state under certain relevant categories or conceive of said objects as meeting certain criteria. In fear, the object must meet the criterion of being harmful or, at least, of being perceived to be harmful. Anger requires that the object be perceived as meeting the criterion that it has wronged me or mine.

What "criterion" means above, functionally speaking, is that in order to be an appropriate object of the emotion in question, the relevant object must meet certain necessary conditions, or, alternatively, must be thought to be subsumable under certain essentially defined categories. For x to be the object of pity, x must be thought to meet the necessary criterion of having suffered some misfortune; for y to be the object of my envy, I must cognize y as at least meeting the necessary condition of possessing something I lack (indeed, generally something that I lack that I would prefer to have, if only upon learning that y has it).

Thus, when we speak of emotions as requiring cognitions, the cognitions that we have in mind—first and foremost—involve subsuming the objects of the emotion under certain categories or, alternatively, perceiving that the object meets certain criteria of appropriateness (harmfulness, for example, in the case of fear; wrongfulness in the case of anger).

Of course, this is not the whole story of what it is to be in an emotional state. Emotional states are temporal affairs; they endure over time intervals; they are episodes. When we detect the object of our emotional state and the relevant cognitions ensue, our perception becomes emotionally charged. It casts the cause or the object of our state in a special phenomenological light; it fixes our attention upon it and alerts us to its significance (e.g., x is dangerous).

The emotions gestalt or organize perception. They call our attention to those aspects of the situation that are pertinent by selectively guiding perception to the features of the stimulus that are subsumable under the criteria of the reigning emotional state.

There is also a feedback mechanism in operation here. Once in an emotional state, the prevailing state further structures our perception by drawing our attention to further elements in the array that are pertinent to sustaining the emotional state that we are in. Alerted by fear to the potential that there is someone or something prowling around our campsite, we scope out the scene in search of further signs of threat which, if found, reinforce both the state we are in and its related feedback processes. In this way, the emotions manage attention over time. The form that this perceptual management takes is to focus our attention upon those elements in a situation that are relevant to (that mesh with the criteria that govern) the presiding emotional state (e.g., dangers with respect to fear; slights with respect to anger).

The emotions can be analogized to searchlights. They direct attention, enabling us to organize the details before us into significant wholes or gestalts. Where the emotional state is one of fear, we scan it for details highlighted as dangerous; where the state is pity, it battens on elements subsumable under the category of misfortune. The emotions foreground such relevant details in what might be called a special phenomenological glow.

Moreover, once we are in the grip of a given emotional state, we not only stay fixed upon the details it has selected out in the first instance; we scan the array for more details with a similar pertinence to our initial emotional assessment of the situation. The emotions manage our attention, guiding both what we look at and what we look for. Moreover, that process of attention management undergoes changes of adjustment. First our emotions alert us to certain gestalts (whose structure of inclusion and exclusion is governed by the criteria relevant to the ruling emotional state), and then the presiding emotion encourages further elaboration of our attention, prompting us to form expectations about the kinds of things that we should watch for as the situation evolves (where the pertinent kinds of things are those that fall into the categories that criterially determine our prevailing emotional state).

So far we have been talking about the emotions and their relation to perception in a pretty abstract way. How applicable is any of this to film viewing?[9] Can this abstract characterization of the emotions tell us anything about the relation of the garden-variety emotions to standard fictional films? I think it can, although in order to see how we must take note of one very large and obvious difference between the activation of emotional responses with respect to events in everyday life versus events in narrative film fictions.[10]

In life, in contrast to fiction, our emotions have to select out the relevant details from a massive array of largely unstructured stimuli. We are sitting in a room reading the newspaper. We hear sirens nearby, alerting us to potential danger. An incipient sense of fear prompts us to rise and to go to the window to search for indications of danger. We smell fire. Warily, we look down to see if it coming from our apartment building. If it is, we rush to the hallway in order to see if the flames have reached our floor. Our mounting sense of fear, in other words, shapes our perceptual itinerary. It organizes the situation for us in a way pertinent to action, which, in this case, all things considered, will probably eventuate in flight.

But with respect to fiction, things stand differently. The emotions are not called upon to organize situations de novo. To a much greater extent than in everyday life, situations in fiction films have already been structured for us by filmmakers. We do not usually rely upon the emotions to organize fictional film events for us as much as we rely upon the emotions to perform this task for us in ordinary life because, in the main, fiction film events have been emotionally predigested for us by filmmakers. That is, the filmmakers have already done much of the work of emotionally organizing scenes and sequences for us through the ways in which the filmmakers have foregrounded what features of the events in the film are salient. In contrast to the way that emotions focus attention for us in everyday life, when it comes to films the relevant events have already generally been prefocused emotively for us by the filmmakers. The filmmakers have selected out the details of the scene or sequence that they think are emotively significant and thrust them, so to speak, in our faces. The means that the filmmakers have to secure this end include camera position and composition, editing, lighting, the use of color, and, of course, acting and the very structure of the script or narrative.[11]

Very frequently in everyday life, when an acquaintance or colleague slights us—perhaps by a passing remark—we are not immediately angry, even if we are hurt, because we may wonder whether the insult was an intentional wrong rather than merely carelessness. But as such remarks recur, anger takes hold and we come to recognize a discernible pattern of nastiness directed at us. In typical fictional films, on the other hand, we rarely have to waver so long. So often, characters wear the meanness of their actions on their sleeve and, if that were not enough, we also have access to the disapproving judgments of the people around them. We not only have a pretty unmistakable gestalt of wrongness thrust in bold relief before us, but we also have the reaction of surrounding characters to reflect and to reinforce our assessments of the situation.

Thus, it is hard not to respond (initially) with anger to the father in *Shine* (1996) when he refuses to allow his son to accept various scholarships. Generally in fiction films, that is, the detection work that our emotions need to do for us is somewhat minimized because the scenes and characters in such films have very frequently already been made or designed from, so to speak, the point of view of anger to begin with; or, to say it differently, they have been emotively prefocused or predigested for us.[12]

But how is it possible for a character, a scene, or a sequence to be emotively prefocused? Here it is useful to advert to the general picture of the emotions that we developed previously. The emotions, we argued, are governed by criteria of appropriateness. To be angered, the object of our emotional state must be perceived as a wrong done to me or mine. I was angry with Leslie because I regarded his gossip as a wrong done to me. Likewise, if I am angry with a broker because I believe he has squandered my mother's savings, it is because I perceive it as a wrong done to mine (where mine can extend to friends, countrymen, and anyone else, including a fictional character, to whom I bear a pro attitude).

But just as emotions must meet certain criteria of appropriateness in everyday life, so must emotions in response to fictions be governed by criteria of appropriateness. Thus, a film text can be emotively prefocused by being *criterially prefocused*—that is, by being so structured that the descriptions and depictions of the object of our attention in the text will activate our subsumption of the relevant characters and events under the categories that are criterially apposite to the emotional state in question.

Once we recognize the object under the criterially relevant categories— like the harmful for fear or the wrongful for anger—the relevant emotion is apt (under certain conditions to be discussed shortly) to be raised in us. That is, as a result of entertaining the appropriate cognitions, we will be likely to undergo some physical changes: with comic amusement, ideally, we laugh; as we will see in the next section, with horror films our skin may crawl; with suspense films, we tense up; and with melodramas, we may shed a tear.

As well, our attention becomes emotively charged. Our emotional states fix our attention and illuminate it in a special phenomenological glow. Our attention is glued to those features of the object of the emotion that are appropriate to the emotional state we are in. Our emotional state prompts us to survey the event for further features that may support or sustain the presiding emotional state in which we find ourselves. And, protented, our emotively charged state shapes our anticipation of what is to come by priming us to be on the watch for the emergence of further details that are also subsumable under the categories of the dominant emotional state—our anger at a character in the first scene alerts us to be on the lookout for more churlishness from him in later scenes. Or, in summary, a criterially prefocused film text gives rise, in the right circumstances, to *emotive focus* in the audience, where by "emotive focus" I am referring both to the way in which the emotional state of the viewer fixes *and* then shapes her attention.

Central, then, to a theoretical understanding of the relation of the garden-variety emotions to film are the notions of the *criterially prefocused film text* in relation to the *emotive focus* of the audience. On our account so far, a criterially prefocused film text is a standard condition for securing emotive focus. However, it should be obvious that merely presenting viewers with criterially prefocused film texts, no matter how well designed, does not guarantee that spectators will respond emotionally. A criterially prefocused film can be viewed dispassionately. What makes for a passionate response? The notion of a criterially prefocused film text needs to be supplemented, if we hope to propose a theoretical model of the arousal of garden-variety emotions by narrative fiction films.

I hypothesize that what that supplement comes to is a concern or a pro attitude on the part of the viewer with respect to the way in which the depicted situation in the fiction is or is not going. That is, in addition to being criterially prefocused, the narrative must invest the viewer with certain concerns about the fictional characters and events (and their prospects) in the film. These concerns or pro attitudes function like the desires that are found in many everyday emotions, and when added to the mental content or conception of the object, derived from the criterially prefocused text, the combination, all things being equal, should elicit an emotional response (including emotive focus) from viewers in accordance with the criterial features of the film text that the filmmakers have made salient.

The structure of our emotional involvement with narrative fiction films, then, typically comprises a criterially prefocused film text plus certain concerns or pro attitudes, and together, in the standard case, these are apt to elicit broadly predictable responses (including emotive focus) in standard audiences (which, by stipulation, bars sociopaths). The criterially prefocused film text embodies a conception of a situation from an emotively relevant point of view. But a conception of a situation may not alone be sufficient to motivate an emotional response, if the audience is otherwise indifferent to what is going on. To prompt an emotional response and to secure emotive focus require that the audience be engaged by concerns—certain pro and con attitudes—about what is going on in the story.

This hypothesis presupposes that film narratives can enlist audiences in preferences about the way in which a story might go. This assumption should not be problematic. *Potemkin* (1925) enlists a pro attitude in the audience toward the crew of the battle cruiser which leads them to prefer that the fleet not destroy them. In *High Noon* (1952), the intended audience prefers that the sheriff survive. This is not to say that films always defer to the preferences that they engender in audiences. With *You Only Live Once* (1937), we may prefer that Eddie (Henry Fonda) escape, but he doesn't. Nevertheless, the special emotional *frisson* that attends the end of this film is a function of the fact that the filmmakers encouraged viewers to form a pro attitude toward another outcome.

Typically, narrative fiction films develop in such a way that spectators have a structured horizon of expectations about what might and what might not happen. And in addition to a sense of the possible outcomes of the ongoing courses of events, one also, generally under the guidance of the filmmakers, has convictions about what outcomes one would, in a certain sense, prefer to obtain in the world of the fiction versus those she would prefer not to obtain. In some cases, the preferred course of events correlates with the express goals and plans of the protagonists of the story; what they want to happen—say, delivering life-saving medical supplies—is what the audience wants to happen. However, in a great many other cases, the film may proffer preferred outcomes independently of the express goals and plans of any of the characters. That is, the film may have its own agenda, as in the cases of all those fictional lovers who never wanted to fall in love in the first place.

But however motivated, audiences evolve concerns regarding the situations portrayed in films, and when those concerns are threatened, we tend to react with dysphoric (or discomforting) emotions, whereas when the concern in question is abetted by narrative developments, our emotions tend to be euphoric.[13] Which particular dysphoric or euphoric emotion is engaged, of course, depends upon the way that the film text is criterially prefocused. For example, considering some dysphoric emotions, if a character toward whom I bear a pro attitude is wronged—as when the character Zane, played by Charlie Sheen, in *The Arrival* (1996) is fired—in such a way that the injustice of the event is made criterially salient, then, all things being equal, I will feel anger; whereas if presented with the criterially prefocused misfortune of a group that has elicited my concern—say the victims in a disaster movie— then I am apt to feel pity for them.

Similarly, euphoric emotions of different sorts are also likely to evolve in accordance with the way in which the film text is criterially prefocused in those cases where our concerns or desires about the direction of the relevant courses of events are satisfied. When a character toward whom we bear a pro attitude overcomes obstacles, saliently posed in the film—as when the sheriff finally defeats the shark in *Jaws* (1975)—then we are likely to respond with admiration; whereas the manifestation of virtually limitless power by an agency of which we approve—for instance, nature or a god—will tend to evoke reverence.

My proposal, then, for analyzing our emotional response to fiction films is that a criterially prefocused film text is apt to elicit an emotional response from audiences where the audiences are encouraged to adopt pro attitudes to certain developments in the story. Where story developments mesh with those preferences, the response is likely to be euphoric; where they clash, the emotional response is apt to be dysphoric. Moreover, the emotional response involves engendering emotive focus in the audience and this emotive focus guides our reception of ongoing and anticipated screen events on a moment-to-moment basis.

Furthermore, if this hypothesis about our emotional involvement with fiction films is roughly correct, it suggests a certain direction for cinema research. To analyze the way in which a film arouses an emotional response from viewers, one needs to first determine the way in which the film or film segment is criterially prefocused. Here the critic, using herself as a detector, begins by noting the emotion the film has elicited in her. Perhaps she feels a global sense of pity. Next, using the criteria of the emotion in question as a hypothesis, she can review the way in which the filmic material is articulated in order to isolate the pertinent depictions or descriptions in the film that instantiate the concept or meet the criteria of the pertinent emotion.

Additionally, she will want to determine which features of the film are designed to engender pro attitudes in viewers, along with determining what those pro attitudes are. By following this procedure, one can pith the emotive structure of the film.

To "pith the emotive structure of the film" here means finding the aspects of the depictions or descriptions of the object of the emotion that satisfy the necessary criteria for being in whatever emotional state the audience is in. This is what explaining the emotional state of the audience generally amounts to (along with identifying the depictions or descriptions that give rise to the concerns and preferences the audience is meant to bear to developments in the narrative).

Of course, this order of research may not always be practicable. In some cases, the analyst may not be able to identify with precision his or her emotional response to a film or film segment. In that event, the analyst is better advised to take up the salient depictions or description in the text with an interest in seeing what they foreground. Then, after evolving some hypotheses or questions in this regard, the analyst can compare what the film has foregrounded with the criteria for the better-known emotional states. This may lead to a clarification of the emotional address of the film or film segment under examination.

Needless to say, the emotional address of some films may be designedly ambiguous, while other films may introduce novel emotional timbres. But even in these cases the methodology that I am recommending is still somewhat serviceable, since it will enable us systematically to get a rough sense of the general contours of the emotional ambiguities and novel emotional timbres of the films in question.

Undoubtedly, often when we are watching films that are remote from us in time and place, we will not be able to depend on our own emotional responses to the film because we do not have the appropriate cultural background. This is exactly where film history and the ethnographic study of film have an indispensable role to play. Film historians and ethnographers can supply us with the background necessary to make the emotive address of films from other cultures and other periods in our own culture emotionally accessible to us.

Emotion and Genre

The framework for analyzing the relation of film and the emotions advanced above is general in the sense that it is supposed to be useful for analyzing responses to characters, sequences, scenes, and whole films. A great deal of our experience of film viewing is attended by garden-variety emotions in response to many different units of film articulation, ranging from single gestures and looks to the sorts of chase sequences that can last for half the length of a film. Attempting to illustrate the feasibility of the preceding method for every kind of case would require more detail than a chapter allows. But perhaps empirical credibility for my theoretical proposals can be derived by illustrating what these hypotheses might facilitate with respect to the analysis of certain genres.

As I have said, emotion is engaged on a moment-to-moment basis throughout much (if not most) of our experiences of film. We track much of the unfolding action in films via what I have called emotive focus. My theory is intended to be instructive in analyzing virtually every instance of our emotional engagement and emotive tracking of cinema. However, there are certain dimensions of cinematic articulation, notably genre films of various sorts, where emotive address is particularly pronounced and obvious. Thus, at the very least, my theory should have something informative to contribute to the study of the relevant genres.

Some genres seem to traffic in certain specifiable emotions essentially. That is, certain genres appear to have as their abiding point the elicitation of specifiable emotional states in audiences. For example, Aristotle thought that the arousal of pity and fear was an essential feature of Greek tragedy.

Of course, all popular film genres engage emotions, generally a range of emotions. However, some genres appear dedicated to raising particular, predetermined emotional states in audiences just as Aristotle thought that Greek tragedy was predicated upon provoking pity and fear. That is, whereas all genres tend to evoke anger, joy, hatred, and the like, in addition to these emotions some genres also aim at arousing specific emotions in spectators as a condition of being an instance of the very genre in question. Or, to put it differently, raising various preordained emotions in spectators is the *sine qua non* of certain film genres. In these cases, the genres in question aim at the production of a particular emotion whose tincture colors the film as a whole.

Sometimes these genres are named by the very emotion it is their purpose to arouse. Suspense and horror are examples here. Moreover, other genres, like melodrama, though they are not named by the emotion whose point it would appear they are predicated upon provoking, nevertheless aim at arousing a roughly specifiable, preordained emotional response from spectators. This emotional response is dominant in the sense that it lends its aura to the film as a whole.

Suspense, horror, and melodrama, then, are three genres where films count as instances of the relevant genre only if they are dedicated to eliciting certain specifiable kinds of emotions from spectators. If my theory is to be even minimally convincing, it should have something to say about genres like these. Thus, for the remainder of this chapter, let me quickly review some of the applications of my theory to these genres.

Melodrama

The first step in applying our theoretical framework to a genre is to identify the dominating emotion that the genre aims to instill in audiences.[14] The term *melodrama* is perhaps an unwieldy one, and it may be difficult to isolate a single package of emotions that applies to everything that someone might be willing to classify under this notion. However, there is a relatively clear class of melodramas, often called "tearjerkers," that take as their subject matter what are loosely called "interpersonal relationships" and that appear to call forth certain massively recurring emotional responses. Three examples are *An Affair to Remember* (1957), *Back Street* (1932), and *Stella Dallas* (1937).

The fact that melodramas like these are often referred to as *tearjerkers* gives us an initial clue concerning their emotive domain. It should be something, all things being equal, that should warrant crying. Of course, crying can be elicited by many stimuli and can accompany many emotional states. Two such related states are sorrow and pity. Moreover, it should come as no surprise to the informed viewer that pity is the relevant tear-producing state that comes into play in the vast majority of melodramas.

Pity, of course, requires as a criterion of emotive appropriateness that its object be persons—we do not pity snowstorms—who have suffered misfortune. Thus, we expect from such melodramas that they be saliently comprised of misfortunes *suffered* by the protagonists.

I emphasize suffering here because the protagonists must feel the pain of their circumstances. Indeed, part of their misfortune is the pain that they feel as a result of their circumstances. Moreover, this misfortune—including the pain that, in part, comprises it—should not be seen as a matter of just desserts. We do not usually feel pity for villains who deserve to be annihilated. Melodramatic pity involves bad things happening to good people, or, at least, disproportionately bad things happening to people of mixed character.

It seems to me that the melodramatic emotion is not merely pity in the typical case of film melodrama. The standard film melodrama is not just a study in victimology. As already indicated, the ill-fortuned characters we weep for in many melodramas are of a certain sort. They are not victims pure and simple. They are people whom we admire; indeed, often we admire them for the way in which they negotiate their misfortune.

One important, recurring motif here is that the victim of melodramatic misfortune often accepts her suffering in order to benefit another, often at the expense of satisfying her own personal desires and interests. Sometimes, in fact, the character's misfortune is a result of the sacrifices she has made on behalf of others. For example, Stella Dallas's (Barbara Stanwyck) misfortune is the loss of her daughter, though she, in fact, has herself engineered this state of affairs on the basis of her belief that this will guarantee her daughter the best possible life.

Thus, we do not merely pity Stella Dallas. We admire her as well. The emotion that wells up in us as she watches her daughter's wedding from afar is not merely a result of pity, but is compounded of admiration as well. Often such emotions are called bittersweet. Perhaps the part that is pity is bitter (or dysphoric), but the part that we feel in response to Stella's noble self-sacrifice is sweet (or euphoric). To attempt to reduce our emotional states in cases like this to pity alone ignores the euphoric component in the response. We don't just feel bad about Stella, we feel good about her, too. That is because the dominating emotional response to the typical melodrama involves admiration—often motivated by a display of self-sacrifice—in addition to pity.

Were melodrama only a matter of pity—of witnessing horrible things happen to people—it might strike us as a particularly sadistic genre. It does not, I think, because typically the misfortunes in melodramas also provide the occasion for characters to exhibit noble virtues amid adversity, encouraging the spectator to leaven pity with admiration. A film of suffering unrelieved by virtue would be more likely an exercise in avant-garde realism than a melodrama. Melodramas are not all dark from the perspective of our emotional responses. Triumph is blended with tribulation so that pity comes in tandem with admiration.

In *An Affair to Remember* the female protagonist, Terry (Deborah Kerr), is struck down by a car on her way to a long-awaited rendezvous with her lover Nicky (Cary Grant). Their meeting, atop the Empire State Building, is supposed to symbolize their commitment to each other. Terry fails to make the appointment because of her accident. Terry's old boyfriend (Richard Denning) wants to tell Nicky what has happened, but Terry won't allow him. She feels that if Nicky learns that she has become disabled, his reaction will be pity, not love. Her silence is, in other words, principled. She does not want to take advantage of Nicky's sense of obligation. We may feel that Terry's course of action is ill-advised. But we admire her for her principles at the same time we pity her. Meanwhile, Nicky is becoming more and more embittered.

Perhaps the most emotionally wrought scene in the film comes at the end. Nicky still does not realize that Terry is disabled. He visits her apartment to deliver a shawl to her that his grandmother has bequeathed to Terry. He is still very hurt and angry. But just as he is about to leave, he realizes that Terry is disabled, that that's the reason why she missed their rendezvous, and, we presume, he also realizes that she didn't inform him because of a self-sacrificing desire to "protect him."

None of this is said. The audience infers that this is what is going on in Nicky's mind. Compactly, in a few seconds of screen time, this device encourages the audience to review the whole saga of Terry's adversity and nobility, jerking tears from man and woman alike. (I'm sniffling even as I write—and I don't have a cold.)

Similar scenes of recognition and acknowledgment are frequent in melodramas. The most moving scene in *Back Street* (1932), I think, occurs when the son learns the sacrifices his father's mistress made in order to sustain their relationship, while in *What's Eating Gilbert Grape?* (1993) the "viking funeral" of Gilbert's mother stands as a commemoration to her ultimate maternal integrity, despite all her other limitations. As in the case of *An Affair to Remember,* recognition/acknowledgment scenes like these serve to remind the audience not only of the bad things that have befallen the protagonists, but of their virtues as well. Pity attaches to the misfortunes, while admiration attaches to the virtues.

Even the ending of *Letter from an Unknown Woman* concludes on a note of admiration. Once the pianist learns of the self-sacrificing love of the unknown woman, he no longer acts the cad; he rides off to a doomed duel, shedding his selfishness and recognizing that, since the best thing in his life has just passed away, the only appropriate action is to join her in death. We pity their demise, but admire their willingness to die for their love.

Melodrama, then, frequently is rooted in engendering a compound emotion, comprising pity and admiration. The depictions and descriptions in a film like *An Affair to Remember* are criterially prefocused by making, on the one hand, misfortune, and, on the other hand, character virtues—especially self-sacrifice—salient to the audience. This, in turn, prompts spectators to be moved to feel pity and admiration, at least in cases where the audience has a pro attitude toward the characters. In *An Affair to Remember,* this is secured by portraying Terry and Nicky not only as very attractive and desirable people, but by establishing them to be persons of superior wit and culture (this is done especially in the voyage section of the film).

Once this pro attitude is in place, misfortune strikes, encouraging us to pity them, especially Terry, while at the same time providing a dramatic forum for Terry to exhibit her self-sacrificing nobility (finally to be joined by Nicky's when his recognition of that nobility leads him to love her all the more).

Horror

Like melodramas of the tearjerking variety, horror films are also designed to elicit a compound emotion.[15] And also like the tearjerker, one of the constituents of this emotional response is pretty evident. If melodramatic tearjerkers can be said uncontroversially to be aimed at eliciting pity from spectators, little argument seems required to establish that horror films are designed to provoke fear. Harmfulness, of course, is the criterion for fear. Thus, the depictions and descriptions in horror films are criterially prefocused to make the prospects for harm salient in the world of the fiction. The relevant harms here take the form of threats—generally lethal threats—to the protagonists in the horror film, and the locus of these threats is standardly a monster, an entity of supernatural or sci-fi provenance whose very existence defies the bounds of contemporary scientific understanding.

These monsters possess powers or propensities that make them threatening to human life. Most often, they are also hostile to the human protagonists in the relevant films. Usually they are bent on destroying or enslaving the humans. Moreover, they have certain capacities or advantages—such as great strength, cunning, indomitable technologies, supernatural abilities, or even invisibility—that are not easily deterred. This makes them particularly dangerous and fearsome. Here the fear that the audience emotes with regard to the monster is not fear for its own survival. Our fear is engendered in behalf of the human characters in the pertinent films. We cringe when the Werewolf of London stalks his prey, not because we fear that he will trap us, but because we fear for some character in the film. When the outsized arachnid in *Earth vs. the Spider* (1958) awakens to the beat of rock 'n roll music, we fear for the teenagers, not for ourselves.

But though fear is a necessary condition for horror, it is not sufficient. Many films conjure up fear on the basis of scientific improbabilities without

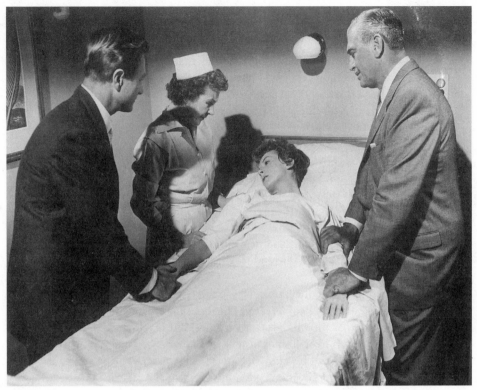

Terry (Deborah Kerr), disabled and hospitalized in *An Affair
to Remember* (1957).

counting as horror films. Examples include time travel films where merciless
fascists from the future are arriving in the here and now to gain a foothold,
or *When Worlds Collide* (1951). Fear, in short, is not the whole of horror, just
as pity is not the whole of melodrama.

Though fearful, our emotive response to the oncoming planet in *When
Worlds Collide* is different from our reaction to the monster in *Species* (1995),
Xtro (1983), or *The Relic* (1997). For we not only find those latter entities fearsome, they are also disgusting. Were a part of their anatomy to find its way
into our mouth, like the tentacles of so many slimy aliens, we would want to
gag and to spit it out.[16] The thought of ingesting a piece of such creatures
invites nausea. If we touched one of them, we would try to scrub our hands
clean at the soonest opportunity. Think of the zombies in *Night of the Living
Dead* (1968), or the giant, dribbling snails in *The Monster that Challenged the
World* (1957).

We find the monsters in horror films repulsive and abhorrent. They are not only fearsome, they are somehow unclean, reviling, and loathsome by their very nature. Vampires, for example, are frequently associated with vermin and disease.

Monsters generally fall into the category that the Bible calls abominations. Even if such monsters were not dangerous, their very being is such that we would wish to avoid them and to refrain from touching them. The very thought of them is repelling—enough to make our flesh crawl, our spine tingle, and our throat choke shut. The most suitable expletives for them are "Ugh" and "Yuck!"

Thus, the objects that comprise the objects of our emotional response in horror films elicit a compound reaction in terms of fear and disgust. The fear component of our response is grounded in the fact that in the world of the fiction these monsters constitute clear and present dangers. They are harmful. But they are also disgusting, and the emotive criterion for disgust is impurity. Thus, the depictions and descriptions in horror films are criterially prefocused in terms of foregrounding the harmfulness *and* the impurity of the monsters.

The harmfulness of the monsters is usually exhibited readily in their behavior. They are killing people, eating them, dismembering them, or taking possession of either their minds or their souls. But in addition to their evident harmfulness, horror-film monsters are also impure. Their impurity, in turn, can be manifested by means of several generally recurring strategies, usually involving the violation of standing cultural categories in various ways.

For example, horror-film monsters may be categorically hybrid, mixing different biological or ontological orders. The creature in *The Relic* blends various species, being part reptile, part human, and part (?) water buffalo. As the very title of the film signals, the zombies in *Night of the Living Dead* appear to be members of an ontologically self-contradictory set of things—creatures that are both living *and* dead at the same time. Many horror-film monsters violate defining characteristics of the categories they supposedly belong to. The giant spider alluded to earlier is at least a thousand times bigger than the largest possible spider.

Moreover, many horrific monsters are incomplete examples of their category—they are so often missing parts like arms, legs, eyes, and even heads. Or sometimes they are heads or just brains without bodies. And last, some horrific beings are altogether so formless that it would be hard to assign them to any category. The Blob is formless throughout the film of the same name. But, of course, many horrific creatures, like vampires, can assume formlessness at will or start out formless before they take over some else's body.

The monster in *From Beyond* (1986) is designed in such a way that it exploits a number of these strategies for projecting horrific impurity. Edward

Zombies in George Romero's *Night of the Living Dead* (1968).

Praetorius (Ted Sorel) has developed a machine whose sonic vibrations give him access to another dimension inhabited by noxious, ill-tempered creatures that resemble lampreys. During his first penetration of this alternative dimension, his head is bitten off. The police assume he is dead and they arrest his assistant as a suspect. Encouraged by a psychiatrist to work through his trauma, the assistant restages Praetorius's experiment. As the alternative dimension becomes manifest, it turns out that Praetorius is not dead. He has gone over to live on the other side.

However, as is par for the course in mad-scientist movies, all is not well with Praetorius. His mind has melded with that of some other-dimensional being. He is evolving into a new kind of hybrid or composite entity. On Praetorius's second manifestation, much of his human body has disappeared into a mass of tissue. He is half a face attached to a gelatinous, decomposing mound of flesh. Not only is he mostly amorphous, but he can dissolve at will into oozing goo. Part of his horrific signature is his ability to go in and out of formlessness, formlessness of a sort that is all the more sickening for being sticky and saliva-like.

Praetorius cannot merely transform himself from bodily articulateness to formlessness, he can also take on parts of different genera. So the sucker of a giant leech can burst through his human forehead. Thus, in addition to exploiting the line between form and formlessness, Praetorius is also a categorically hybrid creature—sometimes displaying parts of several species simultaneously and sometimes changing from one kind of creature into another sequentially.

The categorical distinction between inside and outside is also contradicted and breached in Praetorius's biology; his extended pineal gland waves about externally like an antenna. Sometimes Praetorius has one arm, sometimes two. In addition to all his other problems, then, he is also at times categorically incomplete.

The creature Praetorius has been designed by the filmmakers of *From Beyond* as if in an attempt to touch all the bases when it comes to horrific impurity. There is something to disgust virtually everyone in Praetorius's makeup (both biological and dramaturgical).

And, perhaps needless to say, Praetorius is also quite dangerous. Like so many other mad scientists he, in concert with other-dimensional creatures who also inhabit his body, take it into his (their?) head(?) to conquer the world. His great intelligence, amplified by his experience of other dimensions, poses a great threat to humanity as does his superhuman strength and telekinetic prowess. He represents the greatest potential harm humanity has ever known, so the film avows, and the portal he has opened to the other world must be closed.

Looking at a horror film like *From Beyond* from an analytic point of view requires dissecting, so to say, the way in which the monster has been designed to engender a horrified emotional response from audiences. One proceeds by noting how the monster has been composed and set into action in accordance to the criteria appropriate to the emotion of horror. In *From Beyond,* Praetorius's attributes rehearse the themes of impurity and danger in many dimensions. By saliently posing these criterially prefocused attributes, the filmmakers encourage the audience to subsume or to assess them under the categories of the impure and the harmful in a way that is apt to promote emotive focus of a horrific variety. Moreover, if my hypothesis is correct, once this sort of emotive focus takes control, the audience keeps surveying the image of Praetorius for further evidence of impurity and danger, thereby sustaining the operation of their ongoing emotional processes.

Suspense

Suspense is not exactly a genre unto itself, since suspense is an emotion that is often elicited in many other genres.[17] In *An Affair to Remember,* we feel suspense about whether or not Nicky will see that Terry never abandoned her love for him. And in so many horror films, suspense is engendered over the question of whether or not Earth can be saved from the onslaught of flying saucers, rampaging zombies, pod people, birds, or whatever. In *The Arrival*, which is a science-fiction horror film, suspense is generated over the question of whether the alien attempt to transform ("terraform") the atmosphere of earth can be unmasked. Suspense, it would appear, is a genre classification that cuts across other genre classifications.

Nevertheless, we do talk of suspense films. These, roughly speaking, are films, perhaps of almost any other genre, that either contain arresting or memorable suspense scenes as major parts of the narrative, or that conclude with a rousing suspense sequence, or, maybe most paradigmatically, films that are organized virtually in their entirety around resolving certain dominant, suspenseful questions, such as "can the assassination be averted?"

Suspense is a future-oriented emotion. In everyday life, we don't normally feel suspense about what happened in the past. I don't feel suspense about the outcome of World War II, since I already know it. Suspense is a posture that we typically adopt to what will happen, not to what has happened.

But suspense is not an emotion that takes possession of us with respect to just any future event. I do not feel suspense about whether or not I will go to work tomorrow because I think that it is highly probable that I will go and, moreover, I want to go. In everyday life, suspense takes over where the odds are against—or at least up in the air—concerning something that I want to happen, or, conversely, where something that I do not want to happen seems probable. If it looks like the candidate whom I oppose is either likely to win or has just as good a chance of winning as the candidate I support, then I feel suspense over the outcome of the election. But if the candidate I oppose cannot possibly win and the candidate I favor cannot possibly lose, then there is little room for me to feel suspense.

Suspense concerns probabilities. It is not simply a matter of uncertainty. I am uncertain about the outcome of many future events, but I do not feel suspense in regard to them. Suspense only takes hold where the probabilities seem to be running against some outcome that I prefer, or, to put it the other way around, where the probabilities are running in favor of some outcome that I would rather not obtain. Moving from everyday life to film fiction, for example, as the townspeople are savaged by the outlaws, we feel suspense, since what we want—the rescue of the villagers—is unlikely because the cavalry is still miles away.

The emotion of suspense takes as its object some future event whose desired outcome is improbable, or, at least, no more probable than the undesired outcome; indeed, with suspense, the undesired outcome is characteristically much more probable than the desired outcome. That is to say that the emotive criteria appropriate to regarding an event with suspense is such that the event promises that an undesired outcome appears likely, while the desired outcome seems unlikely. Thus, in constructing suspense episodes, filmmakers must criterially prefocus their depictions and descriptions in such a way that the audience's desires and the probabilities that attach to them come apart.

Perhaps the ways in which filmmakers structure events so that certain outcomes appear probable and others improbable requires little more explanation than the ways in which they make the plights of the characters in melodramas pitiable, or the monsters in horror films fearsome. The rescue of the heroine in the burning building is so unlikely because the flames are so high and the hero is so far away and anyway he is engaged in a losing battle with four implacable villains. Her life hangs on a slender thread, stretched to the breaking point. However, the answer to the question of how filmmakers dispose audiences to prefer certain outcomes over others may be less obvious.

In order to mobilize suspense in an audience, a fiction filmmaker has to get the audience to care about one of the outcomes of the course of affairs she is narrating. She has to engender the audience's concern in such a way that the audience desires the outcome that the narrative depicts as vastly improbable, or, at least, no more probable than the countervailing alternative. But is there any fairly reliable way for the filmmaker to do this? After all, the filmmaker is designing her movie for an audience most of whose members she does not know personally. She has no access to their private preferences and desires. How can she be fairly certain that by characterizing a situation one way rather than another, she will enlist the audience's concern in the way that she needs to in order to make the scene work in terms of suspense? This is a general problem that confronts all suspense filmmakers. Moreover, it has a straightforward solution that is in evidence in virtually every suspense film ever made.

In order to encourage the kind of concern that is requisite for suspense, the filmmaker has to locate some shared stratum of interests and preferences in diverse audiences about whom she has little or no personal knowledge. That is, she has to find some common interests or preferences in the audience such that they will support the suspense response. Here, morality turns out to be the card that almost every suspense film plays. Morality supplies a fairly common set of sentiments that are apt to be shared by most typical viewers. Thus we find in most suspense films that the object of the emotion is an event whose *evil* outcomes are probable and whose *righteous* outcomes are improbable, or, at least, no more probable than the evil ones.

When the train is no more than ten feet away from the heroine strapped to the tracks, the evil machinations of the villain seem inevitable. Likewise, in *Secret Agent* (1936) when "the General" is about to push the kindly old gentleman, misidentified as a spy, over the cliff, we find ourselves in the grip of suspense because averting the murder seems impossible (Ashenden [John Gielgud], the only person who could stop the event, is half a mile away in an observatory, watching the assassination, in anguish, through a telescope) at the same time that we regard the deed as immoral (in part because we share Ashenden's scruples and perhaps, in part, because we realize that the evidence that the old man is a spy is not only slim, but contradicted by his altogether generous, open demeanor). Similarly, in *Speed* (1994) suspense takes over for much of the film because there seems to be no way that the hurtling bus won't be blown to smithereens, killing all of the innocent passengers. In films like *Ransom* (1996), suspense seems to become most excruciating just when it appears that the villain is going to get away.

Of course, the sense of morality that operates in such films is not always the same as the morality that rules our everyday affairs. Often we feel inclined toward projects in films that we would never endorse in "real life." For example, caper films represent persons involved in perpetrating crimes that we do not usually condone. However, it is often the case that films shape our ethical responses to them in a way that diverges from our everyday moral judgments.

Perhaps the most important lever that filmmakers possess for influencing our assessment of the morality of scenes in suspense films involves character portrayal. That is, we tend to accept the projects of characters in suspense films who strike us as virtuous. With caper films, for example, we find that the protagonists in such fictions are standardly possessed of certain striking virtues; and in the absence of countervailing virtues in their opposite number, or possibly given the emphasis on the outright vice of their opponents, we tend to ally ourselves morally with the caper. The virtues in question here—strength, fortitude, ingenuity, bravery, competence, beauty, generosity, and so on—are more often than not Grecian, rather than Christian. But it is because the characters exhibit these virtues—it is because we perceive (and are led to perceive) these characters as virtuous—that we cast our moral allegiance with them.

If the protagonists are represented as possessed of some virtues and their opponents are less virtuous, altogether bereft of virtue, or downright vicious, suspense can take hold because the efforts of the protagonists are morally correct in accordance with the ethical system of the film. Of course, it is probably the case that generally the actions of the protagonists in typical films are morally correct in accordance with some prevailing ethical norms shared by the majority of the audience. However, in cases in which this consensus does not obtain, the protagonist's possession of saliently underlined virtues will project the moral valuations of the fiction and, indeed, incline the audience toward accepting that perspective as its own. Thus it turns out that sometimes even an antagonist can serve as the object of suspense, as long as he or she is presented as possessed of some virtues. In fact, at the limit, I suspect that even a vicious character and his plight can become the object of suspense when he is portrayed as an utterly helpless victim, since the audience's sense of rectitude recoils at the prospect of harming truly helpless victims.

Typically the criteria that an event in a fiction film will meet in order to serve as an appropriate object of suspense involve morality and probability. The depictions and descriptions in suspense films criterially prefocus the events they characterize in terms of outcomes in which the triumph of evil is likely while the prospects for righteousness are slight. Making these features of the courses of events in a fiction film salient is apt to elicit emotive focus in accordance with the criteria appropriate to suspense. Thus, spectators in the grip of suspense fix their attention on the details that contribute to the probability and morality rankings of the unfolding actions in the story. Moreover, once in the thrall of suspense, their emotive focus avidly tracks the fluctuating probabilities in the contest between moral good and evil on the screen.

Analyzing a suspense sequence or a suspense film, then, involves isolating the thematic and stylistic choices that play a role in the criterial prefocusing of the film text. With suspense, those will be the elements of depiction and description that lead the audience to make the relevant assessments concerning the probabilities and moral values of the alternative outcomes of the unfolding action.

Analyzing the ways in which horror films elicit the emotion after which the genre is named also involves attending to the way in which the film text is criterially prefocused. However, in this case, the relevant emotive criteria are not probability and morality, but harm and impurity, and the object of the emotion in question is a being, the monster, and not an event, as it is with respect to suspense. Thus, the horror analyst will attend to the way in which the monster is structured to bring properties in accordance with the criteria of harm and impurity to the fore, and to the way that the plot affords opportunities both to allow the monster to display these properties and to permit the human characters an occasion to talk about and to describe them.

With melodrama, criterial prefocusing is again crucial, though the criteria appropriate to what we might call the melodramatic emotion—a compound of pity and admiration—are misfortune and virtue (generally of an other-regarding and often of a self-sacrificing sort). Pithing the structure that gives rise to the melodramatic emotion involves attending to incidents that set forth the misfortunes and virtues of characters and to the ways in which these are emphasized dramatically, narratively, and cinematically.

Concluding Remarks

In this chapter I have proposed a sketch of a theoretical framework for analyzing the relation between film and what I have called the emotions proper (or, alternatively, the garden-variety emotions). I have also attempted to show the significance of this program for the analysis of various genres that are universally acknowledged to traffic in certain well-known emotional states.

Throughout, I have repeatedly stressed the importance of criterial prefocusing for eliciting emotive focus. My hypothesis has been that by criterially prefocusing the film text—where the criteria in question are the ones appropriate to certain emotions—filmmakers encourage spectators to assess or to subsume the events onscreen under certain categories, namely the categories pertinent to the excitation of the relevant emotional states.

Through criterial prefocusing we could say that the filmmaker leads the horse to water. But the circuit is not completed until the audience drinks. In order for that to occur, the audience must cognize the film text in the ways that the filmmaker has made salient through criterial prefocusing. That means subsuming the onscreen events under the intended criterially governed categories or, alternatively, assessing the onscreen events in light of the intended emotive criteria. But whichever way you prefer to put it, the audience's faculties of cognition and judgment are brought into play in the process of eliciting an emotional response to film. Thus we see that even when it comes to analyzing the relation of film to the emotions, a cognitively oriented approach to film theory has much to offer.

❧ TWO ❧

Sentiment in Film Viewing

ED S. H. TAN AND NICO H. FRIJDA

Introduction

A father is taken to *Pocahontas* (1995) by his wife and children. At one of the
film's climaxes, the character Pocahontas stands up in public against her
father, a powerful Indian chief, and persuades him not to engage in a revenge
action against the English settlers, thus preventing a terrible war. The father
in the cinema fights his tears in the dark. Looking at his son, he notices that
the boy just watches the scene attentively, and the father feels embarrassed
about his own feelings.

The example represents a very common emotion episode. In situations
like this, most observers will not have difficulty in recognizing the father's
affect as a kind of sentimental emotion, or sentiment for short. Yet, the term
sentiment is not a label that persons readily assign to their own perceived
emotional state. First of all, it has a pejorative connotation. Sentimentality is
silly, and a sentimental emotion is often considered phony, or unsincere, and
this goes all the more if it is an artificial stimulus like film that causes that
affect. Sentimentality is also associated with weakness and femininity in a
sense hostile to women. Second, it is difficult to grasp what a sentiment actually is. There may be considerable variability in the meaning of the term for
various individuals, and from a theoretical point of view sentimental emotions may be blends of several emotions, rather than just one. Perhaps one
of the reasons for the unclarity is that the emotions referred to by this term
are obviously more complex than the more common emotions such as fear,
sorrow, and anger. In addition, sentimentality tends to be associated with the
response to cultural products rather than to real-life situations. Moreover,
the cultural products involved, such as popular literature, theater, and film,
are considered of lower standing. This has not always been the case. Indeed,
a short history of the meaning of the term *sentiment* and the sentimental may
deepen our understanding of what sentimental emotion really is. But before

we proceed, we need to delineate sentiment from other kinds of affect in a preliminary fashion.

Sentimentality is almost invariably linked with crying. There are other emotions in which we shed tears, or at least feel a strong urge to cry, in particular sadness and being moved. But a sentimental emotion is not the same as sadness, although the two go together very well. In sadness, we recognize a loss of some importance. We can be moved to tears without being sentimental, as long as we know what moves us, and feel that its importance matches the intensity of our emotion. By a sentimental emotion, on the other hand, we mean an emotion characterized by an urge to cry or a state of being moved with a strength in excess to the importance we attach to its reason. As we shall see, the urge to cry is in turn associated with a state of general softening or helplessness. A second characteristic of what we refer to as sentiments is that they mostly occur as a response to the fate of others. You watch someone else's fortune or misfortune, and suddenly you find yourself crying, without understanding exactly why the precipitating event would touch you so. Finally, sentimental emotions have a certain measure of gratuitousness. They are not of such a nature as to motivate taking or abstaining from action. Hence, often though not always, the judgment of insincerity or superficiality of the emotions under concern.

Note that one may attach the label "sentimental" to one's own emotion—the father in the *Pocahontas* example may well not have understood where his upsurge of feeling came from—as well as to the emotion of someone else: paraplegic patients tend to weep "too profusely" when visiting relatives leave the hospital.[1]

A Short History of Sentimentalism

Sentimental emotion has not always been regarded as cheap affect, and in some cultures sentimentality or its equivalents have been or are much less taboo than today in our culture. In India, for instance, a blossoming industry has produced sentimental movies for a home mass audience, as we know. It should also not be overlooked that sentiment-prone subcultures can be found next to anyone's door: the popularity of soap television series among all categories of viewers should attest to this. And it is not very long ago that sentiment was considered a sophisticated feeling in this culture. The term "sentiment" in a sense neighboring to its present use seems to date back only to the end of the eighteenth century, when the word first stood for sincere opinion and later acquired the sense of pure and delicate feeling, as in Lawrence Sterne's *A Sentimental Journey through France and Italy*. R. F. Brissenden pointed out that authors of sentimental literature from the Romantic period until the present aimed at elevating the morals of their readership, by appealing to and refining their emotions and their natural feeling for what is virtuous and good.[2] The central theme of the sentimental novel, according to Brissenden, is the virtuous character who finds himself or herself in distress due to circumstances not his or her fault. It is not the events in themselves that are emphasized, but the feelings that characters undergo. Their analysis of intricate and perplexing situations and resulting moral discrimination is highlighted, rather than the doing of good deeds. Annemieke Meijer argues that plots of *sudden reversal* facilitate the theme of virtue in distress: a sudden loss of fortune, a rediscovered child or parent, and other strokes of fate, while meandering or fragmented storylines also make for depiction of strong character emotions. The sentimental novel does not excel in originality. It draws on a collection of conventional situations and stock characters. Purple passages, writes Meijer, are given in tableaux, such as deathbed and reunion scenes.

Although the description of sentimentalism refers to eighteenth-century literature, it is not hard to see striking parallels with a large body of contemporary popular film, and especially with Hollywood melodrama from the 1910s to the 1960s. This type of melodrama is set in the domestic environment of marriage and the family. The leading characters are women. Some arbitrary examples are D. W. Griffith's *Way Down East* (1920), Frank Borzage's *A Man's Castle* (1933), David Lean's *Brief Encounter* (1945), and Douglas Sirk's *All I Desire* (1953).

Robert Lang points out that the melodrama is a drama of identity. The conflict in one way or another centers around the definition of the woman's identity, and her struggle against the forces of male dominance and society's traditional conceptions of the role of women and men. It is the latter "virtue," the traditional conception of women's identity, that is in distress. The emphasis on the woman's view represents the melodrama's potential contribution to cultural dissent. However, even the most vehement melodrama does not directly call for a radical change, in that it does not offer a better alternative.[3] As Thomas Schatz notes,

> Whereas the characters of romantic or screwball comedies scoff at social decorum and propriety, in melodrama they are at the mercy of social conventions; whereas the comedies integrated the anarchic lovers into a self-sufficient marital unit distinct from their social milieu, the melodrama traces the ultimate *resignation* of the principals to the strictures of social and familial tradition.[4]

This does not mean that the melodrama's ending consists of an unequivocal restoration of the order as in the Western or the detective film, where it is due to the male protagonist's action. Here a parallel presents itself between the melodrama on the one hand, and the sentimental novel on the other: it is the analysis of feeling that counts, rather than the action. And in this analysis a "j'accuse" may be implied, as is the case in *Brief Encounter* (1945), a British film, by the way. However, in general, the Hollywood melodrama does not draw the distinction between virtue and vice as sharply as to make it an outspoken accusation, as its precursor, the sentimental novel, used to do.

In contrast to the melodrama, in the Hollywood action and adventure genres the distinction between good and bad resembles an absolute Manichean contrast, as Murray Smith has shown.[5] Hence, in this major respect, these "male" genres may just as well be considered sentimental, especially when the portrayal of the action is complemented by disclosure of the protagonist's feelings, in whatever crude and sketchy form. In line with this, Steve Neale has pointed out that not only the Hollywood family melodrama but, in fact, all classical action-centered film genres also spring from nineteenth-century theatrical melodrama.[6] This is because theatrical melodrama comprises a wealth of genres that have the provocation of strong emotion in common. Like the sentimental novel it obeys a convention of sudden ups and downs. Heavy use was made of perplexing spectacular special effects, and acting was based on prescribed movements that were assumed to pass the character's sentiments on to the audience in a direct fashion. Diderot's idea of creating sentiment through a perfect technique, although more widespread in more serious theater, may have been influential here.[7]

The common root in theatrical melodrama and the sentimental novel, then, may account for the potential of all classical genres to provoke sentimental emotions as the response to the portrayal of some incarnation of *virtue* in distress, be it either damsel or male hero. Sentimentality may be the dominant kind of emotion in the family melodrama, but it is also part and parcel of the Western as well as the gangster, the detective, the screwball, and the musical films. The Hollywood movie, it has been observed by many, is thoroughly melodramatic in a wider sense, in that it is theatrical, excessive, and aims at enlarging emotion.

The Psychology of Emotion in the Film Viewer

From a psychological perspective, cinema sentiment is an emotional state in the film viewer. Elsewhere we have offered a comprehensive account of emotion in the film viewer. It complies largely with Carl Plantinga's proposal for a cognitive-affective theory of film spectatorship.[8] Elsewhere we argued that affect in the film viewer is a genuine emotion from a psychological point of view.[9] We showed that Frijda's general theory of the emotions can explain the film viewer's experience.[10] Here, we can only summarize some major points of the account. Emotions occur when a situation is relevant for an individual's concerns. They consist of an appraisal of the situation's significance and an action tendency. The emotional experience is the awareness of the situation's particular meaning in terms of a relevance for a concern, reality and difficulty, and the felt-action tendency. The action tendency itself consists of an inclination to act in a particular way. For example, fear is an appraisal of a threat of physical harm that cannot be countered, and the urge to run away, to protect oneself, or to freeze. The action tendency in emotion, moreover, is characterized by its control precedence. That is, it strives toward completion at the cost of other ongoing actions and cognitive processes. This is what lends any emotion its force and relative impenetrability to purely cognitive considerations.

Film-elicited emotion, furthermore, consists largely of *witness emotions*. That is, the major affects in film viewing correspond to affects in daily life when we watch people to which we relate in one way or another, who are involved in an emotional situation, but under conditions in which we cannot act, be acted upon, or otherwise participate in the situation except as onlookers. We are concerned about their fate, but have to wait for the outcomes. The viewers of films are led to imagine themselves as invisible witnesses that are physically present in the fictional world. Emotions arising from this awareness may be called *F emotions*, since they are responses to events in the fictional world. Emotions when viewing film may also be evoked by the film as a manmade artifact. *A emotions*, as we have dubbed these, include enjoyment and admiration of the film as a film. We will concentrate on F emotions. Being a witness affords the viewer to take specific positions or attitudes with regard to events. The film narrative controls these attitudes to a large degree. It can stress the viewer's awareness of the significance of the situation in the fictional world to the protagonists. In this case, the protagonist's appraisal is included in the viewer's representation of the situation. The viewer then shares in the feelings of the protagonist. The F emotion here is an *empathetic* emotion, and sympathy, compassion, and admiration are the most common examples. The viewer's knowledge may differ from that of the protagonist. For instance, we experience empathetic fear when the protagonist is in danger without knowing. Many empathetic emotions, including sentimental ones, are determined by some knowledge discrepancy between the viewers and the protagonists. However, in all empathetic emotion, the significance of the situation for the protagonist is relevant for the viewer's emotion. In *nonempathetic* emotion this is not so. As cinema spectators, we enjoy the sight of a majestic landscape or the looks of a protagonist regardless of what they mean to the protagonist's fate and feeling.[11]

Viewer Sentiment and Film Sentiment

Contemporary research in the psychology of emotion on the subject of sentimental emotion is scarce. Still it has added a few insights to the description of sentiment that emerges from a historical account of sentimental cultural products. The first is the distinction between sentimentality in the stimulus and sentimentality in the recipient, which parallels the distinction of emotion in the film and in the recipient generally. The former is a representation of fictional affects in a fictional character, whereas the latter is a psychological state in an empirical individual. So far, no explicit description has been given of the nature of emotions in the viewer. It often seems to be assumed that the viewer's emotion is a reduplication of the one represented in the fiction; this is plainly incorrect. To be sure, tears of sentiment are contagious, as all tears are. And we will shortly see why sentimental emotion is even more contagious than sorrow.

Sentimental emotion *in* the film, however, does not necessarily provoke sentimental emotion in the viewer—if it does provoke any emotion at all— and, conversely, sentimental emotion in the viewer does not only occur in response to sentimental emotion shown on screen. The *Pocahontas* example may be illustrative here again: the father in the cinema cries, while the character Pocahontas is not sentimental at all. We believe that in the typical case the viewer's emotion does not parallel the one observed in the protagonists, for reasons that will be discussed later.

Sentiment and Helplessness: General Effects

Both in common speech and in psychological research, sentimental emotion is associated with an inclination for crying. It is this inclination that in this culture lends sentimentality its embarrassing qualities, especially for men, as in the *Pocahontas* example. Frijda argues that crying is a response to helplessness, rather than specifically to grief.[12] It is, in fact, a submission response, and occurs in confrontation with other people as well as with events the power of which one recognizes; the philosopher Helmuth Plessner labeled crying a "capitulation response."[13] Tears of joy and tears of grief have in common that they occur in situations that are experienced as overwhelming, as situations that one feels unable to control, to deal with, or retain one's distance from. Sorrow that makes one cry concerns a loss one feels is irremediable; joy that makes one cry concerns a gain one feels unable to handle or over which one fails to be the master. Crying is a sign that one yields to the helplessness with regard to the emotional situation at hand, either because one is unable to do something about that situation, or because one gives in to one's felt inability, and perhaps willingly abandons to one's lack of power. In agreement with this interpretation, it has been observed that episodes in which the subject has been struggling with some difficulty end in crying when he or she gives in, or when resistance is not necessary any more. For instance, J. S. Efran and T. J. Spangler argue that the audience of *The Miracle Worker* (1962) cries exactly at these points where the narration lifts a barrier to the protagonist's well-being that it had previously created.[14] Their explanation is that this lifting of the barrier results in some relief or discharge of tension.

However, another, more cognitive explanation seems more appropriate, because it does not use a hydraulic metaphor. Resistance of the subjects ends because some resolution has been met with. That implies that viewers can allow themselves to accept the situation as the fulfillment of an important goal, or have to accept it because it cannot be changed by the protagonist. In response to this cognitive change the subjects may let go and accept their helplessness in the given situation or over the episode.

Elsewhere we have pointed out that the traditional film narrative invokes a number of emotion episodes in the viewer characterized by high levels of interest.[15] Each scene in a film conforming to classical principles of narration sets up a complication and presents a temporary resolution, as David Bordwell points out.[16] The viewer's response to a scene is an emotion episode in which interest and empathetic feelings like hope and fear increase with the difficulties the protagonist meets. It ends with joy or sorrow, and compassion or admiration, depending on the outcome. The viewer's appraisal that there is an outcome, whatever its kind, signals an abrupt break in interest and the sympathetic emotions like those mentioned. This allows acceptance of the state of affairs as it is, a standing-still of expectations, and hence allows for tears, almost as a function of the discomfort caused by the problem dealt with in the scene. This means that any major resolution in a conflict where the stakes are high in a traditional film's action can give rise to some kind of sentimentality. In every film there are climactic moments where interest in the viewer after a steady rise is highest, and where it is broken by the first unambiguous sign of a resolution: the onset of a kiss in the love scene, the resolute turning of the body at a final goodbye, the one gesture that signals acceptance after a long rejection. But sentimental emotion may also readily occur in more offhand scenes, like those of the *Pocahontas* example, that from *Pretty Woman* to come, and that of E.T. when he says he wants to go home.

The location by eminence of sentiment-provoking stimuli in the plot explains why sentiment in the cinema is an aspect of characteristic emotional blends. At moments where a temporary or more permanent resolution is presented, viewers necessarily experience emotions that have the outcome events and the nature of the main characters as their object. First, there is joy as a response to a favorable outcome and, less commonly, sadness where an unfavorable outcome is definitive and becomes part of life. Second, there is relief where hopes are fulfilled and fears are terminated. And third, there are acute feelings toward the protagonist, like pity and admiration, and corresponding feelings toward the antagonist, such as anger and *schadenfreude*. All these outcome-related emotions lend themselves to yielding or submitting on the part of the viewer. We admit that we are smaller than the events taking place and the spectacle we watch, in the magnitude of the sorrow or joy, or of the manner in which the protagonists carry their fate, or of the purity, the completeness of feeling. At least, that may get a sense of being faced with something we have to accept and to submit to, as the way things go. In particular, with respect to the protagonist, it is as if we have to conclude that "your victory or your tragedy is larger than mine, or that of anybody else." It is this part of our understanding of the meaning of events that renders our emotions sentimental.

The outcomes that elicit sentimental emotions are changes for better or for worse in the protagonist's life. The nature of the changes determines which emotions they are. The emotions may obscure the sentimental response from the viewer's awareness; the emotions themselves may be dominant in the viewer's consciousness. They have objects that are readily recognizable in the film, whereas the sentimental aspect is a response to a change in an inner process, that is, an abrupt giving up of coping effort or expectation. Sentiment in the film tends to hide behind pity, gratefulness, admiration, and the like feelings aimed at objects in the fictional world.

Yet, the sentimental is a true emotional variant. It is a variation of emotion in its own right because it has its own mode action tendency. The action tendency in sentiment is to yield to the overwhelming. This accounts for the embarrassing quality of sentiment. The helplessness in sentiment, when recognized, does not conform to the ideal autonomous self that most of us prefer, and is the cause of embarrassment under normal circumstances. But in the dark of the cinema and, more so perhaps, in the safety of the witness position, we are more free to allow ourselves the enjoyment of temporary weakness. That is a second feature showing sentiments to form a true subclass of emotions: they have the appraisal of personal safety, and of being discharged of any obligation to act, as their condition. Both because of the sentimental emotion's action tendency itself, that is, yielding, and the gratuitous safety and our resulting readiness to let go, sentiment in the cinema tends to lift a number of control mechanisms. Hence all other emotions can be intensified as a diffuse effect of sentiment. The fact that sentiment acts as a hidden intensifier may be one of the reasons why people often report that they are astonished about the force of their emotions in the cinema.

Film Themes Provoking Sentiment

So far we have discussed sentiment as a response of helplessness and submissiveness in the face of the overwhelming, and related to the tension-relaxing qualities of the narrative's points of resolution. There are some major emotional themes that are particularly conducive to provoking sentimental emotions. Psychological research into the functioning of these themes is in its infancy, and the ideas that we present are largely speculative. The three themes we think we can identify are the separation-reunion theme, the justice in jeopardy motive, and the awe-inspiration theme.

The Separation-Reunion Theme

The separation-reunion theme is quite common in sentimental films. A child has been separated from the parents (*A Hole in the Head* [1959]; *The King of the Hill* [1993]), is lost (*The Wizard of Oz* [1939]), rejected (*Little Lord Fauntleroy* [1980]), or mistaken for someone else (*Anastasia* [1956]). After many complications it returns home, is accepted again or recognized. The theme acts upon a basic attachment concern. Attachment concerns are desires to seek, retain, or regain intimacy, proximity, and dependency to selected individuals. Such concerns belong to the basic and universal human equipment as shown by Harry Harlow's famous research.[17] They are basic, not only in the sense of being part of the biological equipment, but also in that they are not the result of other concerns such as, for instance, the need for food. John Bowlby has given a complete account of the basis and development of attachment strivings.[18]

For our purposes it is especially important to stress Bowlby's finding that in an individual's lifetime the most intense emotions arise during moments that derive their significance from attachment concerns. The situations activating the concern have to do with the formation, maintenance, disruption, and renewal of attachment relationships. Attachment behavior is not restricted to children:

> In view of attachment behavior being potentially active throughout life and also of its having the vital biological function proposed, it is held a grave error to suppose that, when active in an adult, attachment behavior is indicative either of pathology or of regression to immature behavior. The latter view, which is characteristic of almost all other versions of psychoanalytic theory, results from . . . theories of orality and dependency which are rejected here as out of keeping with the evidence.[19]

To explain why so many people are overwhelmed by witnessing separation and especially reunion scenes, it has to be assumed either that even in individuals with favorable life histories, separations from the parents and especially the mother have left some sensitive mark, or that people as a social species have a hankering for bonding that is never fully satisfied and renders every (re-)union of some importance a "coming home." A third possibility is that most people have strong, though not always as easily accessible, memories of safety, warmth, and acceptance from early infancy.[20] It may be that people have learned that permanent strong bonds are, in fact, rare, and the disappointment is temporarily elevated by the recognition of the possibility as demonstrated by a scene one happens to witness, in film or in reality.

In any case, the sentimental response implies that in our culture there is some difficulty involved with attachment that is suddenly lifted by the stim-

Dorothy (Judy Garland) separated from her family in *The Wizard of Oz* (1939).

ulus. The separation-reunion theme has several variants. One of these is the acceptance variant, which seems to be more effective in provoking sentiment in men.[21] Being accepted as a son or a man by a father, an older brother, or a community of men is a theme that makes male viewers cry in the cinema. For instance, as Lothar Mikos observes about *Pretty Woman* (1989),

> Numerous men report that they cried during a specific scenic arrangement of a situation in the film. Independent of the actual plot, what counts to these men is a particular gesture, understood scenically and accompanied by the transference of emotion. James Morse, the elderly company-owner, lays a fatherly hand on Edward Lewis's shoulder, the honorable broker, as if to say, "Well done, my boy."[22]

Pretty Woman is one film in a long series of even more typical ones dealing with rejection or rebellion followed by acceptance as a man, for example, *Hud* (1962), *Rebel Without a Cause* (1955), and *On the Waterfront* (1954).

Of course, the universality of the separation-reunion theme does not rule out individual differences in the ease with which it may provoke sentiment. People differ as to the degree to which they habitually control their emotion. Some people are better equipped for control than others. For instance, it is known that factors like fatigue, illness, and old age facilitate sentimentality.[23] Also, some individuals may be more receptive to the separation-reunion theme than others, due to differences in life histories, in actual satisfaction of the attachment concern, and styles of coping with being alone, separation, and loss. Some may have a stronger yearning for intimacy and proximity than others. Strong suppression of attachment desires, as in strongly macho cultures or individuals, may likewise enhance sensitivity to the separation-reunion theme (think of Charles Foster Kane and his "Rosebud!," as well as the popularity of strongly sentimental films on losses and separations in love in cultures with rather restricted romantic interchanges in real life).

The Justice in Jeopardy Motive

The second theme recurring over and over again in sentimental film is the justice in jeopardy motive, or, perhaps more generally, the moral rectitude under seduction theme. The world's corruptness obscures the good from view, but that good may on occasion nevertheless rear up its lovely head. The *Pocahontas* scene is one of thousands of examples from traditional movies where the good stands out in the face of evil's massive presence. In the family melodrama, a woman is visited with affliction, and in the end she either chooses to conform to the accepted moral standards or gives in to temptation. In either case it is her struggle with temptation that counts. It looks like a self-inflicted torture, and whatever alternative she chooses her fate will be unhappy. On the other hand, many a theorist has emphasized the clash of historical forces (such as a traditional restrictive moral) with individual protagonists.[24] The protagonist in the family melodrama does not necessarily have to be female. In *Blood and Sand* (1929) the successful toreador Juan Galiardo (Rudolph Valentino) drifts away from his wife and family in law. A *femme fatale* holds him spellbound. Only at his deathbed does he realize how foolish he has been. The melodrama (including the family melodrama) raises the question of what is good and what is evil. The viewer is cornered into a passive role, and tossed back and forth between the moral alternatives, an experience boosted by the genre's characteristic sudden twists.

As already noted, in the more action-oriented genres, the contrast between good and evil is stark, at the cost of the analysis of feeling. In these genres, suspense is the dominant narrative procedure. Noël Carroll has stressed the significance of the justice in jeopardy theme in suspenseful film. In suspense, according to Carroll, viewers are led to expect two mutually exclusive outcomes, one of which is morally correct, whereas the other is morally incorrect or evil.[25] Other research has demonstrated the importance of morality for viewer disposition toward fictional characters. Dolf Zillmann has convincingly shown that viewers side with any character to the degree that he or she acts according to dominant moral standards.[26] In line with this, it may be argued that in popular movies the moral adhered to by protagonists generally corresponds to beliefs and values held by its audience, although the cultural studies of film have found more room for idiosyncratic interpretations of morality, both by film viewers and the industry.[27] In the action-oriented film genres viewers are led to entertain strong hopes and fears associated with morally correct outcomes, which are then played with by the narrative's twists and turns. Paul Comisky and Jennings Bryant varied the subjective probability of the favored outcome in a suspense fragment.[28] They found that the level of suspense was highest when this probability was almost nil, and lowest when the favorite outcome was almost certain.

An essential aspect of appraisal in sentimental emotion provoked by this theme, then, may be that at first sight there is no hope for a just or morally right resolution. The essence of the appraisal is that justice is done in the face of a paralyzing moral conflict, as in the melodrama, or in spite of its opponents' superior numbers, as in the action genre. The parallel with the separation reunion theme is that the viewer's maintaining a belief against all odds, in this case the hope of the triumph of justice, is rewarded in the end. Here again, as in the functioning of the separation-reunion theme, the resolution may be experienced as realistic in the sense that it demonstrates a possibility, and this may lift the viewer's more cynical stable beliefs, even if only for a short time. Thus, the justice in jeopardy theme, as its name suggests, resembles most closely the historical *virtue in distress motive* in sentimental literature and melodrama in a wider sense.

Just as the separation-reunion theme assumes a number of variant shapes, the justice in jeopardy theme occurs in various guises. One is suspicion, in which a good protagonist is suspected of committing a crime of which he or she is not guilty, as in *A Woman's Face* (1941), and a number of famous Hitchcock movies. Another is the rough diamond motive. Dizzie Davison (James Cagney) is an irresponsible, amoral womanizer in *Ceiling Zero* (1935), who sacrifices a colleague test pilot only to be with the latter's date, Tommy (June Travis). In the end, he gives her away to another pilot, who "really" loves the girl. Dizzie takes over the pilot's dangerous flight and he dies. The emotion is intensified as the viewers may feel sorry when they suddenly realize they have had unwarranted negative and aggressive feelings toward the protagonist. Akin to the rough diamond motive is the sensitive beast figure. In *Beauty and the Beast* (1991), *The Elephant Man* (1980), *Young Frankenstein* (1974), *The Hunchback of Notre Dame* (1996), and even in some Dracula films, like Herzog's *Nosferatu* (1979) and Coppola's *Bram Stoker's Dracula* (1992), we find ourselves sympathizing with the sensitive being who in the first instance presents himself as a monster, and has to deal with all the world's offense. In *Ceiling Zero* there is another sentimental motive at work, also based on justice in jeopardy: the self-sacrifice. The same applies to *Maria Goretti*, treating the rape of a steadfast chaste girl, with her attacker then turning into a devout monk. Perhaps the idea of giving up oneself for the right cause is the ultimate resolution of the dramatic conflict that lies at the heart of the justice in jeopardy theme. In the typical case, the protagonists keep the sacrifice secret, as they do not want any returns, and this contributes to even more suffering on their part. A classical example can be enjoyed in *Mata Hari* (1931), where Mata Hari (Greta Garbo) has just shot the man who was to betray her lover Rossanov (Ramon Novarro), and is sentenced to death for this without Rossanov knowing. Rossanov is blinded and he believes they are in a hospital instead of a prison. Hari passes by, descending the stairs on her way to her execution. "Thank you, doctor," she says to a helping guard.

The return of the woman to her husband and family in the Hollywood family melodrama is undoubtedly the best-known example of the self-sacrifice motive. Another is that of virtuous people who do not want to be a burden to others, like Helen (Jane Wyman) in *Magnificent Obsession* (1953), who disappears from her love Merrick (Rock Hudson) after she has become blind. Other women sacrifice themselves for the good of a hero in whose hands is the plight of many, as in Joseph von Sternberg's *The Last Command* (1927), in which the woman saves the general by delivering herself to the bolshevist comrades.

As the example of *Ceiling Zero* shows, self-sacrifice is not limited to women protagonists. In *A Hole in the Head* (1959) Tony Manetta (Frank Sinatra) does not marry the widow, Mrs. Rogers (Eleanor Parker), whom he truly loves, because he is about to be bankrupt and he does not want to involve her, even if she would agree. Perhaps male sacrifice adds more to the heroic character of the protagonist than to his suffering. But the woman's sacrifice in melodrama has likewise been interpreted as an exhibition of courage, stressing the capacity to determine her fate and live with the impossibility of her desires.[29]

Of course, in truly sentimental films a number of themes are skillfully combined. The characteristic twists of the plot contribute not only by themselves to emotion, but they arrange the sentiment provoking thematic episodes into the ideal series. In *Magnificent Obsession,* Helen has become blind as a result of an accident caused by Merrick. When she is blind, he approaches her in disguise, and she falls in love with him. A long time after she has left him, a reunion follows with Merrick who has discovered her whereabouts. Merrick the Irresponsible has turned into a skillful doctor and he returns sight to Helen, undoing the initial harm and emanating as a rough diamond. The quasi-logical match of the initiating and the final event appears to contribute to sentiment because it undoes the long episode of suffering in retrospect, as discussed earlier.

Why the power of this theme in provoking sentimental emotion? Probably, its source is not too remote from the power source of the separation-

The sympathetic vampire (Klaus Kinski) in Werner Herzog's
Nosferatu (1979).

reunion theme. It may well lie in a romantic belief in a just world: we han-
ker for good being good, and the world being just, all experiences to the contrary notwithstanding, and we eagerly welcome any sign that the belief may
be well founded after all.

Perhaps it is significant in this context that the two sentimental themes
mentioned so far tend to be strengthened by the occurrence of misunderstandings in the plot. In all genres, misunderstandings create suspense, as the
viewer has to wait until they are resolved. In an action film, this is the only
function of misunderstandings. Just as misunderstanding in the comedy contributes to the viewer's superiority and felt distance to the characters, in the
tragedy it deepens the viewer's compassion for the protagonist. In sentimental movies, (melodramatic) misunderstandings emphasize the viewer's
feelings of helplessness; the sympathetic protagonist does not know that he
is loved, and acts according to this—which often means that he is working
against his fortune—and we as viewers cannot inform him. When the misunderstanding is lifted by the end of the sentimental film, the viewer is con-

firmed in his or her romantic belief that, after all, in the end the world turns out to be just.

The Awe-Inspiration Theme

The third theme is the least specific because it is not immediately associated with the film story's action or with an understanding of the protagonist's feelings. We will call it the awe-inspiration theme. Being in an environment in which one feels tiny and insignificant, such as a huge coliseum or a cathedral, experiencing the vastness or endlessness of a landscape or empathizing with music may provoke two kinds of emotional response. In both cases, the stimulus is appraised as larger than oneself, and it provokes a tendency of helplessness and surrender, and serious respect as the less-intensive response. On the one hand, the stimulus may be attractive and call forth fascination, a propensity for further contemplation and losing oneself in it. On the other, it may have a repellent quality, eliciting a tendency to shiver and look for shelter. Both variants of awe may be seen as sentimental in the sense that they relate to yielding.

The concern for *fusion*, that is, losing oneself in a stimulus, the longing for giving up one's identity and losing oneself into something greater than oneself would appear to be an equally fundamental desire as that for attachment and for belief in a just world. It may, in fact, have a common root with the attachment concern. One stimulus of awesome sentiment is a filmic representation of an object that in reality, too, makes people fall silent. The wide and dry scenery in *Out of Africa* (1985), *The Sheltering Sky* (1990), *The Passenger* (1975), or *Zabriskie Point* (1970) probably evokes awe, depending on the narrative context, a tendency to lose oneself in it, for example, when an episode of love is set in it and we have lyrical music in the background. Other examples are the lyrical finales in which we seem to dissolve in the sky. A superb craning shot elevates our viewpoint to sky altitude. Here the sentimental response originates in a movement like flying that seems to liberate the viewer from gravity, and from his or her individuality. A recent example is the final sequence of *Breaking the Waves* (1996), where being in the sky has still another, almost metaphysical meaning. This kind of sentiment goes together well with joy or elation, and its diffuse action tendency of undirected energy makes us jump and dance in a context other than the cinema. On the other hand, viewers may be annihilated and experience a sense of loss of orientation and intimidation when the action is set in enormous buildings of an unfriendly regime, such as the SS headquarters in Bertolucci's *The Conformist* (1971), or the Empire's Death Star in *Star Wars* (1977).[30]

Because it is not a feature film, Leni Riefenstahl's *Triumph of the Will* (1934) offers perhaps the prototypical examples of awe-inspiring imagery, as the scenes of the Nazi party seem to aim almost exclusively at liberating

Awe-inspiring imagery in Leni Riefenstahl's *Triumph of the Will* (1934).

the viewers from their individual identity by means of an ongoing show of intimidating environments, deindividualized phalanxes, and solemn ceremonies. Notice that the inspiration of awe and crying often go together in real life, too. Their connection can be observed during religious ritual, and in meetings with pop stars and political leaders. It emphasizes the meaning of crying as submission behavior.

Conclusion

What do the three themes have in common? It may be that they all appeal to possibly idealized, paradisiac childhood memories of being completely accepted or being part of some absolute, uncorrupted purity, or at least to desires for such a state. The feeling corresponding to such a paradisiac state has been designated by Freud as the *oceanic feeling*, presumably stemming from a stage that precedes the development of individuality in young infants, and in which no separation is felt yet between the I and the external world.[31] The child feels completely accepted and part of some absolute unity. To this memory, idealized or based on real experiences, is retrospectively added a quality of uncorruptedness and *purity,* in large part as a contrast to experiences the individual has had later. The memory, then, may acquire a connotation of lost paradise, and stimuli that apply to it may be appraised as overwhelming, and as one the person can or would like to abandon to, as we have seen.

In daily life, but especially in the cinema, the action tendency of sentiment, to give up one's individual autonomy and lose oneself into the greater entity, easily merges with the action tendencies of the other emotions. The empathetic emotions, which are based on an appraisal of events from the point of view of a virtuous protagonist and an understanding of the protagonist's feelings, are especially suited for such a merger. Sympathy is accompanied by a wish to be close to the protagonist, and in the sentimental form of sympathy this tendency neighbors the infatuated desire to be near the protagonist all the time. Pity's action tendency is to care for, protect, and help the other. Sentiment turns this into an urge to feel into the protagonist's state of distress and share the suffering. Likewise, admiration when touched by sentiment assumes the extreme form of almost complete identification.

※ THREE ※

The Sublime in Cinema

CYNTHIA A. FREELAND

Reviving the Sublime

The sublime has been held to be a grand object, often a natural one, that produces in us a characteristic combination of painful and pleasurable feelings of terror plus awe and elevation. Immanuel Kant gives as examples "shapeless mountain masses towering one above the other in wild disorder, with their pyramids of ice, or . . . the dark tempestuous ocean."[1] The term *sublime* has also been used to describe certain artworks and emotional experiences they evoke in audiences. As an aesthetic term it was elaborated by Longinus, refined by Edmund Burke and Immanuel Kant, and applied to the analysis of works by landscape painters, romantic poets, Gothic novelists, and composers like Beethoven.

Are some films sublime? The concept of the sublime had lost its prevalence by the time cinema arose, and it has been little used to describe films.[2] Though the sublime has seen renewed attention lately from continental authors,[3] for those interested in cognitive studies of the arts it may seem to denote only an antique or even a "debased" aesthetic concept.[4] What have we to do with this notion unearthed from the creaky architectonic of the *Critique of Judgment?*

In this chapter I argue that there are certain films best described as sublime and that this concept may facilitate more diverse descriptions of films as artworks. I believe it is plausible to view figures like Burke and Kant as antecedents of the current enterprise of cognitive science. Burke tried, in true empiricist spirit, to locate sources of emotions in the human nervous system and perceptual apparatus.[5] And Kant identified mental capacities relevant to our responses to art—capacities that function to relate humans to the natural world. We have advanced beyond Kant and Burke, but contemporary cognitive studies can still learn certain lessons from them.

My account of the sublime identifies it in terms of four basic features derived from the Kantian analysis. To begin, I outline these basic features, illustrating them with a film example. I then review Kant's account of the psychology of the sublime, before moving on to consider how the sublime might be described in two frameworks of contemporary cognitivism: the recent work of psychologist Ed S. Tan on film emotions, and studies of emotions by various neuroscientists.[6] Both kinds of analysis, I argue, confront challenges in accounting for our experiences of sublime films as works of art.

Four Features of the Sublime

People will cite their own candidates for the cinematic sublime: perhaps the face of Garbo in *Queen Christina* (1933),[7] the burning of Atlanta in *Gone with the Wind* (1939), or the spaceship ballets of *2001: A Space Odyssey* (1968).[8] I am inclined to call a few entire films sublime, and I discuss three of them here: *The Passion of Joan of Arc* (Carl Dreyer, 1928), *Aguirre: The Wrath of God* (Werner Herzog, 1972), and *Children of Paradise* (Marcel Carné, 1944). All are particularly powerful and warrant this special aesthetic characterization.

To call an object "sublime" means, first and most centrally, that it calls forth a characteristic conflict between certain feelings of pain and pleasure—it evokes what Burke labeled "rapturous terror." On the one hand, the sublime prompts a painful feeling sometimes designated as terror, fear, or dread. But the sublime object does not cause merely pain or terror, but also "rapture": we find it exhilarating and exciting. Kant and Burke emphasized that so long as we are safe, the ineffable, great element before us in the awesome object evokes a certain intellectual pleasure of astonishment or elevation. Kant thought that this pleasure was tied to an awareness of features of our moral selves; Burke instead linked it to the power of the artist's creative mind. My account will fall somewhere in between these alternatives.

To illustrate this first feature of emotional conflict, let us consider *The Passion of Joan of Arc,* a uniquely powerful film that offers viewers a sustained experience of heightened feelings. On the one hand the film is very painful and disturbing. Joan's (Maria Falconetti) accusers glare at her with cruel and horrible faces; her funeral pyre is prepared and ultimately consumes her. *The Passion of Joan of Arc* offers a visual depiction of painful feelings that are so extreme they almost pass beyond representation. Joan's intense anguish is matched only by her profound religious faith. This character's penetrating sorrow and deep mysterious conviction are simply there on the screen for us to see, in Falconetti's astonishing and ravishing face. When I say "ravishing," I mean to indicate that another emotion is involved in our experience of this movie, a feeling of awed pleasure. There is something exalting about the film's power and beauty. Dreyer keeps Falconetti's marvelous face under constant and intense scrutiny; it remains luminous even under torture.

This leads me to the second characteristic feature of the sublime object. Something about it is "great" and astonishing. It is bold and grand, to use

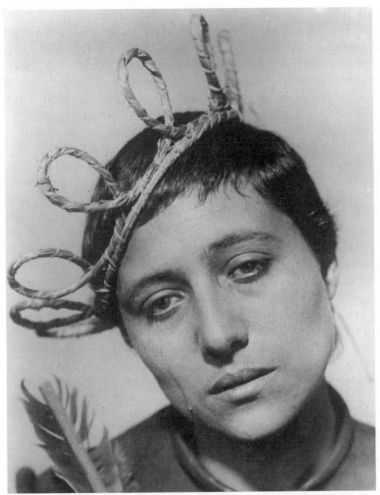

Maria Falconetti as Joan in *The Passion of Joan of Arc* (1928), directed by
Carl Dreyer.

Longinus's language. Or, as Kant puts it, "*Sublime* is the name given to what
is *absolutely great*" (94/248; Kant's emphasis). The sublime object is vast, powerful, and overwhelming. Used about an artwork, "sublime" is a term of aesthetic praise, signifying that the work has a grandeur or a superlative kind of
greatness. This is why accounts of the sublime were so often linked to theories of artistic genius. Kant also makes the interesting observation that in the
case of something sublime, "it is not permissible to seek an appropriate standard outside itself, but merely in itself. It is a greatness comparable to itself
alone" (97/250).

Dreyer's film and the others I shall discuss are great in this sense, highly distinctive and original achievements, so powerful that they merit a special kind of descriptive label surpassing "beauty." To be sure, the film *Joan* is beautiful: it strikingly juxtaposes closeups of faces with the blank white cells of the monastery. But it moves beyond beauty to the kind of grandeur we associate with the label "sublime." This is partly due to its subject matter, but also to the film's treatment of this grand subject matter. Joan of Arc is represented in the film as great and extreme—even somehow unfathomable in her faith and ability to withstand her tormentors. The film effectively depicts a woman who inspires reverence. It is a superlatively great film.

A third feature of the sublime is that it evokes ineffable and painful feelings, through which a transformation occurs into pleasure and cognition. The ineffable feelings are related to the second feature, greatness: something about the sublime object is so powerful or vast that it is hard to grasp or take in, and painful. Kant says that the sublime involves an experience of something "almost too great" to be presented or represented (100/253).[9] In Kant's view, the ineffability of the sublime object is tied to the overload on imagination or senses that it presents to us, hence to its painfulness. But, still, this gets translated into something we can conceptualize and feel pleasure at. Kant puts this point by saying that the sublime is defined as "an object (of nature) the representation of which determines the mind to regard the elevation of nature *beyond our reach* as *equivalent to* a presentation of ideas" (119/268; my emphasis). In more modern terms, we might say that the sublime object presents us with a sensory and emotional experience of some sort that is so extreme, unsettling, or intense that it would be disturbing on its own. But in its context it forces us to shift into another mental mode, cognition, or thought. We become more able to handle the deep feelings evoked by the work, and we put a label on them and on the work. Within this new reflective mode, we categorize the object in some way, and through its painfulness we find it pleasurable, exhilarating, or elevating.

In the film *Joan,* the ineffable element is its unusually great emotional intensity. Feeling is expressed by the film itself (and by its actors) on such a grand level as to be overwhelming. Here I begin to depart from Kant, though, as I shall redescribe the shift he spoke of from the ineffable to the cognized, and from pain to pleasure. I suggest that the shift occurs when we regard the deep and painful feelings evoked by a work as crucial for its success as powerful and uplifting art. We are disturbed by the nearly inexpressible pain and emotional intensity of *Joan,* and yet enraptured by its artistic production of painfulness. This paradox of emotions arises when we conceptualize the film's deep emotional intensity as part of an artistic rendering of a viewpoint on its subject.[10]

A fourth and final feature of the sublime is that it prompts moral reflection. Here again I follow Kant in outline, but disagree on the details. For Kant, the describable aspect of the sublime involves a sense of our own moral capacities and duties. The ineffability is both "out there" in the great natural object and "in us," in our depth of feeling about the object. He regarded our awareness of the sublimity of an object outside ourselves as an awareness of the moral law and of certain of our own moral duties. Hence Kant describes this feature of the sublime as part of a universal teleology of nature (a central topic of the third *Critique*).

Kant held quite subtle and sophisticated views about the relations between aesthetics and ethics. I depart from him because I reject his account of the nature of morality and the sorts of cognition it requires; I simply do not accept his view of how natural (or perhaps aesthetic) objects support our recognition of a supposed universal moral law. So I suggest reconceiving this feature of the sublime as follows. Certain aesthetic objects give rise to the central emotional conflicts of the sublime. The ineffably dreadful and painful experience grounds the pleasure of elevation, because it stimulates our human capacities to value powerful artworks. In particular, we are elevated in engaging through the work in reflection that is somehow about the pain or terror it evokes.

Morality is clearly a concern of *The Passion of Joan of Arc*. Let me review how we shift from the deep emotional experience of this film to an elevated cognition about its power as an artwork. What sustains the viewer through an experience of this film's painful emotions and disturbing visions is our respectful and awed recognition of its power and aesthetic qualities. Shot after shot, in their framing, juxtapositions, and intensity, work together to express a moral vision—the critique of this woman's—Joan's—agonizing pain, isolation, and oppression. The film could be said to underscore Joan's conviction and faith by the very way it presents her, this woman with an exalted face, as someone saintly who rises above the fear of death and the laws of the men who try to condemn her. The representation of so much suffering is indeed painful, but it is justified and made enjoyable within the film's expert construction and through its attitude about such suffering. A range of responses to Joan are depicted within the movie: she bewilders or angers some of the judges, prompts others to ridicule and spit at her, and inspires the peasants to revolt. In the end, I suggest, our aesthetic response to the film (and to the work within it of Falconetti and Dreyer) is like that of the monk who falls at Joan's feet in a kind of awe, terror, and reverence. There is something deeply pleasurable about this film that we can feel even while also being pained at what it depicts.

My brief sketch and illustration of four features of the sublime began with the emotional conflict describable as "rapturous terror." This is closely intertwined with the three other features I have mentioned: greatness, cognition of the ineffable, and moral reflection. These features make the sublime distinctive. I shall next review in more detail Kant's account of how these features were linked, so as to explain further both why I disagree with Kant and how I would locate the four features in films. This will pave the way for my consideration of revisions and updates in our theorizing about emotions of the sublime.

Kant on the Sublime

Kant's "Analytic of the Sublime" occupies an extensive portion of *The Critique of Judgement* (1790).[11] The aesthetic is analyzed here within the framework of Kant's faculty psychology. He describes the beautiful as involving interactions between the faculties of *imagination* and *understanding;* these get activated pleasurably by the beautiful in the rather notorious "free play" he discusses earlier in the third *Critique.* There is a kind of restful contemplation in the beautiful, as opposed to a "mental movement" or even a "vibration" in the sublime (107/258). The sublime prompts "a pleasure that only arises indirectly, being brought about by the feeling of a momentary check to the vital forces followed at once by a discharge all the more powerful" (91/245).

The sublime crucially depends upon a tension between our highest sensible faculty, imagination, and our highest human faculty, reason. Kant speaks of the sublime as involving a kind of "outrage on the imagination" (91/245), because the object is so massive, powerful, or extended that it is beyond our capacity to imagine, that is, supersensible. Such an object might be the "starry skies above" mentioned in a famous passage at the conclusion of the *Second Critique.*[12] Kant similarly describes what occurs when someone confronts the immensity of an overwhelming object like St. Peters in Rome: "For here a feeling comes home to him of the inadequacy of his imagination for presenting the idea of a whole within which that imagination attains its maximum and, in its fruitless efforts to extend this limit, recoils upon itself, but in so doing succumbs to an emotional delight" (100/252). In the end, then, although imagination is outraged, reason emerges triumphant and produces its own distinctive delight, "Respect" (Achtung), the "feeling of our incapacity to attain to an idea *that is a law for us*" (105/257; Kant's emphasis). The sublime experience affords an enhanced sense of ourselves as we experience a feeling of finality independent of nature, but residing in us (93/246). Kant summarizes the psychological tensions involved in the sublime in this way:

> The feeling of the sublime is, therefore, at once a feeling of displeasure, arising
> from the inadequacy of imagination in the aesthetic estimation of magnitude
> to attain to its estimation by reason, and a simultaneously awakened pleasure,

arising from this very judgment of the inadequacy of the greatest faculty of sense being in accord with ideas of reason, so far as the effort to attain to these is for us a law. (106/257)

In Kant's view, the notion of the sublime applies first and foremost to natural objects, not artworks. He says that we do not relate to the sublime object (whether natural or manmade) through application of any *concept* importing a definite end (100/253). But of course the sublime does, interestingly, concern a way in which nature comports to an end—a "higher finality" (92/248) beyond any ordinary teleology, the finality not of nature but of ourselves. The experience of the sublime serves the higher end of reinforcing our human moral nature by calling forth awareness of and respect for the moral law.

Let me now move from Kant's account back to my topic of films. I would like to provide an illustration of the details of the Kantian analysis of the sublime as it might apply to films, while at the same time explaining my departures from his view. Let us consider, then, how Kant's framework might be applied to my second film example, Herzog's *Aguirre: The Wrath of God*. *Aguirre* is interesting to take up here because it is in some sense a film or artwork *about* the sublime in nature. Through its particular representation of sublime landscapes, the film itself becomes sublime.

Aguirre begins with an extraordinary sequence offering a distant, soaring view of the Andes Mountains. It is not simply the scenery here that is sublime, but also the representation of it. Herzog's camera is literally elevated in the opening scene. Viewers seem to float down eerily through cloud-topped peaks and jagged ravines. The sensation of floating, a kind of disturbing yet exciting dislocation, is enhanced by the film's repetitive, high-pitched musical score. From a great distance, the camera reveals a line of miniature humans who can barely be seen. It reinforces feelings of the sublime by making the scenery vast and overwhelming in proportion to the ant-like human enterprise within it. The column turns out to be a long line of conquistadors in armor, women in velvet dresses and starched white ruffs, Indian and black slaves, horses, cannons, pigs, and so on. The magnitude of their endeavor is extraordinary yet still minuscule within nature's overwhelming vastness.

A second sublime landscape in the film is the river that the conquistadors encounter upon their descent from the jagged mountain peaks. They find themselves amid an overwhelming trackless jungle, and ride rafts in danger from rapids and whirlpools. The camera places us there, like the adventurers, on the river and in danger of being sucked under and destroyed. (In one scene, a horse forced off their raft simply disappears into the watery jungle without a sound or a trace.) This film visually displays its sublime landscape, just as Dreyer's film displayed Falconetti's face.[13] Though this landscape is depicted as threatening, strange, and ominous, it also has a terrible serene beauty. It is huge and impressively indifferent to the humans it dwarfs.

Consider, then, how *Aguirre* presents the first two features I mentioned above, the characteristic emotional conflict of the sublime and its related grandeur or scope. The mountains, river, and jungle are grand not just in themselves as natural objects but in the way they function as *Aguirre*'s subject matter. The film depicts these natural objects in ways so as to represent their power, extension, and grandeur, arousing a conflict in emotions of the viewer. Just as *Joan* evokes in viewers pain over the visual display of her suffering, here too the viewers feel great dread. We become almost tortured in waiting for each new disaster to unfold for the characters, watching their snail-paced progress through the vast landscapes. And yet while these aspects of the representation of the landscape and figures within it are overwhelming and painful, other aspects of the film are elevating and pleasurable. So we can speak as Kant did of a "movement" or "vibration" in our perception of this object. It is crucial that we, unlike the depicted conquistadors, are safe as we encounter the jungle. We can enjoy seeing the film's awesome depiction of power, space, and beauty—and perhaps we enjoy even Aguirre's depths of insanity (since of course we are not subject to his murderous tantrums). Watching this jungle as Herzog shows it in the film, we can appreciate intellectually his representation of how it crushes the humans within it, and this can move us to a feeling of loftiness and respect. Their enterprise is shown to be mad, and is defeated accordingly.

This is, however, where I part ways with Kant. For him, the respect the sublime object awakens in us is really "about" ourselves, about our human capacities and our recognition of duty and obligation to the moral law. The third and fourth features of the sublime are crucially connected for Kant, since the switch from painful ineffability to pleasurable cognition is also a shift from sensibility into a moral framework where we feel respect for the moral law. I agree that one aspect of an experience of a sublime film like *The Passion of Joan of Arc* or *Aguirre* involves painful and ineffable feelings. *Aguirre* is very slow-paced; Herzog allows the camera to observe the unfolding of this astonishing natural landscape, so as to express its vastness and convey its magnitude, evoking dread and terror at its power. I suggest that we switch from our somewhat overloaded sensory and emotional experiences of things seen and depicted in the film to a more cognitive, intellectual appreciation of *how* the film depicts its great subject, including moral reflection on its point of view. We are prompted by certain extreme features of the depiction to become aware of and to enjoy our experience on another level. This does not involve "the Moral Law," but rather cognition of the film as a powerful artwork prompting moral reflection. My suggested emendation of Kant is that in describing the shift from the sensory to the cognitive, we should consider the experience of "elevation" as occurring when we shift from the perspective *within* the film to a perspective *about* the film. This shift accompanies the shift from a predominantly emotional or imaginative experience on the sensory level to a more intellectual or cognitive experience including pleasurable reflection on the film's moral point of view.[14]

I now offer a further proposal about how sublime cinema prompts such shifts from the ineffably painful to pleasurable cognition, from dread to elevation. This happens most notably at various moments in the film where we cannot avoid becoming aware of the movie *as* a movie. Although I am happy to describe certain films as a whole as sublime, I also say that certain scenes in these films are particularly sublime or particularly effective. That is, certain cognitive shifts occur at moments of the rupture of representation, when films draw our attention to themselves and to their perspective on what is depicted. These ruptures prompt our recognition of the filmmaker's desire and ability to show us something about a person or landscape.

There are many such moments of rupture prompting such recognition in *Aguirre*. I have already mentioned the effectiveness of the film's opening scenes, where devices of framing and dislocation announce the film's point of view on the characters it is about to show. Another rupture is prompted by the deliberate framing devices in the beautifully composed scene of Aguirre's daughter's death. The filmmaker hides our view of the arrow that has pierced her breast, so that her death is at the same time horrible, painful, yet a mysterious graceful swooning into her father's arms. Again at the film's conclusion, we are shown an extraordinary vision of the mad Aguirre, clad in armor and helmet astride his rickety raft, which has suddenly become awash with skittering small monkeys. The camera reinforces the "viewedness" of this scene when it makes an uncharacteristic move from the slow pace of historical realism into a more modern mode: apparently mounted on a helicopter, it drops far back, jolting us, and then swoops in with frightening speed to circle the mad warrior. Finally it retreats, and restores us to the earlier realist mode of calm detached observation. These shifts remind us we are seeing a depiction and reinforce a particular point of view on the mad conquistador.

The most extraordinary moment of rupture in this film occurs when we witness a deliberately hallucinatory sequence showing a fully rigged sailing ship lofted high into a treetop. The few survivors in the raft, mad from poison arrows, thirst, hunger, and fever, see this vision and say, "That is not a ship." As film viewers, we too cannot be sure whether we see the ship or a hallucination. The scene could be said to "vibrate" as Kant put it. The boat looks real, but the thought of a sailing ship in a treetop goes beyond what seems possible or cognizable.

These ruptures in *Aguirre* prompt a shift from emotions felt primarily

Aguirre, the mad conquistador of *Aguirre: The Wrath of God* (1972).

within the film narrative to reflection about the film. Such devices are also present in *Joan of Arc*, a film that similarly draws attention to itself with its careful framing of scenes—with, for example, compositions of frames depicting a small head in relation to a large white space, or the use of unusual angles of view, from well below a face or far above a scene. *Joan* further prompts an awareness of our presence as "audience" through its frequent depiction of carnival entertainers waiting for the trial to lead to its predestined conclusion. These emphasize the fact that for us, just as for the peasants in the film, Joan's trial and execution provide an entertainment or spectacle.

Kant held that the experience of the sublime occupied a border space between the aesthetic and the moral. I have rejected his insistence that the shift from ineffable to cognized is precisely the transition from imagination to reason's recognition of the moral law. Rather, the sublime art object prompts a shift from sensory, emotional involvement in the object to aesthetic enjoyment and cognitive appreciation. Such appreciation involves awareness of artistry and reflection upon moral matters. Here I am also following Burke: we are prompted by the sublime to feel respect for something human—not for the moral law and our obligations, but for the ability to construct powerful art with a moral vision.

I have also suggested that we are prompted to shift to this recognition when we have a cognitive appreciation of the film as a film, not as mere entertainment or as sensory and emotional spectacle. Recognizing the film's artistry takes us to a level of reflection upon it as a whole, including an appreciation of what it aims to *say* about the painful things it depicts. In *Joan of Arc*, Dreyer provides a fierce critique of Joan's oppression and torture, and *Aguirre* links the painful emotions involved in its visions to a moral assessment of colonizers dominated by greed and the lust for gold.[15] Appreciating the work requires recognizing the moral vision it offers, though not necessarily accepting that vision.

Cognitivism Revisits the Sublime

Kant's faculty psychology frames his account of the sublime. How might a more contemporary psychological theory describe the emotional conflicts of the sublime? Let us consider two broad types of contemporary cognitive approaches to the emotions, first that of a psychologist, and second that of a neuroscientist.

Psychologist Ed S. Tan presents a cognitive analysis of emotions in film in his recent book, *Emotion and the Structure of Narrative Film: Film as an Emotion Machine*.[16] Tan explores cinema-watching as an active, conscious experience combining thought and emotions. Like other cognitivists, Tan sees emotions as adaptive forms of behavior that facilitate organismic response to the environment (232). He seeks to identify images, narrative devices, and so on that will trigger specific kinds of emotional responses in viewers—responses that scientists can study empirically.

Tan treats films as constructed artefacts or "machines" designed with a specific function: they simulate our natural environment in ways to which we respond with appropriate emotions. Talk of "simulation" leads Tan into currently disputed territory about whether films are images, representations, or some sort of "pretend" version of reality.[17] In his view, although film images are illusions, the emotions they arouse are authentic; we can test this by measuring things like viewers' pulses or breathing rates. So Tan criticizes philosopher Noël Carroll for relying solely on the evidence of introspection in deciding whether he felt "real" horror at scenes in *The Exorcist* (1973).[18]

In Tan's view, certain devices of plot, narrative, framing, and so on, are *effective*—they work in predictable ways upon audiences. Being shown suffering, for example, tends to evoke sympathy or empathy (247).[19] Certain aspects of feature films "conduct fantasy" so as to produce particular emotions in response to the scenes and characters. Though Tan does not regard film viewers as passive—since we must process information, actively form certain beliefs, and even act to an extent—he still says that we are "being led along highly structured paths" (236), where both our "maximum" and our "minimum" emotions are controlled: "[Viewers] are at the mercy of the narrative and must undergo each and every event that occurs, pleasant or otherwise, expected or unexpected" (241).[20] He thinks that art films are quite different from narrative feature films, which have entertainment as their primary goal (52/243).

To consider how one might generate an account of the sublime within this sort of psychological framework, we need to examine Tan's distinction between "fiction emotions" and "artefact emotions" (65, 82). Fiction emotions are tied to the "diegetic effect," the illusion of being present in the fictional world (52–56). Fiction emotions would include immediate empathetic responses of ineffable pain evoked by films, such as our empathy for the tortured Joan or dread about the conquistadors' fate in *Aguirre*. By comparison, artefact emotions involve recognition of a film's construction or of its artistry (65); this latter category encompasses aesthetic emotions such as awe at great acting, wonder at cinematography, and so on. Thus artefact emotions might include the pleasurable cognition of greatness I have described as our response to the sublimity of both *Joan* and *Aguirre*.

Tan says that when features of film as artefact come to the fore, they are often regulated by the film to sustain certain narrative effects, that is, to foster the production of fictions (192, 82, 238). He also hints that an experience of the sublime might be available only to certain viewers, since he hypothesizes that artefact emotions are linked to the factor of "cinephilia" (34–35). That is, some artefact emotions are tied to the competences of certain viewers who enjoy the cognitive games of cinema (49); they are less recognized by "most natural viewers." For example, I have suggested that in the sublime we take pleasure in something painful, signaled by moments of rupture in the film's fictive surface, but Tan says that the main reason for most viewers to "direct their attention toward the artificiality of the fiction" is "because the essence of what is being depicted on the screen is not to their liking" (81). I confess to feeling suspicion about this distinction between cinephiles and natural viewers, but I cannot argue with Tan's comment that "more research on the viewer is clearly needed" (65). I believe there are further challenges for a psychological theory like Tan's, so let us now consider how he might describe the effectiveness of a specific scene from my final example of a sublime film, *Children of Paradise*.

This movie can be praised at many levels: cinematic spectacle, dialogue, characterization, narrative complexity, and acting. One thing that makes it stand out as "incomparable" is the presence of the mime Jean-Louis Barrault. Certain scenes he is in are especially effective at prompting emotions of the sublime, and I shall consider one in detail here. In this scene, Barrault plays the character Baptiste, a mime acting in a play he has written. Dressed in Pierrot costume, he enacts despair over the loss of the goddess-statue he worships. Our point of view is that of the represented audience at the theater, but we know more than they: the statue-goddess is Garance (Arletty), the woman Baptiste loves but whom he has lost because he lacked faith in her love. The film is about the nature of art, emotions, acting, and authenticity. It supports the view that emotions like love are "really very simple," deep, and permanent. Baptiste has lost his chance to be with Garance through testing her love too much.

On stage, the Pierrot finds a rope and plans to hang himself, but is diverted when a laundry-maid wants the rope to hang her clothes. We also know that this laundry-maid is really Nathalie (Maria Cesarès), who helplessly loves Baptiste. Distracted, the Pierrot gazes off to the horizon in search of his lost goddess. The camera, which until now has depicted the entire scene from the audience's perspective in the theater, suddenly shifts—and Tan would point to this as a controlling device that directs and produces our emotions. We first see a point-of-view shot depicting Baptiste's view of Garance in the wings flirting with her new lover, Frederique (Pierre Brasseur). A reverse shot shows the pain, shock, and anger on Baptiste's face. His pain is very intense and strange, and our view of him is suspended for an unusually long time. Tan would say that the extended closeup cues particular fiction emotions of pity and empathy.

To go this far only would ignore aspects of this scene and of our response to it that are relevant to what makes it sublime. We do not simply feel certain emotions in empathy with Baptiste. We also have an emotional conflict, because there is something intensely pleasurable and uplifting about the scene and the way it fits into the film as a whole. That is, we have another emotion that is perhaps broader in scope and different from the first emotion, one linked to an appreciation of the film as a work of art. Tan would say that this is a kind of artefact emotion.

Artefact emotions may be most strongly felt during moments of "rupture" like those I described in *Aguirre*. It is possible to identify such moments here as well. *Children of Paradise* prompts recognition of its status as artefact by a doubling of the audience, contrasting us as its viewing audience with the represented audience in the mime theater. Lacking our knowledge and point-of-view shots, that audience may think that Baptiste is still in character when he is suspended in his long moment of anguish. What they see as simply Baptiste's good acting is for us an almost delicious ambiguity or tension. Is Baptiste miming or expressing pain? Does he enact the Pierrot's despair, or his own? And doesn't Barrault play this scene marvelously![21] This tension in this scene is pleasurable because we recognize that the film is using reflexive elements of artistic self-representation to create a powerful emotional effect.

The mime Jean-Louis Barrault as Baptiste in Marcel Carné's
Children of Paradise (1944).

Baptiste's expression is so strange it becomes frightening (indeed, his despair boils over in later mimes where he enacts murderous desires). His suspended stare is so excruciating that it prompts the frightened Nathalie to drop her character in the mime and cry out "Baptiste!" in shock and horror. Her cry startles the theater audience, which does not comprehend what has occurred as we do. Nathalie, too, is forced into a kind of rupture of representation, paralleling the rupture or vacillation in the shift between Baptiste and the Pierrot, and in our own appreciation of the film as both a story in progress and a reflexive artwork.

Tan might say that the sublimity here involves this shift between fiction and artefact emotions. The film works as a machine due to the effective way in which this scene, and others in it, are crafted. Through its careful structure of narrative, music, dialogue, and point-of-view shots, such as closeups of Baptiste and Nathalie, the film prompts our own conflicting emotional responses: fiction emotions of sadness, horror, pity, dread, and shock, combined with aesthetic emotions of awe and admiration. Tan's contemporary cognitivist account tries to describe some psychological laws that film exemplifies. These laws would explain how emotions are produced and what role they play in our human behavioral economy.

On my own revised Kantian-Burkean account, the sublime involves a shift from overwhelmingly painful emotions to pleasurable reflection about a work's moral viewpoint. This point raises a certain challenge for an account like Tan's. The psychologist studying viewers' artefact emotions may need to develop tools to study both their concepts of art (which Tan proposes to do by studying "cinephiles") and their concepts of morality. Like *Joan* and *Aguirre, Children of Paradise* is a sublime artwork not just because it prompts deep emotions but because those emotions are linked to moral reflection. The subject of this movie as a whole concerns the values involved in art, acting, and feeling emotion. The power to create art and beauty is associated with the power to feel deep, sincere, and "simple" emotions like love. Thus Baptiste and Garance are contrasted as "good" with all the other weaker characters in the film. Baptiste is a dedicated master artist whose performances are gripping and gorgeous, and the interruptions of his art (here and later in the film) are horrifying and painful. In this scene there is a unique reflexivity, as the film meditates about art and about moral values through a number of representations, juxtaposing the art of the director Carné with that of the actor Barrault and the mime Baptiste. This artistry and depth are what exalts the film audience.[22]

Cognitive Neuroscience

I turn now to consider a more biologically oriented approach from cognitive neuroscientists who differentiate mental functions according to human evolutionary history. They locate and explain emotions in terms of the development and operation of various systems in the brain and nervous system. Cognitive science replaces Kant's talk about "faculties" with talk of various "emotion systems" that interact with "information-processing systems."[23] The emotions currently studied are often rather primitive, such as a rat's fear of a cat. Still, some of the results are fascinating, and they suggest new ways of accounting for more subtle and complex emotional phenomena, including conflicts between the sublime emotions of fear or terror versus exaltation.

Cognitive neuroscientists challenge aspects of the folk psychologies we inherit from Western thinkers. First, they challenge certain philosophical notions of *rationality* in the tradition, as they break down distinctions between reason and emotion. For example, they maintain that some emotions can bypass cognition and the brain's cortical tissues (although other information-processing is still necessary). Or they note the role played by emotions in making rational decisions.[24] This is interesting because it suggests that both of the key emotions involved in the sublime—fear and elevation—might involve dimensions of feeling as well as of cognition.

Cognitive neuroscientists also challenge the philosophical presumption that emotions are *conscious*. Joseph LeDoux argues that "the conscious feelings that we know and love (and hate) our emotions by are just red herrings, detours, in the scientific study of emotions" (18).[25] Again, I find this suggestive because it might indicate why we cannot always describe or pinpoint our emotions, including perhaps the "ineffable" emotions evoked by a powerful artwork. Nevertheless, some kind of experiencing or processing is going on in response to the work, and it might lead, as Kant thought—though not by the paths Kant thought—to yet other emotions and cognitions.

LeDoux and others also challenge a *voluntaristic* account of emotions. LeDoux writes,

> Emotions are things that happen to us rather than things we will to occur. . . . We have little direct control over our emotional reactions. While conscious control over emotions is weak, emotions can flood consciousness. This is so because the wiring of the brain at this point in our evolutionary history is such that connections from the emotional systems to the cognitive systems are stronger than connections from the cognitive systems to the emotional systems.[26]

Once again this is important because it means that emotions arise in response to things and can "overcome" us, much as the painfulness of what is great in something sublime can "overwhelm" us or "flood" our receptive system. The question next arises whether, if one kind of flooding occurs, a shift to another system can take place?

In other words, how many conflicting basic emotion systems are there, and how do they interact and possibly conflict when we experience complex stimuli? Currently these seem to be open questions. Jaak Panksepp identifies three basic types of emotions and further argues that there are at least eight basic emotion systems in the brain.[27] Others divide our affective/behavioral repertoire into three fundamental basic emotion systems: behavioral approach, fight/flight, and behavioral inhibition.[28] Various scientists agree that the emotions in these various systems in humans may not necessarily involve cognition, but do require information processing.[29] Fear, for example, has been studied in decorticated cats and rats in ways that show that certain stimuli, say, visual ones, get processed by the brain on a basic, urgent pathway leading from the visual tissues through the amygdala to the emotion centers, alerting the animal to danger and altering its physiology accordingly. Meanwhile, in an animal with a cortex, the same holds true but the stimuli are simultaneously sent on the path from vision to the cognition center so as to be more precisely processed and labeled.[30]

And what of the emotions of the sublime—the characteristic combination of exaltation and fear? Recall that "respect" for Kant was a complex, rarefied emotion ("delight") involving our awareness of inadequacy before the moral law. Neuroscientists may not currently study such a complex emotion (nor may they ever wish to), but presumably they believe that even such a lofty phenomenon as the sublime must have roots within our basic, brain-based emotional systems. Interestingly, Antonio Damasio comes close to saying just this, while fending off incipient charges of reductivism: "Realizing that there are biological mechanisms behind the most sublime human behavior does not imply a simplistic reduction to the nuts and bolts of neurobiology. In any case, the partial explanation of complexity by something less complex does not signify debasement."[31]

Somehow the brain is capable of self-awareness of its own kinds of capacities, and it has the ability to organize inputs from various systems into an integrated conscious experience. This is true both for the inputs from different emotion systems and inputs from the emotion and information-processing or cognitive systems. LeDoux suggests that the "pure" states of the three basic emotion systems he describes may be described as *anxiety, panic, or rage,* and *hope or elation.* It is interesting to note that fear, one of the sublime emotions, seems to occur within a separate system from elation. And these systems may operate in distinct ways through different kinds of conjunctions with cognitive processes (or neocortical pathways). This suggests a new approach to discussing conflicts of the sublime experience: such conflicts reflect the simultaneous operation of multiple emotion systems, which themselves might have distinctive kinds of links (and even multiple links each) to our cognitive systems.

Thus it could turn out that the sublime object is being processed in different ways simultaneously by different mental systems. Perhaps after a certain point of perceptual processing of, say, a fearful stimulus, the limits of the more primitive system are reached and so we shift to another emotional system working with another kind of input and another layer of cognitive or categorical analysis. Perhaps within our complexly evolved human brain we are then able to reintegrate the overwhelmingly enormous input into our normal functioning—as a rat or cat cannot—by changing it into an abstraction that we can handle better. Fear arises in one system when our perceptual system begins to break down or be overwhelmed. Elation comes when we gain mastery over the perceived object by integrating it into our rational framework. This rational framework would need to be complex, so as to include the socially constructed notions used in our discourse about art and morality. Here also would have to be located the reflexiveness of our emotions that refer to other emotions. So in experiences of the sublime we combine pain and pleasure that is felt somehow at or about that pain. This is admittedly a very speculative account of how future scientists might redescribe the kind of conflict of the sublime that Kant located between the mental faculties of reason and imagination. But it suggests that there may well be a successor cognitive account for the phenomenon Kant observed.[32]

Kant used the subdivision of mind to ground his theory of moral value. Reason, the "highest" faculty, was also the most valued. Talk of "higher" brain functions in cognitive science tends instead to indicate stages of evolutionary development.[33] Although such language is not typically linked to any framework of moral theory, it can be. There are interesting efforts to draw connections both between recent studies of brain function and behavior and ethical theory. These proposals suggest that there will be a number of new and distinctive approaches to grounding ethics on this new sort of psychology.[34]

Conclusion

The sublime, as I have described it, is an experience involving four key features. At its heart is the emotional conflict between terror or dread and elevation. Second, the sublime involves something great or vast. In speaking of this second feature, I amended Kant's account in two important ways, focusing on artworks, not natural objects, and claiming that the grandeur belongs not only to the world in the work but to the work itself, to the way that world is depicted or shown.

Third, the greatness of the sublime is linked to an overwhelming, painful, ineffable effect the object has on the perceiver. I have described this feature of ineffability by mentioning representations in each film of certain feelings or landscapes that disturb us and strain our capacity for experience (such as Joan's faith and suffering, Baptiste's desperate love, or the conquistadors' dread in the Amazonian jungle). But this ineffable pain turns into pleasure as the object also prompts a shift into cognition. Unique and sublime films prompt our appreciative, awed reflection on how they use the film medium to disturb us in artful ways.

The fourth feature of the sublime is that such reflection is elevating because it includes a powerful moral perspective. I revised Kant by describing this as cognition of how human artists can offer powerful moral reflections in their works. To illustrate our switch or vacillation between the sublime emotions (the rapturous terror), I focused on scenes of rupture, and described how our awareness of the self-referential aspects of filmic art mediate between emotional involvement and more distanced aesthetic and moral appraisal.

I have also outlined challenges that cognitivist accounts face in capturing these four features of the sublime. There are two primary challenges. The first centers on the reflexivity of the emotions of the sublime. It is crucial to the sublime that one somehow feels exaltation, elevation or pleasure *about* what one is overwhelmed by or fears. Empirically based approaches to the study and explanation of the emotions need to capture this reflexive element. The second, deeper challenge concerns the ways in which values enter into our experience of the sublime. When we find a film sublime, we both evaluate it as an excellent, superlatively great artwork, and also are elevated by reflection on the moral issues it raises and its perspective on those issues.

Tan's psychological approach provides a certain basis for discussing the reflexivity of emotions, in describing how artefact and fiction emotions might ramify and interact. I expressed concerns above, however, about whether his "machine" account of films can explain how our aesthetic emotions are tied to active and complex cognitions of moral value. Similarly, neuroscience research indicates that there may be brain-based grounds for emotional conflicts like those of the sublime, even though the details will obviously be different from what Kant envisaged with his primitive theory of mental faculties. Still, neuroscientists may capture what I call the reflexivity of emotions by emphasizing complexity of communication between cognitive and emotion systems and the presence of feedback loops in the brain. Again, like Tan, the neuroscientists, too, face the second challenge, because the meta-emotions of film viewers involve not just our wiring and physiology, but our higher-level cognitions of value. We have these because we are humans using complex concepts that reflect our social organization as beings who make artworks, interpret them, and can understand their moral visions. When we see and react to Joan's suffering we need to have thoughts about patriarchy, nationalism, and religion, just as *Aguirre* requires conceptualizations of colonialism, incest, and madness, and *Children of Paradise* meditates on the values of artistic originality and emotional authenticity. I do not wish to suggest that it is impossible to account for these thoughts about values and their role in prompting our emotions. My goal has been, rather, to say that it will be a complex task to explain what makes certain films sublime.

FOUR

The Emotional Basis of Film Comedy

DIRK EITZEN

On three occasions in *The Shawshank Redemption,* a prisoner, "Red" (Morgan Freeman), appears before a panel of stone-faced parole officers. The first two occasions are separated by ten years in the prisoner's life and nearly an hour of movie time.

"Do you feel you've been rehabilitated?" a parole officer asks.

"Oh yes, sir," the prisoner replies. "I can honestly say I'm a changed man. No danger to society here. God's honest truth."

The camera lingers on the prisoner's face for a moment. Then, in large closeup, a metal stamp thumps its inked imprint on a form in the prisoner's file: "REJECTED."

The third time Red appears before the parole board, it is twenty years later, he is an old man, and we know that the movie is drawing to a close. To the inevitable question, "Do you feel you've been rehabilitated?" he replies, "I don't have any idea what that means. To me it's just a made-up word, a politician's word. . . . So you go on and stamp that form, sonny, and stop wasting my time because, to tell you the truth, I don't give a shit."

Again, the camera lingers on the prisoner's face. In a close-shot just like the first two, the stamp thumps down on the request for parole. This time, however, it comes away from the paper to reveal "ACCEPTED."

Shawshank Redemption is full of instances of pointless brutality, poignant tragedy, and grim irony, but very little humor. Yet here, near the end, is a moment of levity, all the more exhilarating for its unexpectedness. Inevitably, the audience laughs.

In *The Rock* (1996; an entirely different kind of picture even though, by the luck of the draw, it also unfolds in an abandoned prison), Sean Connery and Nicolas Cage play two reluctant heroes (John Patrick Mason and Stanley Goodspeed) forced to infiltrate Alcatraz, which has been occupied by a gang of crazed commandos intent on dropping a horrific chemical bomb on San

Francisco. In one scene Mason has dispatched a bad guy by dropping a large air-conditioning unit on him. As Goodspeed nervously tries to defuse a bomb filled with delicate glass vials of the lethal chemical, the dead guy's feet begin to twitch.

"You've been around a lot of corpses," Goodspeed says to Mason. "Is that normal?"

"The feet thing?"

"Yeah, the feet thing."

"Yeah, that happens."

"Well," Goodspeed says, "I'm having a kind of hard time concentrating. Can you do something about it?"

"Like what?" Mason replies. "Kill him again?"

As in many other moments in this flick, Cage's just-over-the-top delivery coupled with Connery's Bondian badinage gives the violent action an incongruously playful edge. Inevitably, the audience laughs.

Humor, it has been said many times, is not an emotion. A top humor researcher, Paul E. McGhee, points out that the perception of funniness is not always linked to any particular emotional response.[1] Philosopher John Morreal ticks off a list of reasons not to regard humor as an emotion, including the conceptual complexity of comedy and its effect of distancing us from immediate practical concerns.[2] Henri Bergson, in his influential turn-of-the-century essay "Laughter," maintains that laughter and emotions are downright incompatible.[3] So what is an essay on comedy doing in this anthology on emotion?

Four things. First, the two examples offered above are already proof enough that, even if humor is not an emotion, comic moments in movies can be accompanied by the sense of a powerful emotional release. Furthermore, if one defines emotions (as many do) as more-or-less automatic responses that when triggered *incline us to think and act in particular ways*, then humor very definitely is an emotion.[4] When we experience fear, we are alert to the possibility of danger in our surroundings and prepare to fight or fly. That is, we are inclined to think and act in particular ways. The same is true of humor. When we find something funny, we are inclined not to take it terribly seriously or, at least, to view its seriousness from arms' length, and to signal this disposition by smiling or laughing.

Second, certain very typical kinds of film comedy give an emotional kick, but at the expense of impeding the forward movement of a narrative. The enduring success of this kind of humor in Hollywood movies is evidence that emotional responses are even more fundamental to our interest in and enjoyment of movies than our anticipation of what is going to happen next and our eventual satisfaction at seeing a story through.

Third, there has been a lot of empirical research on humor—psychological, physiological, ethnographic, and ethological—that suggests that laughter and smiling are, at root, socially motivating behaviors and not merely the expression of private emotions. Both laughter and smiles appear chiefly in interactive situations. Laughter invites playful engagement and fosters social cohesion. Smiles appease aggression, strengthen social bonds, and facilitate the exchange of warmth and affection. A large part of the pleasure we experience from humor in everyday life, it seems, is not the solitary pleasure of cognitive mastery, wish fulfillment, ego gratification, or any such thing, but a result of the exercise of behaviors that have an important adaptive function in facilitating social affiliation. It is worth looking at humor research to test whether this hypothesis can be extended to movies.

In *The Imaginary Signifier*, first published two decades ago, Christian Metz suggests that our fascination with movies is something so peculiar, so extraordinary, so completely out of line with *reasonable* behavior that it can only be explained as the behind-the-scene operation of unconscious processes.[5] This extraordinarily influential essay has had the impact of inclining film scholars ever since to view our enjoyment of movies as something strange and mysterious. I will take the risk of revealing at the outset that the conclusion of this chapter is the very opposite: our pleasure in movies or, at the very least, of humor in movies is not so strange or mysterious after all. Empirical humor research suggests that our pleasure at comic elements in movies is merely an extension of a particular emotional response to ordinary, everyday experiences. It is a product of evolved habits of mind that shape all of our experiences, not just our experience of movies. It has its foundation in intrinsic emotional responses to certain kinds of potentially stressful social situations that are by no means peculiar to movies, even though some movies serve them up in especially concentrated doses.

So a fourth reason to look at humor research in an anthology that aims to help shift the way film scholars think about movies is because it provides strong evidence against the assumption, still widespread in the discipline, that the pleasures of movies are singular, strange, and somehow unrelated to the pleasures of everyday experience.

One familiar theory of cinematic storytelling holds that popular movies tend to be structured as a series of *problems* (from the viewpoint of characters) or *questions* (from spectators' viewpoint) coupled with their eventual solutions or answers. For example, at the beginning of *The Rock*, a group of commandos stages a daring raid on a military base. One by one, they encounter and overcome a series of obstacles and security measures—"problems" to be solved as they march toward their objective. "What are they up to?" we wonder, and "Will they succeed?"—questions we expect the movie to answer as it unfolds. There is nothing in the scene, or next to nothing, that distracts our attention from the sequence of problem and solution, question and answer. This structuring principle is the heart of most narrative entertainment.

It is a small step from this compelling observation to the conclusion that the chief *pleasure* of movies stems from spectators' anticipation and eventual discovery of solutions to problems or questions posed by the plot. The pithiest and most explicit expression of this theory is Noël Carroll's. Carroll suggests that the main source of the emotional impact of movies is the conceptual comestibility of the question-and-answer structure, which he calls "erotetic narration":

> Unlike those of real life, the actions observed in movies have a level of intelligibility, due to the role they play in the erotetic system of questions and answers. Because of the question/answer structure, the audience is left with the impression that it has learned everything important to know concerning the action depicted. . . . The powerful impression [movies make] is nothing but the exceptional perspicuousness, economy, and clarity of the action in movies which is due to erotetic narration.[6]

In other words, the emotional power of popular movies stems from the intense way in which they satisfy the innate human desire for order, coherence, and meaning.

David Bordwell articulates a more detailed version of the narration-as-problem-solving theory. He argues that a movie creates "gaps," putting a protagonist into a clear predicament but holding back information about possible solutions or likely reactions, forcing the spectator to make guesses or hypotheses about what will happen next. Because the questions posed by the plot of the classical Hollywood film overwhelmingly concern protagonists' likely reactions to the predicaments in which they find themselves, they can be reduced to just one: "What is this character going to do now?" Generally, viewers are permitted to correctly predict the general course of protagonists' actions (because it is "logical"), even though the action is fleshed out in unanticipated and occasionally surprising ways. The spectators are caught up in the process of guesswork, anticipation, and partial satisfaction. This "game" is the glue that holds the classical entertainment film together.[7]

Bordwell is cautious about ascribing all of the emotional power of movies to this game of anticipation and guesswork. Still, he writes, the pattern of response that is typical of the classical fiction film is most compatible with a theory of pleasure in which affect is bound up with expectation and its delayed fulfillment.

> When we bet on a hypothesis, especially under the pressure of time, confirmation can carry an emotional kick; the organism enjoys creating unity. When

the narrative delays satisfying an expectation, the withholding of knowledge can arouse keener interest. When a hypothesis is disconfirmed, the setback can spur the viewer to new bursts of activity. The mixture of anticipation, fulfillment, and blocked or retarded or twisted consequences can exercise great emotional power.[8]

For Bordwell, as for Carroll, the spectator of mainstream entertainment films is motivated primarily by curiosity about narrative developments and by the anticipation of narrative coherence and closure.[9] In other words, the principal pleasure of mainstream movies is in solving story problems.

If the *only* pleasure of movies was in solving story problems, one kind of narrative "problem" would be as good as any other (providing, of course, that the "solution" is neither too predictable nor too abstruse). We might find movies that are full of mundane problem-solving tasks like teaching and writing. But that is manifestly not the case. The questions that drive Hollywood movies are not just questions, they are burning questions. They always carry with them a strong emotional charge. They have to do with situations that have grave consequences for the physical or emotional well-being of characters in the movie. It would be possible to make a movie that is perfectly coherent according to the question-and-answer structure, yet as boring as a drill. Yet, strikingly, that is not what evolved in the classical Hollywood cinema. What evolved are stories that are full of sex, violence, melodrama, fast action, suspense and surprise, fantasy and horror, and humor.

So, it may be that the narrative-as-problem-solving theory puts the cart before the horse. Perhaps the problem-solving structure came about not because audiences get an intense pleasure from solving problems per se but because the problem-solving structure is the most reliable and effective way of generating intense emotional responses in movie audiences. Perhaps this structure evolved not because it was intellectually satisfying but because it provided the most economical framework for dishing up emotionally charged events. The case of comedy supports this hypothesis.

In the opening scene of *The Rock,* in which commandos storm a military garrison, next to nothing distracts from the sequence of problem and solution, question and answer. The same might be said of the funny scene, described earlier, in which Goodspeed tries to defuse a delicate bomb while a dead guy twitches. However, the next to next to nothing in that scene—Cage's acted mannerisms, the out-of-place casualness of the dialogue, and, indeed, the whole business of the twitching feet—is crucially important to our experience of the humor of the scene.

Comic devices in movies—jokes, exaggerated behaviors, parody, gags, and so on—routinely fail to fit neatly into the problem-solving structure that

Carroll and Bordwell describe. They are often unpredictable and incongruous. And even though they may make perfect sense in retrospect, they can
seem to come out of nowhere, rather than posing or answering a question as
most plot elements do. Frequently, as obvious bits of comic performance,
they also distract from or impede the smooth unfolding of a story. Since
support for these claims has been laid out at some length elsewhere, I will
rest my case here upon a single example—the fake orgasm scene from *When
Harry Met Sally* (1989).[10] I could have picked a far more striking example
from, say, *Wayne's World* (1992) or *Ace Ventura* (1994), but I deliberately chose
an example from a comparatively staid romantic comedy to show that, even
when comic elements are clearly embedded in a "classical" question-and-
answer structure, the pleasure we derive from them cannot be entirely explained by their fit within that structure.

Harry and Sally (Billy Crystal and Meg Ryan) are temperamentally poles
apart. He is casual and crude; she is fussy and prim. Because of that, a romantic relationship between them seems out of the question. Because of
that, they have become good friends. Over lunch in a crowded restaurant one
day, Sally asks Harry how he manages his many casual affairs.

"So what do you do with these women?" she asks. "You just get up out of
bed and leave?"

"Sure, he says. "I say I have an early haircut, early meeting, early squash
game."

"You don't play squash."

"They don't know that, they just met me."

"That's disgusting," Sally says.

"I know, I feel terrible," Harry replies between bites, without a trace of
either remorse or irony. "But," he goes on, "I think they have an okay time."

Sally says that he cannot know that, especially since he is out the door so
fast. Harry replies, with a superior smirk, that he does indeed know. (We
already know why, since in an earlier conversation with a male buddy he
boasts about having made a woman meow in sexual ecstasy.) Sally insists
that Harry cannot possibly know for sure whether a woman is truly aroused,
since oftentimes women pretend for the sake of their partners. Harry maintains, with absolute confidence, that there is no way *he* could be fooled.

Sally gazes at Harry with an expression of amused disbelief. After a few
moments, she frowns slightly, then begins to moan. Harry asks, "Are you all
right?" Sally continues to moan, louder, "Oooh, God!" and begins to writhe
in her chair. Harry divines what she is doing and sits back in his chair with
an expression of bemused tolerance. Sally's moans become more and more
emphatic, then turn to gasps of pleasure, then rhythmic cries of "Oh, yes, yes,
yes!" accompanied by thumps on the table. Practically the whole café has by
now turned to watch. We see a series of shots of people staring with unfath-

omable expressions. Harry's look of bemusement turns to one of obvious embarrassment. He gives an awkward little nod of greeting to the staring patron at the next table. Sally's display finally ends with an ecstatic groan, then she picks up her fork, smiles sweetly at Harry, and pops a forkful of salad into her mouth. A woman at another table looks up to a waiter, indicates Sally, and says, "I'll have what she's having."

A good deal of this scene makes sense according to the hypothetical question-and-answer structure. For example, what drives the whole movie is the question, "Will Harry and Sally ever sleep together?" This scene points toward the answer, with its obvious indications of Harry and Sally's growing intimacy. Another question that sustains this particular scene is, "Who is going to win this argument?" or "Will Harry ever see the error of his ways?" Sally's daring conversational gambit pretty much gives her the last word in this debate, and that spells the end of the scene as well. So questions undeniably provide much of the impetus of this scene.

Unexpected answers also account for part of the humor. What comeback can Sally possibly make to Harry's smug dismissal of her verbal arguments? Surprise! Public humiliation. However unexpected it may be, Sally's fake orgasm is also obviously a decisive answer. Similarly, the final line of dialogue in the scene, "I'll have what she's having," brings satisfying resolution to the scene by punctuating Sally's demonstration with a kind of "touché!" Even though the line is utterly unpredictable, it puts a nice finishing touch on the question, "Who is going to win this argument?"

Still, much of the humor in this scene has nothing to do with such questions and answers. In fact, the funniest thing about the scene is the almost unbelievable social gaucherie of loudly faking an orgasm in the middle of a crowded restaurant. The choice to have a character so blatantly violate social conventions comes from completely outside the system of questions and answers. It is something extra. And as the treatment of the scene makes apparent, that something extra is of profound interest to viewers. We dwell for more than a minute on Meg Ryan's oohing and ahhing—far more than is necessary to pose or answer any question. In fact, the extended fake-orgasm sequence essentially brings the story to a halt. We also see a great many more reaction shots than are necessary to simply get the story across. All this "excess" serves to emphasize the social dimensions of the scene: the stunning inappropriateness of Sally's behavior, the stares she is attracting, her calculated obliviousness to the scene she is making, and Harry's acute embarrassment. Furthermore, because Ryan's actions violate our expectations about what is plausible and likely, they call attention to themselves as a bit of comic performance as do, in their own way, all the underplayed reaction shots in the scene. It is all these extra elements—not just surprising kinks in the string of questions and answers—that make this scene so funny.

The point of this example, to reiterate, is that what makes us laugh at movies often has very little to do with their problem-solving structure, however thoroughly it may be mixed up with it. And yet humor has always been so much a part of Hollywood movies that it is obviously one very important attraction of them. Since the narrative-as-problem-solving theory does not account for this attraction, how can we explain it?

This simplest answer is this. What the average moviegoer wants most of all from movies is not narrative per se but strong and concentrated affective responses. Movies can provide a powerful emotional kick in a safe context. This is what mainstream audiences have always been most eager to pay for in movies—not just the pleasure of seeing a problem through, but the concentrated experience of emotions that are not often triggered in day-to-day affairs: sadness, horror, fear, excitement, the happiness associated with the climax of a romance, the thrill of having survived a brush with death, and, as in the example offered here, the funny side of inappropriate behavior. I submit that this is the pressure that most influenced the shape of the classical Hollywood cinema.

Besides comedy, this theory accounts for other nonnarrative attractions of movies, such as spectacle, melodrama, and horror. It also makes a certain amount of historical sense because it aligns the Hollywood cinema more closely with amusement park attractions, variety shows, video games, nonfiction television, and other popular nonnarrative entertainments. Furthermore, it explains why we can find the same movie enjoyable twice in a row—something problem-solving theories of narrative have trouble explaining. We can experience the same emotions the second time through, even if we already know what is going to happen.

Emotion theories have long been plagued by the question of how manifestly imaginary scenarios, like movies, can produce such strong emotional responses. Are we really frightened when we see a violent twister approaching in the movies, or do we just imagine we are frightened? If we are really frightened, why do we just sit there? If we just imagine we are frightened, why do we get so tense? In either case, why are we so eager to pay six dollars or more to subject ourselves to that stress?

One attraction of the narrative-as-problem-solving theory is that it sidelines these questions. If people go to movies mainly to experience an aesthetic response that stems from movies' narrative form, not direct emotional responses to the situations movies present, then questions like those above can be easily dismissed. Why are we frightened by a twister in the movies? Oh, that is an *aesthetic* response, merely *metaphoric* fright. But, as I have showed, problem-solving alone is not enough to explain our laughter at the fake orgasm scene in *When Harry Met Sally*. I suppose that it is also not enough to explain other emotional responses, including our tears during fictional death scenes, our arousal at depictions of romantic sex, and our fear of Industrial Light and Magic tornadoes.

Having used the case of comedy to show that aesthetic responses cannot entirely account for the pleasure of movies, is it also possible to use the case of comedy to establish any tentative answers to the question of how mere shadows on a screen can arouse genuine emotions? Do empirical studies of humor responses suggest any theories for why people seek out not only happy surprises in movies, like Sally's fake orgasm, but depictions of less pleasant experiences, like brutality, horror, and death?

The main contender for a comprehensive theory of film emotions is Dutch scholar Ed Tan.[11] His recent book, *Emotion and the Structure of Narrative Film,* is a new approach to old catharsis theory.[12] It argues, in a nutshell, that when we watch movies we endure moments of dullness (no emotional response) or displeasure (disagreeable emotional responses, such as anxiety) in view of the reward of eventual release from emotional tension. Our interest in movies is generated by our anticipation of such release.

Tan's catharsis theory may account for part of the pleasure of comedy. Our laughter at the scenes from *Shawshank Redemption* and *The Rock* I described is indeed accompanied by a sense of emotional release (even though in *The Rock* our laughter occurs in the middle of a tense scene, not at the end of it). But Tan's theory does little to explain the sustained pleasure we experience from the *buildup* of emotional tension in the fake orgasm scene in *When Harry Met Sally*. Even more crucially, it fails to account for the *immediate* satisfaction we can derive from "painful" emotions in movies, such as sadness, horror, and anxiety.

When I see a violent twister on the screen, I find a certain satisfaction in the moment itself, in the very exercise of extreme emotions in a safe context. I am excited by the spectacle, the emotions of characters in the fiction, the anticipation of disaster, and so on. This excitement can be its own reward. The reward may be compounded by a subsequent release from tension, but it does not depend upon it. What I am eager for when I watch a movie like *Twister* (1996) is the *appearance* of the next violent cyclone, not its *disap*pearance. My interest in the movie is generated not merely by the promise of release from anxiety, but by the anxiety itself. In this regard, a movie can be like a rollercoaster ride. The closest Tan's theory comes to explaining this phenomenon is to suggest that there is an intrinsic pleasure in merely attending to a "concern" (that is, anything that triggers an emotional response). So, for example, it gives us pleasure to watch Nicolas Cage's face as he handles those tinkling glass vials of a lethal chemical because, at some level, people's expressions of emotion always "concern" us.

On this point, Murray Smith has written more extensively.[13] He argues that people are psychologically predisposed to imagine the emotional experiences of other people and that our emotional responses to fiction films make sense in this light. This is probably true, but it does not account for our laughter at Red's parole in *Shawshank Redemption,* which is more an expression of our surprise than a reflection of Red's feelings.

Our laughter in instances like this is immediate and direct, like the vertigo we experience from a helicopter shot in an IMAX movie. It does not need to be mediated by our imagination of a character's feelings. The immediacy of viewers' emotional responses to humorous moments in films and the discreteness of those responses from characters' emotions are two more reasons that it is useful to look at comedy in trying to understand the part that emotions play in the pleasure of movies.

There is a vast literature on humor. Much of it, including an august tradition of philosophical debate that involves such notables as Aristotle, Hobbes, and Kant, is grounded chiefly upon introspection.[14] Introspection is a notoriously unreliable basis for psychological speculations. There is also, however, a tradition of research based upon the observation and analysis of actual situations and stimuli that result in laughing, smiling, and amusement. These studies have spawned highly speculative theories, too, but they have, in addition, resulted in certain widely accepted findings about when and why people engage in humor.

There is overwhelming evidence, for example, that the cognitive and behavioral foundations of humor are innate. For one thing, humor is a human universal. Laughter, smiling, and words to describe amusement are part of every culture. Even though people in different cultures may laugh at different things, they laugh at the same kind of thing and in the same kind of situation.[15] Smiling and laughter develop in the first half year among infants and become a normal response to social stimulation. Infants smile at moving face-like objects even before they are capable of recognizing and distinguishing faces.[16] Children who are deaf and blind from birth laugh and smile in the same kind of situations as other children, which shows that these are not learned expressions.[17] Finally, homologs to human laughter and smiling occur consistently among apes, and in situations we would regard as familiar: rough-and-tumble play, for example.[18] All of these observations suggest strongly that humor is an evolved response, with an adaptive functional basis.

Another very robust conclusion is that humor is a predominately social response. It arises most often by far in and from social situations. For example, a classic study of preschool children found that almost all of their laughter arose from playful interactions with other children and toys, behaviors regarded as socially unacceptable, and verbal jokes (in that order).[19] All of these situations are defined by their social dimension. Freud observed that jokes usually brush up against social taboos.[20] Anthropologists and sociologists have likewise observed that joking behaviors enter cultures at points of social stress.[21] The contagiousness of humor also points to its social basis. Many studies show that canned laughter, the presence of another person, and even the mere assumption that somebody in another room is sharing in a humorous experience all facilitate laughter and smiling.[22] All of this suggests that humor, even if experienced in private, has its functional foundation in social experience.

The developmental and ethological evidence for this conclusion is particularly compelling. The fact that infants smile indiscriminately at human faces from about three to five months of age testifies to the importance of smiling in triggering the kind of social responses that infants need for their healthy development. Observations of infant-mother interactions support this hypothesis. Laughter in infants, likewise, is an invitation for interaction.[23] Among chimpanzees, the laugh homolog almost always accompanies play behavior and indicates that fighting or romping is not meant seriously. The smile homolog sometimes elicits affinitive behaviors, like eye-contact and touching; at other times, it accompanies submissive behavior and appeases aggressive behavior.[24] Although "smiling" and "laughing" behaviors are more discrete among apes than humans, they both appear almost exclusively in interactive situations. They both seem to signal friendly intentions and to invite a friendly response. Together, infant and primate studies provide a strong indication that the basic functions of smiling and laughter in humans include (1) the function of producing social bonding and intimacy and (2) the function of diminishing social tensions by signaling friendly or nonhostile intentions.[25]

Although dozens of competing theories have been put forward to explain the pleasure of humor, most of these can be boiled down to one of three types. The first is *incongruity-resolution theory,* which stems from the observation that a great deal of humor, including most jokes, results from unexpected solutions to conceptual challenges.[26] Like Bordwell and Carroll's problem-solving theories of narrative, this theory holds that the chief pleasure of humor arises from the satisfaction of anticipating and discovering solutions to problems (albeit incongruous or surprising solutions, in the case of comedy).

The second theory is catharsis or *tension-relief theory.* Like Ed Tan's theory of the pleasure of movies, this theory holds that the pleasure of humor stems from the release of emotional tension. This may involve either the solution of an intellectual challenge or the amelioration of a socially stressful situation. Tension-relief theory is sometimes coupled with *safety theory.* This theory holds that identifying with or being the object of humor lessens its funniness because it elevates our emotional investment in the situation, thereby counteracting the release of emotional tension.

The third theory is *superiority theory*. Noting the failure of the incongruity-resolution model to account for the fact that most humor involves some breach of social norms or accepted behavior, this theory holds that humor can be explained as a relatively nonviolent and therefore socially acceptable form of aggression toward others or correction of social deviancy. The pleasure of humor, in this theory, stems from ego affirmation: humor makes us feel part of a privileged in-group or otherwise superior to those at whom our laughter is directed.

These three theories cannot be brought into line. Certain of their aspects can be (the relief of tension is implicit in the resolution of incongruity, for instance), but none of them is fully compatible with any other because each proposes a radically different explanation for the fundamental pleasure of humor. Each of the theories has convincing empirical evidence to back it up. Each has other empirical findings it cannot explain.

Incongruity resolution seems to account quite well for the humor of the scene from *Shawshank Redemption* described at the start of this chapter. Red says just the right things before the parole board twice and is denied parole. The third time, he says just the wrong things, it seems, and gets paroled anyway. The incongruousness of this sets us back on our heels for a moment, yet we quickly recognize it as fitting, both in terms of the story and as a metaphor for the arbitrariness of the penal system.

On the other hand, incongruity resolution fails to explain why Billy Crystal's expressions of bewilderment and embarrassment are so amusing in the fake orgasm scene from *When Harry Met Sally*. Superiority theory might account for that. Indeed, it is pleasurable to see smug Harry get his comeuppance. But then, superiority hardly seems to account for our laughter at Red's parole. And, as stated earlier, tension-relief theory cannot explain our pleasure in the *buildup* of emotional tension in the *When Harry Met Sally* scene.

I propose (as others have) that there is some truth to all of these theories or that there are some situations in which each of them applies. Sometimes when we sit in a movie theater chuckling, we feel a special bond of affinity with our neighbor, who is also chuckling. We feel like part of a special in-group—*superior*. I suppose this is particularly true of those people who, like me, laugh at such things as the ironic goriness of a corpse being put through a wood chipper in *Fargo*. Sometimes, our laughter signals a relief of *tension*. Indeed, part of the reason I laugh at the scene from *Fargo* is to mitigate its horror. Another ingredient of my laughter at the same scene may be its sheer outrageousness—its *incongruity*. Whoever would expect to see such a horror in a crime drama? . . . Well, in a Coen brothers crime drama, perhaps. (And here, with this special movie knowledge, we are brought back to superiority theory.)

Incongruity-resolution theory, tension-relief theory, and superiority theory each make intuitive sense as a partial explanation of the pleasure of film comedy. But I submit that all three are second-order explanations. The pleasure of humor is innate. That pleasure is one of the psychological levers by which evolution perpetuated behaviors that result in social bonding in humans (like sharing in play) and reined-in behaviors that result in social fragmentation (like naked aggression). In other words, the fundamental reason that we find humor pleasurable is the same as the reason that we find sugar sweet: because we evolved that way.

This theory may seem too general to have much explanatory power when discussing the particular pleasures of film comedy. In fact, many humor researchers treat it as a given. It is nonetheless necessary to state it explicitly here, for two reasons. First, because it makes it clear that in order to understand the psychological and social foundations of comedy, it is especially useful to consider what adaptive functions a sense of humor might serve.[27] This is, indeed, the approach taken by most anthropologists and sociologists who study humor. The second reason is that it implies that film comedy works by triggering emotional responses that are by no means cinema-specific. This is contrary to the oft-assumed notion that the pleasure of the movies is something strange and peculiar to the cinema, something that has little to do with the pleasures of other kinds of experience.

Darwin argued that from an evolutionary perspective emotions have two basic functions in all animals. First, they increase the chances of individual survival through appropriate reactions to emergency events in the environment. Second, they act as signals of the intentions of future actions through various display behaviors, like laughing and smiling.[28] Since laughing and smiling are by and large incompatible with any urgent inclination to immediate action, such as fight or flight, humor must have more to do with the second of these functions than the first. The adaptive advantages conferred upon the species by the humor response must be largely social—for example, the enhancement of our capacity for social interaction or of our inclination to form social groupings.

This is particularly apparent in the most primitive functions of smiles and laughter, those evident in the behavior of apes and young children: namely, the functions of ameliorating social stresses and creating social bonds. Among very young children, laughter accompanies not just any kind of play, but tickling, mock attacks, being chucked in the air, and other playful aggressions. As children grow older, their laughter extends to flatulence, deliberate misbehavior, and other breaches of social nicety. In all of these instances, laughter ameliorates social stress by signaling nonthreatening intentions and stakes out social boundaries through playful interactions. These functions are very apparent in most instances of humor, even among adults, as a great many scholars of humor have remarked.

Humor is very closely connected, on one hand, to aggression and humiliation and, on the other, to a sense of relief or of cementing one's social standing. We smile or laugh when we succeed at a practical joke or win a particularly tough point in a game of tennis. The humor, in those instances, is in a sudden relief of tension that affirms our sense of social self-worth. We also find humor in embarrassment, when we are the victim of a practical joke or fall down in public. The humor here is an attempt to diminish or distance ourself from our loss of face. We also laugh when someone else is embarrassed. We might laugh sympathetically, to show solidarity. We might laugh casually, in a way that distances us from that person's humiliation. We might even laugh derisively, in a way that figuratively casts the person out of our social sphere altogether. In all of these cases, we are attempting to relieve a social stress.

Derisive laughter is sometimes said to increase rather than diminish social stress. It is obviously a form of aggression and can therefore be seen as a challenge to social stability. But derisive laughter is also a substitute for more direct or violent aggression and thus prevents a more serious tear in the social fabric. When we mock someone, we smile to show that our hostility is not to be taken "seriously." When someone mocks us, we smile to show that no "serious" threat is intended in return. So, even when humor is hostile, it helps to preserve against the breakdown of social affiliations.

It seems quite likely, then, that one of the evolutionary cornerstones of humor is the function of helping us deal with socially induced stress. Humor accomplishes this by allowing us to hold situations that threaten our social standing or self-esteem at emotional arms' length. I can conceptually step back from a stressful situation (so long as there is no imminent danger of actual harm in it) by framing it in a way that distances me from it. In the words of emotion theorist Nico Frijda, humor is "detachment from a previously mobilized concern."[29] For example, when I take an embarrassing public pratfall, I can reduce the stress of feeling clumsy and undignified by establishing a context for the event that is "funny" rather than damaging to my self-esteem. The same is true if I witness someone else fall. By laughing at the mishap, I show that I do not take it seriously, which diminishes the stress of the situation for both of us. In adopting a humorous stance, I take a perspective outside the immediate concreteness of the situation in which I am involved. This can involve a rationalization—deliberately adopting a different intellectual frame, as in the case of irony—but it is based upon an automatic emotional response that is part of our biological hardware.

Humor is one natural, evolved response to emotionally charged social situations. We laugh to defuse a threat or an insult. We laugh in response to feelings of personal inadequacy, especially when we are in public. We laugh when we are embarrassed or when someone else is embarrassed. Contrary to popular belief, Hollywood movies are not primarily about happy endings; they are about just such emotionally charged personal and social situations. They are about skirting or surviving a series of potential disasters. We know a movie is over when there is no longer any imminent danger of embarrassment or pain. We get pleasure from happy endings, of course, but we do not go to movies just for the endings; we go for the process of getting there. The classical Hollywood cinema is not defined by happy endings, it is defined by deferred happy endings or sustained emotional high points. It is primarily about seeing characters squirm in dangerous, painful, or embarrassing situations. Because humor is one natural response to such situations, it is natural that we experience humor in Hollywood movies.[30]

Granted, a movie pratfall is an *artificially mediated* pratfall, and therefore different in important ways than a pratfall in the flesh. Movies present our sense of humor with some special challenges and some unusual reassurances. For one thing, movies can dish up occasions for humor with a frequency that is seldom if ever found in everyday experience. For another, film affords unique possibilities for "play" in its presentation. The humorous scene from *The Rock* discussed earlier, for example, is funny not just because of how Cage's character (Goodspeed) responds to the situation in which he finds himself, but because of the way Cage the actor plays the scene. Part of the humor is in the style of the *discourse*. Filmmakers' control of framing, shot juxtapositions, sound mixing, and so on all add cinema-specific dimensions to the possibilities for play in and through discourse.

When watching a movie, we are also safe from embarrassment or harm, which makes us freer to respond with humor to situations observed than in everyday experience, where laughing at someone's misfortune has to be seen as a potentially real insult. In this respect, watching a movie is comparable to observing an everyday situation from behind a one-way mirror. Fiction films afford still another level of safety as well—the reassurance that what we are seeing is "just a movie," a scenario played out by actors in which, despite our "willing suspension of disbelief," we know that no one really comes to harm.[31]

Despite these differences, however, the humor we experience at movies is merely an extension of a particular emotional response to ordinary, everyday experiences. It involves the same cognitive strategies. It produces the same emotional responses. It is predicated upon the same innate human tendencies, the most fundamental of which, I have argued, is a predisposition to respond to certain kinds of potentially stressful social situations in a way that changes their emotional valence to a nonthreatening one.

This theory explains the eternal funniness of the pratfall. It explains the humor surrounding the twitching dead guy in *The Rock*. It explains our amusement at Sally's fake orgasm in *When Harry Met Sally*. One thing this theory still does not explain is our laughter at Red's parole in *Shawshank Redemption*. Red is not humiliated in that scene or subjected to any kind of stress we might find funny. Nor is anyone else. Red does break the "rules" by frankly giving the parole board a piece of his mind, but that is not what is funny. What is funny is how our expectations are momentarily turned upside down by his being granted parole. This is mainly an aesthetic response: the incongruous resolution of a story situation.

The resolution of incongruity is an aspect of a great deal of humor that cannot be dismissed. It explains a lot of the sight gags and verbal wit in movies, as well as amusing story twists like Red's unexpected parole. This aspect of many humorous situations—the surprising or incongruous resolution of problems—is perfectly congruent with Carroll and Bordwell's theory that movies give us pleasure by satisfying our penchant for problem-solving. This is part of the pleasure of play. It is part of the pleasure of jokes. It is no doubt, likewise, part of the pleasure of watching movies.

Still, in evolutionary, developmental, and psychological terms, this is a secondary pleasure and one that is predicated upon the success of our social problem solving skills.[32] It makes sense to suppose that the emotional kick that problem-solving gives us is what motivates our interest in problem-solving, in the first place, as Bordwell and Carroll both acknowledge. Movies can give us a similar emotional kick in plenty of other ways as well, such as music, dramatic special effects, showing facial emotions, depictions of sex, and so on. The history of film comedy amply illustrates this. There are lots of instances of incongruity-resolution humor in Hollywood movies—verbal wit, sight gags, and so on. But these moments are literally overwhelmed by the number of humorous situations based upon aggression, embarrassment, off-color gags, and other violations of personal dignity or social convention.

By and large, then, comedy in the cinema seems to serve the same purpose as humor in everyday life. It produces pleasure by first posing a potentially challenging or stressful situation and then permitting us to view it as play, as something not intended to do "serious" insult or injury. The pleasure we experience is not a consequence of the release of tension, as catharsis theory suggests. It is rather a more fundamental emotional response associated with the "play frame" itself, a response that produces feelings of social connectedness and self-esteem and diminishes feelings that our social standing or personal competence may be challenged.

II

Film Technique, Film Narrative, and Emotion

✎ FIVE ✎

Local Emotions, Global Moods, and Film Structure

GREG M. SMITH

Until recently there were only scattered essays and one book attempting to apply cognitivist assumptions to film and emotions.[1] The very question seemed strange: how could cognitivism, with its emphasis on rational processes, hope to explain the irrational world of filmic emotion? Yet in the past few years several landmark books have appeared which pose compelling answers to that question.[2] It now seems easier to discuss a cognitivist perspective on film emotions.

Overturning long-held Romantic notions about the opposition between emotion and cognition, a cognitivist can emphasize emotions as a structured complement to cognitive processes. Emotions, to this way of thinking, motivate people to move more quickly toward their goals. Whether the goal is to remove oneself from a threatening lion's presence or to achieve intimacy with a loved one, emotions provide us with an impetus that logical deliberation alone cannot provide. Emotions are not dysfunctions that interfere with our rationality; instead they are functional processes. Emotions, to the budding cognitivist perspective, are functional action tendencies that motivate us toward goals and that are shaped by our situational expectations.[3]

While I agree with the thrust of this argument, I believe we must ask, In what ways is it productive and counterproductive to view the emotion system with these assumptions? The relatively straightforward fit between traditionally cognitivist concepts (such as goals and expectations) and the functionalist explanation of emotions is tempting. Before we embrace a particular understanding of the emotion system to guide our investigations into film, however, we should investigate if our current cognitivist assumptions leave out important parts of the emotion system.

The emotion system is more complex—messier, if you will—than such functionalist assumptions would indicate. While retaining a cognitivist understanding of emotions as structured phenomena, I wish to muddy the waters by portraying the emotion system as based on a looser connecting principle (associations), not on the tight trajectory that links action and goal. As important as action tendencies, "object" orientation, and goal orientation are to the emotion system, they are not the whole story.

This chapter attempts to add an associationist model of the emotions that parallels, but is not identical to, the functional one emphasized in film cognitivism thus far. This model enlarges the focus of our attentions from the emotions proper to include other emotion-related states such as "mood," and I argue that these less intense states are as vital to understanding filmic emotion as are more prototypical emotions. In the first half of this chapter I articulate this alternative model of emotions in some detail, so readers more interested in film than emotion theory perhaps should skim this argument and move fairly quickly to the second half, where I discuss what this model's assumptions might tell us about emotions and film narration.

While film cognitivism is in its early stages, we need to make sure that our basic conception of the emotion system does not needlessly limit our understanding of filmic emotions. This chapter sketches an approach to analyzing the emotional appeals of particular film texts, an approach that can provide nuanced insight into the broad range of complex emotion cues within a film. The first step toward creating such an approach to films is to ensure that our theoretical understanding of the emotion system is not too narrowly defined to discuss the breadth of emotional experience.

Film Cognitivism and Emotion Thus Far: The Emotion Prototype

Emotions are a real-world category, and, like many real-world categories, they are arranged around a prototype. Trying to determine if an egret is a bird, under ordinary circumstances, involves comparing the individual to a prototype (e.g., a robin). It is much simpler to recognize that there are numerous similarities between the egret and the robin than it is to ascertain if an egret has all the Linnaean factors required to classify it as a bird: Does it have feathers? Does it lay eggs? Is it warm-blooded? Prototypes allow us to recognize category members quickly and efficiently.

What, then, are some of the characteristics of the prototype of emotion? The emotion prototype is structured according to the principles that film cognitivism has embraced. Emotions are prototypically thought of as being action tendencies: for example, fear spurs us to run away from a menacing animal. Such emotions have a goal (to remove the animal menace from our presence). Emotions are intentional, in Franz Brentano's term; they have an object (I am not merely afraid; I am afraid *of* something).[4] Definitions of emotion rooted in cognitive philosophy tend to have some combination of these central characteristics of the emotion prototype: an action tendency, an orientation toward objects, and a goal orientation. Film cognitivism has inherited these assumptions.

These assumptions makes prototypical emotions seem not unlike other goal-oriented phenomena that film cognitivists have explained. David Bordwell,[5] for instance, has argued that canonical narrative form (in the classical Hollywood cinema) tends to put individual protagonists in pursuit of a clear goal. The actions characters perform to achieve their goals become the basis for the forward movement of the plot. Spectators make hypotheses about what will happen next based on their expectations. Seen in this way, the connection between comprehending film narration and experiencing film emotions seems more straightforward, since expectations, goals, and purposive actions are at the heart of both processes.

Relying on the prototype of emotions has helped film cognitivists Noël Carroll, Ed Tan, and Torben Grodal provide admirably specific accounts of filmic emotions. Carroll is able to discuss with considerable particularity the characteristics of the monster, the central object of horror in the horror film. Tan's model explains how spectators assemble narrative information into cohesive emotional scenarios, and this model provides specific, testable hypotheses concerning how actual viewers understand characters' actions, motivations, and goals.[6] Grodal's system provides a rich array of terms to describe the emotional experiences of a spectator identifying with characters as those characters try to achieve their goals.[7] Considering the emotions using prototypical assumptions helps these theorists to describe filmic emotional experiences with insight and specificity.

With these advantages come certain disadvantages, however. If one understands filmic emotions as object-, action-, and goal-oriented, then this privileges the portion of the film that most clearly fits these criteria. For Carroll, Tan, and Grodal, this means that filmic emotions are inextricably character-oriented. Dramatic characters provide clear objects for our emotions. They have goals, and they pursue them through a course of action. Because of the tightness of fit between the functions of characters and the functionality of emotions, these theorists privilege our understanding of characters' actions, motivations, and goals over other considerations. For Carroll the key to understanding horror is to understand the qualities of a particular kind of character: the monster. Tan argues that action/plot structures and character structures are the primary determinants guiding our emotional expectations. Grodal places strong emphasis on the identificatory link between spectator and character as crucial to understanding filmic emotion. The prototypical understanding of emotion helps foreground the importance of characters and actions in filmic emotions.

But what about other features that are less clearly object-, goal-, and action-oriented? What about style, for instance? Carroll, Tan, and Grodal all recognize that style helps films provide their emotional appeals. However, none of them give style a central place in their system's concept of emotion.

Carroll provides an indicative case. Instead of examining the *mise en scène* or musical conventions of horror films, he concentrates on the qualities and actions of a particular character: the monster. In Carroll's wide-ranging career, he has clearly paid much attention to style. However, when he examines film music,[8] a stylistic element that is less clearly person-centered, he notes that its primary function is to "modify" the more important emotional cues provided by character, plot, situation, and so on. All of these theorists agree that style has a valuable modifying role, but their assumptions about emotion (as object-, action-, and goal-oriented) keep style in a secondary role. In each cognitivist theory the dominant mechanism engaging filmic emotions depends on characters and their actions.

Considering that the Hollywood cinema encourages us to concentrate on characters and relegate stylistic matters to the background, this approach makes sense. But should we, as critics examining filmic emotions, follow this foregrounding of character and action? The answer is not obvious. Perhaps broadening our understanding of the emotion system beyond the prototype may provide richer readings of films and their emotional appeals.

The emotion system is accessed by emotion states that do not fit the emotion prototype so clearly. Depression, for instance, is not a functional action tendency. If I am so depressed that I am immobile, it is difficult to view such an emotional, self-perpetuating state as being an "action tendency" toward a goal. Emotion states such as depression do not promote the subject's well-being, and yet a depressed person alone in his or her room is experiencing an emotion state that is no less forceful simply because it is not functional. Emotion states can have nondirected expression (like depression) and can be elicited by extremely diffuse stimuli (like a sunny day). If I feel happy because it is a sunny day, my emotion has a cause, but the "object" (everything surrounding me) is too diffuse to be an object in any strongly meaningful sense.

Wait a minute, you may interject. Depression and positive feelings on a sunny day are not clearly *emotions*, one could argue. Such states are a far cry from the fear one experiences in being chased by an animal or the love one feels for Mother. These may be emotion-related or emotional *states*, but many would argue that such less-focused, less-intense, and less-cognitively elaborated states are not emotions proper. For instance, Carroll (see chapter 1) notes the existence of bodily states that have an affective tendency, but he brackets these off from emotions proper.

To bracket off these emotional states from the "real" emotions, I would argue, tends to encourage the critic to afford them less attention. Subtle critics well versed in the research on emotion and the body (including Carroll, Tan, and Grodal) may acknowledge the existence of such related states, but it is easy to let such states slip into the background, since they are not truly considered to be emotions per se. Such emotion states tend to be excluded from the primary mechanisms in filmic emotion theories.

This exclusion does make a certain sense, if one is trying to explain the major mechanisms governing filmic emotions. Providing an explanation for intense, focused filmic emotions seems intuitively to be more important than explaining lesser emotional states. Intuition can be deceiving, however. A better measure would be to determine if the emotion system reacts similarly to both prototypical emotions and other, more diffuse emotional states. If it does, this would argue for the potential usefulness of expanding our concept of the emotion system to include nonprototypical emotion states. For the moment, let us entertain the possibility that just because certain emotional states are at lower levels, are less focused, and are less forceful than the emotion prototype does not mean that they are less *important* to understanding how the emotion system works.

The Emotion System: An Associative Model

We need a model of the emotions which links responses and stimuli in flexible but stable connections. The model proposed here asserts that associations can provide just such a linkage, and that the primacy of associations is supported by the physiological and neurological structure of the emotion system.

Emotions are what may be called multidimensional response syndromes.[9] They are groups of responses (including action tendencies, orienting responses, and expressions) connected to several possible eliciting systems. Emotions differ from reflexes in that they can be expressed through differing responses, depending on the individual's predispositions, the characteristics of the social situation, and cultural mores. A person might respond to embarrassment by blushing, cringing, making a self-deprecating joke, or deflecting attention away from oneself. One cannot specify with absolute certainty which of a group of responses a specific person might have to an emotional situation, but one can enumerate a group of likely responses.

Not only can emotions provoke a range of responses, but the emotion system can also be invoked by several possible subsystems. Those subsystems that have been discussed as being important to eliciting emotions are facial nerves and muscles, vocalization, body posture and skeletal muscles, autonomic nervous system, conscious cognition, and the nonconscious processing by the central nervous system. Each of these plays a part in the general process of producing emotion.

Psychologists have investigated these six areas in search of the underlying bases of emotions.[10] Various researchers have found that all of these systems have a contributing or mediating effect on the emotion system, but none of these subsystems is sufficient to cause emotion by itself. Only one of the components of the emotion system has been shown to be necessary to emotion: the limbic system in nonconscious central nervous processing.

The limbic system is a highly interconnected neurological center that receives information from a wide range of input systems. Its function is to evaluate that information, to provide an emotional coding based on this evaluation, to trigger an initial response, and to monitor the stream of emotional stimuli and responses (in conjunction with conscious processing). The limbic system (particularly the amygdala) is the common neural pathway traveled by emotional data.

This model therefore locates the connection between stimuli and emotional responses in nonconscious processing. The limbic system makes an initial emotional evaluation of stimuli received from the other subsystems, and it does so without assistance from conscious processing. The limbic system "shades" the data with an emotional "coloring" and produces an action response to the situation. After the initial evaluation, the limbic system and conscious processing interact to monitor and coordinate the processes of emotional expression and emotional experience. The limbic system (amygdala) is the core of the emotion system.

The limbic system's structure provides us with clues concerning how the emotion system is structured. Since none of the emotive subsystems except the limbic has been shown to be necessary for emotion—yet all of them contribute to emotion in some way—a simple model of an emotion system is not possible. The emotion system requires a model that allows multiple causes without fixed sequencing, since all potential causes except one can be circumvented. Since no one of the subsystems has been shown to be sufficient to cause emotion (not even the limbic system) without help from the others, the model must allow for joint causation.

I propose an associative network model of the emotion system which is consistent with the highly interconnected structure of the limbic system.[11] In my model, the various components of the emotion system are connected by a series of associative links. Emotions and emotion states (the nodes of the system) are tied to particular thoughts and memories as well as patterns of physiological reactions. Conscious cognitions (such as memories, social mores, and emotional labels), autonomic and central nervous system patterns, action tendencies, vocalizations, and facial patterns are all interrelated.

For example, a node in the network labeled "fear" might be associated with a childhood memory of falling from a height, a trembling voice, running, increased heart rate, increased right frontal hemispheric activity in the brain, and widened eyes. If only one of these six systems is activated, the chances of the fear node being activated in an associative network is small. If two are activated, the chances of being afraid increase, perhaps providing an "as if" emotional experience.[12] As more nodes are activated (i.e., as more channels of input provide emotion cues), the emotion is more likely to be experienced and expressed. Whether or not an emotion occurs in a situation depends on how many channels of emotion provide emotion cues and how intense those signals are.

This yields a system that is flexible—one that is not tied to any particular input channel but can receive emotion cues from any of several different sources. There are many possible ways to access the emotion network, since any one component can initiate an emotive sequence of events, but no single one of them (except for the limbic system) is required.

Yet the system is not flighty; it does not activate the "fear" node every time one's heart starts beating faster. To experience and express an emotion requires redundant cues, such as those that occur most frequently in the rich environments of real life. In most everyday emotional occurrences, multiple stimuli (such as cognitions, facial expressions, and body postures) provide overlapping cues telling us what emotion is called for. The associative model of the emotion system relies on the redundant cuing of the real world to elicit forceful emotions, but it also explains the lesser emotional phenomena produced with constrained stimuli in laboratory conditions.

The notion of an associative network model is supported at the neurological level because the limbic region of the brain is so richly interconnected.[13] This interconnection among various emotion-eliciting subsystems makes the emotions different from the sensory systems. There is only one channel for visual input (the eyes), but having several input channels makes the emotion system simultaneously more complex and better protected. This distributed system insures that if any path becomes inoperative, other paths can compensate. Unlike the senses whose inputs come through specific localized channels, the emotions must handle a broad range of stimuli from a variety of sources. A distributed network of interconnections ensures that the emotions can still provide their motivating urgency even if some input channels are not functioning properly. If a threatening stimulus does not gain the attention of one subsystem, other systems monitoring the environment can also instigate an emotional action to deal promptly with the threat.

The associative model begins with the parallel processing of cognition and emotion. Sensory data are sent to the cortex for conscious processing while the same data are sent to the emotional center of the brain (the limbic system) to gain feeling tone. One process is primarily cognitive, the other primarily emotive, but both begin simultaneously. Once cognition and emotion are separately activated, the two processes begin to interact heavily. Neither cognition nor emotion requires the other as a prerequisite, but, once initiated, the processes are almost always yoked together, particularly in strong emotions. Thoughts become one of the inputs to the emotion system, and emotional signals are sent to the cortex for processing. In a model based on interconnection, the link between cognition and emotion becomes crucial, providing an explanation for the malleability of emotional expression and behavior. Parallel processing of thought and feeling allows a person to react quickly to an emotion subsystem, but the interconnectivity permits us to inhibit or intensify feelings based on social situations.

Significantly, this connection between conscious thought and the limbic system allows the emotion prototype and scripts to shape emotional experience and expression.[14] Such cognitive scripts allow us to store a rich set of information about an emotion: what responses are appropriate, what kinds of objects tend to be causes of the emotion, and the script of how the emotion tends to change as it progresses. This information is fed into the limbic system, altering the responses it calls for in the autonomic nervous system, the face, and so on. These subsystems report their altered functioning back to the limbic system, and a cycle is in place that alters emotional experience in light of the emotion prototype and emotion scripts. Cognition and emotion begin as parallel processing, but they soon begin to exchange data.

This interchange between separate cognition and emotion systems helps explain how action-, goal-, and object-orientation can be *prototypical* characteristics of emotions and yet not *necessary* to them. Cognitive concepts of emotions (prototypes and scripts) powerfully organize and direct our emotional experiences by interacting with the emotional core of the system. These cognitive schemas are important in assuring the efficiency of emotional responses, providing scripts for how we should interpret and respond to fearful or loving situations. The emotion prototype is useful in the majority of real-world situations we experience. When we are afraid, usually we are afraid *of something* and we want to take action accordingly. The real world, however, is also full of hidden and partial information. The emotion system needs to be able to respond to such cues, even if they don't fit the prototype. A network based on associations allows this flexibility, giving us a lower-level experience of emotion which encourages us to examine our world more closely for possible emotion cues. An unexpected snapping of a twig in the forest or a dissonant musical interval in a film may be enough to trigger a fear association.

Treating the emotion system as if it functioned according to the prototype would make the model in this chapter considerably simpler. To do so would be to treat emotion more like cognition, as it is traditionally understood. Leaving out considerations of nonprototypical emotionality, however, would rob this model of some of the complexity that makes the emotion system more responsive. The flexible emotion network allows us to create a variety of associations with an emotion (a gray rainy day, a slouched posture, a frown, an oboe playing in a minor key, all associated with sadness) which can cue us to experience and express an emotion, even if the situation does not fit our prototypical understanding of what the emotion is. Because of the flexibility of such associations, the emotion system cannot be limited to the prototype.

The system outlined here uses the emotion prototype, but it does not rely solely on it. While fully acknowledging the importance of the emotion prototype, an associative network model relies on neurological structures in asserting that associations are the foundation of the emotion system. Since nonprototypical and prototypical emotion states both rely on the same highly interconnected emotional core (the limbic system), prototypical structures might be viewed as a special kind of association that is organized around goals, objects, and action tendencies. Associations are the building blocks of the system, the basis for all emotional functioning.

In summary, I propose an associative network model of emotions with multiple sources of input (such as facial feedback, autonomic nervous system, and conscious cognition) feeding into a system of emotion "nodes" and interconnections. No one single input is required to initiate the emotion, but if several different subsystems are initiated, it is likely that the emotion node attached to them will be activated, even if the stimulus and the emotional response are not purely logically connected. This emotion system can be initiated without relying on conscious cognition. Emotional evaluation takes place in parallel to the conscious assessment of stimuli. If the emotion system's signals become strong enough to reach consciousness, emotional experience results. Once both conscious thought and the emotion system are initiated, they tend to interact through a highly interconnected linkage, allowing thought to influence the course of an emotion and vice versa.

The system is not completely malleable; there are undoubtedly system limits. It is impossible to raise the system threshold so high that one cannot feel emotion, nor is it probable that one can significantly alter the emotional evaluation that occurs before conscious awareness. Given certain limits, however, the emotion system is remarkably flexible. Associations can link emotions to seemingly unconnected objects (as Freud noted in fetishes), and the emotion system can connect emotions that appear to be opposites. A rollercoaster aficionado can tie enjoyment to the fear activated by falling, and horror-film fans can have rollicking fun when their uncontrollable startle reflexes are jolted. Because associations are the basic connective tissue of the emotion system, this provides the network with the necessary flexibility to become well suited to an individual's environment.

Mood

Before I discuss how to apply insights from this model to filmic emotional appeals, let us consider one more finding, this one concerning emotions and time. Memories of emotional episodes seem to indicate that emotions can have considerable longevity. According to my memory, I was angry at my boss for a full day, or I was happy all weekend long. However, memories of emotions are notoriously suspect sources of evidence about actual emotions. Humans can be remarkably bad at remembering specifics of their own experiences, and for good reason. Instead of storing all the details of our experiences, it is much more efficient to put a summary, a condensed version with a clear label, into memory. If a script labeled "jealousy" covers much of our experience during a particular episode, then we can label that memory as a jealous episode, even if that label does not fit all the emotional ups-and-downs we felt. Recalling an emotional experience often brings to mind the way we labeled that experience as much as the details of that occurrence.

Once again the power of the emotion prototype is important. Prototypes and scripts organize not only the way we interpret our surroundings but also the way we store and retrieve information about our experiences. Emotional memories are better at providing evidence about our emotion scripts than furnishing the details of emotional experience. This may be particularly true of the way we remember emotional duration.

More precise attention to emotional experiences and expressions as they occur is yielding a different picture of emotional longevity than the one we tend to remember. We do not remain angry for an entire day. Instead, evidence suggests that emotions are relatively brief states, measured in seconds rather than hours or days.

Studies indicate that emotional expression changes frequently during an emotional episode. Paul Ekman observed that most emotional expressions on the face last between one-half and four seconds.[15] Other subcomponents of the emotion system (for instance, the autonomic nervous system) change less rapidly. Heartbeat frequency does not alter as quickly as facial expression, and so emotional expression has different longevity in different subsystems. Emotional longevity may differ from emotion to emotion. For instance, Pio Ricci-Bitti and Klaus Scherer suggest that sadness tends to last longer than fear.[16]

Although there is variation in emotional longevity among emotions and emotional subsystems, overall the duration of emotions seems to be relatively brief. This has been found by researchers with quite different methodologies, from studies of EEG patterns to observations of marital interactions.[17] Studies have found fairly little variation in emotional duration across European cultures, suggesting that there may be limits to the system's emotional longevity.[18] When one examines actual emotions in progress rather than self-reports of memories, one discovers that emotions are relatively brief states.

The counterintuitiveness of this important finding needs some explanation. How can we seem to have a coherent long-lasting emotional attitude toward a situation when we experience a series of short bursts of emotion? The answer lies in an additional faculty of the emotion system. The emotion network can also orient us toward our environment.

Emotions not only provide urgency to a chosen course of action; they also can provide urgency to the way we gather information. Surprise, for instance, is an emotion-related state that quickly prepares an organism for response when that organism is not already in an appropriate preparatory state. After evaluating the stimulus quickly, the orienting state of surprise is immediately followed by the appropriate action-oriented response (such as fear or joy). Such an orienting response is a preparatory state that encourages us toward the more action-oriented emotion state.

Orienting emotions tend to be preparatory states. They ready the body and turn the attention toward particular stimuli, thus changing the way we interpret our environment. The orienting function of emotions highlights those portions of our situation which are emotion-congruent. For instance, a person in love might interpret the day's weather in relation to his or her positive feelings, and so a lover might perceive a sunny day very differently than an angry or fearful person. The orienting function of emotion encourages us to seek out environmental cues that confirm our internal state. We interpret our environment in light of the orientation provided by our emotions. It is this crucial orientation that provides a consistent framework for brief emotional experiences.

The primary set of orienting emotion states is mood.[19] A mood is a preparatory state in which one is seeking an opportunity to express a particular emotion or emotion set. Moods are expectancies that we are about to have a particular emotion, that we will encounter cues that will elicit particular emotions. These expectancies orient us toward our situation, encouraging us to evaluate the environment in a fashion congruent to our mood. Moods influence us to interpret our environment as consisting of emotion-producing cues. A cheerful mood leads one to privilege those portions of one's environment which are consistent with that mood. Moods act as the emotion system's equivalent of attention, focusing us on certain stimuli and not others.

These expectancies are themselves low-level emotional states that tend to be more diffuse and longer-lasting than emotions. They are not emotions per se but tendencies toward expressing emotion. A mood, therefore, is a longer-lasting but less forceful emotion state whose orienting function encourages us to express a particular group of emotions. While they are not as intense as emotions, their longevity helps make them a crucial part of the emotion system.

Moods have an inertia. They tend to keep us oriented toward expressing and experiencing the same emotion. They encourage us to revisit the stimulus again and again, each time refreshing the emotional experience with a new burst of emotion. These surges of emotion in turn support the mood, making us more likely to continue to view the world emotionally. A fearful mood puts us on emotional alert, and we patrol our environment searching for frightening objects. Fear makes us notice dark shadows, mysterious noises, and sudden movements and thus provides more possibly frightening cues. Once we see a frightful sight, this bolsters the mood and makes it more likely that we will continue to evaluate future stimuli as frightening, thus sustaining the fearful mood. This cycle continues as long as emotional stimuli are present.

A mood requires these brief, stronger doses of emotion in order to continue. If the mood cannot find emotional stimuli, however, the mood will eventually extinguish. Without dark shadows or other cues providing opportunities to experience fear, our fearful mood will gradually subside. Mood, therefore, is in a partnership with emotion. A mood is a predisposition that makes it more likely that we will experience emotion. Mood supports and encourages the expression of emotion. At the same time, brief bursts of emotion encourage the mood to continue. Without occasional moments of emotion, it would be difficult to sustain a predisposition toward having that emotion.

The emotion system, then, is a combination of longer orienting tendencies and briefer emotional states arranged into a process that allows us to evaluate and act upon our environment. Brief emotions allow us to respond quickly to changes in the environment. We can constantly reevaluate the complexities of changing real-world situations and respond with appropriate emotion. However, the orienting capacity of the system acknowledges that most situations do not change second by second. Most environments change only incrementally, and therefore a consistent emotional stance toward that environment is required. Brief periods of emotion can provide the urgency and speed needed to deal with sudden changes in the world, but they cannot provide the steady emotional orientation required to deal with a stable environment.

Mood provides that consistency of expectation, which means that we do not constantly have to attend to the variability of our emotional experiences. Mood helps us select stimuli that are most likely to be important. It filters out extraneous emotional stimuli and gives coherence to events, which usefully simplifies our experiences and our memories. Long-lasting mood and brief emotion combine with external stimuli to create emotion episodes, which allow us to store our experiences in memory as consistent units. Together these different temporalities help give the emotion system a sophisticated combination of flexibility and efficiency, speed and stability, adaptability and coherence.

The Emotion System and Film Structure

What does this understanding of emotion suggest to the person interested in filmic emotions? Given the flexibility of the emotion system I just described, it would seem difficult for a mass media form to elicit emotional responses with any degree of consistency across a wide range of viewers. If the emotion system is so highly flexible that it provides for such a range of emotional responses, how can films be structured to elicit dependable responses from a wide variety of audience members? If emotions are such brief states, how can a film maintain a consistent emotional appeal throughout its running time? What part do the emotion prototype and emotion scripts play in film, and how do emotional stimuli that are not part of the prototype factor into a film's emotional appeal? Having summarized my basic model of the emotion system, I now turn to presenting a useful approach for analyzing the textual structures that narrative films use to make emotional appeals based on the associative model.

Following Kristin Thompson's usage, I am formulating an *approach* to film criticism, not a *methodology*. An approach is "a set of assumptions about traits shared by different artworks, about procedures spectators go through in understanding all artworks, and about ways in which artworks relate to society." I am not outlining a method ("a set of procedures employed in the actual analytical process").[20] An approach guides the critic, but it is no substitute for the critic's activity. Instead it relies on and encourages the critic's close attention. The goal of this approach, which I call the *mood-cue* approach, is to help critics to be able to see and articulate the cinematic structures that appeal to audience emotions.

I argue that the primary emotive effect of film is to create mood. Because it is difficult to generate brief, intense emotions, filmic structures attempt to create a predisposition toward experiencing emotion. Moods prepare us to express or experience emotion. They are orienting states that cause us to interpret stimuli in a particular emotional fashion. A mood encourages us to look actively for opportunities to express and experience bursts of emotion. If we do not find any opportunities to experience these brief emotions, our particular mood will erode and change to another predispositionary state.

In order to sustain a mood, we must experience occasional moments of emotion. A mood makes it more likely that we will experience such moments, since mood predisposes us to treat stimuli as possible emotional elicitors. Therefore mood and emotion sustain each other. Mood encourages us to experience emotion, and experiencing emotions encourages us to continue in the present mood.

Film structures that attempt to elicit mood can take advantage of the various means of access to the emotion system. Films provide a variety of redundant emotive cues, increasing the chance that differing audience members (with their differing preferences of emotional access) will be nudged toward an appropriate emotional orientation. Redundant cues, including facial expression, narrative situation, music, lighting, and *mise en scène,* all collaborate to indicate to the viewer what emotional mood is called for. The viewer need not focus conscious attention on each of these elements. The associative network of the emotions is activated by some of these cues, and this creates a low level of emotion. If a film provides a viewer with several redundant emotive cues, this increases the likelihood of moving the viewer toward a predispositionary mood state.

This emphasis on emotive redundancy echoes the Hollywood cinema's tendency toward narrational redundancy of story information. Just as it repeats its commentary through character, event, and environment to assure that viewers will comprehend the necessary story information, the classical film gives us redundant emotional data to insure that we are cued toward the appropriate emotional orientation. A mournful mood can be signaled by character dialogue, lighting, music, *mise en scène,* facial expression, and narrative situation, and generally it is cued by some combination of these elements. Just as narrational redundancy exists because viewer attention frequently varies, emotive redundancy exists because the viewer's emotion system can be accessed through a variety of associative channels.

Redundant cues can fairly reliably create an emotive predisposition (a mood); once that mood is created it has a tendency to sustain itself. A mood is not entirely self-perpetuating, however. It requires occasional moments of strong emotion to maintain the mood. One cannot look for an opportunity to express an emotion indefinitely; emotional experiences are required in order to reinforce the mood.

Films use emotion cues to prompt us toward mood, a predisposition toward experiencing emotion. Moods are reinforced by coordinated bursts of emotion cues, providing payoffs for the viewer. These payoffs may occur during narratively significant moments (like obstacles), or they may occur in instances that do not advance or retard the plot progress. Cues are the smallest unit for analyzing a text's emotional appeals. Emotion cues of narrative situation, facial and body information, music, sound, *mise en scène,* lighting, and so on access the emotion system in prototypical and nonprototypical ways. Films call upon prototypical scripts when asking us to interpret characters' actions, given their narrative situations and their facial expressions. But emotion cues also provide the possibility of nonprototypical access to the emotions, and therefore they tend to be used redundantly so that they may more predictably gain access to the flexible emotion system. Emotion cues are the building blocks used to create larger narrational structures to appeal to the emotions. Mood is sustained by a succession of cues, some of which are organized into larger structures, some of which are not.

The basics of the mood-cue approach to analyzing a film's emotional appeal are simple. The critic's task is paying attention to small emotion cues and how they are coordinated. A basic assumption is that a film will encourage viewers to establish a consistent emotional orientation toward the text (a mood), and so the critic looks for highly coordinated sets of emotion cues that will communicate the proper orientation to the viewer. Once the mood has been established, the mood must be bolstered by occasional bursts of emotion, and so the critic looks for a series of emotionally marked moments that will sustain or alter the basic emotional orientation. The critic should pay attention to how long-term mood and brief emotion interact across the film. Both emotional associations and emotion scripts are centrally important factors in analyzing the film's emotional appeal. The critic should pay attention to how prototypical scripts shape our experiences of cinematic emotions while simultaneously being sensitive to the many possible cues that can activate the emotion system nonprototypically.

Informativeness, Goal Orientation, and Emotion Markers

Using these few basic components, the mood-cue approach allows us to discuss with particularity the different ways texts make emotional appeals. Although this approach does not prescribe a set of narrational structures to search for in the text, I have found that applying this approach tends to produce new terms that describe narrative structures. In the brief case studies that follow, I will introduce neologisms such as emotional informativeness and emotion markers. The purpose is less to nominate these terms as the keys to understanding filmic emotional appeals than to demonstrate that the mood-cue approach is literally productive. While it allows us to analyze emotional appeals with particularity, it simultaneously begins to produce a vocabulary for describing emotional film structures. Rather than imposing a top-down terminological system onto the text, this approach values the structures uncovered by the bottom-up process of examining and comparing particular texts. Using the mood-cue approach across a variety of texts will slowly produce a more specific language for describing filmic emotional appeals.

If the assumptions guiding the mood-cue approach are correct, we cannot reduce a film to its most narratively significant elements (actions hindering or furthering a character's goal achievement). Few texts can rely only on narratively significant moments to provide mood-sustaining emotion. We should therefore be able to find highly coordinated bursts of emotion cues that have little or no effect on the overt diegetic aim (the achievement of a goal).

Applying the mood-cue approach to several films, I have found such bursts, which I label "emotion markers." Emotion markers are configurations of highly visible textual cues for the primary purpose of eliciting brief moments of emotion. These markers signal to an audience traveling down the goal-oriented path of a narrative, cuing them to engage in a brief emotional moment. These emotional moments reinforce the mood's predisposition and encourage the mood to continue.

It is important to recognize that the emotion marker is not there simply to advance or retard the narrative's progress. Obstacles to a goal may contain several strong emotion cues that provide significant payoffs for the viewer, but I wish to distinguish such obstacles from what I term "emotion markers." The emotion marker is neither an informative device offering more detail about the story nor an authorial commentary on the diegesis. The primary purpose of an emotion marker is to generate a brief burst of emotion. Often such moments could be excised from a film with little or no impact on the achievement of narrative goals or the state of story information. However, these markers fulfill an important emotive function in the text. For the viewer engaged in an appropriate mood, they give a reward that helps maintain that predisposition toward expressing emotion.

Let us look closely at what would seem to be an intensely goal-oriented, action-driven sequence: the opening of Steven Spielberg's *Raiders of the Lost Ark* (1981). The initial sequences of the film follow Indiana Jones (Harrison Ford) through the jungle and into a booby-trapped cave in search of a golden statue. These sequences are packed with redundant cues that signal an appropriate emotional orientation toward the film, as the mood-cue approach would predict. The mood is suspenseful, apprehensive of the imminent attacks of jungle savages or the swift triggering of hidden death traps. The musical score is an unsettling mix of unusual melodic intervals and percussion; the environment is full of deep shadows, and the camera tracks behind Jones. One of Jones's trail guides tries to shoot him from behind, and Jones saves himself with a quick lash of his whip, establishing his character's skill with the weapon. That whip helps Jones and his remaining guide cross over a deep pit, only to have their support slip, almost plunging the guide to his death. This whip-and-pit obstacle must be crossed again on their way out of the cave. These obstacles use multiple emotion cues (musical stingers,[21] facial closeups) to signal emotional expression of fear, both serving important narrative functions (impeding progress toward the goal and providing the setup for future narrative occurrences) and providing emotional payoffs. Perhaps not surprisingly, the opening sequence of *Raiders of the Lost Ark* contains many redundant cues that can appeal to our flexible emotion system and evoke an appropriate mood orientation.

Along the way are moments that are highly emotionally marked without

Indiana Jones (Harrison Ford) flees the booby-trapped cave in the opening scenes of *Raiders of the Lost Ark* (1981).

serving such significant goal-oriented narrative function. One of the guides traveling through the thick jungle uncovers a grotesque stone idol and screams, accompanied by the loud flapping of a flock of flushed birds and a musical stinger. Clearly this is a concentrated organization of emotion cues coordinated to prompt a startle reflex in the viewer, but unlike the previously discussed emotional elicitors, this emotional marker neither hinders nor helps the protagonist's progress toward his goal. Neither does it provide new story information. What this moment does do is provide a reliable burst of congruent emotion which helps maintain the sequence's suspenseful mood. This is the primary purpose of the stone idol scare.

It is difficult to argue, given the interconnected nature of narrative, that any moment has absolutely no bearing on goal progress or story information. The stone idol scare may have some minor contribution to the state of story information (letting us know that Jones is near the place where the golden treasure is housed), but clearly the functionality of this narrative incident exceeds its narrative informativeness. The main purpose of the stone idol is to shout "Boo!" to the audience, marking this moment as fearsome. This emotional marker is a sort of red herring, a scare precipitated by something that poses no real threat to the narrative goals. However little function it has in retarding or forwarding the narrative, the stone idol scare primarily bolsters the mood's predisposition toward emotion, a necessary function given the structure of the emotion system.

A primary task for a film's early sequences, according to this approach, is to establish a emotional orientation that will guide the audience through the film, encouraging them to evaluate cues in mood-congruent ways. Establishing this mood requires coordinated cuing, potentially involving a broad range of cinematic signifiers. Some of these cues are coordinated with the pursuit of broader narrative goals, but we must also pay attention to the cues that do not have a bearing on narrative outcomes. Even a highly goal-oriented and plot-heavy film such as *Raiders of the Lost Ark* needs emotion markers (highly coordinated bursts of emotion cuing that do not advance the plot) to bolster the mood. The concept of emotion markers reveals that the need for structured appeals to the emotions exceeds the functional information that is organized by narrative goals and actions.

Using a range of goal- and nongoal-oriented cues,[22] each text builds an emotionally interpretive framework guiding our hypothesis formation concerning what kinds of emotion cues a film will use and how these cues will be structured. Comparing how different texts arrange their cues begins to give us a language for classifying and discussing filmic emotional appeals. For instance, we can classify a text's framework as following more or less consistent genre expectations. In addition, film texts can be classified according to how densely informative they are regarding emotions. The concept of densely informative emotional narration gives us a way to begin talking about the differences between a highly manipulative film such as *Raiders* and a seemingly more subtle film, such as Bill Forsyth's *Local Hero*.

A film with dense emotional information attempts to elicit emotions with great frequency and specificity. These texts use many redundant cues and use them frequently in a highly foregrounded manner. *Raiders of the Lost Ark* is such a densely informative text, providing us with many cues as to how to respond. For example, *Raiders* strongly marks the introduction of each major Nazi character, using loud musical stingers, low-angle dolly shots, and menacing facial features to mark them clearly as characters to be hated. Such coordination of many redundant emotion cues is characteristic of a densely informative film. A sparsely informative text would provide fewer redundant cues. These terms are necessarily comparative, and so they help us to see connections and differences among films which are not always apparent.

These terms allow us not only to compare different films but also to describe variations in how single films cue emotions. For instance, a film does not maintain a uniform level of emotional informativeness. Instead, its level of emotional information varies. Even a densely informative film like *Raiders* does not provide the same quantity of emotion cues throughout the film. Texts are more densely informative at certain points and less densely informative at others. *Raiders* stages the Nepalese barroom brawl without music, helping to make it a less emotionally marked sequence than the chases and confrontations at the film's climax.

Texts also may be classified according to how strong or weak their goal orientation is. A highly goal-oriented narrative like *Raiders of the Lost Ark* presents actions moving toward a clear series of goals (rescue the damsel, find the ark). Such narratives provide easier comparisons with prototypical emotion scripts. Given clear goals, it is easier to label the emotional states of a character like Indiana Jones and to make sense out of other emotion cues. Just as the density of emotional information may vary across a film, so may the level of goal orientation vary throughout a film. *Local Hero* (1983) openly lays out a clear narrative goal: to purchase a Scottish town to prepare the way for the construction of an oil refinery. McIntyre (Peter Riegert) is designated to bring about the deal, and in the initial stages of the film he pursues that goal in a businesslike fashion. However, the middle portions of *Local Hero* do not share this strict pursuit of the overt narrative goal, making the viewer more dependent on subtler emotion cues, not on a goal-oriented emotion prototype. Later the film returns to its earlier strong goal orientation.

In the terms outlined here, *Local Hero* is a less densely informative film with varying degrees of goal orientation. It is a film with relatively few clear generic expectations (perhaps films about quaint magical communities or films about technology encroaching on old value systems are the principal intertextual points of comparison). As such, the film was referred to as a "mood film" or a "slight" or "subtle" film by reviewers.[23] The textual approach and the terms outlined here helps us better specify how such a "mood film" is constructed, which I will examine in some detail.

Local Hero begins with a clear narrative goal orientation communicated through a fairly standard series of scenes. In a board meeting we are given an expository summary of the importance of the refinery and this particular Scottish site. We see McIntyre in his office preparing to leave for Scotland, letting us know through dialogue that he's not particularly excited about his assignment to this job. These scenes are standard instances of character and situation exposition, each with a slight twist foregrounded in the *mise en scène*. The board meeting is conducted entirely in a whisper, so that Happer (Burt Lancaster) is not awakened. McIntyre discusses his assignment with officemates only a few feet away, but he uses the telephone to communicate. In each situation the actual narrative information is almost overshadowed by an unexpected element emphasized in the *mise en scène* (the sleeping Happer, the telephones and glass walls). *Local Hero* presents straightforward narrative exposition while upstaging this information with comic cues, creating a goal-oriented framework while simultaneously signaling the appropriateness of a comic mood.

McIntyre arrives in Scotland and initiates negotiations with a solicitor to buy the entire village. The solicitor says he will handle the situation and suggests that McIntyre spend some time getting to know the area while the solicitor negotiates. At this point the narrative pursuit of McIntyre's overt goal grinds to a halt because there are no obstacles. The townspeople are delighted to sell the land, and Knox Oil and Gas is delighted to pay for it. The solicitor stalls so not to appear too eager, but we are shown that there are no known forces opposing the achievement of the goal. *Local Hero* at this point becomes a significantly less goal-oriented text.

What we are left with is a series of comic cues and markers. McIntyre and his assistant eat a meal, squirting juice into their eyes as they dine. A loud motorcycle whizzes by, nearly hitting McIntyre and the assistant. We hear overhead the solicitor and his wife giggling during sex play. The early goal-oriented scenes prepared us to expect such comic cues, and when the primary goal pursuit vanishes, this comic mood must be supported by a continuing stream of emotion cues and occasional emotion markers (like the loud motorcycle zooming past). These cues are usually not highly redundant or marked, but in the absence of the clear initial goal they serve as the primary emotional elicitors in this sparsely informative text.

Local Hero does not lose all goal orientation when McIntyre reaches the village, however. Instead, it replaces the initial goal (to buy the village) with a much less concrete goal, a goal that can be pursued in small increments through this series of sparsely informative cues. The outcome of most of the Scottish portion of the film is to change yuppie careerist McIntyre into a gentler, more easygoing fellow who learns to fit in with the town's slower rhythm (paralleling the film's change to a less strongly goal-oriented narrative). McIntyre's dress becomes progressively more casual; he loses his watch in the ocean; he learns to pause before leaving the hotel to avoid being run over by the motorcyclist. We learn slowly about McIntyre's conversion through a series of accumulating details presented in brief vignettes.

The classical cinema is traditionally concerned with change in its protagonists. In order to achieve the overt narrative goal, classical protagonists must often undergo character change themselves. This internal change makes the achievement of the action-oriented goal possible. In this fashion, overt goal orientation and character change are inseparably linked.

In *Local Hero*, however, character change and the overt narrative goal are separated. When the pursuit of the land deal comes to a halt, McIntyre begins his transformation to a less driven person. This transformation, once isolated from the clear initial narrative goal, becomes a goal in and of itself, but this goal is pursued intermittently in brief comic cues. Instead of character change being organized by the pursuit of an action-oriented narrative goal, *Local Hero* presents its hints about McIntyre's metamorphosis as part of a relatively unhierarchized series of comic moments. Vignettes giving us details about McIntyre are not marked more pronouncedly than other vignettes primarily concerned with the townspeople. The overt narrative goal established early in the film no longer lends its narrative force to organize the scenes in a strong linear progression toward the goal's achievement. Instead, the progression is intermittent rather than strongly goal-centered, episodic rather than simply linear, sporadic rather than steady. *Local Hero* does not abandon its goal orientation entirely, but the text becomes less strongly organized around goal achievement during most of the Scottish portion of the film. This relatively weaker goal orientation makes labeling filmic emotions less clear-cut.

On first impression *Local Hero* does not seem to be a particularly fast-paced text. On closer examination one discovers that it presents a remarkably speedy series of emotion cues. These cues are brief (McIntyre's assistant practicing holding his breath underwater, snippets of conversation with bit players) and are rarely redundant. These fragmentary cues fit the brevity of the audience's emotional experience and allows the filmmakers to string together a rapid-fire series of emotion cues. Although *Local Hero* is not fast-paced in its progression toward a goal (thus explaining the impression of the movie as a "gentle" film), without the benefit of a goal-oriented emotion prototype or strong genre framework the film must put together a rapid succession of emotion cues in order to sustain the comic predisposition. The fact that these cues are not highly marked or redundant helps us position *Local Hero* as a "subtle" film.

Local Hero uses music selectively to help convey its "subtle" quality. Highly foregrounded music (such as the music in *Raiders of the Lost Ark*) would too obviously telegraph its emotional appeal, so *Local Hero* almost entirely abandons music when McIntyre arrives in Scotland. Music is used only occasionally in the early Scottish portions of the film, and then it functions as a transition device when the film moves to a very different time and space. Because such music cues are so clearly motivated functionally, they are not foregrounded as highly visible (or rather, audible) emotion cues.

Music is next heard in the film as a clearly marked diegetic source while people dance. Only after the community dance scene does *Local Hero* use highly foregrounded nondiegetic music. Not coincidentally, the appearance of nondiegetic music occurs when *Local Hero* resumes its initial goal orientation. Immediately after the community dance scene, the solicitor discovers that the beach is really owned by an old man who refuses to sell. This is the first obstacle to the initial goal's achievement, and we encounter it three-fourths of the way through the film. The final quarter of the film is goal-oriented and uses highly foregrounded nondiegetic music.

In summary, *Local Hero* spends the majority of its time in Scotland without a strong goal orientation and without musical accompaniment. Music is first introduced as a brief and functional transition device. Then music is used in a fashion clearly motivated by the diegesis (dancing). Finally, *Local Hero* uses nondiegetic music to signal emotional responses, and it uses it redundantly in conjunction with such emotion cues as lighting and *mise en scène*. A film that early on used few redundant emotion cues relies on more and more redundancy later in the film. This progression allows us to label *Local Hero*'s emotional appeal as "subtle" (unlike *Raiders*'s) and yet takes advantage of the emotional power provided by redundant cuing late in the film. The early lack of redundancy sets our expectation for relatively sparse emotion cues, and the gradual progression toward more and more redundant emotion cues near the film's climax provides a significant emotional payoff.

This small exercise in analyzing a subtle "mood film" emphasizes the fact that such textual qualities as density of emotional information and level of goal orientation are comparative terms. We can only say that one text is more densely informative (emotionally) than another. We cannot point to these qualities in the texts without using intertextual comparisons. For example, *Raiders of the Lost Ark,* a much more densely informative text than *Local Hero,* uses a progression of gradually more foregrounded music similar to the one in *Local Hero.* After the initial whiz-bang find-the-treasure-and-escape scenes, *Raiders* becomes relatively silent musically, using music only as a transition device. The next action sequence, the Nepalese barroom brawl, is done without music at all. When Jones and Marian (Karen Allen) enter the marketplace, we hear exotic Eastern music motivated by the diegesis. Only after this diegetic music does *Raiders* return to a relatively dense use of musical cues. This pattern of increasingly prominent music (beginning with no music, then music as transition, then diegetic music, and finally nondiegetic music) is the same as the one *Local Hero* uses to make "subtle" emotional statements.

Notice that very different kinds of texts can use similar patternings of emotion cues. The *Raiders* score has a subtle progression of its own, but its foregrounded redundant cues (e.g., stingers introducing Nazis) help make *Raiders* a more densely informative text. Texts are not either emotionally informative or emotionally uninformative. They are more or less densely informative compared to other texts.

The comparisons between such seemingly dissimilar films as *Raiders of the Lost Ark* and *Local Hero* make the point that the mood-cue approach can help us talk about similarities and differences in emotional film structures

Enroute to purchase a quaint Scottish fishing village, high-powered oil
executives Oldsen (Peter Capaldi) and Mac (Peter Riegert) pause to help a
wayward bunny. From Bill Forsyth's *Local Hero* (1983).

with more precision. These brief case studies are meant to be indicative of
how a critic might examine a film text, guided by the assumptions of this
analytic approach.

The associative model of emotions discussed in this chapter provides the
key assumptions for the mood-cue approach to analyzing a film's emotional
appeals. This model suggests that films initially work to establish a mood (an
emotional orientation toward the film) through early clusters of emotion
cues. The viewer progresses through the film, tending to pick up cues that are
congruent with the established mood. Scripts based on real-world emotions
and previous cinematic experiences create expectations that guide the viewer
in making hypotheses concerning what kinds of emotion cuing will follow.
The mood must be bolstered by occasional highly concentrated bursts of
emotion cues, or the mood will be extinguished. Scripts and the emotion prototype help us label appropriate emotional states, and coordinated patterns
of emotion cuing encourage us to execute these scripts on our own emotion
systems.

The critic guided by this model should examine how the multiple cues in
the early portion of a film establish a mood. Then he or she should note the

scripts that guide the viewer in understanding the film's emotional progression, paying particular attention to the series of highly concentrated moments of emotion cuing that reaffirm and realign the viewer's emotional orientation toward the text.

The advantages of the mood-cue approach are several. This approach recognizes that the emotion prototype and emotion scripts provide strong explanations for most emotional experiences. Much of my analysis of *Local Hero* depends on goal orientation, a prototypical quality of emotions. I believe that learning more about specific emotion scripts (such as the particular characteristics of concepts of fear and sorrow) is one of the most vital areas for emotion research, and I applaud the continuing efforts of psychologists, cognitive philosophers, anthropologists, and sociologists who are helping us to articulate these shared scripts. However, this approach asserts that actual emotional experiences can be messier than our action- and object-oriented prototype. The emotional appeals of *Local Hero* and *Raiders* do not depend solely on plot-significant actions. An associative model of emotions reminds us of the importance of the vast range of signification outside a character's action trajectory toward a goal, and the mood-cue approach begins to give us a language to describe these structures.

In order to access the emotion system, cues need not be linked to representations of human actors in any strong way. Emotional associations provided by music, *mise en scène* elements, color, sound, and lighting are crucial to filmic emotions, and this approach provides a way to talk about their importance without necessarily harnessing them to onscreen representations of persons. If we are ever to understand the cultural and social nuances of the interactions between film and real-world audience members, we need to begin by more fully understanding the complex range of emotional appeals that films make.

SIX

Emotions, Cognitions, and Narrative Patterns in Film

TORBEN GRODAL

Film viewers prefer to experience narratives that strongly activate the mind and body, that move and touch, that cue the production of adrenaline and elicit visceral reactions. Such feelings and physical reactions are linked with narratives that offer stimulating cognitive problems and scenes of spectacle and intrigue. The phenomenal world of narratives, consisting of cognition and bodily reactions, is a central concern of directors, actors, and viewers, but has not received much attention from film theory. In film theory the investigation of filmic emotion has been based on romantic and psychoanalytic theories, which hold that the apparent content of films is only a veil.[1] For psychoanalytic theory, true content resides in the unconscious regions of the mind and concerns themes like castration and Oedipal trajectories. From this perspective, thoughts and emotions are opposing forces. Reason is linked to reality, while emotions are negations of this reality.

Recently, however, a number of books and articles have shown that a description of emotions based on physiology and cognitive psychology provides far more satisfying results.[2] Emotions and cognition are two aspects of the way our embodied brains function. Our bodies and minds have developed in the context of evolution. In this process, our emotions have been developed to represent our interests and goals, and function to implement them by means of strong motivating forces controlling our attention and actions. At the same time, our cognitive skills enable us to analyze the situations that hold interest for us, and help us to achieve our goals.

The central theme of this chapter is that feelings and emotions are motivational forces, and therefore should be described not only in close relation to their causes, but also in relation to their role as motivation for potential actions. This is not only the case for strong emotions such as love and fear, but also for the feelings and activations that accompany our mental processes. These will be described more fully in the body of this chapter, and include the feelings of reality or unreality that guide the simulation of action

tendencies, vividness and salience which focus attention, and feelings of
familiarity and unfamiliarity that influence our response to characters and
scenes. It follows that the film-viewing experience must be described as a
process, a mental flow, with bodily reactions as sounding boards. The flow is
a double one: audiovisual data flow from eyes and ears to the brain/mind,
and narrative events flow forward in the diegetic world from beginning to
end.

Important aesthetic and emotional functions are linked to the ways in
which the flow can be constrained or blocked. For example, the actions of
characters can be blocked, as in melodramas or tragedies. However, blockage
of another sort occurs when images are transposed from those experienced,
within the context of fiction, as "concrete" phenomena with physicality, into
those of a mental or lyrical sort, whether this is brought about by an associative, nonnarrative montage or by other redefinitions of the reality status
of the images. This chapter illustrates such processes using examples from
Steven Spielberg's *Raiders of the Lost Ark* (1981) and *E.T.: The Extra-Terrestrial* (1982), two mainstream films that exemplify central narrative prototypes.

Salience, Vividness, Excitation, Emotion, and Arousal

The impact of a film on the viewer may be divided into two different, although interrelated, aspects. One aspect, the *quantitative,* is the activation
of perceptual and cognitive qualia (mental representations and activities)
linked to particular experiential configurations such as "buffalo" or "green
grass." The other aspect is *affective-motivational,* the strength with which
given sensations activate the mind and the magnitude of the emotions triggered by a film scene.

We may often experience a fusion between what a film element represents and the feelings and emotions it evokes. This affective activation has
some special properties, for example, the possible excitational "spillover" to
the following shots, irrespective of their content, resulting from an excitational inertia that may allow an excitation to outlast its cause. This quantita-
tive-motivational fusion is connected with an activation of the body and the
nervous system, and is molded by the way in which the different perceptual
and cognitive activities are integrated within global schemas that, in the narrative, govern the concerns of its protagonists.

The "quantitative" activation exists on different levels of complexity. The
activation may be a local one, such as the fluttering of birds on the wing at
the beginning of *Raiders of the Lost Ark.* The sound is integrated somewhat
into global relations (creating an atmospheric ground for a tense scene), but
it is also an "attraction" in its own right. The local activation may be based
on a situation: when Indiana Jones (Harrison Ford) and Marion (Karen

Allen) arrive in Cairo, the first shots show a "tourist panorama," a view across the rooftops of the city. Nearby we see children laughing at a little monkey, which then spills red wine on the tablecloth; it jumps on Marion's shoulder, obviously irritating and frightening her despite her attempt to hide her dismay. The affective activators—the children's laughter, Marion's distress at the spilled wine, the displeasure caused by the monkey—create arousal by pooling their individual affective charges. At this point in the narrative the situation has no link to global narrative concerns, but later the negatively charged associations linked to the monkey will become important. The arousal from the episode will spill over into the next sequences and, at the same time, the monkey will be charged with affect in the mind of the viewer: this affect will be reactivated when the monkey reappears.

At the global end of the spectrum of activations we find phenomena that acquire their importance in relation to broad narrative complexes. When the Germans and Belloq (Paul Freeman) steal the ark from Jones in the Tanis episode of *Raiders of the Lost Ark,* the full emotional importance of the deed is linked to the narrative totality. The center of the narrative complex is Indiana Jones's personal commitment to protecting the ark. However, the emotional effect will be enhanced if the viewers are acquainted with "grand" historical narratives (Nazism, World War II, the invention of the A-bomb) and Jewish biblical narratives. The emotional charge of these themes is activated as support for the narratives. Such charges are sometimes "partial activations" in that they may be nonconscious or may exist at the periphery of our attention.

Terms for some of the positions on the hierarchy from local to global activations will prove useful for analysis. *Vividness* is the power of the isolated percept, while *salience* is the effect of the percept in context.[3] Often the vivid features will also be salient. *Excitations* are local activations linked to central human concerns, say, an isolated view of a wound, a kiss, or the spilling of wine. *Emotions* are activations linked to global narrative concerns, like Elliott's (Henry Thomas) sorrow when E.T. apparently dies. Global narrative frames integrate vivid, salient and exciting phenomena into a fabric of anthropomorphic concerns.

The affective impact of the mental or narrative flow is supported and enhanced by the autonomic nervous system and the reticular activation system. The autonomic nervous system acquired its name because it is normally "autonomic," that is, outside voluntary control: it regulates pupils, tears, salivation, heartbeat, stomach, bladder, vasoconstriction and vasodilation, the secretion of adrenaline, and so on. The sympathetic branch of the autonomic nervous system supports outward-directed coping (e.g., hunting and other types of object control), whereas the parasympathetic subsystem typically supports activities like eating, digestion, relaxation, and erotic contact.[4] The reticular activation system (RAS) located in the brainstem induces neuronal firings which lead to increased brain alertness, for instance, enhanced attention[5] and an amplification of emotions.[6]

Although autonomic reactions are outside the direct voluntary control of the film viewer, they function in close relation to conscious experience of the themes and situations of films. However, it takes time to induce autonomic reactions, which are slow and unspecified compared with the visual perception of film scenes, and it takes time for the autonomic reactions to wear off. Although a given level of arousal is elicited by a specific scene, for example, Indy and Marion's experiences in Nepal, the arousal is still present in the viewer when the protagonists arrive in Cairo, where the arousal will be reinterpreted and relabeled in the context of this new, romantic setting.[7] Often mechanisms of distancing by means of comic reactions or double focus will further relabel arousal. This occurs in *Raiders of the Lost Ark,* when excitement linked to a crisis—being surrounded by hostile Germans—is amplified by romance (Jones freeing Marion from ropes), and further amplified by comically induced arousal when she is tied up once more, this again slightly controlled by distancing.

The aesthetic orchestration of arousal is the combination of the different activations, from vividness and salience via excitation to the creation of global narrative frameworks. In some of Spielberg's films, for example, the situations and objects of everyday life—the spilling of food, the mutilation of toys—are made vivid and salient by the camerawork, thus boosting the excitation of arousal. The affective flow is then integrated into global narratives that elicit emotional patterns, such as the problematic bonding relations featured in *E.T.* and other Spielberg films. Or, to take another example, in the Indiana Jones series excitation is related to the activation of strong feelings of tactile unpleasantness resulting from the protagonist's contact with snakes, spiders, and other "creepy-crawlies." These thrills add additional fuel to the tensities (reactions) elicited by the treasure-hunting scenes. The orchestration of arousal may be seen in a pure form in the final scene of *Close Encounters of the Third Kind* (1977), in which the extraterrestrials present themselves to Earthlings near the base of Devil's Tower; there vivid and salient visuals, music, and a series of reactions shots are integrated into a narrative theme of contact, greeting, and recognition.

Bio-forces, Intentional and Feeling Agents, and the Affective Energy of Film

The central activating mechanism of narrative films is the characters, representations of living beings with distinguishable characteristics. In their most elementary form, we may metaphorically describe characters by an analogy with physical forces. Characters are sources of energy fields that the spectator experiences as living beings due to innate psychic mechanisms. The linguist George Lakoff has described the way in which many of the metaphors used to describe sexual interaction are mappings from the domain of physical forces, for example, attraction and repulsion.[8] Comic strips make this evident in the way they are drawn, when the attraction or repulsion of characters is manifested in lines, figures, and shapes drawn to represent physical forces. The psychologist A. Michotte carried out a series of experiments that showed that persons tend to attribute anthropomorphic qualities such as animate motion, intentions, and causality, even to the experience of (for instance) the motion of abstract dots and squares. This indicates that we often organize and understand phenomena by subsuming them under the schema of animate beings.[9] Some computer games encourage their players by inviting them to control the way in which a cheese eats dots, or by an appeal to anthropomorphic features such as "kill," "feel pain," "live," and "die." These phenomena indicate that an activating "meaningfulness" emanates from a relatively small set of "animistic" mental schemata: having "intentions," "perceptual capacities," the "ability to feel pleasure and pain," "eating," "excreting," "copulating," "caring," possessing "force," and the two overarching states, having "life" or being "dead." These are basic features of higher living beings, and often attributed to phenomena in the physical world. Cartoons may activate a sense of animation by using a small subset of these qualities, even in abstracted form.

This tendency to anthropomorphize extends to important aspects of our affective response to characters. The psychologist Edward Hall has described the way in which humans and animals possess certain innate, although to some extent culturally modifiable, demands for space.[10] Proximity creates arousal; it will also provide body heat and olfactory clues to the bodily presence of others and will eventually lead to tactile experiences. The visual and acoustic cues of proximity may, by association, be tied to the proxemic cues of body heat, olfaction, and tactility so that these associations may be activated by visual cues alone.[11] A special aspect of visual closeness is the viewer's intake of nonverbal communication. Smiles or angry expressions or a happy or angry tone of voice have a direct impact on the viewer.[12] Visual attention by means of the direction of the glance is a powerful tool for energizing.[13] A mechanism of a more complex kind is "empathy" and "identification" with characters.[14] Empathy and identification are central for human bonding and caring and probably rely on innate dispositions.[15]

Narrative patterns in films are mechanisms in which fictional actions and changes in fictional situations transform the arousal induced by the spectator's engagement with characters. In the following pages I shall demonstrate that the emotions are cued by these characters, or bio-forces, and that the perceived transformations of characters during the narrative flow have their origins in our mental functioning.

The Mental Flow from Perception to Simulated Enaction

When a viewer attends to a film, this initiates a mental flow; this flow is a fundamental frame for understanding the emotional impact of film. Processing occurs in roughly this fashion. First, a given film frame/shot activates ear and eye. These perceptual clues are then processed in the rear part of the brain by a series of filterings and synthesizations to model three-dimensional objects.[16] If this construction of objects is successful it will lead, via a series of mental processes (for instance, matching what is seen with memorized information), to a mental representation of what is seen and heard. This in turn induces affective reactions in part determined by attention and the activation of memories and associations. The film reception processes will then activate representations of possible actions and perhaps induce muscle tension and an activation of the frontal and prefrontal brain areas linked to motor action.[17] For example, when Indiana Jones enters the seaplane, both he and the viewers see a snake. The sight activates associations, for example, snakebites, and affective reactions to these possible scenarios. In turn this activates avoidance reactions, either mental tendencies toward possible future actions or concrete actions.

The direction of the flow has an ecological explanation: our brain and body have evolved as tools for survival, and therefore a film will often have a stronger emotional impact if what we see is related to survival or to human bonding, power, or sexuality, within a framework in which emotions and possible actions are intertwined. Narratives typically consist of an episode or a series of episodes that link perceptions to actions via preferences as expressed in emotional reactions. When Indiana Jones sees a huge boulder rolling toward him, he tries to avoid a painful encounter by running away. Such a scene can be understood by children or adults all over the world. Indiana Jones's reaction, and that of the viewer, are the rational consequences of activated emotions and derive from the imprints of evolutionary history, not from "Oedipal" or "patriarchal" problematics as some psychosemioticians would claim.

This flow from perception via cognitive and emotional processing to (simulated) action I will call the *downstream,* thus indicating that it is the typical flow supported by innate architecture. The downstream will support the bottom-up processes. (In physical terms, the downstream starts in the senses, goes to the rear half of the brain, then activates central association areas. The process furthermore flows forward to the motor centers, then flows "down" in the outgoing, muscle-directed nerves.)

Conversely, viewing processes may also be induced centrally, as when we "look for" something or expect something to happen. Our minds will then "control" our visual perception and bodily movement, and our expectations will (by means of top-down mechanisms) guide the processing of what we see and hear. All kinds of expectations play important roles. The goals the narrative sets up cue our expectations of future events, just as expectations cued by genre conventions are important for our response to narrative situations. This becomes readily apparent in the famous scene from *Raiders of the Lost Ark,* where we are surprised when, anticipating a sword fight between Indiana Jones and his Arab opponent, the film challenges our expectations as Indiana uses a more modern, less chivalrous weapon—a pistol—to shoot the man down. Nonetheless, our narrative expectations and our desire for certain narrative outcomes, surf, so to speak, on the constant "downstream" of perceptual input that moves toward enaction (whether character action or the viewer's mental simulation of action), always guided by the narrative. The kind of mental downstream characteristic of real-world situations is enhanced by the film-viewing situation favorable to such a perceptually induced downstream. Unlike real-world situations, in which we must search for perceptual cues, the film—to a degree—selects perceptual input for us and indexes our focus of attention according to the flow of narrative actions which make some aspects of the scene salient.

In its simplest form, the flow occurs as a stimulus-response pattern, for example, when Indy sees the huge boulder and therefore starts running. The flow is more sophisticated, however, when, for instance, an overarching goal governs a whole series of actions. In *Raiders of the Lost Ark,* Indy works toward capturing the ark from the Germans. This goal serves as the controlling stimulus for many different acts: going to Tibet, to Egypt, and to Greece. When the protagonist pursues a goal, we experience the narrative not as a stimulus-like series of events, but as teleological, controlled by intentions. The narrative becomes a "push-pull" machine. The immediate circumstances function as causal push-percepts, as when Indy tries to avoid snakes or is wooed by a female student with a declaration of love on her lashes. The more distant character goals serve as pull-percepts for the protagonists.

When narratives activate goals, they mobilize very powerful mental-motivational mechanisms used by humans to perform complex tasks. (These mechanisms are based in special frontal brain modules.) If someone decides to become a doctor, to travel to India, to go on a hunting trip, or to make a piece of pottery, this goal controls a multitude of subgoals, and even controls the adjustment to unforeseen events. The hierarchy of goal-directed actions extends from individual acts, such as moving one's hand toward an object, to macronarratives like a journey toward an overarching goal.

Our experience of the downstream is molded into three modes: *telic* (teleological), *paratelic*, and *autonomic*.[18] First, the telic mode occurs when we experience voluntary, goal-directed actions and thoughts, as when we empathize with Indy as he pursues and takes possession of the lorry carrying the ark. Our attention, thoughts, and muscular activation are directed toward goals we believe we have chosen freely. Second, the paratelic mode is activated when experiences, actions, and thought take place without an explicit goal, in relation to the protagonist's moment-to-moment experiences. The purpose of telic actions is often excitation-reduction: Jones is excited about capturing the ark and wants to reduce that excitement by possessing it. On the other hand, paratelic situations enhance excitations, as when dance scenes elicit erotic desire, a love song increases romantic feelings, or fast-paced action scenes increase pure excitement. Such nontelic endeavors are exemplified by rhythmic and repetitive activities that employ "primitive" subject-centered processes instead of telic object-centered processes. The first shots of *E.T.* provide an example of a perception-based paratelic situation, in which we perceive phenomena for which we initially have no telic framework. Art films of the 1960s often feature heroes who aimlessly wander, driven by inner, paratelic forces rather than exterior goals.

The third mode of "downstream" viewer experience, the autonomic, is activated when characters become victims of exterior forces such as history, nature, or fate, and are unable to affect outcomes. The viewer and character react to such situations with tears, shudders, or laughter. Whether a given situation calls for telic (voluntary) actions, a display of paratelic activity, or an acceptance of involuntary, autonomic reactions is a matter felt by the viewer. The shifting modes that accompany viewer experience are an aspect of the narrative orchestration of arousal. An example of a scene that elicits such a shift is in *Raiders of the Lost Ark,* when Indy first experiences fearful despair in the snakepit but then resorts to telic coping and goal-directed action.

Films may induce the feeling that we are looking "upstream," against the ordinary direction of experiential flow, when they present images that represent an early stage of the process and block flow at that point. This may occur in certain abstract films, in which forms and light fluctuations seem to suggest figurative content but finally resist transformations into figurative forms (as in parts of Norman McLaren's abstract films). Framing, focus, editing, and motion may also temporarily blur or block the viewer's perception of forms, which may then be perceived as abstract patterns. This process also occurs in narrative films, as in, for example, *Once Upon a Time in the West.* Here the first flashback to Harmonica's (Charles Bronson) past is shown in a sequence of images completely out of focus. Such nonfigurative visual effects highlight the mechanisms of the eye and visual cortex.

Films may block the downstream flow a little further down when the film presents highly charged images that allow for no "outlet" in symbolic or

Indiana Jones (Harrison Ford) and Marion (Karen Allen) in the pit of vipers.
From Steven Spielberg's *Raiders of the Lost Ark* (1981).

actual actions. Their elicited activation consists of primary visual analysis and associational thinking, but without simulated enaction. The first shots of *E.T.* exemplify such a block. We initially see some objects identifiable as pine trees, a spacecraft, and a rabbit. The images provide sharp lines of contour; their vividness and salience emphasize the primary visual mechanisms, and at the same time activate a web of associations as we try to forge links and categorizations as clues to "meaning" (for instance, the pine tree and rabbit signify benign nature). The night atmosphere evokes "lyrical" feelings based on the enactive reduction characteristic of the human experience of nocturnal space. Later, when we are given more narrative information, the block is removed and the lyrical atmosphere changes into enactive tension with an autonomic undertow.

Processing may be blocked yet further downstream and reversed to the "lyrical-associative" stage of the flow, as in a freeze-frame. In a freeze-frame, the drive toward completion of the action is halted, and the image loses its temporal anchoring and becomes part of an atemporal, associative structure. Music videos or various kinds of montage sequences will also evoke nonnarrative associational structures. Associative structures will also be activated in an unblocked flow, and the emotional experience will differ depending on whether the associations serve focused actions or are cut off from a temporal enactional flow.

When the narrative is unblocked, mental flow will typically lead to the solution of the narrative problems and finally to narrative closure. It has been argued that narrative closure is an ideological device. However, such claims must be tempered with the understanding that narrative closure is intimately linked to innate human features, namely, our ability to structure the world in actions which can be completed.

The aesthetic orchestration of the flow will be experienced as modal qualities: if a film induces vivid or salient perceptions without any (nonperceptual) anthropomorphic or narrative concerns, we experience one type of modal quality which I will call *intense;* this is illustrated again by aspects of the first sequence of *E.T.* If a film presents salient sights and sounds that activate associations charged with affect, such as the presence of snakes or the monkey's spilling of wine in *Raiders of the Lost Ark,* the modal quality may be called *saturated.* If the film induces action-readiness, for instance, as a muscular tension when Indiana Jones tries to escape the boulder thundering toward him, the modal quality may be called *tense.* If the film induces autonomic outlet, like tears, laughter, or shivers, as in the sublime scenes of confrontation with religious or cosmic powers in *Raiders of the Lost Ark* or *Close Encounters of the Third Kind,* the modal qualities may be called *emotive.*

Most viewers find it unpleasant or tiresome to view film sequences which, for prolonged stretches of time, block the narrative "downstream," as many art films do. Such viewers find perceptions and memory activations pleasant only if they lead to tense actions or to powerful autonomic outlet, as in melodramas like *E.T.,* horror movies, or comedies. The first sequence of *Once Upon a Time in the West* (1969) is a borderline case. It strongly emphasizes vivid and salient sights and sounds and activates saturated memories with no enactive outlet. Had the buildup of arousal continued for much longer than it does, offering no narrative macroframe and no corresponding possibility of enactive outlet, most viewers would probably find the film "dull" and "pointless." However, other viewers find the narrative schemata typical of the mainstream cinema too obvious and repetitive, and prefer art films with their intense perception and saturated activation of associations. Such viewers will tend to have an expertise in film viewing or a general cultural knowledge that supports an activation of associations felt to be an active, gratifying response.

A way of mediating flow and block is the use of montage or other lyrical blocks of enactive flow in combination with kinetic "enactional" energy provided by musical rhythms and melodies. "Mainstream viewers" often accept a lyrical block of the narrative flow—in fiction films or music videos—if simultaneous music on the soundtrack stimulates the feeling of an unblocked flow.

Emotions, Canonical Film Narratives, and Ecological Conventions

There exist several different descriptions of what constitutes a narrative.[19] A description that puts weak constraints on what counts as a narrative would be the following: an audiovisual narrative is a film recording of sequences of time-spaces in which animate beings are usually present and where events (both visual and aural) are often linked to the concerns of the animate beings. Such a description allows for fluid limits to nonnarrative descriptions and would posit the needs of animate beings and their concerns as necessary elicitors for viewer activation.

We may view sequences of a fiction film, documentary, or news report for their "unfocused" attractions. Early cinema was often based on "astonishing" attractions, while Sergei Eisenstein saw film as a "montage of attractions."[20] Some aspects of the Cairo episode of *Raiders of the Lost Ark,* for example, are unfocused attractions. What is perceived is activating (e.g., picturesque) but does not point to acts other than that of looking or, as in the case of the monkey spilling red wine, to an experience of saturated affect. The different attractions elicit a paratelic arousal that will eventually be molded, or "labeled," by more focused narrative sequences.

However, the strong activation of the emotions demands a narrative in a more specific sense. Central narrative prototypes, or canonical narratives, consist of one or several central beings, a series of emotion-evoking conditions, and a series of actions to alter conditions and to evoke preferred emotional states in a forward-directed time. These characteristics derive from the role and functioning of emotions. Emotions are motivating activations of the body-mind, linked to possible preferred actions or to the possible actions of other agents. The psychologist Nico Frijda characterizes emotions as "modes of relational action readiness, either in the form of tendencies to establish, maintain, or disrupt a relationship with the environment or in the form of modes of relational readiness as such."[21] The fusion of arousal and a specific action tendency is what Frijda and others see as the central aspect of emotions. Arousal may be cued by many different stimuli and situations, and the arousal will be molded into emotions by the cognitive appraisal of what kind of action is required to deal with the arousing phenomena. If Indiana Jones sees a poisonous snake, his emotional arousal may be felt as anger if he intends to attack and believes that he has the ability to do so successfully. However, the arousal may be molded into fear if he doubts his ability to vanquish his foe, or into despair if he gives up attempting to cope. Therefore, cognitions about situations determine the type of emotions felt and the emotions in turn motivate further cognitions and actions. In the evocation of tense emotions, the cognitive labeling of emotion requires the orientation provided by a centering character or characters. Emotions like anger, fear, or love make full sense only as action tendencies, as cognitive labels on action options. Such labels, in turn, are formed in reference to the concerns of characters.

Audiovisual narratives provide schemata and scenarios with which viewers (and listeners) conceptualize and evaluate actions and desires and comprehend the narrative. If Indiana Jones or the viewer had no preferences about what outcomes were desirable, probable, or possible, there could be no emotions; the activation and arousal would be diffuse and saturated, as in lyrical or art films. Such films or film sequences present arousing images and sounds without a clear narrative progression or central protagonists, and without eliciting strong preferences for specific outcomes. For this reason, the vivid and salient activation and the saturated excitement cannot be transformed by narrative actions. Therefore, they cannot be labeled according to an action readiness, but only appreciated in saturated form. Frijda calls such affective states "moods."[22]

A *canonical* narrative—the typical fairytale, for example—is a story in which actions take place in forward-directed time, are linked to the concerns of a central protagonist, and are molded by causes, consequences, intentions, and actions. It is canonical because its "flow"—from the perceptual awareness of a situation, to cognitive, emotional and motivating appraisal, to an enacting outlet—corresponds to a central way in which we function mentally. Narratives are schemata by means of which we systematize our experiences and guide our acts and expectations.[23] The canonical narrative is the most economical way of linking perceptions, emotions, preferences, and actions together. If we were to rearrange events contrary to canonical narrative structures, for example, by showing the result before we see its cause, the proper downstream activation would not occur. We cannot experience the same tense, suspenseful arousal from a narrative with an outcome already decided and carried out. If one's purpose is to evoke strong feelings of suspense or tension, one must present events with a canonical forward-directedness.[24] On the other hand, if the purpose of a narrative is to evoke what

Frijda calls moods, those saturated feelings with no "phasic structure,"[25] the architecture of the fiction must be different, allowing for more causal and temporal ambiguity.

Raiders of the Lost Ark is constructed of a series of "successful" actions, in that the emotional preferences of the protagonist are actively achieved. Other films, however, are constructed such that the actions meant to achieve goals are temporarily or even permanently blocked. Some of the great moments of *E.T.* occur when the protagonists are unable to act and thus achieve outlet by autonomic response (i.e., crying). These include the scene in which E.T. is supposedly dead and the dramatic farewell scene at the end of the film. Like *Close Encounters of the Third Kind, E.T.* has an abundance of vivid and salient cosmic images, and offers basic ("sentimental") feelings of abandonment and powerlessness. The central wish expressed in the film is that E.T. be able to "go home," but since his home is distant and mysterious the viewers and Elliott are capable of few actions that can implement such preferences. In addition, that Elliott's father is missing is beyond the boy's enactive control, also resulting in his sorrow. Therefore, the film elicits a passive, autonomic outlet for this immense arousal. In both prototypical and mythical fashion, the arousal is created by combining central human concerns (bonds of family and friendship, life and death) with natural themes (nature, sun, cosmos).

In *E.T.* the protagonists are passive, but they are so mainly because they are victims of a diffuse "fate." It is therefore possible to experience a passive acceptance of destiny, and simultaneously to abandon oneself to the sublime themes of death, separation, and nature by means of autonomic reactions. Other genres, for example, horror, will often feature antagonists who represent purely negative and powerful forces and protagonists reduced to passive-defensive reactions. Such narratives, with their forward-directed temporal flow and focusing protagonists, will resemble canonical narratives in some respects. However, the role of the protagonist in these cases is that of victim, and therefore the narrative events may not construct clear-cut goals, and may elicit a somewhat unfocused chain of negative affects. The tense "resistance" to the evil forces exists in combination with strong autonomic reactions.

The Real, the Concrete, the Familiar, and Their Reverse

As argued above, emotions consist of relational action readiness. Another essential element in the orchestration of arousal are feelings of reality or unreality. A film elicits feelings of reality to convince us that certain viewed phenomena are subject to manipulation and control, to the tense acts that are implicit in action readiness.[26] If we judge a given object or event to be impervious to such tense acts, other kinds of feelings are activated. Feelings linked to other levels of reality (for example, memories, dreams, hallucina-

tions, mirrors, or films within films) indicate the special status of these phenomena. Films may use such indicators as elements in the emotional orchestration, for example, by temporarily blurring the distinction between the
real and a memory or dream. The feelings activated by memory-images or
dream-images are not subject to enactment. Of course, the past is sealed off
from enactive relations, except by psychoanalytic sessions in psychothrillers,
for instance, or in science fiction films which represent alternative conceptions of linear and irreversible timespace. Because they are not subject to
enactment, strong feelings cued by the past will therefore often need a "sentimental" autonomic outlet. Even when images of the past lead to action in
the film's present, as in Harmonica's revenge for his childhood trauma in
Once Upon a Time in the West, the different reality status of the cause of the
feelings cues autonomic responses in addition to (simulated) tense revenge
actions (in this particular film supported by melodramatic images and music). Films such as *Close Encounters of the Third Kind* feature "orchestrations"
of feelings dependent on shifts between different levels of reality status.

A subset of the feelings of reality stems from the relation between concrete and abstract, token and type, individual and species. We can only act as
individuals; as a species we must give up our enactive identity and allow
arousal to achieve autonomic outlet, perhaps as participation in a collective
identity. Humans meet extraterrestrials in *E.T.* or *Close Encounters of the
Third Kind* on a species level. Therefore, the viewer may have autonomic
reactions such as tears, shivers, and so on, as responses to narrative events.
Often films will activate "sentimental" feelings by having individual characters act as representatives of roles or groups, for instance as "mother," "son,"
"man," "woman," "American," or "hero." Melodramas often feature characters larger than life, and we may only engage with them psychologically by
giving up our sense of individual voluntary action.

Elements of documentary films may be experienced in a similar abstract
way. If "real" elements are linked to actions or to specific processes of infor-
mation-dissemination, they will be experienced as real. However, documentary representations will evoke lyrical feelings if scenes, objects, and persons
are presented without links to actions or information-giving processes, because in these cases the representations become "abstract" objects of attention. Jean-Luc Godard and other New Wave directors excelled in transpos-
ing "real" documentary footage into an abstract, timeless, and lyrical mode.
The represented objects and film scenes are transformed into types and paradigms, and lose their sense of concrete reality.

With much the same effect, perceptual processes may also be transposed
from something "concrete" into something abstract and mythic.[27] Salient
symmetries and framings, like those in the first sequences of *E.T.,* activate
perceptual processes isolated from enaction. Techniques like freeze-frames,

The diminutive alien of *E.T.:The Extra-Terrestrial* (1982).

slow-motion, or blurred focus often indicate transposition to a mental status not subject to enaction. This transposition—from a tense, concrete level
to an abstract, autonomic mode—is often used to achieve narrative closure;
protagonists and situations are transposed from "reality" to emblems or
symbols. The transposition from the concrete to the abstract and symbolic
may also be performed by narrative means, for instance, by the use of visual
metaphors derived from natural phenomena. Example are "waves," "wind,"
"clouds," "fire," and "fog," all used to elicit human emotions such as love, passion, hate, or fear.[28] The use of fog at the beginning of *E.T.* serves as an example. Such transposition of opportunities for concrete enaction into vehicles
for mental phenomena cues autonomic reactions. In *E.T.,* the children bi-

cycle up into the sky and are silhouetted when they pass the setting sun. By means of the abstraction of the sun in this scene (its enormous size and its abnormal role as a background for human figures) and the silhouetting of the children, the images are perceived as partly "mental" and thus beyond enactive outlet. The abstract, mental angle is underlined when the sun theme is echoed in the final image of the film, where E.T. is partly silhouetted by a sun-shaped, luminous background.

The transposition of time from concrete to abstract cues similar effects, for example the return of the missing pilots and sailors unmarked by age at the end of *Close Encounters of the Third Kind*. Such a transformation blocks concrete enaction and cues autonomic responses. Science fiction films indulge in the temporal distortions that may be characterized as sublime; these distortions often have the purpose of "enhancing" tense feelings with an undertow of autonomic reactions. Such temporal distortions are frequently linked with the expansion of spatial perspective. An enactive block might be combined with the perceptual charge of a mountain scene, for example. In space films we are often given "passive," low-angle views of gigantic space ships (which seem to make human agency insignificant), while the limitless dimensions of cosmic space similarly combine perceptual excitation with the blockage of narrative enaction.

We view films with a perceptual-cognitive "drive" to construct unambiguous cognitive representations of spaces and objects as a precondition for action and orientation. This drive elicits another subset of feelings related to the construction of filmic "reality." Sometimes in films the arousal cued by perceptual and cognitive puzzles is used in isolation from other affects,[29] but often perceptual-cognitive ambiguity is used to enhance our response to global narrative themes. For example, fog, rain, or twilight in a romance or mystery are used both to make perception difficult (in the sense that we cannot see clearly) and to enhance emotional response. There is a huge survival premium linked to unambiguous representations, and thus a strong arousal linked to perceptual and cognitive ambiguities or blockages. Many different art forms, from op art to crime fiction to horror films, use this kind of arousal in various forms.

Supernatural events and objects ranging from celestial beings to ghosts, vampires, and magical weapons are important in the construction of filmic "reality" and are often used to elicit autonomic response. Things supernatural exceed normal causal relationships, and thus block the means by which protagonists ordinarily control their relationship with the world. For example, when ghosts can be seen but not touched, or vice versa, this dissolves the normal synthesis of perceptual modalities. Furthermore, the motives of supernatural beings are often obscure. For this reason, and for the reason that they lack certain perceptual dimensions, we cannot interact with such creatures. This enactive block may have the consequence of producing autonomic reactions such as tremors, sweating, goose flesh, intestinal reactions, or tears of subjection, whether experienced positively in the sublime, or negatively when evil forces conquer, or ambiguously, as when the spirits of the ark are let loose in *Raiders of the Lost Ark*.

Another pervasive kind of feeling, one which in part determines action readiness, is the feeling of familiarity or unfamiliarity.[30] As a general rule, the more we are exposed to a given phenomenon, the more the phenomenon will be felt as "familiar." Familiarity encourages positive feelings and reduces antagonistic arousal and action readiness.[31] Familiarity also provides a background against which the impact of new, "unfamiliar" phenomena are felt. When viewers see Indiana Jones's familiar face in unfamiliar environments, the film enhances arousal, just as many science fiction films cue complex arousal states linked to familiarity and unfamiliarity.

Emotion Filtering by Narrative Genre

The various film genres use mechanisms of reception to filter emotions activated in the viewer by the narrative action. This occurs either by negating the emotions or by creating an affective distance.[32] The "forces" that evoke empathic identification with characters are modified and constrained by various means and thus enable more sophisticated types of emotional modulation. Central devices for creating distance are "schizoid numbness," comic functions, and double focus through distance.

Many films, for instance splatter films, have actions so appalling that most viewers will try to distance themselves from a full empathic identification with even the positive characters. This will lessen the negative affect of the experience. Such viewers will experience the film with a kind of schizoid numbness, an emotional dissociation from the narrative experiences.

Films based on a comic-reception strategy constitute a much larger group. A central device for relabeling viewer emotions is to cue comic response to the affect the film elicits; this negates empathic reaction to the emotions. After finding Marion in a tent in Tanis, Indiana Jones first frees her and then ties her up again. His action "ought" to evoke pain and anger in the viewer in empathy with Marion and in protest against Indiana's cool reason. However, because the scene is interpreted as an intertextual joke based on a long tradition of sheik films, and thwarts our expectations so surprisingly, the viewer negates empathic arousal and laughs "cruelly" at the anger shown by Marion.

A third way of filtering emotional involvement is by fostering affective distance. This can be achieved by setting dual or multiple foci of attention.

Or, to take another example, the simplest way of maintaining affective distance is to increase optical or acoustic distance to the emotion-arousing events. Interfering with points of affective identification also increases distance. *Raiders of the Lost Ark* begins with a reflexive joke; Paramount's mountain, a part of the corporate trademark, changes into a mountain in the fictional world of the movie, thus indicating that the film is "made," "unreal," and creating distance on the part of the viewer. Some of what follows in the credit sequences serves the same function, for example, a "self-conscious" silhouetting of the hero, thus presenting an image of a figure larger than life. Later in the film, Indiana's surprise shooting of his would-be duelist in Cairo and the untying-retying of Marion in the tent in Tanis also point to distance-creation by a comic use of intertextuality.

Why do filmmakers use emotion filters when, at the same time, they employ all of the emotion-activators they can muster? A central reason for this is their intention to amplify rhetorically some aspects of the film. In order to keep a "balance," filmmakers put isolating boundaries on various activations, for example, by indicating the special status of a given film event. Adult viewers of *Raiders of the Lost Ark* are provided with an excuse to enjoy such a matinee subject because it promotes itself as a game in which they may self-consciously participate.

Conclusion

Film reception activates most of the human faculties, and the experience is therefore a complex one. As we have seen, however, there are strong functional links between the different faculties because perceptions, cognitions, emotions, and acts are developed together to serve the preferences of the viewer. A good example of this is the way in which feelings function both as shorthand representations of cognitive evaluations of the reality status of occurrences, and to support attention. The canonical narrative is the superior example of the means by which these faculties are encouraged to work together. The canonical narrative links viewer response to central human concerns, whether the concerns of protagonists working toward goals, or those of agents who become the victims of melodramatic forces. Canonical narratives are linear because the interaction of cognition, emotions, concerns, and actions function by means of a linear phasic flow, supported by nonlinear and atemporal association networks.

The commercial cinema has become a cinema in which the dominant products are fictional, canonical narratives designed to evoke strong emotion. This development has been interpreted as an expression of a Western, male, white hegemony. However, as I have argued, canonical narratives and their melodramatic, passive variant use our mental faculties in a form that suggests innate and thus universal mechanisms at work, mechanisms similar, and in some cases identical with, those skills with which we make sense of and act in the world around us. A political or cultural critique of films would do better to concern itself with content rather than form.

Many of the narrative and visual techniques used to activate "deviant" or "alternative" reality status were developed during the Romantic period and brought later to the world of filmmaking. The Romanticists believed that the strong (subjective) emotions and feelings released by such mental and perceptual phenomena as dreams, memories, perceptual or existential ambiguities (mirrors and supernatural phenomena), and so on, indicated levels of reality which were opposed to the prevailing social order and to rational scientific thought. Important segments of film and literary criticism have inherited a Romantic epistemology and hold that strong feelings of special reality status indicate the true, subconscious, nonrational dimensions of existence. Then the aesthetic play with feelings of reality status becomes more than a game; it is a negation of a rational world. Nevertheless, as I have argued, emotions and feelings are part of a rational holistic framework that has developed to enhance survival. The subjective feelings, when not blocked, are motivators for rational actions and thoughts. Fortunately, these emotions and feelings can be used for aesthetic purposes as well, to elicit arousal in viewers and to provide the pleasure of experiencing the diverse realities films offer.

SEVEN

Movie Music as Moving Music: Emotion, Cognition, and the Film Score

JEFF SMITH

There is a scene at the end of David Lynch's film *The Elephant Man* (1980) that never fails to move me. In this scene, John Merrick (John Hurt), the pitifully disfigured title character, decides to end his own life through a simple gesture that most of us take for granted. After an evening sojourn to the theater, Merrick unpiles the pillows from his bed, gently pulls back its covers, and then crawls in to lay his heavy head down to die. In doing so, Merrick performs a suicidal act. Both we know and he knows that by sleeping in this position Merrick will literally be suffocated by the weight of his own body. The scene, which is motivated by Merrick's yearning for normality, his desire for social acceptance, and the sad recognition that his gnarled and disease-ravaged body ultimately precludes that acceptance, is beautifully played out by both director Lynch and actor John Hurt, and no matter how many times I see the film, it brings a lump to my throat.

Yet while the guileless spectator in me reaches for the tissues, the analyst in me asks why this scene produces such an emotional response. Can my response be attributed to the drama of the scene or the highly evocative music that accompanies it? In other words, am I moved by my experience of Merrick's plight, by the plaintive strains of Samuel Barber's *Adagio for Strings,* or by some combination of the two? Does Barber's music merely enhance the scene's emotional features or does it provide an affective charge all its own? Can my response be reconciled with contrasting responses from other spectators, such as indifference or derision?

Similar questions are raised by a famous scene from Stanley Kubrick's *A Clockwork Orange* (1971). As Alex (Malcolm McDowell) undergoes the Ludovico treatment, he watches a film assembled out of nauseating footage from porno films and newsreels. Although Alex witnesses filmic representations of rape, genocide, and nuclear destruction, he is most horrified by the use of Beethoven to accompany this film. Alex protests this desecration of his beloved "Ludwig van," but is told that the music acts as an emotional en-

John Merrick (John Hurt) in David Lynch's *The Elephant Man* (1980).

hancer. While the spectator of this film-within-the-film may not share Alex's personal affection for Beethoven, she may nonetheless wonder why music is really necessary to Alex's therapy. After all, what could Beethoven's music possibly add to images that are already so sickening in themselves?

The scene from *A Clockwork Orange* described above not only reveals a central conceit of Kubrick's film and Burgess's novel—that Beethoven and other figures of Western culture might be implicated in Alex's "ultraviolence"—but it also exposes a commonplace assumption regarding the dramatic importance of film music. Although the film score plays a number of narrative and structural functions, it is often assumed that its most important function is as a signifier of emotion. As a number of scholars point out, music in film frequently serves to represent the emotional states of characters, suggest the prevailing mood of a scene, and prompt an appropriate emotional response from spectators. The latter would seem especially significant in the *Clockwork* example since it appears to be the *only* putative reason for using Beethoven in the first place.[1]

Yet despite the familiarity of these assumptions, the connection between film music and emotion remains somewhat mysterious. Much of the difficulty in theorizing this relation comes from the way in which film music's emotive character is yoked to its narrative or representational functions. Describing Alfred Newman's central theme for *All about Eve* (1950), Claudia Gorbman summarizes some of the conceptual difficulties involved in sorting out the film score's dramatic functions: "Does this melody, first heard over the credits, and subsequently at most emotional moments where Eve (Anne Baxter) appears, signify Eve herself, or Eve's emotional impact on her 'audiences' (the characters and filmviewers she manipulates), or is it simply a signature for the film *All About Eve*?"[2] More important, though, Gorbman's question also hints at the absence of a theoretical framework that might delineate and specify the film score's function as an emotional signifier.

In this chapter I address these questions by outlining a cognitivist framework for theorizing the relation between film music and emotion. Hypothesizing any relation between film music and emotion, however, depends partly on how we define music itself as an emotion stimulus. In other words, in order to pose questions about film music and emotion, broader questions about the relation between music and emotion must first be answered.

For this reason, I will approach the issue on two separate fronts. First of all, drawing upon work in music theory and analytic philosophy, I will situate the emotional significance of film music within a more general theory of purely musical expressivity. My contention here is that spectators make sense of film music's affective properties on a number of different levels, and that these levels can best be understood within a combination of cognitivist and emotivist theories of musical affect. Cognitivist theories of musical affect assert that music can signify emotional meanings to listeners, but cannot arouse them. Emotivist theories, on the other hand, contend that music not only can but also sometimes does arouse emotional responses in listeners.

Second, using research done in the disciplines of music theory and psychomusicology, I will look at two processes that are central to our emotional experience of film music: polarization and affective congruence. The first of these refers to an interaction in which the specific affective character of the music moves the content of the picture toward the emotional pole communicated by the music. The second interaction, affective congruence, refers to a type of cross-modal confirmation in which the spectator matches the score's affective components to the emotional shading of narrative. While this type of interaction seems relatively routine in cinema, cognitive research shows that its effects are not. More than the sum of its parts, affective congruence produces a degree of emotional engagement that is stronger than either that produced by the music or visual tracks alone.

Why propose a cognitive account of film music and emotion? On its face, one rather simple reason is the prevalence of cognitivist assumptions in music theory. The most influential work in this area over the past twenty years either explicitly or implicitly adopts a cognitive slant to questions of music reception.[3] Although I do not wish to overstate the case, the unifying element of this diverse body of literature is the basic assumption that listeners mentally model musical structures and "chunk" musical information in their processing of any musical soundstream. Of course, the predominance of any theoretical school is no guarantee of its validity or explanatory power. After all, if popularity was the only criterion for the validity of a hypothesis, then this same argument could easily be used to support psychoanalytic theories of cinema at the expense of cognitive accounts. Rather, I simply note the prevalence of cognitive music theory to suggest it is both a natural place to begin one's research and a tradition of music scholarship that is well worth engaging.

Yet while cognitivist assumptions have guided much of the work done in music theory and analysis, they have had very little purchase in the study of film music. As I have pointed out elsewhere, much of this current work on film music is more clearly situated within the doctrinal confines of post-structuralist and psychoanalytic theories of cinema.[4] In laying out discussions of the film score's dramatic functions, many of these scholars adopt a kind of folk model of musical affect rooted in the widespread association of music and emotional expression.[5]

As Murray Smith notes, however, folk models of emotional engagement may be widely used and understood, but they generally lack the comprehensiveness and systematicity associated with a full-blown theory.[6] To illustrate the pertinence of Smith's remarks to the study of film music, I propose that we take a closer look at a typical instance of this school of criticism. Samuel Chell's analysis of *The Best Years of Our Lives* (1946) provides a useful reference point for this discussion insofar as it explicitly adopts the assumptions of poststructuralist and psychoanalytic film criticism, but ultimately uses an analytical approach much closer to the folk model.[7]

Chell begins his essay by situating film music within the context of Metzian and Oudartian concepts of subject positioning. For Chell, music serves as one of many means of "suturing" the spectator into the fictive world, albeit one that works at an entirely emotional level. By creating an emotional bond among film, character, and spectator, the film score authorizes the spectator to "claim" the emotion depicted on-screen as his own. In this way, the score serves to bind viewers to fictions; it not only represents the characters' emotions, but it also reproduces this emotional response in spectators. In Chell's account, music operates as a kind of textual inscription of the spectator's response insofar as the emotional curve of the film's music aurally reflects the emotional experience of the spectator.

Yet when Chell finally gets around to analyzing the music for *The Best Years of Our Lives,* he finds very few examples that function exactly in this way. The one instance cited by Chell occurs in the scene where Wilma (Cathy O'Donnell) declares her love for Homer, the disabled veteran played by Harold Russell. Chell writes:

> During the scene, the "Wilma" theme is gently caressed by the violins, supplying the embraces of which Homer is physically incapable, until his loving "good night," at which point the theme is resolved on a radiantly shimmering unison tonic note. Even as the note is being sustained, the woodwinds provide a lingering echo of the theme as we see Homer cry. Homer's tears are likely to mirror our own, for the music has released us from the unresolved tensions of the opening title theme which has become associated with Homer's estrangement.[8]

More commonly, Chell will describe a given musical theme or orchestration as "sprightly," "somber," "bright," or "eerie," and then will impute that particular emotional quality to the character or scene associated with that theme. In cases such as these, Hugo Friedhofer's score simply communicates the emotional qualities of a scene, but does not necessarily replicate that emotion in the audience.

In fact, one of Chell's most crucial examples, the climactic scene in which Fred Derry (Dana Andrews) reexperiences the war in a grounded B-17, functions as just the opposite of an "emotional bond." In this scene, Fred climbs into a warplane about to be scrapped for housing materials. As he sits in the nose of the plane, Fred's wartime traumas, which are the source of persistent nightmares earlier in the film, come rushing back to him. This is signified on the soundtrack through the sounds of plane engines and musical figures that simulate diving runs and the rat-a-tat of machine guns. Here Friedhofer's music not only tells us what Fred remembers as he sits in the plane, but also communicates the emotional turmoil occasioned by the memory. Yet unless we are willing to grant that Friedhofer's score recreates the trauma of our own wartime experience, then this is an example in which music communicates emotional disturbance to the spectator but does not arouse it. This is not to deny that spectators have emotional responses to fictions, but rather to suggest that the spectator's emotional experience is often different from that depicted in fictional characters.[9]

Thus, while Chell's actual analysis of *The Best Years of Our Lives* has much to recommend it, the psychoanalytic underpinnings of his account all too often lead him to collapse the score's affective functions into a broad, undifferentiated association between film music and emotion. In this respect at least, cognitive approaches to film music can improve on psychoanalytic accounts to the extent that they can specify and catalog the film score's affective functions, namely music's ability to enhance the emotional responses of spectators, to signify the emotional states of characters, and to convey the overall mood or tone of a scene. As we will see in the next section, this range of functions depends on a crucial distinction between communicating an affective component and evoking it. Cognitive theories of film music are not only better equipped to make that distinction, but they are also better suited to explaining the correspondence between film music's affective functions and the levels of emotional engagement that are operative in any kind of spectatorial response.

Emotion and Music: Cognitivist Theories versus Emotivist Theories

There is perhaps no more contentious issue in the study of music than the question of how it expresses emotion. Generations of philosophers, aestheticians, and theorists have debated this subject and the literature on it is voluminous. Although a complete review of this literature is beyond the scope of this chapter, it may be useful nonetheless to indicate the diverse range of views on this subject. Some theorists, such as Susanne Langer, suggest that music attains semantic significance through its symbolization of emotion. Such symbolization, however, differs from that of language in that music lacks anything resembling a vocabulary. For Langer, music reflects only the morphology of a general feeling state, but it does not express more particularized emotions, such as anger or melancholy. On this view, certain effects of music are so similar to emotions in their shape or form that some listeners naively mistake them for the latter.[10] Others, like Diane Raffman, modify Langer's arguments by asserting that emotion in music is "ineffable" in that it is expressed in musical rather than linguistic discourse. For Raffman, music's expressiveness arises from a delimited class of peculiarly musical feelings, such as beat strength, metrical stress, and prolongational tension. Since these musical feelings can only be approximated in language, the affective components of them which elude description are by definition considered ineffable.[11] Still others, such as Eduard Hanslick and Igor Stravinsky, deny that there is *any* meaningful relationship between music and emotion.[12]

At least initially, then, there appears to be a group of theories that question the validity of my project from the very outset. According to these theories, the notion that music is emotionally expressive is either (a) erroneous or (b) understood solely in terms of musical structures that lie outside the realm of verbal or written language. If we take these theorists at their word, then music's emotional expressiveness would be fundamentally different from that of cinematic narratives. While we might assert that films like *Dark Victory* (1939) or *Terms of Endearment* (1983) make us sad, such sentiments would not hold true for the music that accompanies these films.

Yet while these theoretical positions lie at the heart of the debate regarding musical affect, they prove to be largely irrelevant to the notion of *film-*

musical affect. For one thing, as Raffman points out, the association between music and emotion is a brute psychological fact, one that can be proved with a fairly high degree of consistency and intersubjective agreement. As such, inquiry into the relation between music and emotion is a perfectly valid area of psychological research even if it lies outside the realm of aesthetic or analytic philosophy. For another, most objections to the linkage between music and emotion are premised on a notion of "pure" music—in other words, music that makes no reference to any object, property, or sensation outside itself. Film scores, however, clearly do not fit this constraint. Since they accompany cinematic narratives, film scores must be considered a species of *program* music. Most film music not only refers to the emotional properties of the narrative, but also refers to specific places, times, characters, and themes in its fulfillment of various dramatic functions.

Moreover, for similar reasons, the objection that music lacks an intentional object also falls by the wayside. According to this view, emotions typically have an external object at which the feeling is intentionally directed. Such objects may be real or imagined, but they are specifiable. For example, I may be afraid of evil spirits, I might be saddened by the death of a loved one, or I might get angry at a driver who cuts me off while going to work. In each case, I can point to the source of my anxiety. Pure instrumental music, however, would seem to lack this sense of intentionality insofar as it resists the notion that it is *about* anything. As such, even if we grant that music is expressive in some way, its lack of intentionality suggests that it also lacks the finer shades of expressive meaning that we usually associate with real-world experience.[13]

Even if we concede this point with regard to pure instrumental music, it is irrelevant to the emotional expressiveness of film music. Why? Because film is a representational art and, as Peter Kivy points out, intentional contexts are indeed possible in representational arts.[14] Although the external objects themselves are not real, we can be saddened by the death of a character, we may get angry at a villain's actions, or we may be elated by the hero and heroine's embrace at the end of a film. Here again the presence of narrative enables the film score to circumvent the problem of expressive ambiguity, much as a text or title does in other musical works. Thus, because cinema is a representational art, the appropriate question to ask is not whether the musical accompaniment to a film can produce finer shades of emotional meaning, but rather what the film score itself contributes to that process.

Having sidestepped the objections of formalists and "ineffabilists," we are free to explore other candidates for a theory of film-musical expressiveness. Of those that remain, the two most significant are the cognitivist and emotivist accounts of musical expression. Over the past fifteen years, the strongest advocate of the cognitivist position has been Peter Kivy.[15] In developing his theory of musical expressiveness, Kivy draws a crucial distinction between *expressing* something and *being expressive of* that thing. Using the photograph of a sad-faced Saint Bernard, Kivy argues that the dog in the picture does not feel sadness nor do we in looking at it, but its face is nevertheless expressive of sadness, and we typically recognize this emotional quality in our descriptions of the photograph. Music, according to Kivy, operates in much the same way. Although it might be theoretically possible for music to express the emotional states of a composer or listener, Kivy suggests that music does not ordinarily do so and is more accurately described as being expressive of a particular affective quality.[16]

For Kivy, music realizes its emotional expressiveness through particular formal elements, such as melodic contour, modality, tempo, or dynamics. In mentally processing this musical information, the listener's response is not so much affective as it is cognitive in that musical expressiveness lies in our recognition of emotions rather than our affective experience of them. Thus, when we ascribe sadness to a piece of music, we are not aroused to sadness, but instead are applying a set of intersubjective, public criteria for particular musical conventions that are recognized as expressive of sadness. Moreover, as Kivy points out, a musical work's text and title often help to clarify these criteria by offering important contextual cues to a piece's expressive character.[17]

Kivy's theory of musical expressiveness should have obvious appeal for film-music scholars insofar as it provides a commonsense approach to the problem of how film music communicates affect to spectators. By distinguishing between recognizing musical affect and experiencing it, Kivy's work offers a sound explanatory framework for two of film music's most important dramatic functions. Since spectators are able to discern emotional qualities from specific musical elements, they can then use that information to evaluate the emotional states of characters or the overall mood of a scene.

But what of those spectators who demonstrably share a character's emotional state? And what of my own experience of sadness during the last scene of *The Elephant Man*? Even if one grants that my own response to *The Elephant Man* is anomalous, one cannot overlook the shared response audiences have to such emotionally powerful films as *Stella Dallas* (1937), *Breakfast at Tiffany's* (1961), *Field of Dreams* (1989), and *Schindler's List* (1992). Since Kivy discusses music rather than sad scenes in films, one can only speculate about how he might treat instances such as these.[18] However, if we apply Kivy's cognitivist model to such instances, it would appear that film music plays no role in arousing emotions in spectators. Rather the arousal function would seem to depend on other factors, such as our involvement in the narrative situation or our engagement with characters.

Such a position, however, seems both counterintuitive and inconsistent with our everyday experience. More important, this position also runs counter to the film industry's folk wisdom in using such music in the first place. If Stella Dallas's separation from Laurel on her daughter's wedding day was enough to reduce the audience to tears, then there would simply be no need for Alfred Newman's evocative music for this scene. Thus, while a cognitivist account explains one aspect of a score's dramatic functions—its ability to signify moods and emotional states—it is not comprehensive enough to explain an observable response to films, namely that viewers cry during sentimental, poignant scenes that are accompanied by sentimental, poignant music.

The grounds for modifying a strict cognitivist position can be summarized as follows: (1) Kivy's theory does not work as well for film music as it does for "music alone" since the former might be grouped with other kinds of program music; and (2) that music may, at the very least, have a *tendency* to arouse emotion. In order to make the case for an arousal component of film-music audition, let me explain each of these counterarguments in a little more detail.

First of all, film music would appear to be an exception to Kivy's theory insofar as it shares certain traits with other kinds of program music. As I noted earlier, one of Kivy's chief objections to arousal theory is that music lacks an intentional object at which the emotion is directed. This is not true, however, of either film or film music. On the contrary, viewers can point to very specific dramatic situations which they find moving, such as John Merrick's death, Ray Kinsella's reunion with his father, or Stella Dallas's exclusion from her daughter's wedding. Here again, the question of whether the arousal is a response to the music or the narrative situation is a moot point since together they function, in Claudia Gorbman's words, as "a *combinatoire* of expression."[19]

Second, as Colin Radford points out in a response to Kivy's work, one must not confuse the cause of emotional arousal with the object of that emotion. We may become sad or agitated by changes in our hormonal states, but that does not mean that we would describe ourselves as sad or agitated about that physiological change. According to Radford, music operates in a similar manner, that is to say, listeners may experience the feeling of sadness without necessarily saying they are sad about the music. In this respect, both hormonal changes and musical experience are not unlike colors or dreary weather conditions. Just as gray, dull weather tends to depress people, a somber piece of music will tend to make listeners feel somber by being both expressive of that emotional quality and helping to induce that quality in listeners.[20] As Kivy himself points out, the key to understanding this version of the emotivist position rests in Radford's assertion of tendencies toward arousal rather than strict cause-effect relationships. There is no contradiction between Kivy and Radford's positions if we agree that music's tendency to arouse emotion is relatively strong for listeners like Radford and weak for listeners like Kivy.[21]

More important, what the strict cognitivist position overlooks is the extent to which all emotions are composed of both affective and cognitive components, that is to say, a somatic state of physiological arousal and a judgment about the state of affairs in the world.[22] Not coincidentally, each of these components corresponds with an element of musical experience that cognitivist and emotivist theorists seek to describe. Thus, rather than see these two positions as mutually exclusive, it might be better to view them as complementary theories accounting for different aspects of the same phenomenological experience. Judgment and arousal, thus, would comprise two levels of music's emotional engagement with listeners, the former being a necessary aspect of understanding musical affect and the latter a level of engagement that may or may not be activated depending on the specifics of the listening situation.

If we accept these as different levels of engagement, then something crucial to our interpretation of the scene becomes almost immediately apparent: the emotions evoked by the scene are different from those communicated by the scene. Viewed as an expression of Merrick's point of view, Samuel Barber's music conveys the character's feelings of resignation and muted regret. However, the mood the scene evokes, at least in me, is sadness. This may seem like a subtle distinction, but it arises from a judgment that my own emotional response is somewhat different from that signified by the character. Merrick does not weep, sob, or display any of the other behaviors we associate with overt expressions of sadness. In fact, one reading of the scene might be that Merrick welcomes death as an end to his physical suffering, but does so with a bittersweet feeling of remorse for an existence that prevents him from overcoming his physical limitations. And if we lend significance to the film's final images, we might say that Merrick also welcomes death as an opportunity to be reunited in an afterlife with the mother he has never known. Thus, while the simple epithet of "sadness" seems adequate to describe my emotional state, it is inadequate for the emotions depicted within Merrick, whose situation within the film's narrative context is quite a bit different from my position as a spectator.

On this view, Merrick's emotional expression is a good deal more complex than my own since it is bound up with the character's deeply held beliefs about spirituality, corporeality, dignity, and morality. My own response, on the other hand, is largely an effect of the text and rests on my sympathy with the character's unhappy predicament. These judgments in turn produce a change in my physiological state (the welling of tears, a lump in the throat) that I experience as sadness. My display of sadness indicates that the *intensity* of my emotional arousal has produced a level of self-awareness that may or may not be evident in other viewers. In other words, I realize I am emotionally aroused because I catch myself experiencing the physiological changes I noted above.

Since film music can produce a range of possible responses among spectators, a cognitive theory of film music will have to consider the components of recognition, judgment, and arousal that make up any emotional experience. In most instances, the somatic component of our experience is so slight, spectators are said simply to recognize the affective qualities of the film score. Having recognized the music's affective elements, they then use that information to make judgments and inferences about the state of affairs depicted within the diegesis. When the intensity of the somatic component produces discernible physiological changes, however, the film may be said to have aroused an affective response in a spectator. Such responses are not properly assigned solely to the music, but rather to the combination of film music and narrative, each of which will have its own individual emotional valence. Thus, although judgment and affect enter into all forms of emotional engagement with film and film music, each may take precedence over the other at different moments to produce a range of possible responses. And since cognitivist and emotivist theories of music each describe different hierarchies of judgment and affect, both are necessary to understanding the role film music plays in the spectator's emotional experience.

Emotion and the Film Score's Dramatic Functions: Playing the Mood of the Scene versus the Mood of the Character

In the previous section, I sought to demonstrate the roles played by both judgment and affect in the spectator's emotional response to film music. In this section, I will show how these components are correlated with film music's dramatic functions. Although these functions have been described in slightly different ways by a number of scholars, they typically encompass a variety of musical and narrative interactions: Film music (1) provides a sense of continuity, (2) reinforces formal and narrative unity, (3) communicates elements of the setting, (4) underlines the psychological states of characters, and (5) establishes an overall emotional tone or mood. While all of these functions may involve affective elements, the last three are especially important in the film score's overall capacity as an emotional signifier.

Noël Carroll's theory of "modifying music," for example, offers a remarkably lucid and sensible account of film music's role in characterizing actions and establishing moods. Noting that the music and visual tracks exist in a kind of complementary relation, Carroll argues that music acts roughly like a linguistic modifier, and helps to clarify the particular mood, character, or emotive significance of a scene or visual action. The visuals, narrative, dialogue, and sound effects, on the other hand, imbue the film score with a referentiality that it inherently lacks. In Carroll's *Gunga Din* example, the music, which by itself we might describe as bouncy, light, and comic, adds an inexplicit layer of emotive significance to the filmic text. Other cinematic elements, however, help to specify and particularize that expressiveness, and as a result the music, narrative, and visual elements together signify the masculine, devil-may-care bravado of the film's characters and narrative.[23]

One might object here that the film score merely amplifies affective elements within the scene or contrarily that the visual component of cinema is expressive of these more particularized emotional shadings in and of itself. Such objections, however, prove groundless for two reasons. First of all, the complementarity inherent in this relation produces a level of meaning and emotive significance that is qualitatively different from the meanings of the visual and music tracks themselves. Second, as Joseph Anderson suggests, spectators perceive sound and image information as being generated by a single event. According to Anderson, this perception is the result of cross-modal confirmation by which spectators seek invariant properties of an event across modalities. The spectator's propensity to search for patterns leads him to seek congruence between the emotion of the music and the events unfolding on-screen.[24] While the question of whether the emotions arise out of the music or the narrative might be pertinent to an aesthetician, it is moot with respect to the spectator's cognitive experience of this relation.

Yet while Carroll's theory of modifying music is a compelling application of Kivy's cognitivist account, it is incomplete. Establishing an overall mood is but one function of the typical film score. Another function is the use of music to signify the emotional state of a character. A recent guide to film scoring refers to this as playing the character's point of view. To illustrate this idea, the authors cite a scene from Blake Edwards's *That's Life* (1986) in which Julie Andrews's character, Gillian, sits pensively during a family dinner. To highlight the emotional subtext of the scene, Edwards lowers the volume of the dialogue and sound effects and lets Henry Mancini's underscore take over. The music in the scene highlights Gillian's anxiety and communicates that state to the audience, even as her family members remain oblivious to it.[25]

In some instances, composers may be forced to choose between playing the character's point of view or the overall mood of the scene. Composer Charles Fox faced just such a decision while scoring *Nine to Five* (1980). In one scene, Violet (Lily Tomlin) steals a cadaver from a hospital thinking it is the body of the boss whom she believes she has killed. In scoring the scene, Fox had to choose between playing the character's fear of discovery or highlighting the overall comic tone of the scene. Fox's dilemma was, in fact, an outgrowth of the film's narration; Violet believes she is in serious trouble, but the audience knows that she is not. Fox's music initially played the emotions of the scene a little broadly, but he was persuaded by director Colin Higgins to tone down the comic elements and emphasize the protagonists' fear of being caught.[26]

Brad Fiedel's music for *The Accused* (1988) provides still another example of this kind of dramatic function in the scene of Sarah Tobias's (Jodie Foster) brutal gang rape. Murray Smith has previously analyzed this sequence in some detail in order to counter readings of it that rely on the slippery, and sometimes simplistic, notion of identification. Smith instead argues that the film's representation of the rape is actually more complicated and multilayered than when read through the reductive filter of singular identification, and actually interleaves a variety of emotional and attitudinal perspectives.[27]

Yet while I wholeheartedly agree with the fundamental premises of Smith's argument, I feel that he overlooks a crucial element of the scene which might make his point even more forcefully: the music. Fiedel's underscore here seems to be a classic example of playing the character's point of view, and in fact, appears to function much like the music in the *That's Life* example cited earlier. During the rape, director Jonathan Kaplan gradually fades out the dialogue and sound effects and lets Fiedel's music take over. The score quite clearly signifies Sarah's sense of violation, humiliation, and emotional anguish even as most of the other characters in the scene seem oblivious to it. As such, the music provides a point of emotional engagement with Sarah that undercuts the notion that we might identify with Kenneth Joyce (Bernie Coulson), the eyewitness whose flashback introduces the scene. And as Smith himself points out, any reading of the scene that privileges Joyce's viewpoint is either incomplete or wrongheaded.[28]

Finally, although it is less common, music may also be used to signify the emotional valence of a particular setting. Consider, for example, how Bernard Herrmann's music for *Psycho* (1960) characterizes the Bates home not just as an old house, but more specifically as a spooky old house. Likewise, Jerry Goldsmith's music in *Alien* (1979) underlines the strangeness of the planet visited by Ripley (Sigourney Weaver), Dallas (Tom Skerritt), and the other explorers. Similarly, the upbeat funk of Rose Royce's "Car Wash" characterizes the setting of the eponymous film as a lively and jocular workplace.

All of the examples above are perfectly consistent with Kivy's cognitivist model. Each of these cues draws on a set of musical conventions, which are normatively and intersubjectively understood by an audience as expressive of a specific emotional quality. And in each instance, the film score communicates a particular emotion (apprehension, fear, turmoil), but on its own does not necessarily arouse that emotional state in the spectator. Moreover, the narrative context for each cue helps to particularize the affective elements of the music such that the overall emotional significance of the scene is qualitatively different from that expressed by either the music or visual

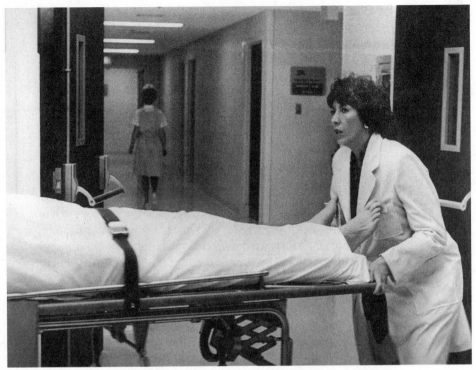

Violet (Lily Tomlin) makes off with a cadaver in *Nine to Five* (1980).

track alone. This is especially true of music that plays the point of view of a particular character. It is through narrative cues and narrational processes that we understand the music as expressive of Gillian's anxiety, Violet's fear, or Sarah's suffering.

The emphasis placed on communicating emotion strongly differentiates cognitive theory from psychoanalytic accounts of film music. As Chell's account makes clear, the suturing effect of film music causes the spectator to claim the emotions associated with the story, setting, or characters as his own. In doing so, film music, in Kathryn Kalinak's words, "binds the spectator to the screen by resonating affect between them."[29] By collapsing textual and spectatorial affect, however, Chell's account would seem to preclude the possibility that spectators might experience emotions different from those of characters. As the preceding examples demonstrate, cognitive theory avoids that problem by distinguishing between the components of judgment and affective arousal that comprise any emotional response. By drawing this distinction, cognitive theory centers on what is arguably the film score's most common function, the communication of affective elements to the spectator. Through this communicative process, the film score encourages specta-

tors to make inferences about a film's events, characters, and setting to facilitate the ongoing comprehension of the narrative. Cognitive theory suggests
that while we may become emotionally aroused in this process, this is not a
necessary outcome of the film score's effect on spectators.

Emotion, Film Music, and Psychology: Polarization and Affective Congruence

Is there any empirical evidence to support this theory of film music and emotion? Well, during the past decade, much of the psychological research on
film music tends to confirm important aspects of this account.[30] This literature supplements an already voluminous amount of empirical research on
questions of musical affect.[31] Although the results of this psychological research are not conclusive, they nonetheless suggest that expressiveness in film
music sometimes involves two processes. The first is known as polarization,
an audiovisual interaction in which the affective meaning of the music moves
the content of the image toward the specific character of that music. The second is called affective congruence and it suggests that the matching of affective meaning in both music and visuals heightens the spectator's experience
of the overall effect.

The effects of polarization have been illustrated in a number of experiments conducted by Annabel Cohen. In the first of these, Cohen tested the
effects of film music on viewers' interpretations of a short abstract animated
film, which depicts the interaction of three geometric figures as they move
in and out of a rectangular enclosure. The film was presented with two soundtracks of contrasting tempo, one *allegro* and one *adagio*. Subjects were then
asked to rate the music and film on bipolar adjective scales, which were
then further subdivided into dimensions of evaluation, potency, and activity. Each bipolar adjective scale consisted of a set of paired terms, such as
calm/agitated, sad/cheerful, villainous/heroic, or serious/humorous. The experiment's results suggested that the music not only affected the perceptions
of each figure, but that temporal congruences between music and image may
have also directed the viewers' attention to certain features of the film to produce an association between the meaning of the music and the attended film
items. In doing so, the music accompanying the film nudged the meanings
associated with each object toward one pole of the bipolar semantic scale.[32]

In a second series of tests, Cohen measured the influence of musical associations on the interpretation of computer-generated visual displays. Here
a bouncing ball that could be varied in terms of its speed and height was
accompanied by music that varied in pitch and tempo. Once again, when
auditory and visual information were presented together, the auditory elements systematically shaped the affective meanings of the visuals. For instance, happiness ratings that were associated by a high fast bounce were

lowered by the introduction of a low, slow melody. Similarly, happiness judgments of the ball were higher when the melody of the soundtrack was organized around a major triad than when the melody was minor.[33]

Finally, in an experiment that tested the influence of musical associations on both referential and affective meaning, Cohen asked subjects to match four excerpts of film music with descriptive titles taken from the record jackets for each respective piece. The results not only showed marked agreement on the appropriateness of three of the four titles, but they also revealed a consensus for semantic differential ratings for all four of the musical selections. Moreover, when two of the selections were used to accompany short excerpts of a film, subjects' semantic differential ratings revealed that changes in both title and musical selection corresponded with measures obtained for the musical selections themselves, which suggests that musical associations influenced both the denotative and affective meanings of each film excerpt.[34]

In each of these experiments, music was shown to influence the interpretation of visual information by moving the affective meaning of the visual event closer to the specific affective character of the music. This process, referred to as "polarization," involved moving the affective meanings of a visual stimulus toward one pole or the other of a bipolar semantic scale. The results of these experiments appear to support the theory of cross-modal matching since the subjects of each used the musical information to create a consistent affective pattern across modalities. The degree to which polarization influenced interpretation, however, depended in some measure on the nature of the visual stimulus. On the one hand, when the emotional meanings of the film excerpt were ambiguous, the effects of polarization became even more pronounced.[35] On the other hand, when visual and aural information clearly conflicted, visual information took some precedence over aural cues. In other words, the effects of polarization were more muted in such instances, and the music simply shaded the affective meaning of the visuals.

Returning to some of the examples I cited earlier, we can now see how the process of polarization helps to structure the communication of musical affect in films. When music is used to suggest an overall mood, as in Carroll's *Gunga Din* (1939) example, the spectator makes judgments about the affective character of the visual and aural information presented to her and then uses the emotional meanings of the music to interpret the visual information of the scene, and vice versa. In Carroll's example, the music itself is characterized as bouncy, energetic, and light. Recognizing these emotional meanings in the music, the spectator then uses this evaluation to interpret the battle scene that the music accompanies. The overall effect is that the music moves the scene toward certain semantic poles that are part of the spectator's cognitive schemata. The battle scene is thus viewed as "jaunty" and "comic" rather than "ponderous" or "tragic."

Polarization operates in a similar way for scenes in which the music signifies the emotional states of a character. In the *That's Life* example, the spectator uses the emotional meanings of the music, its sense of foreboding and
anxiety, to interpret Gillian's demeanor during a rather mundane dinner
scene. In the *Nine to Five* example, on the other hand, the spectator uses the
affective meanings of the music to understand Violet's fear. The reasons why
we interpret the musical affect as character-oriented rather than as a contribution to an overall mood is largely determined by the film's larger processes
of narration. We know, for example, that Gillian has just been told she may
have a malignant tumor. We also know that Violet believes she is covering up
evidence of a murder that did not happen. In each case, the film's regulation
of knowledge influences our judgment of the music's affective qualities and
encourages us to attach them to a specific character rather than the scene as
a whole.

Like polarization, affective congruence involves an interaction of visual
and musical information such that the latter influences interpretations of the
former. Unlike polarization, however, affective congruence does not involve
changing or shifting the affective qualities of the image so much as it does
heightening and intensifying them. Through affective congruence, subjects
feel emotional characteristics more strongly than they would with either
image or music alone.

Although there has been comparatively less work done on affective congruence than on polarization, there are some studies which are of interest
here. Using the Sandra Marshall and Annabel Cohen study as a point of de-
parture, George Sirius and Eric F. Clarke developed an experiment designed
to test whether music and image combined in an additive manner or produced semantic effects characteristic of a true audiovisual percept.[36] For this
study, subjects were asked to rate a group of musical excerpts and computer-
generated images on twelve bipolar adjective scales. The images were three-
dimensional graphics of geometrical figures and the musical examples were
specially composed in the styles of specific musical and film genres, such as
disco, Spanish, thriller, and spaghetti Western. Although Sirius and Clarke
stress that their conclusions are provisional, the results of their study nonetheless indicated that music had only additive effects on the relation between
sound and image.[37] Music that was perceived as especially expressive simply
raised the evaluative scores for the audiovisual combination in which it was
featured, regardless of the specific visual extract that was used. When the
visual extract was semantically ambiguous, polarization structured the interpretation around the affective qualities of the music. However, when the
semantic values of the visuals were more pronounced, the additive effect of
the music simply heightened the affective meanings that were present in
both visual and audio inputs. In other words, the additive effects of the

music simply intensified the subject's impressions of affective meaning such that the combination was greater than the audio or visual percept by itself.

The heightening effect of affective congruence is further reinforced by Marilyn Boltz, Matthew Schulkind, and Suzanne Kantra's study of film music and memory. Although the experiment focused on the extent to which background music influenced subjects' ability to remember filmed events, the authors discovered an interesting correlation between musical moods and event outcomes. The mere presence of music itself was not enough to improve memory skills. Rather, the study showed that it was only when music was temporally and affectively congruent with an event outcome that spectators' recall was significantly enhanced. Most tellingly, even when subjects were unable to identify a tune, the playing of it often enhanced a subject's ability to recall the episode that it accompanied. The authors' interpretation of these results suggests that the affective meanings of music direct the spectator's attention to the underlying mood of a scene. Film music, in other words, directs our attention to patterns of activity that correspond with the affective qualities of the music. Through the process of cross-modal confirmation, the shared affective meanings of music and visuals direct attention to shared formal features which in turn reinforce and engender the affective meaning of the scene. In this way, mood congruence produces an audiovisual percept that is both coherent and strongly encoded with associations. Both of these conditions facilitate the mind's ability to retrieve the audiovisual information encoded in short-term memory.[38]

Although the results of these studies are even less conclusive than those of polarization, the first indicates the tendency of affective congruence to heighten the emotional meaning of audiovisual combinations while the second gives some idea of how that heightening effect is achieved. More important, however, these results support the hypothesis that film music can arouse an emotional response as part of a *combinatoire* of expression. The additive effects of affective congruence are especially important here since it suggests that when an emotionally powerful visual track is combined with an emotionally expressive soundtrack, the heightening of affective meanings achieves an intensity that can produce a physiological response in spectators. The evaluation of this physiological response in turn produces a sense of self-awareness that the spectator attributes to the emotional expressiveness of the film. Thus, to return to the *Elephant Man* example, it is specifically the affective congruence of Samuel Barber's emotion-laden music that heightens the scene's affective meanings, and in turn arouses my visceral response to John Merrick's death.[39]

Yet while psychomusicological research offers interesting insights into the question of film music signification, one must be careful about the weight one places on this evidence for a number of reasons. First of all, as Cohen points out, the extent to which music shapes the spectator's understanding of the image is less predictable than one might expect.[40] Thus, the conclusions of researchers typically describe certain tendencies of musical cognition rather than causal mechanisms. This is, of course, consistent with the common proposition that music, unlike language, has no semantic dimension. However, since the researchers only show a degree of intersubjective agreement that is more or less greater than chance, one cannot draw any sweeping conclusions from this evidence.

Second, by using a semantic differential scale, researchers presuppose certain crucial assumptions of the cognitivist model. Rather than investigate the moods that music might arouse, these experiments only test the subject's ability to recognize affective qualities and identify them with some degree of intersubjective agreement. Thus, one reason these experiments tend to confirm Kivy's model of musical affect might be that they are already predisposed to do so. More important, though, the use of semantic differential scales also constrains the kinds of interpretative skills that subjects might bring to the listening situation. Experiments that use more open-ended questions show that affective qualities are frequently linked to elements of musical representation. In a test performed by Philip Tagg, for example, subjects were asked to listen to a brief piece of film or television music and quickly jot down their impressions of what they thought might be occurring on-screen. A typical response showed verbal-visual associations with affective qualities, like "brightness" and "romance," but also with more representational elements, like "white dress," "meadow," "slow motion," and "shampoo."[41]

Finally, in trying to achieve proper experimental conditions, subjects are often tested in ways that are fundamentally different from a typical moviegoing experience. For one thing, researchers use films and music specially created for the experiment. In some of Cohen's experiments, for example, she used simple animation in the form of bouncing balls or geometric figures to play the function of "character." The results are interesting for what they tell us about music's ability to shape the meaning of nonnarrative events, but obviously these are quite unlike a typical cinematic experience. Similarly, many experiments use only short excerpts to test the relation of cinematic and musical signification. Again the results can prove useful, but the experimental conditions are very different from the temporal unfolding of most cinematic narratives. Usually, these experiments test a subject's ability to recognize localized emotional meanings, and may be more applicable to the individual cue rather than an entire score.[42]

That said, there is still something to be gleaned from psychomusicological research. In developing a theory of film-musical affect, I believe that the contributions made by psychomusicology are twofold. First of all, psychomusicological research tends to support the hypothesis that spectators quite commonly recognize emotional expressiveness as one of film music's dramatic functions. Second, psychomusicological research affords us a more precise description of the spectator's phenomenological experience. Cohen's research suggests that the spectator's activity is best understood in terms of an associationist model that is quite compatible with the theory of expressiveness outlined earlier. Cohen defines this associationism in terms of four features. The first is that associationism is sensationalistic in that it identifies the most fundamental components of mental life with sensory experience. For Cohen, music is sensationalist in that it has direct access to emotions. The second trait is that associationism is mechanistic. By this Cohen means that complex cognitive configurations are predicted from underlying sensations. This is important in the understanding of musical affect in that it is consistent with the hypothesis that music independently adds meaning to an event. Third, associationism is reductionist in that the events to be analyzed decompose into simpler percepts. In cinema, this reductionism refers to the fact that it can be separated into visual and music elements, each of which is processed by a different cognitive mechanism. Last, associationism is connectionist meaning that ideas, sense data, memory modes, and other mental elements are associated together through simultaneous or contiguous experience. The film score's frequent use of themes and leitmotifs is consistent with a connectionist account of musical cognition. More important, both denotative and affective meanings can be accounted for by this connectionist principle in that film music acquires its meaning through prior associations with characters, settings, and ideas and then transfers these meanings to the sequences of the film that it accompanies. Thus, while analytic philosophy provides important clues to the mystery of film music's emotional expressiveness, psychomusicology enriches that account by offering us a more precise description of the ways in which spectators make sense of music's expressiveness within an audiovisual context.

The specific reasons why film music may evoke one response in me and a different response in other spectators are quite complex. One reason is music's lack of emotional specificity, which itself opens up the possibility for different emotional responses to the same piece of music. That music can communicate one thing about a character and evoke a slightly different response in a spectator is partly a consequence of this generalizability. Whatever emotional specificity a film score has is derived from its placement in a narrative context and is not an inherent quality of the music itself. And even when placed within a narrative context, music's tendency toward abstraction opens up the space for a range of emotions within spectators. Other reasons for the variance of emotional responses involve factors specific to the individual spectator. As John Sloboda notes, these would include such things as a spectator's prevailing mood before viewing the film and the extent to which a narrative situation might relate to one's private foibles, fears, desires, and anxieties (i.e., while I view *The Elephant Man,* the film might activate a fear of disfigurement not shared by other audience members).[43]

While I have focused somewhat narrowly in this section on the processes that influence affect comprehension, it is important to remember that these processes are frequently linked to other cognitive activities, such as memory retrieval, mental modeling, narrative comprehension, and cross-modal confirmation. Further research might explore the ways in which polarization and affective congruence influence these activities. A particularly promising avenue of research concerns the relationship between film scores, film genres, and cognition. There is some strong evidence to suggest that the musical styles and conventions used in certain genres have a strong influence on spectators' interpretations of visual material, especially those that involve making inferences about future narrative developments. Moreover, since certain genres are often associated with particular moods, music that activates genre schemata may predispose spectators toward certain affective meanings in the visuals they accompany. In other words, romantic music may lead viewers to recognize affective qualities such as warmth, tenderness, or passion. Horror music may predispose viewers to judgments of fear, terror, and anxiety within a scene. Comic music may yield a greater activation of lightness, buoyancy, and merriment. If this could be demonstrated, research in this area might provide a more precise understanding of how both polarization and affective congruence operate.

Similarly, one might also explore the ways in which the spectator's emotional engagement may be mediated by a film score's other narrative functions, such as its use of leitmotifs or its association with other artworks. Take Bernard Herrmann's score for *Vertigo* (1958), for example. In the scene where Scotty (James Stewart) and Madeleine (Kim Novak) embrace atop a rocky peak overlooking the ocean, Herrmann's music not only conveys the characters' passionate feelings for one another, but also evokes a feeling of epic grandeur within the spectator. The latter is arguably the result of the score's referencing of Wagner's "Liebestod," which parallels Scotty and Madeleine's romance with that of the mythological lovers Tristan and Isolde. Likewise, whatever feelings we might have for Nora Ephron's lovers in *Sleepless in Seattle* (1993) may well be intertwined with the nostalgic warmth felt for both the 1958 weepie *An Affair to Remember,* and the soundtrack of well-known love songs used to underscore the couple's romance. A more comprehensive theory of musical cognition ought to account for these extratextual and extramusical associations and their relation to certain aspects of emotional engagement.

Conclusion

The association between music and emotion is one that pervades both academic and professional discourses on film scoring. Composer Elmer Bernstein, for example, sums up this position by saying, "Of all the arts, music makes the most direct appeal to the emotions."[44] Critic Simon Frith adds, "Music, it seems, can convey and clarify the emotional significance of a scene, the true, 'real' feelings of the characters involved in it."[45] This link between music and emotion is manifested in some of the dramatic functions that film music performs. The three I have emphasized—the signification of characters' emotions, the communication of an overall mood, and the arousal of emotional responses in audiences—comprise a structure of film-musical affect that corresponds with different levels of emotional engagement. These different levels of emotional engagement can be best understood through a combination of cognitivist and emotivist theories of music, which suggest that there are subtle distinctions in the way that film music communicates, evokes, and provokes emotions in spectators.

More important, though, this structure of musical affect is supported by two processes central to a phenomenological account of musical cognition. These processes, which are known as polarization and affective congruence, involve the spectator's judgment about specific kinds of audiovisual interactions. In polarization, the affective qualities of the music move the visuals toward one side or the other of a bipolar semantic differential scale. In affective congruence, the matching of musical and narrative affect heightens and intensifies the emotional qualities of the cinematic signifier such that they exceed those of the musical and visual components in themselves. Such processes may seem relatively routine, but they are nonetheless integral to a number of larger aspects of narrative comprehension, such as the discernment of character motivation, the anticipation of future narrative developments, and the encoding of important narrative information in spectators' memories.

The emotional power of film music is demonstrated in any number of ways ranging from its ability to move audiences to laughter or tears to its ability to evoke specific scenes, images, and characters when heard apart from the film it accompanies.[46] As Philip Sarde points out, when film composers meet with directors, "We all talk about the same thing: emotions."[47] Understanding this emotional power, however, will prove difficult as long as film music remains shrouded in a veil of mystery and ineffability, both in terms of what music signifies and how it might relate to a spectator's unconscious. I believe the best way to pierce that veil is through a careful theorization of the various processes of film-musical cognition. Along this path, we will gain not only a better understanding of what film music contributes to a film, but also of the emotional expressiveness of cinema as a whole.

 **EIGHT**

Time and Timing

SUSAN L. FEAGIN

Bill: "Ask me what is the most important part of comedy."
Bob: "What is the most . . ."
Bill: "Timing."

As everyone knows, humor derives much of its effectiveness from timing. Anticipation, tension, suspense, surprise, boredom, puzzlement, and many other responses to films depend to some extent on timing as well. In the most simplistic terms, a shot of the exterior of a house may set the scene for the action of a film, but if that image persists for two minutes and nothing else is presented to hold the audience's attention, spectators are likely to become restless and bored. At the other extreme, viewers may become frustrated and perturbed when a rapid montage of images is presented so quickly that they literally do not have time to recognize the individual images. I shall stretch the use of the word *image* to refer not only to a static image but also to a portion of a film that can be experienced as, or thought of as, a unit. A closeup of a person's face, an event such as a sword fight, and a scene that takes place in a particular room of a house may each count as an image, and there will virtually always be a variety of promising and useful ways to individuate images within a given film for the purposes of appreciation, criticism and analysis. In this chapter I examine how certain temporal features of a film— the duration of and the durational relationships between and among images in a film—can affect spectators' emotional or feeling responses to a film in ways that enrich their experiences of it.

A canonical ordering of the presentation of the frames of a film is essential to its identity as that film.[1] The sequencing of images can therefore be exploited to influence a viewer's emotions or feeling responses to it. Sequencing is one type of temporal feature of a film. It has to do with the order of images but not their duration or durational relationships. The durational features of a film are what I call "timing."

Timing takes two forms. One is the *duration of an image,* that is, the length of time an image persists, which may affect a viewer's responses. In an early scene of *Raiders of the Lost Ark,* for example, Indiana Jones (Harrison Ford) is chased by numerous foes through a crowded Cairo bazaar. At one point, the teeming mass of people parts like the Red Sea to reveal an impressively clothed, swashbuckling, saber-twirling foe who is shown brandishing his sabers menacingly and skillfully for a significant length of time. Here is an important figure, viewers think, a suitable challenger to Jones whose skills with a whip are likely to be tested in interesting ways. The duration of the image, that is, the length of time spent showing the dexterity of Jones's foe, may have cognitive and affective results. A reasonable cognitive effect would be the belief that an action-packed battle between the whip and the sword is imminent. A reasonable affective effect would be the anticipation, with some trepidation, of a contest that has the potential to involve a lot of blood.

The second type of timing encompasses *durational relationships* among images, including the relative duration of images earlier in the movie, the length of time elapsed between or among them, and the length of time elapsed between them and the present image, which may itself have a significant duration. So what happens in *Raiders of the Lost Ark?* After the extended display of swordsmanship, a cut to Jones's face captures his condescending look that says, "You are so-o-o-o lame," whereupon Jones casually pulls out his gun and shoots the saber man dead. The relatively lengthy buildup contrasts with Jones's quick dispatch of his rival to humorous effect. *Raiders,* a film of adventure in exotic lands, uses timing to nod (in this and other scenes) to the American western, spoofing both. As in other aspects of life, including telling a joke, timing may be good or bad, effective or ineffective. I use "timing" to refer to durational features of a film when they are relevant to these and other assessments of how successful, unsuccessful, subtle, or obvious a film is. A film may lack timing, so that it does not have the effectiveness it could have, but to simplify the discussion below I concentrate on the timing that a film does have and how it contributes to the effectiveness of a film.

Timing thus includes both more and less than what Seymour Chatman calls "discourse-time," which is "the time of the presentation of [plot] events in the text."[2] If "the time of presentation" here refers to actual elapsed real time, it includes only one temporal feature, duration, and not how temporal relationships among various parts of the film influence audience responses. Further, there is an ambiguity in Chatman's definition of discourse-time and hence in the distinction between discourse-time and "story-time," which he defines as "the time sequence of plot events." Story-time is defined in terms of sequencing, which concerns only the ordering of events rather than their duration or relative duration. To make the contrast with story-time one might expect discourse-time to be defined in terms of sequencing also. In any case, sequencing is a temporal feature of a film or set of events, but it is not part of what I call "tim*ing*."

What Alexander Sesonske calls "screen time," "the actual elapsed time of the film" (as well as, I imagine, parts of the film), has the same limitation as the first construal of discourse-time, that is, it does not include actual or relative duration of, or between, two or more images in a film.[3] Conversely, both "discourse time" and "screen time" are broader than my conception of timing in that they include actual elapsed time when it does not play a role in determining what a film is about or in explaining the effectiveness, or lack of effectiveness, of a film. A film may simply not use timing as a way to say or show what it does or to affect audience responses.

As these brief remarks indicate, my interest is not merely to call attention to the explanatory role of timing in relation to affective responses to films. I am ultimately interested in what it is to appreciate a film, and specifically, to appreciate it as a work of art. I have argued elsewhere that appreciating a work of *literature* is a temporally extended process that involves both affective and theoretical components.[4] Appreciating a *film* as a work of art, I propose, involves these same components. The qualifier "as a work of art" will be problematic for some; it is not necessary to rehash debates about the concept of art here, which would get in the way of the ultimately rather straightforward points I wish to make about the effectiveness of timing in film, and how sensitivities to timing enable one, to use the vernacular, to get more out of it.

In a large number of cases, one's appreciation of a film will be fuller and richer both theoretically (cognitively) and affectively when one responds to it in ways that are affected by the duration of and durational relationships among its images. The theoretical component consists of an account of the work which describes what the work is about—what it "means" or says, what it shows or expresses, and how it fails at any of these. An account of a work will, ideally, explain how its parts work together to show or say what they do. Nothing in this description of the theoretical component of appreciation should be taken to require or even suggest that there is only one true or correct account of a work or one true or correct method of interpretation. The affective component comprises emotions, feelings, moods, and affective components of desire. Similarly, there is no presumption that only one set of responses is appropriate to a work, especially if one accepts a variety of interpretive approaches, each of which may foreground aspects of the film that are not recognized as significant by the others. Different methods of interpretation may see a work as having different functions, so that different responses are shown to be appropriate. Even within a single interpretive model different individuals may well have different but equally appropriate responses, just as the responses of the same individual will likely vary with repeated encounters with the same work. The theoretical and affective components come together in appreciation, which involves not merely knowing or coming to know what a work means or says, how to interpret it, and what is valuable about it. Appreciating a film, experiencing it in richer and fuller ways, involves getting the value out of it, that is, *using* it to do what it is supposed to do. And part of what it is supposed to do will often be to evoke emotions, feelings, moods, and desires, that is, to have those kinds of effects on the human psyche. Thus, part of what needs to be explained in the theoretical account of a film is how certain affective responses contribute to the film's doing what, according to this account, it is supposed to do.

I will first explain in greater detail the nature of timing as distinguished from other temporal and nontemporal features of a work and provide a few reflections on why it is difficult to describe and easy to overlook the roles timing plays in generating affective responses to films. The next section explores how timing can affect one's emotions, feelings, and so on indirectly, through cognitive means, that is, by introducing or altering a viewer's beliefs, thoughts, and ideas. Finally, I describe how timing can produce affective responses directly, that is, independently of cognition. I also use *Stranger than Paradise* (Jim Jarmusch, 1984) to provide the primary, but not the only, examples to illustrate how one's responses to a film can figure in an account of what that film is about and how one's responses and reflections on one's responses enrich one's appreciation of it.

Finally, I would like to explain why I present examples the way I do. Since my ultimate concern is with appreciation as an activity ranging across a period of time, I present emotions and affective responses as well as thoughts and ideas as being part of that activity and as occurring in a certain sequence. The examples are oversimplified in order to make the conceptual points clear, whereas actual responses to films are less neatly identifiable and individuated. Further, in the examples I describe cognitive and affective sequences as if they were my own or as if "we" have them. I am not suggesting the responses described in the examples are the only appropriate responses to the film being discussed, as if any reader of this chapter and I have some special status when it comes to such things. Rather, the responses constitute one appropriate set of responses that illustrate how duration and durational relationships can be affectively effective.

What Is Timing?
Elicitors and Conditioners

Two types of reasons are commonly given to explain why one responds as one does to a particular portion of a film. Responses can be partially explained by describing the portion of the film to which one is responding, what I call the elicitor. Responses can also be partially explained by referring to properties of the viewer—beliefs, ideas, abilities, capacities, past experiences, moods, attitudes, personality and character traits, and no doubt numerous other psychological states or conditions. I call these conditioners; they are *psychological* states or conditions of a viewer. No two people ever have all of the same psychological states and conditions, and responding to films in ways that count as appreciating them, fortunately, does not require that they do. Some responses may typically require a viewer to have a certain set of beliefs, amount of information, kinds of values, and possibly to have had certain kinds of experiences. In other cases, however, viewers may think of ideas and thoughts as they try to develop an account of what the film is about, an account that is developed partly on the basis of how they respond to it, rather than as a necessary background condition for having those responses. The sorts of psychological conditions I call "sensitivities" are especially important for understanding the role of timing in producing responses. Sensitivities are dispositional states or conditions such that if one were to encounter a certain kind of thing one would respond in a certain kind of way. Dispositional states are not to be understood behaviorally, simply as a relationship of stimulus to response, but as features or properties of the psyche of a person which account for or explain why one has the behavioral tendencies.

Curiously, timing is neither an elicitor, that is, a part of a film experienced at a given point in time, or during a brief period of time we can call the "experiential present," nor a conditioner, a psychological state or set of states of the perceiver. Timing is a property of a film, in particular, the duration and durational relationships between and among parts of a film to which one is exposed when the film is presented in its canonical mode. When timing is involved, one's responses cannot be explained merely by appealing to elicitors and nontemporal conditioners. Timing works because of what happens to the viewer (or what the viewer does) during the temporal interval. The length of that interval—the duration and durational relationships between and among images in the film—will be part of the explanation why one responds the way one does.

This ontological peculiarity of timing, its dependence on temporal relationships, is one reason it is difficult to isolate the role it plays in generating responses. Furthermore, it is also difficult to determine whether the *particular* duration and durational relationships among parts of a film are effective or whether it is only content and sequencing that produces one's cognitive and affective responses. The affective potential of timing may always be at least partly a function of the content that is timed the way it is. Finally, every part of the film must occur for some length of time or other and in some durational relationships or other to other parts of the film. It is easy to overlook how the duration and durational relationships of an image help establish what a film is about and why it is effective.

Temporal and Nontemporal Factors

Psychological states or conditions of a viewer, including beliefs, unasserted propositional thoughts, and ideas, may function merely as a cognitive stock. A cognitive stock functions like an acquired pool of beliefs, ideas, and thoughts. As a pool, it functions nontemporally: *when* one acquired the beliefs is irrelevant; the only important thing is that one has them. If such beliefs and ideas cannot reasonably be assumed to be part of the common mentality of a film's audience, the film may need to introduce them in some way, and it very well may not matter when, during the film, one acquires them. Certain sensitivities that are deeply entrenched and virtually permanent aspects of a viewer's psyche may also affect that person's responses. Such affective sensitivities are not part of a cognitive stock, but rather dispositions to respond affectively to certain sorts of things. Some assumptions about affective sensitivities in general are pretty reliable: that one will be repulsed by bodily mutilation, fascinated by explosions, or moved by the innocence of a child. On the other hand, a film may refer visually to another film or genre of films, relying on viewers to have seen or at least know about the relevant referent. For example, when the invading spaceship appears in *Independence Day* there is a shot of a traffic jam with people fleeing everywhere. Any viewer familiar with science-fiction movies of the 1950s will likely be amused by this parody of the genre.[5] It really doesn't matter when you saw your last 1950s sci-fi flick; it matters only that you recognize the convention. Such conditioners function nontemporally as do sensitivities that never go away. Some sensitivities, however, are only temporary. Indeed, the very fact that some are temporary entails that timing influences responses.

Sequencing

Sequencing is the order of the presentation of events of a narrative or story. This order, the order of the discourse, may or may not be the same as the order of events in the story.[6] Significant cognitive effort may be required to understand a story given the temporal disparities between narrative time and story time. *Pulp Fiction* (Quentin Tarantino, 1996) no doubt enjoys some of its popularity because of the way one's understanding of the story develops along with one's understanding of the structure of the film. Several years earlier, *Mystery Train* (Jim Jarmusch, 1990), an art film of a somewhat more esoteric variety, also presents consecutively different points of view on the same set of events (discourse-time) that would have been experienced simultaneously by the characters themselves (story-time). *Night on Earth* (Jim Jarmusch, 1991), in a slight variation on the theme, presents consecutively what happens to several cab drivers in five cities across the world during the same period of the night. Interestingly, the screen time of each episode is almost the same as its story time.

Sequencing is a temporal feature of a film because it is the order in which various aspects of a story are told, and hence revealed to the viewer in and through time. Timing has to do with length of time (duration) of an image and relationships between and among various lengths of time relevant images persist. Simply put, sequencing concerns what came before and what came after; timing concerns how long, how long before, and how long after, and how these interactions affect audience response. Timing presupposes sequencing, since the duration and durational relations of the presentation of actions and events are dependent on the images of a film appearing in a certain sequence. Sequencing does not, however, presuppose timing; rather, it makes timing possible.

Indirect Effects of Timing: Cognitive Mediation

Timing affects responses *indirectly* when it is responsible for generating cognitive states or activities that in turn figure in the production and perhaps maintenance of emotions or affective responses. That emotions in particular have cognitive components is these days pretty much a received view in spite of residual disagreements about the nature of those components (whether they take the form of beliefs or "unasserted thoughts," and exactly which beliefs are connected with which emotions). I understand cognitive states to include not only beliefs and unasserted (propositional) thoughts but also ideas whose content is not propositional but captured simply by the words (theoretically, minus any affective implications) that identify them. Beliefs figure in one's understanding or interpretation of a film, what one takes the film to be about and to express. Some thoughts, questions, and ideas may occur as part of the process of trying to understand a film even if they are ultimately rejected as not part of the account one wishes to give. Many films, from detective stories to art films, are designed to puzzle and challenge viewers, at least for a while. Thus, awareness of and reflection on the nature of the process of trying to make sense of such films may be part of their point, and hence count as contributing to one's appreciation of them.

Duration is the length of time the same image is shown, or shown in a particular way. Sameness may exist on many levels and to many different degrees, so that what counts as "the same" is clearly subject to interpretation. Timing can be indirectly significant when some aspect of a film continues longer than one might expect, enabling one to contemplate more subtle aspects of the story and the characters and to think about why the shot continues for so long. In contrast, fast-paced montage and rapid cross-cutting often work directly to create feelings of excitement, so that an effect can be produced without requiring the audience to think.

Most films, Jim Jarmusch says, "don't trust the audience, cutting to a new shot every six or seven seconds."[7] *Stranger than Paradise*, an early film by Jarmusch, employs timing in a way that contrasts sharply with rapid cuts. Shot entirely in black-and-white, it begins with a stationary shot of a young woman standing next to her suitcases on a scrubby knoll overlooking the airport. I notice that it is an unusual vantage point, and probably one that, in reality, would be inaccessible to the ordinary traveler. At any rate, travelers don't generally wander off with their luggage to such a place. The distinctive sounds of airplane engines are heard as she watches a plane move into position to taxi off. Such thoughts pass through my mind rather quickly, but the scene is still on the screen. That's puzzling: why am I still looking at this when nothing much is happening? Is something else going to happen? Why does the camera linger? Just as I restlessly start to wonder how much longer this will go on, I see the young woman gathering up her bags and suitcases. I reflect that maybe now something is going to . . . Cut to black.

The cut to black elicits responses. It is surprising, a little jarring, and it even provokes a bit of a smile. I am surprised by the cut to black because it is unusual to find this type of device in a contemporary film. The abruptness of the cut also has a decisiveness about it that contrasts with the unhurried length of the scene. It is a little wake-up call that gives rise to more thought. The director knows what he's doing after all, amusing me since I had questioned the basic competence of the director. It is almost as if he knew I would do that, and had his reply ready.

Films that require only the usual sensitivities will, of course, be more popular because more people will readily respond to them, and they will not have to stretch their minds in ways a film such as *Stranger* requires. The sensibility that is expressed in *Stranger,* focusing for relatively long periods of time on something or someone who is not doing anything—not doing anything that matters—also has been taken up by others. Brooks Adams begins his report for *Art in America* on the 1997 Whitney Biennial with a description of a video he takes as emblematic of the most prominent artistic sensibilities of the show. The video in question focuses on a stationary tortoise for approximately ten minutes and then it "heaves itself up suddenly, after what seems like an eternity, and slowly trundles off screen." Adams characterizes the video as having a "cooled-out, laid-back tempo, . . . the new rhythm of creation in the decentered, off-on-your-own '90s." He also points out what should not be surprising for film or video, that you have to sit through the videos to get any "real sense of the show."[8] Sitting through them is the only way to experience how timing functions within them.

A doleful atmosphere pervades *Stranger than Paradise:* gloomy and bleak,

Willie (John Lurie) and Eva (Eszter Balint) discuss possibilities in Jim
Jarmusch's *Stranger than Paradise* (1984).

but with occasional unconscious comic effects.[9] The characters, of course,
are not conscious of the comedy. As the movie progresses, Eva (Eszter Balint),
whom we saw at the airport, stays with her cousin Willie (John Lurie) for several days in his small and dingy apartment. After Eva leaves to visit her aunt
in Cleveland, Willie's friend Eddie (Richard Edson) drops by. They exchange
a few words about Eva's leaving, and Willie offers Eddie a beer. Eddie accepts.
Willie gets a beer for each of them from the refrigerator. They sit. Each opens
his beer. One takes a sip. They sit in silence. Then the other takes a sip. Then
the first again. They drink at the same time. They sit in silence. Another sip.
Cut to black.

Referring to *Stranger than Paradise*, Jarmusch has said, "That's what I like
most about that film: the moments between dialogue when you understand
what's happening between people without them saying anything."[10] His focus is on character, and one thing that tells us a lot about these characters is
how they spend their time. But the ways characters spend their time are generally cut out of a film when they basically don't do anything for long periods of time.

Stranger proceeds with a number of scenes that have a pace similar to the
first one, each separated by a cut to black. Printed on one of the black screens

is "One year later." This announcement evokes a little chuckle as you realize the incongruity of taking a lot of time within each scene to show that nothing is happening, and virtually no time at all to indicate that a whole year has passed.

The film in general produces an uneasy feeling that things are slightly, almost imperceptibly "out of sync," a temporal metaphor that is particularly apt since time and timing, as one comes to realize, are part of what this film is about. This observation, as part of the account I develop of the work, starts to color what I notice. Temporal peculiarities show up in nontemporal ways. The time of the action is somewhat obscure. The black-and-white photography alludes to an earlier era, and the cuts to black are reminiscent of the era of silent films. The hats that Willie and Eddie wear look like something out of the 1950s, as does the dingy, spare apartment (reminiscent of though much smaller than the one occupied by the Kramdens on *The Honeymooners* show). There is a calendar tacked up on the wall, almost too high for Willie to see. No matter: nothing is written on it. When Willie finds out his cousin Eva is supposed to stay with him for ten days and not just one, he protests that it's not possible because it will interrupt his life. But, of course, there's nothing going on in Willie's life to interrupt. Through a fluke of timing Eva comes upon a great sum of money. Attempts by each character to reunite with the others are foiled by a simple case of bad timing. What few events fill the time of the movie could hardly be more contingent and accidental from the "story" point of view. Their separate lives are by chance braided together for a time and then the braid becomes frayed at the end.

Direct Effects of Timing

As we have seen, duration and durational relationships among parts of a film can plausibly be the source of thoughts and ideas, which then trigger feelings or figure in an emotional response. It is also plausible to think that durational factors can influence affective responses *directly*, without producing cognitive intermediaries. Thus, one can link timing with the production of feelings and moods such as melancholy, tension and relaxation, joyfulness or well-being, anxiety or boredom, which do not require a cognitive source or component for being the psychological state they are. Our psychological vocabulary for identifying and individuating affective responses that are not emotions is, unfortunately, woefully inadequate and unsystematic. Nevertheless, my suspicion is that such responses are probably just as common as, even if not more pronounced or intense than, clearly delineated emotional responses to film. Separating cognitive and noncognitive sources of affective responses is, as always, difficult, and as we have seen, they blend together in one's account of the work so that they reinforce one another.

Instead of producing or altering one's cognitive states, timing may exploit

the affective potential of cognitive states that viewers can already be expected
to have, as does Alfred Hitchcock in *Notorious* (1945) where T. R. Devlin (Cary
Grant) is looking for evidence in the wine cellar. We know he is in danger of
being caught; we are nervous, apprehensive, and perhaps fearful that he will
be found out. In such cases, timing does not change one's beliefs but intensifies and extends the viewer's apprehensiveness by bringing those beliefs to
the fore.

It is pretty obvious how simple duration can produce a response. A
sound heard briefly may produce only an idea or thought, heard continu-
ously for a longer time it may become irritating, and if it persists for hours
it may become almost unbearable. A stimulus at T1 may alter the psychological state of viewers by having an effect on how one is disposed to respond to
the very same stimulus at T2, which then affects how one responds to that
stimulus at T3, and so on. Thus, the very same stimulus might produce a
variety of responses at successive points in time because viewers' sensitivity
to the stimulus is heightened from being exposed either constantly or repeatedly to it for a lengthening period of time.

A scene at the beginning of *Sling Blade* (1996) provides an example of
how simple duration can produce an affective response directly. All is quiet;
nothing much is going on. One patient then takes a chair and starts dragging
it across the room over to the windows. The noise from the chair scraping
against the floor is disturbingly intrusive and unpleasant, breaking the atmosphere of isolation and quiet among the patients—and viewers. Viewers
readily recognize that the patient's actions are a breach of decorum, and that
anyone with common sense would not persist in the activity. In a conventional film the chair-dragging scene would likely be just long enough to get
some such idea across, requiring only a brief exposure to the irritating sound,
and then cut to the next scene to continue the narrative. In *Sling Blade*, however, we follow this patient dragging his chair all ... the ... way ... a- ...
cross ... the ... floor. We don't merely recognize that the chair-dragging is
irritating in the way we briefly experienced; we experience the irritation ourselves.

Yet the irritation is coupled with amusement, as we realize the filmmaker
is playing a little joke on us. Beliefs and assumptions about how films usually operate, and about how this scene diverges from usual practices, condition one's responses. We become aware of those conventions, as we so often
do with conventions, when they are breached. In this case, the joke is on us,
but we are also in on the joke.

Durational relationships among experiences may also influence responses
directly. Speeded-up action or fast motion almost inevitably appears comic
and produces amusement. A sudden, explosive event produces a startle response. Actions or events appearing with increasing frequency may generate

anticipation or anxiety, depending on the nature of the event. Some direct affective sensitivities may well be explainable by what David Hume called a "natural connexion," or what we might say is "hard wired." Just as we are wired in such a way that certain events produce (physical) pain, it is plausible to think that we are wired in such a way that some durational relationships among events produce certain kinds of responses.

The cuts to black in *Stranger* may not only produce surprise but also a low-level startle: the first one catches me in mid- (though unhurried) thought and abruptly ends the cognitive freedom I felt due to the length of the opening scene. Startle responses do not require cognitive mediation, and sensitivities to a cut to black may be heightened by the length of the previous scene and then lowered by repetitive use of the technique.[11]

When the duration of a shot makes one feel slightly out of sync, Jarmusch makes us not just understand but also feel what the movie is about, just as Brooks Adams says one needs to watch the videos to feel the pace, the sense of time, that characterized so many of the works in the Whitney Biennial. In *Mystery Train*, Jun explains to his girlfriend Mizuko when she asks why it is taking so long to get to Memphis, "There's a time difference in America." Having sensitivities to the oddball timing of *Stranger than Paradise* enables one to get the value out of it. Oddball or conventional, timing is an important feature of films and an important part of their power to affect viewers' feelings and emotions. Indeed, appreciation of virtually any film is enriched by having feelings and emotional responses to it.

Desire, Identification, and Empathy

NINE

Narrative Desire

GREGORY CURRIE

The ending is inevitable: dramatically, commercially, morally, geopolitically. Ilsa (Ingrid Bergman) must stay with Victor (Paul Henreid). This is wartime and sacrifices must be made, and Rick (Humphrey Bogart) has the compensation of an exciting future resisting the Nazis alongside a morally braced Captain Renault (Claude Rains). The idea that it was unclear to anyone—let alone the writers—how the story would end is as incredible as it is appealing, and Richard Maltby has demonstrated its falsehood.[1]

But for all its evident rightness, the ending does not satisfy all our desires. After all, we want Ilsa and Rick to be together, and our sustained interest in the narrative depends largely on this being so. There is here, as in so much filmic and other fiction, a conflict of desire, the logical structure of which I hope to tease out.

There are conflicts of desire which we experience in connection with nonfictional things, and I will say something about the structural relations between the conflicts which arise in these different settings. But there are causal relations as well: in particular, film can engender desires that look outward at the world: a benign example is Woody Allen / Allan Felix, the Bogart/ Rick-fixated character in *Play It Again, Sam* (1972). There are also claims of media-inspired misogyny and violence.[2]

I don't aim to decide here what the causal connections are, and as a philosopher I am not especially well placed to contribute to what is, after all, a complex empirical question. My questions—or two of them—are more guarded: how *might* films and other fictions engender desirings? How *might* the desires so engendered be harmful?[3] And I shall suggest that some of what we regard as healthy, even aesthetically sophisticated desiring with respect to fiction would be highly undesirable desiring with respect to the real world.

A great deal of recent film theory has been concerned with desire. But most of that work neglects two central issues. First, no serious attempt is made to clarify the logical structure of desire, its relations to other kinds of states, and the kinds of relations there can be between different desires. Accordingly, I want to spend a good deal of time focusing on conceptual issues. Second, no serious attempt is made to develop theories of filmic desire in a way that would render them empirically testable, or to find empirical support for the background psychological assumptions (often drawn from psychoanalytic theorizing) used in building theories of filmic desire. Accordingly, I shall place some of this discussion in the context of evidence we have concerning the emotional and other reactions of subjects to fictional narratives. I shall also cite some evidence for the thesis that what we imagine can affect how we behave.

Having been so critical of the opposition, it would be delightful to wheel in a complete and convincing alternative. Unfortunately I do not have one. What follows is, at best, a series of vague suggestions about the direction in which we ought to proceed.

The Framework

One difficulty that the following discussion poses is that of finding the right terms in which to represent a complex set of distinctions. I want to distinguish what I shall call *character desires* and *narrative desires,* to distinguish, say, wanting Ilsa and Rick to stay together and wanting *Casablanca* (1942) to be a narrative that has Rick and Ilsa staying together. These are two kinds of desires that one can have when one confronts a work of fiction. But then I want to make a further distinction between the kinds of desires that we have when we confront the fictional and the kinds of desires we have concerning our family, friends, and fellow citizens, trees, books, and cars, ourselves and the really occurring events that all these things are caught up in. It is tempting to think of this distinction as the distinction between fiction-focused and world-focused desires, with the two halves of the previous distinction (character and narrative desires) fitting neatly into the fiction half of *this* distinction, thus:

```
fiction                          world
  │        ╲
  ▼          ╲
character      narrative
desires        desires
```

But this will not do. One reason is that fictional narratives, and sometimes fictional characters, too, are things of the real world. Othello may be a creature of imagination, something that simply does not exist, but *Othello* is a real thing, and wanting, say, for *Othello* to end happily is as much desiring something about the real world as wanting the friendship and respect of your fellow creatures. We can get around this difficulty by distinguishing, instead, between fiction-focused and nonfiction-focused desires, with reality crossing the boundary between the two, since *Othello* would count as belonging to the fictional-but-real. And those real people who appear in fictions, as Christopher Wren appears in *Hawksmoor,* would belong to the same category.

But there is another dimension we need to take into account. I shall suggest later that it is important to see a role for the interplay between character desires and narrative desires outside the realm of the fictional altogether; we construct and tell narratives about ourselves and about each other, and we have certain desires concerning the outcomes of those narratives—desires that can be in conflict with the desires we have concerning ourselves and each other. So we need to recognize the following categories:

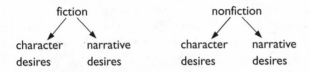

This has the advantage of displaying a symmetry between the fiction and the nonfiction cases that I shall come back to when I talk about immoral and pathological desires. But I need to represent yet another distinction. The desires I have concerning my friends and those I have concerning fictional characters differ not merely in belonging to different focus-groups; they differ also in such a way that one hesitates to call the ones concerning fictional characters *desires* at all. The problem is a familiar one: desires require a background of belief, which is lacking in the case of, say, Anna Karenina. I don't believe she exists, so I don't believe she can be harmed, so how can I desire her not to be harmed? And even if the fictional character is real, as with Wren, the character's plight in the story is one I don't believe the character concerned really was in. How can I worry/be concerned about someone in situation *S* when I don't believe they ever were in *S*?

This is a problem I've had my say on elsewhere, and I don't wish to impose an uncomfortable burden of theory by repeating that here.[4] Instead, I shall simply distinguish between desires *in the scope of an imagining,* and desires not so restricted. My desire that Anna Karenina thrive is in the scope of an imagining; my desire that my child thrive is not. There are additional complexities here: for example, I can have desires in the scope of imagining concerning my child, if my child becomes the subject of a little fictional story I tell myself about him. But to keep the picture manageable I will be satisfied with the following, which could be further articulated:

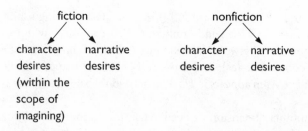

Notice that my narrative desires on the fiction side are never within the scope of an imagining (or so at least I shall assume, once again for the sake of a manageable taxonomy).[5] My desires concerning fictional narratives are desires backed by the right kinds of beliefs: I rightly believe *Casablanca* to be a real thing, and I have all sorts of appropriate beliefs about it.

A second issue that needs to be confronted in order to give us an adequate framework is the relation between desire and emotion. I focus here on desires, but much of what I shall say generalizes to cover at least many emotions. How are desire and emotion related? The question is complicated by the fact that "emotion" names a heterogeneous class of states, not all the members of which have essential connections with desires. Certain low-level emotions, like the startle response, for example, have causes and effects that bypass the cognitive parts of the mind (those that lead to decision and action), and hence are explicable without reference to desire or to belief.[6] At the other end of the scale, emotions become hard to distinguish from pure evaluations, as with deploring Michael Corleone's (Al Pacino) progressive moral anesthesia while at the same time somewhat unwillingly admiring his icy resourcefulness. At this end, emotions look like beliefs of an evaluative kind. In thinking about desire and the emotions it will be useful, therefore, to concentrate on certain cases of emotion: my rationally explicable fear of large, fierce, and unrestrained dogs, your anxiety about getting the Chair of Cultural Hermeneutics, Albert's jealousy of the handsome, wealthy, and talented Gustave.

One thing common to these cases is that they involve beliefs and desires: I believe the dog is a likely cause of harm to me and desire not be harmed, you desire the chair and believe you have only a limited chance of getting it, Albert desires possession of the qualities Gustave has and to which he, Albert, believes himself entitled. But in these cases, an emotion is not just a combination of beliefs and desires. It involves feelings as well, that is, states with *phenomenology*. It makes sense to ask, "What is it like to be afraid of that dog, anxious about the job, jealous of Gustave?"[7] Different feelings go with different emotions, and there is a debate about the extent to which a given emotion can have a feeling (or correlated activity in the nervous system) uniquely its own.[8] But once we take into account states with content (beliefs

Renault (Claude Rains), Victor (Paul Henreid), Rick (Humphrey Bogart),
and Ilsa (Ingrid Bergman) gather at Casablanca's airport in the final scene of
Casablanca (1942).

and desires) as well as states with phenomenology, we can discriminate emotions more finely than any plausible taxonomy of feeling can. Fearing the dog may feel no different from fearing a burglar or ill health, yet they are discriminable emotions. So feelings are, at most, constitutive of emotions; they are not identical with them.

If my fear of the dog gives me an unpleasant feeling, it is presumably in virtue of my believing that I am in danger from it and wishing not to be (simply imagining a threatening dog might do it as well: the kind of case I would describe as an emotion "within the scope of imagination"). So we might say that an emotion of this kind (in the occurrent rather than the dispositional sense) is an episode of causation: contentful states (beliefs and desires) causing states of feeling. And so desires are part of what we have to specify when we describe an episode of emotional disturbance.

But while desires are essential to emotions (or at least to the emotions I am concerned with here), desires can exist independently of emotions. They do so when they fail, as they often do, to cause significant feeling or affect.

Desire is therefore a more basic category of mental state than emotion is. But desire and belief, while distinct, are not so easily separated, either in definition or in fact. An explanation of belief presupposes the notion of desire, and vice versa,[9] and a creature with beliefs must necessarily have desires as well. A creature capable of actions needs two things: a representation of what the world is like and a representation of what it wants the world to be like. Only with those two things in place is it sensible to speak of the creature seeking to bring about a change in the world. The first representation constitutes the creature's belief-state (the totality of its beliefs), the second its desire-state. Take away either, and action is impossible, and without the capacity for action there is no room for either belief or desire.

Like desires, beliefs and emotions can lie within the scope of an imagining. Thinking I shall attend the faculty lunch today, wanting to stay in my room and work, and getting upset at the thought of the time wasted are examples of, respectively, real belief, desire, and emotion; thinking that Captain Renault underrates himself morally, wanting Rick not to give Victor away, and getting upset at the thought that he might are examples of, respectively, belief, desire, and emotion within the scope of imagining. So what I am going to say about desire, within and without the scope of imagining, could be said all over again about belief, and about emotion.

Character Desires, Narrative Desires

Go back to *Casablanca* and the satisfaction of desire. We want Ilsa and Rick to stay together, but we would be dissatisfied if things turned out that way. So we have a conflict in our desires—something that is relatively common. What sort of conflict is this? Perhaps it is of the common kind: we desire that lovers be united, but also that a marriage survive. We may also suspect that Victor will be a more effective opponent of the Nazis with Ilsa, and Rick a more effective one without her. All that conflict is describable within the confines of our thoughts about the action of the film: its events and characters. It is a conflict within what I am calling "character desires." It is also a case of what I called "desiring in imagination": Ilsa and Rick don't exist, their meeting in Paris never occurred, and we know that. We imagine these things, and it is within the scope of that imagining that we desire conflicting outcomes. But otherwise, the case as I describe it is structurally like the kind of conflict of desire we experience in real life, where there is a range of (real) alternatives that confront a group of (real) people, but where each alternative involves something we don't want.

Casablanca would be a more interesting case from my perspective if the viewer's conflict in desire was one that went beyond characters to include narrative. The cases that most obviously do this are cases of tragedy. We desire that Desdemona flourish, and that Othello see how Iago is duping him.

But an *Othello* in which these things happened would, other things being equal, be a worse play than the *Othello* we have. Here, the fact that we want Desdemona to flourish but would be disappointed if things turned out that way is not easily explained as a conflict within character desires. It is not as if there is strong reason describable in terms of the characters and events of the story for Desdemona being destroyed; she has, after all, done nothing wrong. To the extent that we desire the outcome that the play actually gives us—an outcome involving Desdemona's destruction—our desiring concerns narrative. It is the desire for a tragic narrative. We thus desire something which, if it is to be satisfied, requires the destruction of Desdemona, though that is not something we desire in itself. Here the conflict in desire is not a conflict structurally like the kinds of conflicts we most commonly find in our desires concerning real events and people, for it is a conflict between desiring something for a character and desiring something for a narrative.

The conflict is also notable insofar as *it is a conflict we find desirable*. A typical reaction to *Othello* is not adequately described by saying that the disappointment and anguish caused by witnessing Desdemona's destruction are compensated for by the satisfaction of our narrative desire, for the success of the play does not depend merely on the strength of our narrative desire being greater than that of our character desire. Rather, we seem to experience a further, higher order desire for there to be such a conflict, and for the conflicting desires to be resolved as the play resolves them. That desire is then wholly satisfied. Again, this is not commonly thought to be a feature of desire concerning real-world outcomes, whatever other complexities such desires may involve.

If a conflict in desire is wholly a matter of conflict within the class of character desires, then it is also wholly a matter of conflict among desires within the scope of the imagination. But if the conflict is, as with *Othello,* a conflict between character and narrative desires, then it is going to involve both real desires and desires within the scope of imagination. For narratives are real things and the desires we have concerning them are real desires. To desire that *Othello* be a narrative with a tragic ending is to desire a real-world outcome, one the satisfaction conditions of which are that a certain proposition, namely that *Othello* have a tragic ending, be true. And indeed this proposition is true. But character desires are not like that. My desiring that Desdemona flourish is not a desire that is satisfied if it is true that Desdemona flourishes: since Desdemona doesn't exist, that proposition isn't—and couldn't be—true. That desire is satisfied if it is part of the narrative of *Othello* that Desdemona flourish. This distinction gives us a way of characterizing what it is for a desire to be within the scope of imagining. A desire that *P* occur is within the scope of imagining if and only if the satisfaction of the desire depends, not on it being true that *P,* but on it being part of a narrative that *P.*

Questioning the Distinction

Someone might question my distinction between character and narrative desires, saying that all the desires we have in relation to fiction are narrative desires. They might argue this way: a desire to the effect that the hero do X is really a desire to the effect that the narrative make it so that the hero do X. Characters are not, after all, autonomous beings; they are imaginary creatures who have no existence outside the narratives in which their activities are described.

But this admirably simplifying proposal cannot be right. What we commonly call "wanting Cordelia to be saved" cannot really be a case of wanting it to be the case that the narrative of *King Lear* has it that Cordelia is saved, for that desire would be satisfied by the discovery that the authorship of Shakespeare's version and Nahum Tate's had been transposed. Wanting it to be the case that the narrative of *Lear* has it that Cordelia is saved is certainly a desire—Dr. Johnson seems to have possessed it[10]—but it is not the desire most of us recall after the performance when we say that Cordelia's death is shocking and horrible. Our desire is one within the scope of an imagining. We imagine that Cordelia and the others are real, that their fates are undecided (or at least unknown to us) until they are revealed on stage.

Tragedy indicates that at least some cases of conflict in desire provoked by fictions are cases involving character as well as narrative desires. I said that *Casablanca* might not be a case like that, that our response to it may be fully describable as a case of conflict within the class of character desires. But if we do recognize cases—like *Othello*—of conflict involving desires of both kinds, it is not implausible to suppose that even *Casablanca* is, to some extent, a mixed case. Even if Victor were dead and Rick's usefulness to the Resistance not compromised by his liaison with Ilsa, wouldn't we still want them to separate at the end of the movie? Wouldn't that still be in some sense the more interesting, the more satisfactory, and hence the more desirable outcome? But even if the answer is no, conflicts between character desires and narrative desires of one kind or another are common in fairly standard filmic narratives; they are not the exclusive domain of elevated tragedy.

As Noël Carroll has emphasized, filmic and other narratives standardly operate by raising and answering questions.[11] And the questions that narratives raise serve to hold our attention only so long as we have a stake in the answer. We have to desire, to some significant degree, that things turn out one way for a character rather than another in order to be held by the question whether they will turn out that way. And that, very often, is how it is with us when we confront a narrative.

But here as elsewhere we don't simply desire outcomes: we desire knowledge of them also. If we desire happiness for the character, we typically desire the knowledge that the character is happy. But such desires for knowledge are typically narrative desires and not character desires, for we do not think of ourselves as in a position to learn from the characters themselves about their fates. We expect instead to learn about these things *from the narrative*. That, at least, is my view, but I am sorry to say that it is not very widely shared. Writers on film, and on fiction generally, often say that the viewer imagines herself to be in a position to learn about and from the characters directly rather than via the mediation of the narrative. I shall discuss two expositions of this view, both of which are interesting because they, quite unusually, adduce experimental evidence in favor of this view instead of simply assuming that the view is correct.

Richard Gerrig and Deborah Prentice have recently suggested that the viewer of the film is best thought of as occupying (in imagination) the position of a *side-participant,* as Captain Renault is a side-participant in the final conversation between Rick and Ilsa in *Casablanca.* This is, to say the least, an implausible suggestion. Gerrig and Prentice say that it is a "defining criterion" for the possession of the role of side-participant that "the speaker formulates his or her utterance with the specific intention that the side-participant be informed."[12] But if anything is certain about the fictional world of *Casablanca* it is that the conversational exchanges between Rick and Ilsa here (as elsewhere in the film) are not intended by them to be heard *by us.* On the contrary, it is fictional in that story that much of what they say is utterly private and would not be said if they thought they were being overheard by a vast audience of strangers. Further, it does not seem likely that we imagine ourselves as side-participants in these exchanges; if we did our response would very likely be one of embarrassment, or confusion about how, if at all, we ought to respond.

Now, somewhat puzzlingly, Gerrig and Prentice admit that "the intention to inform us is, of course, not Rick's—he doesn't know we exist."[13] How could this be consistent with their claim that we are side-participants, given that on their account it is definitive of side-participation that "the speaker formulates his or her utterance with the specific intention that the side-participant be informed"? Gerrig and Prentice go on to say that the scriptwriter or director is the real source of the intention, but that "we behave as if Rick had intentions with respect to us." Two things could be meant here. The first is that, irrespective of what is going on in our minds, our behavior is that of people who are side-participants in conversations. But this reading—though it is strongly suggested by their words—is a nonstarter because viewers of film engage in almost no *behavior* that would be relevant one way or another to deciding this issue. The second is that, while we know that Rick is not really intending to address us, we imagine that he is. But I have already argued that we do not imagine this. Importing that act of imagining would be entirely out of keeping with the rest of what we are to imagine. For example, we are to imagine that at least a good deal of the time Rick and Ilsa speak in private, or at least only within the hearing of one or two others. We are quite clearly *not* to imagine that they are knowingly speaking in our presence.

Gerrig and Prentice claim to have empirical support for their view. They conducted an experiment in which they had their subjects read a passage from a fictional story designed to induce in them a desire that one of the characters be punished. In a second excerpt, subjects discovered that the character was punished—but in a much more alarming way than one would expect, given the first extract. Subsequent testing then suggested that subjects who had desired revenge now felt guilty in light of the harm done the character. But of what relevance is this to the specific thesis that Gerrig and Prentice offer? Surely the evidence supports only the weak claim that consumers of fiction do have desires and emotions concerning fictional characters very like the desires and emotions they have concerning real people, with the same potentiality for regret and other responses. The evidence says nothing about whether—and, if so, how—such consumers, in experiencing these desires and emotions, conceptualize the source of their information about the characters.

A theory similar to that of Gerrig and Prentice has been offered by Paul Harris. Harris argues that the familiar psychological state of being absorbed by a fiction is to be explained in terms of the audience adopting an imaginary point of view within the world of the fiction: a point of view "relative to the geography and the temporal sequence of events within the narrative."[14] In support of this Harris cites the following experimental data:

1. Morrow and colleagues showed that subjects reading that a character is moving from room to room were quicker to answer questions about the room to be entered rather than about the room just left, and even slower to answer questions about the rooms not on the itinerary.[15]

2. Glenberg and colleagues showed that subjects reading about an athlete running round a track were able to answer the question whether the word "sweatshirt" had occurred in the narrative more quickly if the runner had, according to the story, put on rather than taken off the sweatshirt before beginning the run.[16]

3. Black and colleagues presented subjects with the sentence "Bill was in the living room reading the evening paper." These subjects subsequently read sentence (a) faster than sentence (b):
   (a) Before Bill had finished the paper, John came into the room.
   (b) Before Bill had finished the paper, John went into the room.[17]

It will be good at this point to have some labels for the competing theories. Let us call the theory espoused by Gerrig and Prentice and by Harris the *direct* theory, because it says that we imagine ourselves directly related to the characters and events of the story. And let us call the theory I adopt the *nondirect* theory, because it denies this. How do the data just described relate to our two theories? I claim that the evidence does not favor one of these theories over the other. It is *common ground* between the two theories that readers are "cognitively focused" (Harris's phrase) on the events described in the narratives they read. In particular, the advocate of the nondirect theory does not claim that the reader has no interest in or concern for the characters and events of the fiction; she claims only that in being interested in and concerned about those characters and events the reader does not imagine being located at the places and times where the characters and events are located.

Consider the cases of the character moving from room to room. If I am engaged by the fiction, my attention shifts from (fictional) place to (fictional) place as the character moves, and may—as seems to be the case here—run ahead of the character, anticipating his destination. But it does not follow that I am imagining being in the room on which my attention is focused. Similarly, if I am imagining the athlete running, and he is said to be wearing a sweatshirt as he runs, then as I imagine him running I shall (if I am attentive) imagine him running in a sweatshirt. I need not imagine myself where he is in order to be cognitively focused on the sweatshirt sufficiently for it to affect my response to a question about that item. In other words, we have to distinguish between the issue, "On what is the reader cognitively focused in the story?" and the issue, "Where, if anywhere, does the reader imagine himself to be located?"

Case 3, however, is at first sight more problematic for the hypothesis of impersonal imagining that the other two cases. For the difference between sentences *a* and *b* concerns an indexical expression; *a* differs from *b* in that it contains the indexical expression "came" rather than "went." Indexical expressions—like "I," "here," and "now"—contribute to the truth conditions of sentences in a way which depends on facts about the speaker. Thus the referent of "I" shifts according to the identity of the speaker, and the referent of "here" shifts according to the location of the speaker. Similarly, if I say that someone *came* into the room, this has to be understood as meaning "entered the room I was in at that time," whereas if I said that he *went* into the room I would be saying that he was moving away from my location, or so you might suppose. In that case, subjects being (apparently) more tuned into *a* than to *b* would seem to be best explained in terms of *a*'s more adequately reflecting their own (imagined) perspective on the action than *b* does.

This is certainly one explanation for the result, and I assume it is the one that Harris adopts because it is the explanation that favors the direct theory. But I do not believe it is the only possible explanation. I begin by noting that we do, in fact, quite commonly use expressions like "came" and "went," not in reference to our own location but in reference to the location of another, in situations where it is not likely that we are imagining ourselves to be in those locations. Suppose my friend Norbert has told me about a visit he had from the dean, just at the moment when he, Norbert, was smoking a cigar, an activity banned in our building. In reporting these events it would be very natural for me to say, "At that moment the dean came in," and very unnatural for me to say, "At that moment the dean went in." Would this be because I was imagining being there? This seems hardly plausible. Norbert's story is sober truth rather than fiction, and I believe that "came" rather than "went" would be the appropriate term whether I was imagining this or not. And the reason, once again, that "came" would be appropriate here is surely that the way I am telling the story causes the hearer to be cognitively focused on what is going on in Norbert's room.

In that case, the subjects' preferred readiness for *a* over *b* need not be explained by supposing that the subjects imagined themselves to be where Bill was. However, this claim of mine ought to be relatively easy to test. While it would be natural, in retelling Norbert's story about the dean, for me to say "came" rather than "went" it would *not* be natural for me to say, for example, "the dean came here" (assuming that, as I tell the story, I am not in Norbert's room). However, if Harris is right that readers of the Bill-story imagine themselves to be where Bill is, they ought to respond preferentially to, say,

(a) Bill was reading the paper here,

over

(b) Bill was reading the paper there.

I predict that they would not. I predict that, if anything, readers would find *b* more natural than *a*. I conclude that none of the evidence cited by either Gerrig and Prentice or by Harris supports the direct theory over the nondirect theory.

Narratives and Real Lives

I have been speaking as if narratives and narrative desires are something that we need take account of only in regard to fictions. Obviously enough this is not so; there are, for example, nonfictional narratives, and one can have desires concerning how they will turn out. What is perhaps not so obvious is whether narrative desires in these kinds of cases are capable of having the same kind of independence from our desires about real people that our narrative desires (where the narrative is fiction) can have from our desires about fictional characters. I may desire that tomorrow's paper bring good news about the hostage crisis, but I have that desire because I wish the hostages well. In this case, what I really want is something for a person, and what I desire about a narrative is dictated by that. We have seen that that is not how it is with *Othello*. But in real life (as well as in fiction) there is the *Emma* phenomenon. Emma Woodhouse might resist the suggestion that she had anything but the interests of the parties concerned at heart, but we may suspect that those people are to some extent characters in a narrative of her designing, that at least part of what she wants is a certain outcome to the narrative which is not simply the product of the overall best for the characters as Emma judges it—that, after all, is what makes Emma's behavior morally troubling. And so it frequently is with us: we want, to some degree, a narrative outcome that goes against the interests of the protagonists.

More troubling still would be cases of genuine narrative pathology. Jon Jureideni at Women's and Children's Hospital in Adelaide is developing a theory of the rare condition unsatisfactorily called Munchhausen's by proxy syndrome. Jureideni argues that the condition involves a pathological form of narrative desire; a baby is ruthlessly recruited to play a role in a narrative of illness, medical emergency, and heroic intervention within which the perpetrator plays a starring role. It is an important part of this proposal that the perpetrator (mostly, so far as we know, the mother) need not wish harm on the infant; rather, she is in the grip of a narrative desire strong enough to overcome resistance to the dire consequences of the narrative's enactment, much as we, safely within the scope of an imagining, are prepared to sacrifice Desdemona for a well-wrought narrative.

Someone might question my transfer of narrative to things and events of the real world. To speak of narrative desires in connection with the fictional is unproblematic, because fictional things and events generally have no existence outside the narrative. But for anyone but the most extreme antirealist, this is not so of real things and events. You and I are not characters within a story in anything like the sense that Holmes and Watson are. So what justifies us in carrying over the character/narrative distinction from fiction to the real world?

The answer must be in terms of the explanatory power of the theory that results, and there do seem to be cases that are illuminated by the transfer; I take it that Emma-style cases show that, and so may pathologies like Munchausen's by proxy syndrome. Rather more difficult is the question, "How can we characterize narrative desire in such a way that the notion does not collapse into triviality?" If we say, for example, that desire is narrative when its possession is in some way dependent on telling stories, most desires will turn out to be narrative simply because testimony plays such an important part in belief-formation, and desires always require a background of belief. This is a complicated issue deserving extended treatment it cannot receive here, but this is a first shot at a more discriminating characterization.[18]

Emma wishes Harriet and Mr. Elton to marry, and her so desiring is a case of narrative desiring on the following grounds. First of all, it is an instrumental desire: a desire she has, not (or not wholly) for that outcome itself, but because that outcome will facilitate other outcomes that are desired for themselves. Second, those other outcomes are of two distinctive kinds. One is that Harriet marrying Mr. Elton should take its place in a *pattern* of likewise desired events; part of the pattern in this case is that Emma should have brought it about that Harriet marries Mr. Elton. The other is that this pattern of events should be *known about by Emma*. So my preliminary proposal, stated generally, is that the desire that *P* is a narrative desire if that desire subserves the desire that there be a pattern of events of which *P* is a constituent, and that this pattern should be an object of knowledge.[19] Such a characterization avoids trivializing the idea of narrative desire, but it is still a relatively undemanding one. It is possible, in this characterization, for someone to have a narrative desire without possessing the concept of narrative.

Can we also say something about the circumstances under which narrative desires concerning real-world things take on a pathological or at least morally troubling aspect? The question is an important one for us, because one aim of this chapter is to probe the ways in which desires that are unproblematic in a fictional context may become problematic in a real-world setting.

The best answer I can give at the moment is this: A sufficient (but not a necessary) condition for a narrative desire concerning real-world things to be troubling is that it should lead to an action that *either* the agent recognizes is against the interests of that character (and which therefore may also override a narrative desire the agent has) or that the agent could reasonably be expected to recognize is against the interests of that character. Whether Emma's fault is describable in terms of the first disjunct or the second is perhaps unclear; if Jureideni is right, the agent whose action displays Munchausen's by proxy syndrome is deficient in the second way. With both kinds of case, the contrast with fiction is striking: there does not seem to be anything troubling about wanting, on balance, that *Othello* should make it the case that Desdemona is destroyed while wanting, but less intensely, that Othello not destroy Desdemona.

I have indicated an asymmetry between fiction and nonfiction narrative desires. In some writing on narrative there is a tendency to downplay that asymmetry. It is important, therefore, to insist upon it. The relation between narratives and characters in the fiction case is quite different in one important respect from the relation between narratives and characters in the nonfiction case. It may be that we are doing whatever we are doing partly because we are telling (or have told) ourselves, or each other, or someone stories about what we plan to do; if the story was absent or different we might be doing different things; it is not the case that without the story we could not be here.

But without *Casablanca*, there is no Rick, no Ilsa, and no question about what they will do. In the real world, narrative and action are causally related; in fiction the one is logically dependent on the other.

Changing Desire

So far I have considered narrative desires in a fictional setting, and in the setting of real people and events. Let us, finally, bring these two together. How might the experience of fiction change our desires outside the context of the fictions they present? How, in particular, might fiction (especially filmic fiction) change the desires I have concerning real people and events? In many ways: By making available thought-contents that were not previously available to the subject; by vividly depicting a state of affairs and thus giving specificity to a previously inchoate desire; by depicting a certain state of affairs and eliciting a pleasurable sensation from the viewer, causing the viewer to desire a state of affairs relevantly similar to the depicted one. I would like to focus here on one other way that movies can bring about change in desire, because it connects with what I take to be an important fact about the nature of imagination.

If we think of the imagination as a private inner world quite cut off from reality and without implications for behavior, it is possible to defend a strongly liberal conception of the mimetic arts by insisting that such arts engage the imagination alone. But if we think once again in evolutionary terms, this is unlikely. A complex mental organ like the imagination is not likely to be disconnected from our capacity to act; if it were, it is hard to see how the imagination could have contributed to our fitness. True, not every feature so contributes: the heaviness of the polar bear's coat slows him down and makes it harder to catch prey; it is there because engineering a warm coat required weight.[20] But it does not seem that way with the imagination. I suggest that the imagination is a mechanism designed to help us improve our performance.

It is worth noting, first of all, that the imagination is a capacity not wholly divorced from our capacity to act. Sometimes what we can imagine reflects our own physical limitations, as can be seen in the case of people with certain kinds of restricted physical capacities due to brain lesions. When patients with impairment on one side of the body due to Parkinson's disease are asked to report the speed at which they can imagine performing a finger-sequencing exercise for both hands, they report a slower speed in imagination for the impaired hand, and the time differences for these imagined cases closely match the time differences for their actual performance. Also, imagining doing things can make it easier for us actually to do those things, a fact often exploited by athletes seeking to improve their performance. Astonishingly, imagining undertaking physical exercise can, in the right circumstances, re-

sult in increases in maximal muscle force comparable to (though less than)
the increases produced by actually exercising! And there are many skills besides directly athletic ones which seem to benefit from practice *in imagination* as well as in reality.[21] These connections between imagining moving and
really moving are paralleled in the case of imagined experience: imagining
seeing and attending to things has all sorts of effects on one's capacity actually to see and attend to them.[22] In that case it might be (though I know of
no direct evidence for this) that *desiring* things in the imagination (the sort
of desiring involved in narrative desires) has connections with one's tendency actually to desire them. In particular, desiring something in imagination might make one more prone to desire it in reality. If we suppose, plausibly, that it is relatively common for people to desire, to some (perhaps very
limited) degree, to do things they know or believe are wicked, then works of
fiction that encourage us to desire wicked things in imagination (to desire
that someone suffer or be humiliated) may have the effect of strengthening
those wicked desires to the point where they become the desires on which
the agent is prepared to act.

There are further possibilities. Might narrative desires be harmful in themselves rather than because they lead to other directly harmful desires? If we
focus on cases like wanting *Othello* to be a narrative in which Desdemona
suffers, the answer seems to be no: there is nothing directly harmful about
that. But suppose the narratives we read and watch suggest to us *other* narratives: narratives in which *we* play roles, and in which *others* play roles at our
behest, perhaps in situations of coercion? Kendall Walton has emphasized
how games of make-believe—games that involve playing out a narrative,
though sometimes a spontaneous and relatively unstructured one—can be
made more vivid by the introduction of props.[23] Walton's primary examples
of props are inanimate things like snowmen and hobbyhorses. But children
sometimes recruit other people as props in their games; Daddy might be a
bridge over which the explorers imagine walking, and the explorers might,
to make their enactment of the bridge-walking narrative more vivid, really
walk over Daddy. Indeed, anyone who acts out a part in a narrative of my
choosing can be considered a prop, be their part an active or a passive one.
Now in any case where we recruit a person to our purpose, the possibility
arises that there is coercion involved. If certain kinds of movies and other
fictions (examples come readily to mind) are capable of prompting the desire
to reenact that narrative, and if the narrative involved requires or would at
least be rendered more vivid by the participation of someone in a degrading
role, then there could be cases where a person's degradation arises, coerced
or not, from a narrative desire.

Conclusion

In thinking about film and desire it is important to be clear what kinds of desires we have in mind. I have suggested a taxonomy of such kinds, and some connections between them. And I have also suggested that desiring in relation to filmic and other fictional narratives needs to be seen in the context of a theory about the natural capacities and functions of the imagination.

TEN

Identification and Emotion
in Narrative Film

BERYS GAUT

When film viewers are asked to describe their emotional reactions to films they often appeal to the notion of identification. They say things such as "I could really identify with that character," "the film was no good: there wasn't a single character I could identify with," or "I felt so badly about what happened to her, because I strongly identified with her." It is part of the folk wisdom of responding to films (and to literature) that audiences sometimes identify with characters, that the success or failure of a film partly depends on whether this identification occurs, and that the quality and strength of emotional responses depend on identification. It seems that any theorist interested in our emotional reactions to films must give an account of the nature of this process of identification and explain its importance in shaping responses. And there would appear to be no room for denying the existence and importance of spectatorial identification.

Yet film theory has exhibited a curious reaction to this folk wisdom. On the one hand psychoanalytically inspired theories have responded positively to these claims but treated them in hyperbolic fashion. Drawing on Lacan, such theories hold that the child is constituted as a subject through an act of identification with her own image in the mirror at the age of 6 to 18 months; the power of cinema in giving an impression of reality and as an ideological device lies in its ability to re-enact this basic process of identification. Film identification according to Jean-Louis Baudry has a dual aspect:

> One can distinguish two levels of identification. The first, attached to the image itself, derives from the character portrayed as a center of secondary identifications, carrying an identity which constantly must be seized and re-established. The second level permits the appearance of the first and places it "in action"— this is the transcendental subject whose place is taken by the camera which constitutes and rules the objects in the "world."[1]

While they acknowledge the existence of character identification central to the folk theory, psychoanalytic theories thus demote it to a secondary status. The notion of the identification of the viewer with an invisible observer becomes central, an identification that constitutes the identity of the viewer as an illusorily unified, ideological subject. Besides this sidelining of the notion of character identification, the dominant trend in psychoanalytic theories also departs from the folk view in regarding the viewer as becoming a fetishist, sadist, and voyeur through his acts of identification.[2]

Those film theorists and philosophers who draw on analytical philosophy and cognitive science generally have little time for such psychoanalytic construals of spectators' responses. But rather than simply stripping out the psychoanalytic components from the notion of identification, they have in most cases rejected the claim that identification occurs at all. Noël Carroll writes that "identification . . . is not the correct model for describing the emotional responses of spectators";[3] Gregory Currie argues that identification does not occur in the point-of-view shot;[4] and even Murray Smith, who has some sympathy with the idea of identification, generally presents his own concept of engagement not as an analysis of identification but as an improved concept with which to replace it.[5]

This suspicion of the notion of identification by theorists of a cognitivist stripe is striking given the widespread use of it in ordinary viewers' reports of their interactions with films, and indeed of the use of the notion more generally in ordinary life, as when we talk of identifying with our friends. And it also fuels the accusation by psychoanalytic theorists that the cognitive paradigm is peculiarly unsuited to account for emotional responses to films. For if the cognitive view rejects appeal to a central notion required to explicate spectators' emotions, how can it give an adequate account of those emotions?

This, then, is the situation that confronts anyone interested in the notion of identification in film. The task of this chapter is to rehabilitate the notion of identification for cognitivist theories of film, to show that the notion does not suffer from the deep conceptual confusions alleged against it, and to demonstrate that it has explanatory power in accounting for spectators' emotional responses to films. The argument will require several new distinctions to be drawn, but these involve refining the notion of identification, not abandoning it.

The Concept of Identification

The notion of identification can seem deeply odd. Its etymological root is of "making identical." Thus it would seem that when I identify with a character I merge my identity with his, which would "require some sort of curious metaphysical process, like Mr. Spock's Vulcan mind-meld, between the audience member and the protagonist."[6] This is not just deeply odd but actually impossible: two people cannot be made (numerically) the same without ceasing to exist. But here, as quite generally, etymology is a bad guide to meaning. Any argument exploiting this etymology to show that identification does not exist would be like an argument that noted that "television" has as its etymological root "seeing at a distance," argued that we do not literally see things at a distance when we look at a television screen, but only their images, and concluded that televisions do not exist. The question is not what the etymology of the term is but of what it means, and the meaning of a term is a matter of its use in the language.

So how do we use the term "identification" when we apply it to a character in a fiction? One use is simply to say that one cares for the character. To say that there is no one in a film with whom one can identify is simply in this usage to report that one does not care about what happens to any of the characters. But in such a use, the fact that I identify with a character cannot *explain* why I care for her, for such a purported explanation would be entirely vacuous. The natural thought here is that identification in the explanatory sense is a matter of putting oneself in the character's shoes, and because one does so one may come to care for her. But what is this notion of placing oneself in someone else's position?

Psychoanalytic and Brechtian theories, given their belief in mainstream cinema as a form of illusionism, might naturally hold that just as the viewer is somehow under the illusion that the cinematic events are real, so she is somehow under the illusion that she is the character with whom she identifies. But that would credit the viewer of a film with an extraordinary degree of irrationality; it would hold that she does not believe that she is sitting safely in the dark, as is clearly the case, but that she believes she is swinging from a rope on a mountaintop, or shooting at villains, or otherwise doing whatever the film represents the character as doing.

A more plausible version of this story would hold that a "suspension of disbelief" occurs in the cinema: the viewer believes that she is not the fictional character, but that belief is somehow bracketed from her motivational set. In such cases the viewer reacts *as if* she believes that she is the character depicted, even though she does not in fact believe this to be the case. But then many of the viewer's reactions to the film fail to make sense under this assumption: for instance, since characters in horror films rarely want to suffer the terrors that torment them, viewers who identify with these characters should storm out of the exits at the first appearance of these films, for on this construal of identification they should react as if they believed they were these characters.[7]

A better version of the identification view would hold, rather, that the viewer *imagines* herself to be the character with whom she identifies. This, then, is part of the explanation of why she comes to care for the character, if she indeed does. But this formulation raises new worries, for it may be objected that it makes no sense to talk about imagining oneself to be someone else. Arguably there are no possible worlds in which I am identical with some other person—they are simply worlds in which I possess that other person's properties without being him. So how can I imagine being another person? Similar worries apply if one holds that it makes no sense to think that I could be different in some radical way from the person I am (I could not have been a tenth-century female Eskimo, for instance). The reply is that even if one accepted claims of this kind, it would not follow that one could not imagine things that the claims hold are impossible. We can, in fact, imagine things that are not just metaphysically but even logically impossible—for instance, that Hobbes actually did square the circle (as at one time he thought he had done). And we do that not infrequently in responding to fiction—we may be asked to imagine people going back in time and conceiving themselves, we may be asked to imagine werewolves, or people turning into trees, or intelligent, talkative rats complaining about lordly, overbearing toads.

However, there is still a problem with holding that one imagines oneself to be another person when one identifies with him. As Richard Wollheim has noted, if I imagine myself to be a particular character (say, Jeeves), then since identity is a symmetrical relation, this is equivalent to the claim that I imagine Jeeves to be me. But the two imaginings are very different projects: in the former case I imagine myself in Jeeves's position, serving and manipulating Bertie Wooster; in the second case I imagine Jeeves surreptitiously taking over my life, and I become disconcertingly butler-like.[8]

What we should conclude from this is that the act of imaginative identification involves imagining—not, strictly speaking, being that other person, but rather imagining being in her situation, where the idea of her situation encompasses every property she possesses, including all her physical and psychological traits (so we imagine the world from her physical and psychological perspective). Hence what I do in imaginatively identifying myself with Jeeves is imagining being in his situation, doing what he does, feeling what he does, and so on. And that is clearly different from imagining Jeeves being in my situation.

Wollheim has objected to this construal of identification: he holds that since I do not imagine myself to be identical to Jeeves, the account would allow me while imagining myself in his situation to imagine meeting him, which my imaginative project surely rules out.[9] And it is indeed true that my imaginative project rules this out, but that is in fact compatible with imagining myself to be in Jeeves's situation. For as we have understood the notion of a person's situation, it comprises all of his properties; these include not just his contingent properties but also his modal properties, such as necessarily not being a number, necessarily having the potential for self-consciousness, and necessarily not being able to meet himself. Thus Jeeves (fictionally) has the property of necessarily not being able to meet himself, that is, necessarily not being able to meet Jeeves. Hence, were the question raised of whether I could properly imagine myself meeting Jeeves when I am imagining myself in his situation, I ought to rule out imagining meeting him. For I ought to imagine possessing those of his properties which are relevant to this situation, in particular the modal property of being unable to meet Jeeves. Thus Wollheim's rejection of the account of identification in terms of imagining oneself in another's situation looks plausible only on an overly narrow understanding of someone's situation that excludes certain of his modal properties.

This account of identification also fits how we talk of imaginative acts. We frequently talk of understanding someone by imagining ourselves in her situation, of putting ourselves in her shoes. And we come to understand her by imaginatively projecting ourselves into her external situation, imaginarily altering those aspects of our personalities which differ from hers, and then relying on our dispositions to respond in various ways, so as to work out what other things she might reasonably be supposed to be feeling.[10]

Even on this construal of imaginative identification, however, the idea that identification occurs in films seems to encounter fundamental difficulties. It is often supposed that one of the central cases of cinematic identification is when we are shown a point-of-view shot; here surely we are asked to identify with a character: we literally take up her perspective. But this claim has met with a barrage of objections. Currie has urged that if identification occurred in the point-of-view shot, then the viewer would have to imagine that what happens to the character happens to her and that she possesses the most obvious and dramatically salient characteristics of the character, and it would have to be that she has or imagines she has some concern with and sympathy for the values and projects of the character. But none of these, says Currie, need be the case. I often do not imagine any of the events happening to the character happening to myself, nor do I imagine myself having any of his characteristics, nor need I have the least sympathy with him—consider, for instance, the frequent use of point-of-view shots in horror films, taken from the perspective of the killer.[11] Smith has also argued that the point-of-view shot need not give access to the character's subjectivity: indeed, the point-of-view shot in horror films often functions to disguise the killer's identity.[12]

These points about point-of-view shots are well taken, but they do not force us to abandon the claim that identification can occur in such cases. Once we construe identification as a matter of imagining oneself in a character's situation, the issue becomes pertinent of *which aspects* of the character's situation one imagines oneself in. As we have seen, we should construe the situation of the character in terms of what properties she possesses. Her physical properties include her size, physical position, the physical aspects of her actions, and so on. Her psychological properties can be thought of in terms of her perspective on the (fictional) world. But that perspective is not just a visual one (how things look to her); we can also think of the character as possessing an affective perspective on events (how she feels about them), a motivational perspective (what she is motivated to do in respect of them), an epistemic perspective (what she believes about them), and so forth. Thus the question to ask whenever someone talks of identifying with a character is *in what respects* does she identify with the character? The act of identification is aspectual. To identify perceptually with a character is to imagine seeing from his point of view; to identify affectively with him is to imagine feeling what he feels; to identify motivationally is to imagine wanting what he wants; to identify epistemically with him is to imagine believing what he believes, and so on. What the objections rehearsed above force us to see is that just because one is identifying perceptually with the character, it does not follow that one is identifying motivationally or affectively with him, nor does it follow that one imagines that one has his physical characteristics.

This may seem to distort the concept of identification. Surely, it will be urged that the notion of identification is a global concept that is, we imagine, being in that person's situation in all respects, and in talking of aspectual identification we are in effect abandoning the notion of identification.

On the contrary, if identification were global, it could not in practice occur. Even a fictional character has an indeterminately large number of properties (most of which will be implicit, not explicitly stated by the text or film), and a real person has an infinite number of such properties. It would not be possible to imagine oneself as possessing all of these properties. And, of course, one does not do so: one picks on those characteristics that are relevant for the purpose of one's imagining. Nor should someone hold that even though one does not imagine all these properties holding of oneself, one ought to do so. For even if one held (which I earlier argued against) that identification with a character requires you to imagine being identical with that character, it is not in general true that one is required to imagine all of the consequences of one's imaginings. As Kendall Walton has pointed out, very often fiction requires you not to imagine such consequences; Othello speaks extraordinarily poetic verse, while saying that he is plain of speech, and yet no one notices this. Why is this so? To raise the question would be to ask a "silly question"; even though in the real world there would be an answer to this question, there is no answer in the world of the fiction.[13] What we are to imagine is shaped by the knowledge that we are looking at an artifact designed to prescribe certain imaginings, and our imaginings are shaped by the demands of the context.

It has sometimes been objected that the idea of identification is much too crude a notion, reducing the possibilities of our relations to characters to either being identified with a character or distanced from her, and thus we need to abandon the notion.[14] Once we recognize the existence of aspectual identification, we can see that recognition of these complexities is well within the grip of the notion of identification. Since we have distinguished different aspects of identification, we can hold that the fact that we are perceptually identified with a character does not entail that we are affectively identified with her—the fact that we are imagining seeing from her perspective does not *require* us to imagine wanting what she wants, or imagine feeling what she feels. It then becomes a matter of substantive theorizing to investigate under what conditions one form of identification fosters another. It would be surprising, given the complexity of film art in general, if one could find any invariant, law-like principles for linking different aspects of identification together. But that leaves plenty of space for investigating how one form of identification may tend (other things being equal) to promote another form, or for how certain film techniques may tend to enhance some kinds of identification.

So far we have been following out the implications of the thought that identification involves imagining oneself in another's situation. This idea of imaginative identification is, however, not exhaustive of all that people mean when they talk of identification. Consider the idea of empathy, which is naturally thought of as a kind of identification, and a very important one at that. If someone has a parent die, identifying with the bereaved person characteristically takes the form of taking on her feelings, sharing them ("I feel your pain," "I know what it's like to undergo that loss"). But note that this is different from the notion of affective identification as we have characterized it. That required the viewer to *imagine* feeling what a person (or a character fictionally) feels; empathy requires the viewer *actually* to feel what a person (or a character fictionally) feels.

Now it is plausible that empathy requires one imaginatively to enter into a character's mind and to feel with him because of one's imagining of his situation.[15] But that is to say that empathic identification requires some form of imaginative identification; it is not to conflate the two phenomena. It is possible to identify with a character affectively, imagining his sorrow, anger, or fear, yet not empathize with him, since one does not actually feel sorrowful, angry, or afraid with him. In fact, it is only those theorists who allow for the possibility of feeling real emotions toward merely imagined situations who can even allow for the existence of empathic identification with fictional characters (though they can, of course, allow for such identification with real people). The idea of empathic identification is that one feels toward the situation that confronts the character what the character (fictionally) feels toward it; and since that situation is merely fictional, the possibility of real emotions directed toward situations known merely to be fictional must be allowed.[16]

The final notion we need to discuss is that of sympathy. As earlier noted, sometimes to talk of identification with a character is simply to say that one sympathizes with him. But if we want to retain identification as an explanatory concept, we should mark this off as a distinct usage. And, in fact, sympathy and empathic identification are distinct notions. To sympathize with a character is in a broad sense to care for him, to be concerned for him. (We need not care for him merely because he is suffering sympathy in the narrow sense since one can talk, for instance, of having sympathy with the goals of a political party, even though that party is not suffering.) This care can be manifested in a variety of mental states: fearing for what may befall him, getting angry on his behalf, pitying him, feeling elated at his triumphs, and so forth. These states need have no relation to what he is feeling: I may pity him because he has been knocked into a coma in a road accident and is feeling nothing; I may be angry on his behalf for what has been done to him, even though he may be stoical about it; I may fear for what will befall him, even though he is sublimely unaware of the imminent danger in which he stands. Empathy, in contrast, requires one to share in the feelings one ascribes to him: I am empathically angry if and only if (I believe or imagine) that he is angry, and the thought of his anger controls and guides the formation of my anger.[17] So if he is in a coma and not feeling anything, nothing counts as empathizing with him. Since most people are concerned for themselves, empathizing with them will involve sharing this concern, and hence sympathizing with them. But the co-occurrence of sympathy and empathy is contingent on the psychology of the person with whom we are empathizing and sympathizing, rather than showing that these two kinds of dispositions to feel are the same.

These distinctions also allow us to answer an influential objection to the idea of identification advanced by Carroll. Carroll holds that identification with a character requires one to feel what she is feeling. But, he points out, the correspondence between what the viewer feels and what a character feels is normally at most a partial one. A woman is swimming in the sea, unaware that she is in imminent danger of attack by a shark: she is happy, we are tense and fearful. Oedipus feels guilt for what he has done: we do not feel guilt, but pity him. And Carroll holds that a partial correspondence of feelings is insufficient for identification.[18]

Insofar as Carroll is discussing the notion of identification here, it must be that of empathic identification, for he is discussing what the audience actually feels, not just what it imagines feeling. So, even if successful, his critique does not undermine the notion of imaginative identification. Moreover, because we have seen that the activity of identification is always aspectual (and therefore partial), it cannot be an objection to identification that the correspondences between what the audience is feeling and what the characters are fictionally feeling are only partial. For identification always is partial.[19] Further, what Carroll's examples show is that our responses to characters' situations are often sympathetic (we are concerned at the swimmer's situation, even though she does not recognize the danger and so feels no fear), rather than empathic. But this point hardly shows that empathy never occurs: when the swimmer does recognize the danger and panics, we then share her fear.

Carroll objects to this last move: he holds that we do not share the swimmer's fear because her fear is self-directed, whereas our fear is directed toward her. However, this objection fails to see the significance of the imaginative element involved in empathic identification. That is, we have to place ourselves imaginatively in the swimmer's situation in order to empathize with her. Thus when I imagine the shark's attack on the swimmer, I am imagining the shark's attack on me (since I am imaginarily in her situation), and hence I can share the swimmer's fear, since in both cases it is self-directed.[20]

Identification and Film Techniques

So far I have defended the concept of identification from the claim that it is mysterious or incoherent by distinguishing different kinds of identification: on the one hand, imaginative identification (imaginarily putting oneself in another's position), which is in turn subdivided into perceptual, affective, motivational, epistemic, and perhaps other forms of identification; and on the other hand, empathic identification, which requires one actually to share the character's (fictional) emotions because of one's imaginarily projecting oneself into the character's situation. On the basis of these different kinds of identification, one may come to sympathize with the character (this sympathy, as we have noted, is sometimes itself thought of as a kind of identification, but we shall treat it as one possible upshot of identification, since one can sympathize with someone without employing any sort of imaginative projection into his position). I have also deployed these distinctions to defend the claim that identification occurs in films against the sorts of objections that are often raised against it. Given these distinctions between different kinds of identification, we can now examine in more detail the role of identification in our relations to films.

As earlier remarked, the point-of-view shot is often thought of as the locus of character identification in film. In fact, it is the locus of perceptual identification (the viewer imagining seeing what the character fictionally sees), and it does not follow that the viewer identifies with the character in all other respects. The example of a shot in a horror film taken from the point of view of the killer shows that there is no necessary tendency to empathize with the character whose visual perspective we imaginarily occupy. However, since we now have the distinction between affective and empathic identification in place, we can see that there may be a tendency to affective identification resulting from this shot: that is, other things being equal this shot may get us to imagine what the character is feeling (though we need not actually feel it ourselves, i.e., we need not empathize with him). Consider the shot in *The Silence of the Lambs* taken from the point of view of Buffalo Bill, who is wearing green-tinted night-glasses, looking at Starling (Jodie Foster) while she flails around in the dark, desperately trying to defend herself from him. Certainly, we have no tendency here to empathize or sympathize with Bill—our sympathies lie entirely with Starling—but the shot does tend to foster our imagining of Bill's murderous feelings (partly because we can see their terrifying effect on Starling).[21]

The point-of-view shot, besides being an instance of perceptual identification and having a tendency to foster affective identification, also fosters a kind of epistemic identification. For the latter requires us to imagine believing what the characters fictionally believe; and some beliefs are perceptual. However, the idea of epistemic identification is broader than that of perceptual identification, since we may occupy the character's epistemic perspective by virtue of having our knowledge of what is happening restricted to her knowledge (this is characteristic of the detective film, for instance).[22]

Though the point-of-view shot is the characteristic form of perceptual identification in film, it is not the only type. This is demonstrated by another shot from *The Silence of the Lambs*. Consider the scene in which Starling and the other FBI agents are in the autopsy room with one of Buffalo Bill's victims, who has been partially flayed by him. It is only towards the end of the scene that we are finally shown the corpse itself; up to this point we are confined to watching the investigators' reactions, particularly Starling's. Watching Foster's finely nuanced performance, which registers barely controlled disgust and fear modulated by pity for the victim, we are invited to imagine what she sees without actually being shown it. The result is that what we imagine her seeing is very likely worse than what we are finally shown, since each viewer, watching the emotions registered on her face, is invited to imagine something that will justify these emotions, and so tends to imagine whatever would make these emotions appropriate to her: each imagines her own private nightmare scenario. Thus the expressive reaction shot, as well as the point-of-view shot, can cue the spectator to imagine seeing from the character's point of view.

Furthermore, as the example also shows, the reaction shot can be a more effective vehicle for affective and empathic identification with a character than is the point-of-view shot.[23] The reaction shot shows the human face or body, which we are expert at interpreting for signs of emotion, and through the art of a consummate actor like Foster we can obtain a very full sense of what the character is feeling. Hence we are provided with a large amount of information with which to engage accurately in affective identification.

Moreover, if we are confronted with visual evidence of an individual's suffering, we have a strong tendency to empathize and sympathize with her. Tales of mass disasters in distant countries also have the power to move us to empathy and sympathy, but generally more effective is a confrontation with the individual visage, with the particularities of an individual's plight etched in her expression. Recall the way, for instance, that aid agencies employ photographs of individuals in states of distress as a way more effectively to convey their message of mass suffering.

As noted earlier, the point-of-view shot also has some tendency to move us to affective identification. But it has the disadvantage of having less information to convey about what the character is feeling, and because of the absence of a shot of the face, has less power to move us to empathy and sympathy. The point-of-view shot has in fact fairly crude options available for the conveying of feelings. It may employ a shaking camera to convey unrest and uncertainty (think for instance of the hand-held, jiggling shots in Cassavetes' *A Woman Under the Influence* [1974], which convey something of the troubled minds of the married couple). It may employ low-angle shots to convey a sense of being dominated by other characters (think of some of the low-angle shots of Kane [Orson Welles] in *Citizen Kane* [1941]). Even more radically, the entire *mise en scène* may be set up so as to convey a character's troubled state of mind (think of the shot from the crazed artist Borg's perspective of the dinner guests in Bergman's *Hour of the Wolf* [1968]). If we contrast these fairly simple options with the subtleties of Foster's reaction shot in the autopsy scene, we can see that on the whole the reaction shot is more important than the point-of-view shot in mobilizing affective and empathic identification.

Epistemic identification also has a tendency to foster empathy, though in more indirect ways than does the expressive reaction shot. If our knowledge of what is fictional in the film corresponds to a high degree with that of a particular character, there is a tendency to identify affectively and to empathize with that character, even if we are antecedently not disposed to do so. Consider a scene in which we follow the movements of a group of criminals engaged on a job; we watch them being vigilant, stopping lest they be discovered, being alarmed at dangers, being hopeful about the success of the crime, and so on. In these cases where we have the same epistemic point of view on the events as they do, we can easily find ourselves empathizing with them and wanting their crime to succeed, even though normally we would not want this.

A more complex example of this phenomenon occurs in Harold Ramis's *Groundhog Day* (1993). Pete the weatherman (Bill Murray) is caught in a comic version of Nietzsche's eternal recurrence, condemned to live the same day over again and again until he gets it right. Our feelings for Pete are initially complex: his humor is hip and funny, but his cynicism is upfront, too, and our affections are divided between him and his colleagues. As the film progresses we increasingly empathize and sympathize with him. This is partly because he grows morally and becomes a more attractive figure. But it is also because we are stuck in the same epistemic situation as he is. No one apart from him and the viewer realizes that the scenes we are seeing have been played out many times before: we thus share the knowledge about what is happening with him and find it increasingly difficult to look at the world from any other point of view than his because we know that all the other characters do not appreciate what is going on. Here epistemic identification tends to foster our empathy and sympathy with the character.

In addition to these factors, there are others that tend to foster empathy and sympathy. First, empathy and sympathy are mutually self-reinforcing. To empathize with a character involves feeling what fictionally she is feeling; since most characters have a concern for their own welfare, by empathizing with them one will also be sympathetic to them, that is, one will be concerned for them. Conversely, if one is sympathetic to a character, one will tend to align one's emotions with his, feel what he feels, and so empathize with him.

Second, and more obviously, we tend to sympathize with characters who are represented as having various attractive traits. A wide range of traits can foster such responses: characters may be witty (as is Pete the weatherman), physically attractive, interestingly complex, and so forth. In Neil Jordan's *The Crying Game* (1992) our sympathies are mobilized toward Jody (the British soldier, played by Forest Whitaker), Fergus (the IRA member, played by Stephen Rea) and Dil (the transvestite, played by Jaye Davidson) by their vulnerability: Jody is vulnerable because he appears to be in imminent danger of being killed by the IRA yet is in Northern Ireland for no better reason than that he needed a job; Fergus is vulnerable because he does not believe in the credo of violence to which he is ostensibly committed and is himself then endangered by it (and his vulnerability is displayed in his remark to Jody that "I'm not good for much"); and Dil is vulnerable because of her marginal social and sexual situation. Besides these kinds of character traits that can promote empathy and sympathy, the knowledge of who is playing the character can also materially engage our feelings. Hitchcock, for instance, was master at deploying this technique. Considered in terms of his character traits, Scotty

Dil (Jaye Davidson) and Fergus (Stephen Rea) in Neil Jordan's
The Crying Game (1992).

(James Stewart) in *Vertigo* (1958) is a fairly unsympathetic character; but we are encouraged to empathize with him partly because of our epistemic identification (up to the point of Madeleine/Judy's [Kim Novak] flashback we are unaware of the plot that has been hatched against him, and are largely confined to his knowledge of events) and also because he is played by James Stewart, with his long history of playing folksy, sympathetic heroes.

So the notion of identification can be refined so as to avoid the objections frequently leveled against it, and this refinement allows us the creation of theories of some complexity by examining the relations between different kinds of identification. The refined notions still allow for an important connection between identification and emotion. This is displayed partly in the constitutive connection between empathic feelings and identification: empathy is feeling what a character feels because one imaginatively projects oneself into his situation. And the connection between identification and emotion is also displayed in some causal connections: as we have seen, epistemic identification tends to foster empathy, and affectively identifying with a character, particularly when her situation is vividly imagined, tends to produce empathy with him. Thus the common view that there is an important connection between identification and emotional response to films has received a partial defense, based on distinguishing different notions of identification. However, the theorist's claim that the point-of-view shot lies at the heart of cinematic identification has fared less well. It certainly constitutes a characteristic form of perceptual identification, but it is not the only form: the reaction shot, too, can invite us to imagine seeing from a character's perspective. And while the point-of-view shot may have some tendency to get us affectively to identify with the character concerned, it is not as effective in this respect as the reaction shot, and the latter is vastly more effective in engaging our empathy and sympathy.

Identification and Learning

Identification, then, plays an important role in our emotional responses to films. It also plays a significant part in teaching us how to respond emotionally to fictionally delineated situations. There are at least two basic forms that this kind of learning may take. The first is that through empathy our emotional reactions mirror those of a character, and that as she grows emotionally we do, too, learning to respond to situations in a way that we and she would previously have found inappropriate. The second basic type of learning results from identifying with a character, but coming to realize that her reactions are in some ways inappropriate to her situation, and discovering that there is a deeper perspective on her situation, different from her own. In the first case, both we and the character grow emotionally together; in the second only we may grow while the character remains much the same. The first possibility is illustrated by *The Crying Game*; the second by Max Ophuls's *Letter from an Unknown Woman* (1948).

In *The Crying Game* we are led after the traumatic death of Jody to identify (epistemically, affectively, and empathically) with Fergus, who is traumatized by Jody's death and eager to escape the IRA. Jody has asked Fergus to take care of his lover, Dil; Fergus has seen a picture of her and found her very attractive. He falls in love with her, she performs oral sex on him, and at the turning point of the film she appears naked before him: Dil is a man. Fergus is aghast, strikes Dil, throws up in the toilet, storms out. Since the audience has been epistemically closely identified with Fergus throughout, they are also likely to be astounded by the discovery (Jaye Davidson's impersonation of a woman is extraordinarily convincing). The rest of the film is the story of how Fergus comes to accept the fact that he loves Dil, even though Dil is male ("I preferred you as a girl"), and goes to prison for her sake.

The Crying Game is thematically very rich, engaging with issues of race, gender, and love. What is interesting for our purposes is how Fergus is represented as coming to accept that he loves Dil, even though his heterosexuality was not previously in doubt. Love transcends mere gender boundaries; not only is that a theme of the film, but the audience is also positioned to *want* Fergus and Dil to continue their erotic friendship, even after it is clear that Dil is a man. Because we are multiply identified with Fergus and because Fergus comes to accept his love for Dil, we too are encouraged to accept it. Here identification with a character whose attitudes toward homosexuality change fundamentally in the course of the film also encourages the audience through empathy to want the relationship to work out, and thus also encourages them to question their attitudes toward homosexuality.[24] This, then, is a particularly clear example of a film that deploys identification to get audiences to reconsider their emotional responses and to learn from a fictional situation.

Letter from an Unknown Woman is on the face of it a film that falls well within the conventions of the "woman's picture." Lisa (Joan Fontaine), the unknown woman of the title, loves Stefan (Louis Jourdan) from a distance and is enamored of his musical prowess, the sense of culture and mystery that he brings to her cramped bourgeois life, when she first encounters him at puberty. Yet she talks to him only a handful of times and goes to bed with him only once, from which she conceives a son. For the sake of that son, she marries an honorable man, whom she respects but does not love, but throws it all away when she meets Stefan years later. Yet Stefan does not recognize her, and she leaves his apartment distraught, apparently having finally seen through his superficial charm and having grasped the fact that she was no more than another conquest to him. Yet the film is structured around the letter she writes to him while she is dying, a letter that reveals her still-hopeless infatuation with him, a letter that avers the great good that could have come out of their love—if only he could have remembered her, if only he could have recognized that she was his true muse, the woman who could have lent meaning to his life. Stefan, reading the letter, apparently accepts his responsibility and his failure, goes off to fight a duel with Lisa's husband, and thus departs to his certain death.

On the face of it, the film is a paradigm melodrama, a picture that intends not so much to jerk tears as to ladle them out in bucketfuls. And there is no doubt about the audience's multiple identification with Lisa. Hers is the voiceover, and almost all the scenes in flashback are those in which she features; she is quiet and beautiful with a childlike charm and an impressive determination. The audience is thus epistemically, affectively, and empathically identified with her, and there is no doubt about the resulting sympathy that they are encouraged to feel for her. Yet in a real sense, Lisa never learns the significance of what has happened to her. Her dying letter is a testament

Stefan (Louis Jourdan) and Lisa (Joan Fontaine) stand before the gaze of the jealous husband. From Max Ophuls's *Letter from an Unknown Woman* (1948).

to how if only Stefan had been able to love truly, to dedicate himself to her, their lives would have been immeasurably richer. So identification with Lisa on this interpretation of the film would lead to a reinforcement of the romantic attitudes that many of the original audience presumably brought with them when they came to see the film.

There is another way to interpret the film, however. Lisa is an obsessive person, unable to recognize that she is projecting her romantic fantasies onto a figure who does not in the least conform to them, and that she is pursuing these fantasies literally to the death, even though there is abundant evidence that she is deluding herself in a way guaranteed to lead to disaster. For this view there is much evidence in the film. Lisa says things in her letter that are contradicted by what we see: for instance, that "I've had no will but his [Stefan's] ever," whereas in fact it is transparently clear that Lisa has a very strong will of her own (she is willing to throw away her marriage on a chance of being with Stefan), while Stefan wanders through life with little sense of direction (he admits that he rarely actually reaches any place for which he sets out). These and other clues in the film give the audience evidence for a counter-perspective in the film, a point of view that is not Lisa's, which shows us that Lisa's views are partly fantasized distortions of her true situation.[25]

On this second (and I think better) way of interpreting the film, the audience is encouraged to identify with Lisa in several respects but is also provided with evidence that her actions are in certain respects foolish and self-deluded. If it grasps this counter-evidence, then what it has learned from the film is that certain of its romantic values are distorted, tending to encourage potentially disastrous self-delusions. Because the audience so much identifies with Lisa, it should take that lesson to heart; it cannot stand back and think that what has been shown about Lisa's values has nothing to do with its own, since it has seen those values enacted in a woman with whom it has closely identified. This, then, is the second way that identification with a character may teach an audience about correct emotional responses. On this model, the character does not grow emotionally, but the audience does because of the way it has discovered that its values are flawed. Here identification plays a more indirect cognitive role than on the first model: to learn what it is appropriate to feel, the audience has to be prepared to detect the existence of a counter-perspective to that of the character. But identification functions to drive the lesson home, to show that the values and attitudes under attack are the audience's own, and thus to create the possibility of a real, lived change in their basic commitments. As this possibility illustrates, the Brechtian idea that identification must always function so as to render the audience uncritically receptive to conventional values is false. Identification may work in an appropriate context to drive home some hard lessons.

I have argued that philosophers and film theorists who reject the centrality of the psychoanalytic paradigm should not also reject, as they all too often do, the idea of identification. Despite the criticisms that have been laid against the coherence and the explanatory power of the concept, it does in fact have a valuable role of play in understanding our emotional responses toward films. As used by audiences to describe and explain their reactions to films, it is undoubtedly somewhat crude. But once we make necessary distinctions, the concept can be refined so that it plays a valuable part in film theory and in the analysis of individual films. Abandoning the idea of identification because of its deployment in psychoanalytic theory is worse than throwing the baby out with the bath water. It is a failure to identify with the baby.

ELEVEN

Gangsters, Cannibals, Aesthetes, or Apparently Perverse Allegiances

MURRAY SMITH

> I am not more certain that I breathe, than that the assurance of the wrong or error of any action is often the one unconquerable *force* which impels us, and alone impels us to its prosecution.
>
> EDGAR ALLEN POE, "The Imp of the Perverse"

The subject of perversity is one that has often been seen to have an intimate connection with the cinema—either in terms of certain film genres which are said (by some) to pander to "perverse" tastes and desires (pornography, horror), or, more broadly, in terms of the general conditions of spectatorship in the cinema, which are said (by some) to engender voyeurism, fetishism, and even sado-masochism. The furor surrounding David Cronenberg's *Crash* (1996) might be seen as a condensed emblem of all these associations. Though these are subjects I will inevitably traverse in the course of this chapter, my target will be a broader and more inclusive notion of "perversity."[1] "Perversion" is technically defined as turning or being deflected "from what is right, good, proper" (from the Latin *pervers*, "askew")[2] and has as much force in phrases like "perverting the course of justice" as in arguments about the nature of sexual perversion. So I will base my arguments on an understanding of the term "perversion" which refers essentially to the *deliberate violation of moral precepts*.

   At the most general level, my concern will be with the ways in which, and the reasons for which, we are interested in representations of deliberate wrongdoing, or "wickedness of will," as one recent study characterizes perversity.[3] More particularly, and in line with the subject matter of this volume, I want to consider the nature of our emotional responses to representations of "evil" and perversity; to ask whether, and under what circumstances, we are appalled and horrified by such representations, or delighted by them, or perhaps ambivalent in our responses to them. I shall argue that there are a variety of aesthetic approaches to perverse subject matter, each of which in-

vites a different kind of response. I describe a number of such aesthetics, in
each case outlining the kind of emotional response they seek to elicit. Finally,
I bring together the various explanatory factors invoked in the course of the
discussion in order to provide an alternative to the psychoanalytic explanations that are put forward almost automatically for both the making and
viewing of perverse material. Before getting into the meat of the argument,
however, a few matters concerning background assumptions need to be
briefly discussed—concerning the notion of perversity, and the relationship
between morality and emotion.

Perverse Allegiance

Why would matters of morality—whether "straight" or "perverse"—be of
pertinence in an examination of our emotional responses to films? For the
simple reason that moral evaluations and judgments frequently underlie our
emotional reactions. It is common nowadays to assume a "cognitive" definition of emotion—one that characterizes emotions in terms of both bodily
arousal and cognitive judgment (as well as expressions and action tendencies, among other possible elements). What is less often stressed is that many
of the cognitive judgments integral to emotions have an ethical character: in
reacting with anger to some item of government policy—say, lowering in-
come taxes but raising sales tax—the moral judgment that this policy is un-
just, that it will hurt the vulnerable but help the privileged, is integral to the
anger. Or, in feeling pride, I must feel that the object of pride is morally worthy—that the action in question shows determination or generosity, for example. Many of our emotional responses to both actual and fictional events
are in this sense morally saturated. And if perversity is defined as the deliberate violation of a moral precept, then morality must enter into "perverse"
emotional responses as much as it does into "straight" responses.

In most contexts, the word "perversion" and its siblings carry an in-built,
negative moral charge—think of the force of calling someone a "pervert." It is
important to recognize, however, that there is a nonmoral, descriptive sense
in which we might talk about perversion. *Functional* perversion occurs when
some part of the human anatomy, or even an artifact, is used to perform some
function other than the function it standardly does serve (whether by human
design or evolutionary selection). Functional perversity might be seen as an
equivalent within the domain of culture of what Stephen Jay Gould refers to
as evolutionary "exaptation."[4] Exaptation involves the use of some feature of
a species to perform a "new" function that enhances its fitness for the environment. The feature either evolved to perform some other function or was
not an adaptation in this sense at all but a by-product or "nonaption," which
has come to perform a (new) function. Examples include certain birds that

use their wings to cast shadows enabling them to detect fish, or the evolution of feathers as a form of insulation, "exapted" for the purposes of flight.[5]

If evolution itself is apt to throw up such possibilities, it is hardly surprising that we find a similar dynamic at work on the level of cultural and individual behavior. Many sexual perversions fall into this category of functional perversion: not only fetishism or anal intercourse and other "paraphilias,"[6] but also something as commonplace as kissing (insofar as the main function of the mouth is to allow us to ingest food).[7] The point of saying that kissing is a perversion is to reveal, however, the absurdity of—but also the difficulty of avoiding—the moral condemnation of many "perverse," "unnatural" practices. One of the complexities of discussing sexual perversity in particular is that the term invariably brings with it the implication not only of functional but of moral perversity: that the functional violation or innovation is to be condemned because it is harmful, either to individuals or society as a whole (or, on the other hand, to be celebrated as an act of freedom and creativity). My focus here will be on moral perversity, and only on sexual perversity—or particular sexual perversions—insofar as they have been regarded by particular communities as morally, and not merely functionally, perverse.

We can also make a distinction here between what we might call *first-order* and *second-order perversity*: first-order perversity involves a direct taking of pleasure in that which is morally or socially proscribed, while second-order perversity involves taking pleasure in some action *because* it is so proscribed. The first-order pervert just likes (say) using iron filings as a culinary seasoning, or prefers sex with a dead body or an inert dummy over that with a responsive human agent;[8] the concept of first-order perversity recognizes the existence of impulses and desires not morally or socially sanctioned. The second-order pervert, however, enjoys the transgressiveness of what she knows will be looked upon as "perverse."[9] Second-order perversity—the kind captured in the phrase, "you're just being perverse"—is my primary concern here, even where particular cases seem to involve both first- and second-order perversity.

Moral perversity understood in this broad sense is an enduring subject of fictional representation, both filmic and literary. A key aspect of this phenomenon concerns the way in which viewers and readers of fictions depicting "perverse" acts and agents are invited to respond to them (cognitively, conatively, emotionally); and especially whether and in what circumstances we are invited to endorse them. This issue—what is often discussed as the question of our "identification" (or lack of it) with represented characters—is one I have analyzed in earlier work, though without tackling the particular case of the perverse act or character. So before we can delve further into the mysteries of perversion, we need to take a brief detour through some essential, if perhaps less immediately alluring, material.

One of the fundamental distinctions that I argue we need to make in thinking more precisely about "identifying" with characters is between, on the one hand, *alignment* and, on the other, *allegiance*.[10] Under the rubric of alignment, I include all of those aspects of textual structure that pertain to our access to the actions, thoughts, and feelings of characters. Under the rubric of allegiance, by contrast, I include those aspects of the text that pertain to our evaluation and emotional response to characters. Simply put, then, the contrast between alignment and allegiance is one between the narrative information that a text provides us with and the way a text directs our evaluation of this information. Allegiance refers to the way in which, and the degree to which, a film elicits responses of sympathy and antipathy toward its characters, responses triggered—if not wholly determined—by the *moral structure* of the film. Most basically, the moral structure of a film works in terms of whether characters are presented as "good" or "bad," but there are more subtle possibilities—a film may withhold obvious judgment, allowing only tentative patterns of allegiance, or ironically undercut judgments it has set up. These other possibilities—graduated reactions, contradictory responses, ironic detachment—will all be important in considering perverse allegiance. Perhaps I should also add that I conceive of the evaluative attitudes of sympathy and antipathy as end points on a continuum, not a simple dichotomy. We often assess characters as more or less bad or virtuous, rather than simply categorize them as wholly good or evil; the concept of allegiance recognizes the possibility of such graduated responses.

Now it might seem that the two processes of alignment and allegiance are inherently tied to one another; indeed, most film criticism and theory routinely conflate them. This is a mistake, however. *Typically,* alignment with a character is conjoined with sympathy for that character; few films, and least of all mainstream films, align us with wholly unsympathetic characters. This is one reason why it is easy to conflate alignment and allegiance. But this is a contingent rather than necessary relationship: the very notion of the *anti-hero* in modern fiction depends on the possibility of our being aligned with an unsympathetic character. Mike Leigh's *Naked* (1994) provides us with a reasonably good example: a (moderately) despicable character with whom we are informationally aligned. For more extreme examples, we can turn to contemporary horror: a film like *Maniac* (1982) aligns us with a character who undertakes a series of horrific murders, rapes, and scalpings. Assuming that our moral engines are firing on all cylinders, we will be utterly repelled and disgusted by the film's protagonist. So sympathetic allegiance is not *automatically* produced by alignment with a character. What counts in how we evaluate and respond emotionally to a character with whom we have been aligned is not merely *that* we have been aligned with him, but *what* we discover about him through that alignment.

Two objections to the notion of allegiance, as I have briefly defined it here, will help us to move back toward the subject of perversity. These objections will also allow me to refine and elaborate the concept of allegiance. The first objection is that I conflate moral desirability with other forms of desirability. Berys Gaut argues that

> for the most part the notion of allegiance gets cashed out in terms of one's moral approbation or disapprobation of a character. But I can clearly identify with characters because of many other qualities besides their moral ones: they may be physically attractive, witty, interesting, wild, or whatever. Smith . . . takes films that encourage us to ally ourselves with morally reprehensible characters as tending to get us to reconstrue our moral assessments, whereas all they need be doing is showing that our sympathies can be based on other than moral characteristics.[11]

The second objection is that I take no account of what might be called *perverse allegiances*—that is, responses of sympathy to characters on the basis of their embodiment of socially or morally *undesirable* traits. "The fact that [Smith's model] does not account for the fact that some spectators may favour the bad guys is a minor flaw," writes one student, perhaps somewhat disingenuously.[12] What the two objections share is the idea that I define "allegiance" too narrowly—either by tying it exclusively to morality or by tying it exclusively to "moralism," by which I mean the unyielding application of a particular moral code to the actions of others, a consequence of which is intolerance of lifestyles embodying different moral precepts. The second objection implies that the concept of allegiance, at least as I have set it out, makes prim "moralists" of us all, responding only in the most upright fashion and, what is more, in complete agreement with one another.

In *Engaging Characters,* I try to take account of perverse allegiances (without naming them as such) by pointing out that allegiance often takes place on the basis of traits that we *wish* or *desire* to possess, rather than those that we do actually possess. Such wishes may take the form of desires that are socially or morally proscribed; indeed, the desire, and the pleasure arising from an imaginary experience of fulfilling it, may arise as a resistance to such social and moral constraints. This is the definition of perversity given to us by Poe in his "The Imp of the Perverse," where he argues that when acting perversely we perform deeds "merely because we feel we should *not*."[13] Socially and morally "unacceptable" desires are then, precisely, "perverse" desires that can form the basis of perverse evaluations, emotions, and allegiances. For example, one might enjoy imagining some form of physical revenge, not merely in and of itself, but precisely because it violates the precepts of (New Testament) Christian morality. This sort of perverse delight is one that takes not only the depicted action as its object but also what one takes to be the normative reaction to the action (revulsion, condemnation, and so on); we might think (metaphorically) of such perverse delight as a contrary of normative guilt.[14]

Let us acknowledge that the notion of perverse allegiance—responses of sympathy to characters on the basis of their embodiment of socially or morally undesirable traits—describes a real phenomenon. But how significant or widespread a phenomenon is it? I want to cast a skeptical eye over apparently perverse allegiances, asking just how genuinely perverse these texts and the responses they invite are. My suspicion is that perverse allegiance is actually rather rare, and that most fictions that elicit perverse allegiances do so only temporarily or strategically, ultimately eliciting morally approbatory emotional responses. This is not to deny that there are fictions that straightforwardly solicit our perverse allegiance in the purest sense—fictions that ask us to approve of and delight in actions that are socially or morally proscribed: de Sade obviously comes to mind, as do some variants of hardcore pornography. (And if there are readers who would dispute these examples, then it should still be clear that we can at least imagine fictions designed to elicit perverse allegiance.) There are also films, like *Man Bites Dog* (1992), which supposedly satirize our appetite for the gruesome and the perverse, while (at least arguably) pandering to that appetite in a way that the target of the satire in fact rarely does—cases where perverse allegiance may be an unintended effect of the film. Moreover, individual spectators are fully capable of taking perverse pleasure in representations that were not designed for that purpose— think of a pedophile watching *Home Alone* (1990), for example, or a necrophiliac watching documentary footage of the aftermath of a massacre.

But such cases are not the focus of my interest, which is, rather, the way in which and the degree to which major aesthetic traditions and popular genres of fiction can be said to tap into morally perverse desires and solicit perverse allegiances. A number of psychoanalytic arguments have been made— and indeed, in certain quarters, taken on the status of received wisdom—to the effect that many of the types of fiction which we were accustomed to thinking of as nothing more than "harmless entertainment" or innocent escapism in fact feed and feed off perverse desires.[15] My argument is not that there are *no* examples of fictions designed to elicit perverse allegiance, but that they are actually exceptional and unusual, and that the major popular traditions that appear to elicit them (like horror) often reveal underlying structures that are more complex but also more conventionally moral than these psychoanalytic arguments have suggested. I will make this argument by posing what seems to me to be a key question with regard to what we might provisionally define as cases of perverse allegiance. In such cases, do we feel an allegiance with—a sympathy for—a character *because of* the perverse act that they engage in or *in spite of* that act? This is a key question because the truly perverse allegiance is one with a reprehensible character *on the basis of* their reprehensible actions or traits, not in spite of them. In the truly perverse allegiance, we take pleasure (for example) in that which we know causes suffering (first-order perversity), perhaps because we know that it is transgressive of ordinary social and moral conventions to do so (second-order perversity). We do not sympathize with the murderer because he is subsequently beaten up, but because he murders.[16] In order to answer my question, I want to examine several cases, generally focusing upon well-known popular cultural character types—gangsters, cannibals, and aesthetes—and the genres of fiction with which they are associated.

Slumming It

In *The Movies: A Psychological Study* (1950), Martha Wolfenstein and Nathan Leites discuss the prevalence within Hollywood of the late 1940s of what they call the "good-bad girl" and the "good-bad man." These are characters who are—or are revealed to be—essentially "good" or virtuous, and yet who appear initially to be corrupt or "evil" in some respect. Examples of the "good-bad girl" include Gilda (Rita Hayworth) in the film of the same name, Vivian Sternwood (Lauren Bacall) in *The Big Sleep* (1946), and, extrapolating to Hollywood films of other eras, Vivian Ward (Julia Roberts) in *Pretty Woman* (1990).[17] Moreover, such "girls" are attractive to the male protagonist largely because of their "badness"—invariably their explicit sexual allure—though ultimately the hero discovers that "he can take [her] home and introduce [her] to Mother."[18] This, of course, represents one pattern in the typical development of the *femme fatale:* domestication.

In the case of the "good-bad man," the "badness" typically resides in a propensity to violence rather than sexuality. But this again conceals a more morally desirable and virtuous core to the character. This dynamic is often articulated through the relations between the protagonist and other characters. In *The Roaring Twenties* (1939), for example, the James Cagney character is not a good character in all respects—he's a gangster, after all—but he is not *malign* in the way that the Humphrey Bogart character is. Eddie Bartlett (Cagney) is depicted as a good man who slides into racketeering because of harsh social conditions (he returns from World War I to find his job gone); and Prohibition itself is presented as a foolhardy and unpopular law, the bootleggers being described at one point as an army of freedom fighters. George Hally (Bogart), however, is presented as mean, self-interested, and vindictive from the start, taking pleasure in killing a young enemy soldier just prior to the armistice. So the Bogart character gives us a kind of license to ally ourselves with the *relatively* good Cagney character. Again we can find this pattern in much later films: consider the contrast between "bad-boy" Henry Hill (Ray Liotta) and the vicious and psychotic Tommy De Vito (Joe Pesci) in *GoodFellas* (1990); or the relative desirability of hired killer William Munny (Clint Eastwood) in *Unforgiven* (1992) compared with the sadistic and arrogant sheriff, Little Bill (Gene Hackman).

We might summarize one of the basic satisfactions offered by melodramas in terms of *comeuppance,* in which we "see the villain perform a sequence of progressively more heinous acts and then get what is coming to him."[19] Just deserts are meted out to the various characters according to their real moral natures—virtue rewarded and villainly punished—and part of our satisfaction is derived from responding emotionally in what we regard as a morally sound fashion. What then would the point or attraction or fascination of the "good-bad" character structure be? The explanation offered by Wolfenstein and Leites is that this is a structure that "makes it possible for us to eat our cake and have it, since we can enjoy the suggested [immoral] wish-fulfilments without empathic guilt; we know that the characters with whom we identify have not done anything."[20] We might imagine "from the inside" the sense of power Bartlett feels as he gains more and more control over his environment, and respond empathically with a sense of excitement and even pride—not only without guilt, but with an added integral thrill attached to the fact that these fictional actions are illicit.[21] But as Wolfenstein and Leites point out, the characters "have not done anything," in the sense that they are only apparently guilty of the crimes of which they are accused, or, as in *The Roaring Twenties,* there are a host of redeeming factors mitigating the wrongdoing of the character. We might add that they "have not done anything" in the further sense that fictional persons don't perform actual deeds. In our imagination we can indulge forbidden desires (including desires that are only desires because they are forbidden) and experience emotions apt to the actual realization of these desires,[22] while ultimately being reassured that we, like the "good-bad" characters, are attractive and morally worthy. The "good-bad" character structure allows for a kind of imaginative slumming on the part of the spectator.[23]

A similar argument has been put forward by Rick Altman in relation to genre films in general. Altman argues that a committed genre film spectator must be "sufficiently committed to generic values to tolerate and even enjoy in genre films capricious, violent, or licentious behaviour which they might disapprove of in 'real life.'" He goes on:

> When we are in the world, we follow its rules; when we enter into a genre film, all our decisions are self-consciously modified to support a different kind of satisfaction. . . . From one genre to another, the genre spectator always participates in overtly counter-cultural acts.[24]

The key point, then, that I wish to draw from both Wolfenstein and Leites and Altman is the idea of a knowing, self-conscious, imaginative play with the morally undesirable in the domain of fiction. Insofar as the films in question foster an allegiance with characters who are only apparently or temporarily characterized as morally undesirable, however, our allegiances with them are only apparently perverse. Perhaps, though, more authentic cases of perverse allegiance can be found in other kinds of film.

Sympathy for the Devil

The horror film would seem to be a likely place in which perverse pleasures might be lurking—indeed, Carol Clover has argued that horror films are appreciated by their typical audiences precisely for the sadomasochistic pleasures they offer up: sadistic delight in the attacks on hapless victims but also masochistic pleasure in the idea of being so attacked. Once again, though, I am rather skeptical of the extent to which any variant of the contemporary horror film draws us into a sustained, positive, approbatory relationship with morally perverse actions. I will argue that, as in the case of the Hollywood dramas and melodramas I have discussed, we find structures that license our allegiance with characters who are, as it were, only partially evil. I will focus on the case of cannibal and sadist Dr. Hannibal Lecter (Anthony Hopkins) in the film *The Silence of the Lambs* (1990).

In this film we find a variant of the "good-bad" character structure—what I will call, in deference to Gaut's distinction between moral desirability and other forms of desirability, the "attractive-bad" character structure. In such cases a genuinely vicious, corrupt, or immoral character is nevertheless made attractive in some way. Lecter is an excellent example of such a figure. He enjoys not only eating human flesh but also inflicting both physical and psychological suffering. These perverse desires and traits are made abundantly clear in several sequences: for example, when he sucks his breath in rapidly in a chilling gesture of delight at the thought of consuming human flesh. Still more disturbing is the scene in which he at once helps Sen. Ruth Martin (Diane Baker), whose daughter has been abducted, by providing information about her captor Buffalo Bill, while at the same time tormenting her with a series of grotesque asides, metaphorically relating the act of breast-feeding to both cannibalism and sexual lust. Lecter's monstrosity is, then, firmly established.

The question for us, though, is: how does the film ask us to evaluate these monstrous desires and actions? At these moments we are surely meant to be disgusted and horrified by them; according to Noël Carroll, if we aren't disgusted and horrified by the monster in these ways, then the film just isn't working as a horror film.[25] If that were all there were to the case of Hannibal Lecter, there would be little further to discuss. What makes his case more

Dr. Hannibal Lecter (Anthony Hopkins), an evil yet attractive character.
From Jonathan Demme's *Silence of the Lambs* (1990).

complex are the other, attractive traits that also characterize him. In spite
of Lecter's taste for human livers and other body parts, he is on many occasions charming, witty, urbane, genteel, and learned. (Often these traits are
co-present at the very moments that the repellent traits are given expression,
eliciting a decidedly uneasy, ambivalent response from us.) Moreover,
his mentor-like relationship with Clarice Starling (Jodie Foster)—a rather
warmer relationship than she shares with her official FBI superior—also
makes him attractive: some of our allegiance with Clarice "rubs off" onto
Lecter, since she clearly trusts and values his opinion (up to a point). The
bond with Clarice is underlined at the end of the film, where we see Lecter
speaking with Clarice by telephone from the Caribbean island to which he
has escaped, contemplating revenge on Dr. Chilton with the immortal words:
"I do wish we could chat longer, but I'm having an old friend for dinner."
There is no sense of a denial of poetic justice here—in spite of his sadism and

cannibalism, we want things to go well for Lecter, as Gaut might put it, and they do. (As the character Jules [Samuel L. Jackson] remarks in *Pulp Fiction* [Quentin Tarantino, 1994], "Personality goes a long way.") So here we seem to have a genuinely perverse allegiance.

But do we? Do we find Lecter sympathetic and attractive *because* of his taste for human liver? *That* would be perverse. Rather, I would argue that we find him (relatively) sympathetic because he possesses a number of attractive and appealing traits, and in this respect he contrasts with both the other prisoners on his corridor—demented, sex-crazed animals like Migs (Stuart Rudin), who flings semen at Clarice as she passes by his cell—and Dr. Chilton (Anthony Heald), the sadistic doctor who oversees Lecter's incarceration. Moreover, though we hear a lot about Lecter's cannibalistic antics and witness the gruesome aftermath of one of his attacks, we never see him chomping liver or defacing his victims, yet we *do* see him strapped into a device that looks like a cross between an iron maiden and a dog muzzle. Like Alex (Malcolm McDowell) in *A Clockwork Orange* (1971), Lecter is humiliated and degraded by his captors; what is more, these actions are made more salient in the film than Lecter's own vicious actions. The film keeps his immoral traits and actions in the background and stresses his positive attributes through his almost paternal relationship with Clarice Starling. As in the case of the "good-bad" character structure, the internal moral system of the text makes a character attractive *relative* to other characters.[26] In sum, any allegiance we form with Lecter is one that develops in spite of rather than because of his perversity. The perversity of the allegiance is, once again, more apparent than real.

Another factor that plays an important role in the eliciting of these apparently perverse allegiances is the "charisma" of stars, which may play an important role in the legitimation of certain imagined desires and their resultant emotions which the spectator herself might frown upon outside of the realm of the fictional. In many of the examples discussed, it makes a difference that the "bad" characters with whom we sympathize are stars: Cagney, Eastwood, Hopkins. But this is a complex matter, in which there are at least two distinct processes at work. First there is the fact that when a star plays a role, our awareness of the fictional status of the character she plays may be heightened, and this may license our imaginative play with morally undesirable acts to an even greater extent. When we watch Hannibal Lecter, we are really watching Anthony Hopkins–playing–Hannibal Lecter. The presence of a star underlines, in other words, the "playfulness"—unreality, fictionality—of the acts we watch. Second, in the case of stars who are offcast into villainous roles, there is a fund of positive associations that dilutes our sense of "evil" in the character (though given Cagney's associations with gangster roles and Eastwood's with the Dirty Harry character, it is doubtful that this second factor is relevant in the cases of Cagney/Eddie Bartlett and Eastwood/William Munny).

Thus *The Silence of the Lambs* does not quite provide us with an instance of genuinely perverse allegiance. Nevertheless, *pace* Gaut, I think the kind of spectatorship the film inculcates is mildly subversive of moral norms—that is one obvious reason the horror genre is popular with teenagers. I do not doubt the analytic distinction between moral desirability and other forms of desirability; but in our assessments of individuals—real and fictional—it is not clear to me that the two can be easily disentangled. Though we often do make judgments about persons (or characters) that discriminate between aspects of character—I admire this trait, abhor that one, can live with another, am irritated by yet another—we also make "global" judgments of a person's overall character. It is in this way that the *alloying* of good and bad, or attractive and unattractive, traits can force us if not to recast our moral framework of judgment, then at least to question certain habits of moral judgment—the habit of vilifying and valorizing without qualification, or of condemning or condoning outright regardless of context, for example.[27] Am I not inclined to forgive, or at least overlook, the immoral actions of someone whom I like or love rather more than in the case of someone I dislike or detest? Surely our judgments of particular traits and actions continually contaminate or inflect one another. This might not reflect our moral ideals, but it is surely a reality of our moral existence. And it seems to me that films exhibiting the "attractive-bad" character structure trade on just this phenomenon for the sake of either a kind of entertainment (the emotional thrill of imagined-but-controlled danger, of slumming it), or even—though I suppose there will be no shortage of people who will take issue with this claim—for the sake of moral learning.[28]

Paradoxes of the Perverse

My analysis of the two cases discussed above suggests that they are designed to allow for a very mild indulgence, in the imagination, of perverse desires and emotions. These fictions invite us to ally ourselves, up to a point, with perverse actions or characters. But what about fictions that invite not responses of sympathy for immoral agents but amoral responses, such as cases where we are invited to adopt an amoral attitude toward actions that we would expect to evaluate morally?

The Aestheticist and Decadent movements of the late nineteenth century—most famously represented by the work of Poe, Baudelaire, Rimbaud, Huysmans, and Wilde—are often described in terms of amoralism, with their stress on the idea of "art for art's sake," the concomitant rejection of the moral assessment of art, and the (perverse) discovery of beauty in acts of violence and depravity. Aestheticism and Decadence are in part defined by a cultural attitude—or more precisely, a countercultural attitude—which prides itself on an ironic distance from, or subversion of, mainstream values and attitudes. Asked what the beautiful is, Wilde reputedly answered, "What the bourgeois call the ugly."[29] If ever there was a case of second-order perversity, this is it. This rejection of received values can range across the whole gamut of experience—including, as Wilde's remark indicates, matters of style and taste—but what I want to focus on here are instances of detachment from morality; of, as it were, *studied amorality,* the deliberate flouting of morality per se.

The clearest examples of films that invite a Decadent, amoral response come from the 1960s—films like Kenneth Anger's *Scorpio Rising* (1963) and other "underground" films by Jack Smith, George Kuchar, Barbara Rubin, Robert Nelson, Andy Warhol, and Ken Jacobs—a connection made by Jonas Mekas when he described the emergence of a "Baudelairean" cinema in 1965:

> The movies I have in mind are Ron Rice's *The Queen of Sheba Meets the Atom Man;* Jack Smith's *Flaming Creatures;* Ken Jacob's *Little Stabs at Happiness;* and Bob Fleischner's [and Ken Jacob's] *Blonde Cobra*—four works that make up the real revolution in cinema today. These movies are illuminating and opening up sensibilities and experiences never before recorded in the American arts; a content which Baudelaire, the Marquis de Sade, and Rimbaud gave to world literature a century ago and which Burroughs gave to American literature three years ago. It is a world of flowers of evil, of illuminations, of torn and tortured flesh; a poetry which is at once terrible and beautiful, good and evil, delicate and dirty.[30]

Smith's *Flaming Creatures* (1963), the most notorious of Mekas's examples, depicts a large group of transvestite characters, shot in overexposed, grainy black-and-white footage, dancing, cavorting, and engaging in all manner of stylized performance postures and actions, including polymorphous orgies in which sadism and masochism feature. *Scorpio Rising* shows a biker gang engaged in various countercultural activities, culminating in an ecstatic, coke-driven motorbike race in which a biker crashes to his death. The putative amorality of such films is made explicit by Susan Sontag when she argues that Smith's *Flaming Creatures* exists outside "moral space."[31]

If we look more closely at these films, however, we will find that they are not quite as thoroughly amoral as Sontag would have it. Although Aestheticism and Decadence are often defined, as we have seen, by their repudiation of morality, what is being repudiated by these Decadent or "Baudelairean" films is not morality per se, but *moralism.* H. L. Mencken described the work of Wilde as "a sort of moral revolt against the moral axiom," and Wilde himself as "the first unmistakable anti-Puritan, the first uncompromising enemy of the essential Puritan character."[32] Decadence and Aestheticism are not so much amoral as expressive of *anti-Puritanical morality*. They are a reaction against Puritanical morality which is perceived to be intolerant on (at least) two fronts: first in terms of actual behavior, especially with regard to unconventional sexuality; and second with regard to the bounds of propriety in representation. Aestheticism and Decadence underline the distinction between representation and reality, maximizing the space for the knowing play of imagination; Puritan morality, by contrast, tends to literalize representations, treating them as the equivalent of the actions represented (the most extreme forms of Puritanism see no distinction, for example, between fiction and lying). Again Wilde is illuminating: "What is termed Sin is an element of progress. . . . Through its intensified individualism it saves us from monotony of type. In its rejection of the current notions about morality, it is one with the highest ethics."[33] In essence, this is a Romantic moral attitude in which the highest good is self-expression and self-realization through fearless experimentation—but a moral, rather than amoral, attitude all the same. Amoralism, in this context, is a strategic vehicle for an underlying moral project.

There is a paradox here which illuminates the peculiar nature of work within this tradition. The *paradox of amoralism* is that the amoralist's detached treatment of moral issues will always be treated as *immoral* by the moralist—and this is often recognized in advance by the (ostensible) amoralist. So an amoral gesture is often, in reality, an immoral gesture. But this in turn can be construed as a kind of a moral gesture, as an instance of what has been dubbed "moral immoralism"—the holding up of a particular moral doctrine for ridicule, for the sake of a superior moral claim.[34] Aestheticism and Decadence speak a rhetoric of amorality, but in reality they fail to escape the gravity of moral space, and so it is that works in this tradition frequently become the object of heated debate regarding their immorality or morality. Robert Mapplethorpe's photographs of gay sadomasochism provide us with a contemporary instance of the paradox of amoralism. Here it is not only a verbal discourse surrounding the artworks which evokes an Aestheticist sensibility, but also the photographs themselves: "elegant, luxurious, sophisticated, impeccable" are the words Arthur Danto reaches for to describe Mapplethorpe's refined and precise visual style.[35] But Danto goes on to argue that the photographs are "acts of artistic will driven by moral beliefs and attitudes. . . . It would be known in advance that such [images] would challenge, assault, insult, provoke, dismay—with the hope that in some way consciousness would be transformed."[36]

This tension or equivocation between Decadence as genuinely amoral and as confrontational "moral immoralism" can be seen in Mekas's writings on the "Baudelairean cinema." Describing it as "a cinema of disengagement and new freedom," Mekas goes on:

> A thing that may scare an average viewer is that this cinema is treading on the very edge of perversity. These artists are without inhibitions, sexual or any other kind. These are, as Ken Jacobs put it, "dirty-mouthed" films. They all contain homosexual and lesbian elements. The homosexuality, because of its existence outside official moral conventions, has unleashed sensitivities and experiences which have been at the bottom of much great poetry since the beginning of humanity.[37]

Note here that the idea of complete disengagement from society and conventional morality is disingenuous: the films Mekas cites are made to outrage and disturb precisely by frank and unabashed representations of activities that have been labeled "perverse" or immoral. Mekas suggests in another piece that Smith's *Flaming Creatures* cannot simply be trivialized as generic underground "craziness."[38] *Pace* Sontag, then, these films do not exist wholly outside of "moral space." Apparently amoral, they are in reality assaults on moralism, on the intolerance of Puritanical moral doctrines and precepts.

The moral force of this kind of art is, however, precariously balanced between two traps into which it may fall. On the one hand, the confrontational threat posed by the artwork's forthright representation of unsanctioned behavior can become strained and arch: as Richard Ellmann has remarked, "Parisian decadence, pretending candour, was edged with absurdity."[39] In such cases, the moral challenge of such work is deflated by this unintended absurdity; though it ought also to be acknowledged that sufficiently elaborated, such absurdity (a close relative of "camp") can become a legitimate aesthetic end in itself, as in Jan Svankmayer's *Conspirators of Pleasure* (1997).[40] On the other hand, the Decadent artwork may delve so deeply into the domains of the morally perverse that any underlying moral claim is undermined. The representation of what most of society has now come to at least tolerate—homosexuality, bisexuality, group sex—is often conjoined in Decadent works with the approving representation of more questionable practices, such as necrophilia, rape, and nonconsensual sadism—acts that can only be morally justified according to the most extreme versions of moral egoism.[41]

Another contemporary example of aestheticism-as-moral-immoralism— albeit a watered-down, mainstream version of it—is *Pulp Fiction*. It may seem like a stretch to link Mapplethorpe and Tarantino in this way, but that is what I propose. Two scenes in *Pulp Fiction* encapsulate the aspect of the film that connects it with moral immoralism: the one in which Mia mistakenly snorts a large quantity of heroin (instead of cocaine) and has to be revived by a large needle being violently plunged directly into her heart, and the later scene when an innocent character's head is blown off in a car entirely by accident. Both are treated with a kind of ludic, if not comic, attitude, by the film. Indeed, more straightforwardly, these scenes embody a kind of black humor.[42] (Traces of the same attitude are also evident in *The Silence of the Lambs:* at the end of the scene in which Lecter taunts Ruth Martin with his knowledge of her daughter's abductor, he commands her attention again, only to make an irreverent—because irrelevant and trivial—remark about her preppy clothing: "Love the suit." And, of course, there is Lecter's droll declaration of his intention to eat Dr. Chilton at the end of the film.)

Some people get very upset at these scenes. A colleague of mine said something to the effect, "I just don't see how shooting someone in the head is funny." In a more formal context, Noël Carroll has argued that narratives "that muddy moral understanding, as does *Pulp Fiction,* which suggests that homosexual rape is much worse than murder, are morally defective."[43] Right or wrong, the key point here is that a film like *Pulp Fiction* is calculated to elicit such responses. It is precisely the conventional moral sentiments embodied in the reactions I have quoted that the film trades on. The film deliberately brings into play conventional Christian morality through Jules's scriptural harangues, usually delivered to victims just prior to their execution, as if Jules were God himself. The film invites a second-order perverse delight, a delight that takes as its object not only depicted actions but also what we take to be the accepted and responsible moral response to these actions. The scenes invite a "cool" or "hip" response—one that can see comedy in such violent, grim, and immoral actions, which is precisely not tied down by what it regards as the stodgy moralism of mainstream culture, with its anxieties about screen violence and its effects upon the "vulnerable"—the young and the "uneducated" (the working class).

My point here is not to defend the attitude that the film expresses so much as to describe the complex internal structure of this attitude—the fact that it depends implicitly on contrasting itself with what it regards as a "square," moralistic response. The film requires just this kind of Whitehouseian[44] response—imagined or realized—in order for it to be fully enjoyed by the hip audience to whom it is addressed. This is a kind of perverse enjoyment—involving perverse allegiance with Jules and Vincent (John Travolta) as they live out their gangster lives, rubbing out a victim here, accidentally killing an incidental character there—because the delight it evokes is partly founded on the disapproval of the strict moralist. It would be a mistake, however, to see *Pulp Fiction* as expressive of nothing more than a perverse delight in offending a "responsible" audience. This impish quality is only one aspect of the film. *Pulp Fiction* also communicates a delight in the freedoms of storytelling and formal play, of redescribing the world. This is itself a morally

Jules (Samuel L. Jackson) and Vincent (John Travolta), cleaned up
after an accidental shooting, standing with Mr. Wolf (Harvey Keitel). From
Quentin Tarantino's *Pulp Fiction* (1994).

informed attitude, insofar as it is committed to freedom (albeit merely imaginative freedom—the freedom to imagine acts and events that we wouldn't countenance in reality). Unlike the Baudelairean, underground films of the '60s, however, *Pulp Fiction* makes no effort to challenge us with respect to the real social freedoms of minority groups like gays to live their lives openly and without reprisal: in this sense, the "moral immoralism" of *Pulp Fiction* certainly is a dilute version of it.

The Parasite's Perspective

Sexual perversity—or unconventional sexuality—is a thread that connects the Aestheticist and Decadent movements not only with the Baudelairean strain of American underground filmmaking but also with the work of the more mainstream filmmaker David Cronenberg, from early films like *Crimes of the Future* (1970) and *Shivers* (1975) through to mature works such as *Dead*

Ringers (1988) and, above all, the recently released *Crash*. Cronenberg's place within this tradition is further underlined by his adaptation of William Burroughs's *The Naked Lunch* (1991), a novel that Mekas appropriately situates in the Decadent tradition. There is clearly also a strain of confrontational "moral immoralism" in Cronenberg's work. Cronenberg has commented with satisfaction, for example, on the reaction of certain "French critics [who] saw *Shivers* as being an attack on the bourgeois life, and bourgeois ideas of morality and sexuality. They sensed the glee with which we were tearing them apart."[45] Cronenberg's work, however, cannot be fully understood in terms of moral immoralism. His films attempt, I shall argue, to inculcate a genuinely amoral attitude, an attitude that I will explicate in terms of curiosity and fascination.

We appear to have a limitless natural curiosity in and fascination with the bizarre and the horrific. Such fascination and curiosity have an essentially amoral character and can take two forms: the first premised on the human kinship between ourselves (spectators, readers) and the object of our attention; the second on the complete absence of such kinship. This second form of fascination leads us to watch, often in amazement, documentaries about the natural world, depicting the behavior of animals: each species may have its own habits and even social routines, but we don't go about morally evaluating the behavior of the animals depicted. Our curiosity about the mindsets of psychopaths and other morally perverse characters, I would suggest, *can* be of the same type: that is, we can be fascinated by their world because it is governed by such alien, "inhuman" beliefs, desires, emotions, and behavior. Alternatively, amoral fascination may be premised on the underlying humanness of the bizarre and the horrific—a fascination captured in the phrase "there but for the grace of God go I." Robert Solomon argues that (some) horror fictions appeal to us in this way:

> The revolting and disgusting is attractive in its own right . . . because it reminds us of something essential about ourselves. We live in a sanitized society, in which even criminal executions have been whittled down to a clinical, private injection. . . . [Horror] reminds us of our most basic vulnerabilities.[46]

There are those who would condemn these types of fascination as titillating, shallow, ghoulish, or morbid, but an interest in the strange and extreme states that we can either imagine befalling us, or which exist alongside us, seems like nothing more than an extension of curiosity in general.

Fascination and curiosity almost always play a background role in our interest in representations of morally perverse or undesirable agents, including the films already discussed, though there is an aesthetic in which these amoral forms of attention come, as it were, to center stage, placing our normal tendency to evaluate actions and agents in partial abeyance. Cronenberg's *Shivers,* a film described at the time of its release by one critic as "the most perverse, disgusting, and repulsive" film he had ever seen,[47] embodies this kind of aesthetic strategy. In the course of discussing this film, we will encounter a kind of agent rather different from the rogue's gallery of types this chapter has focused on, for the film depicts the horrific infection of the inhabitants of an apartment complex by a virulent, genetically engineered parasite. The parasite—memorably described by Carol Clover as looking "like a cross between a penis and a turd"[48]—is spread by sexual contact and is described in the film as the fusion of a strain of venereal disease with an aphrodisiac. Once infected, the host experiences a rapid and overwhelming surge of libido, undiscriminating in its choice of sexual object (old or young, male or female); this is a genuinely polymorphously perverse parasite. It is easy to see from this description how the film might be regarded as an "attack" on bourgeois sexual mores—that is, as a post-Freudian allegory concerning the way our libido is channeled and constrained by contingent social and moral conventions. This does not, however, get to the heart of the film's aesthetic project.

The film uses the plot premise of the parasites as a way of stripping the characters in the film of their traditional human attributes—complexity, emotion, rationality, morality—so that they, like the parasite that lives within them, become dominated by a primitive, carnal appetite. In effect, the characters become sex zombies. Although the film places at its center a conventionally attractive protagonist (a young, good-looking, sympathetic doctor), it refuses to depict the spread of the parasite through the population in classical fashion, with the protagonist acting as the last bastion of human values—and of sympathy—in the face of the revolting, alien, monstrous threat. By way of contrast, *Star Trek: First Contact* (1997) provides a ready example of this classical procedure, which is articulated in part through a particular use of point of view, well analyzed by Angela Groth:

> The general attitude of the cybernetic collective called the Borg is illustrated by means of a particular form of optical POV [point of view]. The humans they see appear drained of colour, askew as in a convex distorting mirror, and are thus rendered inane and insignificant. . . . The humans as "individuals" are irrelevant. . . . We are expected to feel deeply wounded in our human pride through this inhuman and dehumanizing perspective.[49]

The doughty crew of the Enterprise, of course, combat and conquer the affront and threat to human values embodied by the Borg. This classical formal structure is present in *Shivers,* but drained of expressive force. Cronenberg invests little energy in bringing the protagonist and his defense of "humanness" to life, but rather depicts his struggles alongside the relentless advance of the parasite with a kind of evenhandedness (if not quite equanimity). By the end of the film, the parasite has infected every inhabitant of the apartment complex, and the final shots show the human hosts driving out into the surrounding city, implacable in their inhuman mission to spread the parasite still further. Reacting to the suggestion that this is a bleak ending, Cronenberg has remarked:

> A virus is only doing its job. It's trying to live its life. The fact that it's destroying you by doing so is not its fault. . . . I think most diseases would be very shocked to be considered diseases at all. It's a very negative connotation. For them, it's very positive when they take over your body and destroy you. It's a triumph. [*Shivers* tries] to reverse the normal understanding of what goes on physically, psychologically and biologically to all of us.[50]

The parasites are horrific, inspiring loathing and disgust in us, but not because we are asked to value the characters as individuals in the classical fashion, who are meant to be "flat." The vestiges of the traditional moral structure of the horror film are still in place, but Cronenberg has deflated our typical moral investment to such a degree that we can see things from the parasite's perspective—not in the sense that we come to feel "what it is like to be a virus," but in the sense that we understand events with the interest of the virus in mind. Insofar as we respond to the events depicted with horror, we cannot be said to have relinquished our anthropomorphic perspective entirely. Nevertheless, the film attempts to draw us away from the anthropomorphic—and moral—perspective, asking us to look upon human catastrophe with a kind of detached, amoral fascination. And as with the phenomena of imaginative slumming and of a partial sympathy for the devil, amoral fascination is to be distinguished from truly perverse allegiance.

The Banality of Perfection

In discussing the cases of gangsters, cannibals, aesthetes, and parasites, I have canvassed a range of motivations that might explain our interest in representations of the morally perverse: the play of the imagination, whether for sake of moral learning, or for the innate fascination of imagining experiences that we lack the opportunity or courage to experience in reality; curiosity about the extremes of possible or conceivable experience; and a delight in provocation, whether as a strategy of social distinction and generational identity formation or as a vehicle of moral protest. Each of these has been tied to a particular fiction or type of fiction in my discussion, but it should be obvious that many fictions will elicit more than one of these kinds of response. I do not suggest that these form a unified "theory" of perverse allegiance—but then it is not clear, given the diversity of types of perversion, that a single form of explanation is appropriate or desirable. But what this array of explanatory motivations does reveal is the narrowness of explanations based either on notions of "catharsis" (we engage with perverse material in the domain of fiction because it enables us to give expression to dangerous desires and to vent the damaging emotions these give rise to, in a safe context) or based on psychoanalytic theories (fictions dealing in the perverse allow for the expression, in disguised form, of repressed wishes and fears). I do not want to argue here that fictions do not or could not perform such "psychodynamic" functions, but rather that we need to check what has become a kind of "psychoanalytic reflex response" within film and cultural studies—the assumption that, for any text dealing with matters perverse, psychoanalytic explanations are the primary or even sole fitting form of explanation.

Let me end by adding one further, general argument regarding our moral interest in sympathetic or amoral representations of immoral agents; an argument that has a bearing on the interest and value of all the kinds of filmmaking I have discussed and the kinds of emotional response we have to them. Some may find the argument either trite or disreputable, but I think it has its place within a comprehensive answer to the question I have addressed in this chapter: under what circumstances and for what reasons might we experience sympathetic emotions toward morally perverse or undesirable characters? In an essay entitled "The Positive Desirability of Evil," Colin Radford writes:

> If the wrongdoer ever were to become an endangered species . . . the rest of us would and should cherish its members. Not because we loved them, though I think we sometimes genuinely do love the rogue, and not despite, but because of his or her naughtiness . . . , but because the existence of wrongdoing not only guarantees that both we and the wrongdoer can act well but ensures that our lives are rich, diverse, challenging, puzzling, anguished, worth living.
>
> Heaven would be hell.[51]

It is important to add here that Radford is not arguing for the existence of "more evil" in the world. Rather, he seems to be making a partly conceptual, partly existential argument for the existence of wrongdoing and immorality in the world. Life, he claims, would lack both complexity and intensity without the moral dimension (and the emotional dimension, which, to reiterate, is integrally connected with it). This is the trite aspect of the argument—we are human because we have values and attachments and respond emotionally on the basis of these values. But its being trite doesn't stop it being true.

Whatever one thinks about this in the arena of real social and moral action, it does provide a partial explanation of the appeal of perverse characters—or partially and apparently perverse allegiances with those characters—in the domain of fiction. Fiction is an institution built on our capacity to imagine. Just as fiction provides opportunities to ponder dilemmas that we have not, or have not yet, faced in reality, so it offers us an opportunity to indulge in forbidden desires and imaginings, and, perhaps even more fundamentally, *to recognize the role played by that which we would normally condemn in the satisfaction we derive from acting morally*. In other words, at another level the question I have posed asks us to consider not so much how we might derive pleasure from and approve particular actions that transgress the particular moral values according to which we generally live, as to recognize our "need" for the wrongdoer, a need that is hard to accept or admit to in reality.

TWELVE

The Scene of Empathy
and the Human Face on Film

CARL PLANTINGA

One of the least explored aspects of film and television is their sensory means of communication—their direct appeal to our senses of sight and hearing.[1] Both literature and film present stories with characters, plots, and settings. It is only film (and television) that present those elements through photographic images and recorded sounds. In this chapter I argue that a central way the *visual* aspect of film is significant is in the use of the human face in the *scene of empathy*. For as film theorist Béla Bélazs wrote years ago, the closeup of the human face occupies a central place in the cinema because it hearkens back to prelinguistic communication, "the expressive movement, the gesture, that is the aboriginal mother-tongue of the human race."[2]

Many films feature a kind of scene in which the pace of the narrative momentarily slows and the interior emotional experience of a favored character becomes the locus of attention. In this kind of scene, which I call the *scene of empathy,* we see a character's face, typically in closeup, either for a single shot of long duration or as an element of a point-of-view structure alternating between shots of the character's face and shots of what she or he sees. In either case, the prolonged concentration on the character's face is not warranted by the simple communication of information about character emotion. Such scenes are also intended to elicit empathetic emotions in the spectator.

Often the most significant scenes of empathy in a classical film occur at the film's end. *Yankee Doodle Dandy* (1942), for example, stars James Cagney as the well-known Broadway songwriter, actor, playwright and producer George M. Cohan. The film idealizes Cohan, representing him as witty, honest, loyal, humble, patriotic, and a marvelous theatrical talent. By the film's end, our allegiances are with Cohan, if we have allowed the film to do its work on us. In the last scene, the aging Cohan emerges from the White House of 1940, having just received the Congressional Medal of Honor for his "contribution to the American Spirit." In the streets in front of the White House, he finds a military parade, where the marchers and crowds sing his famous World War I patriotic song, "Over There." He joins the parade but does not sing, upon which the soldier marching next to him asks, "What's the matter, oldtimer? Don't you remember this song?" Soon after we cut to a 21-second frontal shot of Cohan, ending in a fadeout that closes the film. In this shot, the camera tracks back as Cohan marches forward, his face eventually framed in closeup. Cohan begins to sing, though reluctantly at first. His face soon becomes animated, a tear rolls down his cheek, and he robustly joins the crowds singing his own song.

Among film scholars, probably the best-known scene of empathy comes at the end of *Stella Dallas* (1937), in which Stella (Barbara Stanwyck), on a rainy night, watches the wedding of her estranged daughter from the street outside the wedding mansion. However, I foreground the scene of empathy in *Yankee Doodle Dandy* to counteract the assumption that scenes of empathy focus only on female characters and are aimed only at women in the audience. As I note below, some researchers believe that women have a greater capacity than men for empathy. While this may be true, scenes of empathy occur not only in so-called women's films, but in a wide array of genres, and not only in relation to female characters, but also to males. Think of the ending of *City Lights* (1931), for example, in which the Flower Vendor (Virginia Cherrill) discovers the identity of her benefactor in the tattered and embarrassed Tramp (Charles Chaplin), or a scene near the conclusion of *Blade Runner* (1982), in which the replicant Batty (Rutger Hauer), after saving the life of Deckard (Harrison Ford), mourns his own impending death. Scenes of empathy occur in diverse genres in relation to both female and male characters.

In this chapter I describe the use of the human face in the scene of empathy. First, I argue that facial expressions in film not only communicate emotion, but also elicit, clarify, and strengthen affective response—especially empathetic response. This is possible because viewing the human face can elicit response through the processes of affective mimicry, facial feedback, and emotional contagion. Second, I discuss and define empathy to better show how the representation of the face contributes to empathy for film characters. Third, I show how filmmakers use the human face in the "scene of empathy," and describe strategies designed to maximize the affective potential of the human face on film.

Facial Expression and Emotional Contagion

Clearly, film directors use the human face to *communicate* information about the emotions of characters. Noël Carroll has provided an analysis of how such communication functions.[3] Carroll is concerned with the use of the human face in movies in conjunction with point-of-view editing. In a point-of-view

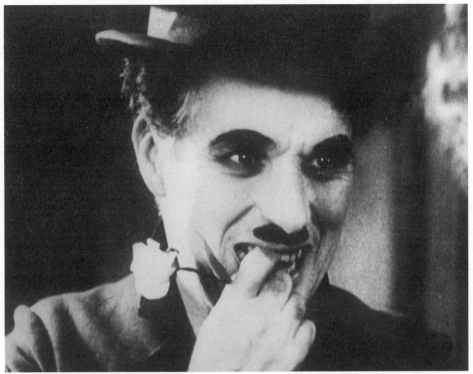

Charlie Chaplin's embarrassed smile at the end of *City Lights* (1931).

structure, a shot of the character's face—what Carroll calls, following Ed Branigan, a point/glance shot—is juxtaposed with a point/object shot, or a view of what the character sees. Carroll calls the point/glance shot a "rangefinder" because it enables us to identify the "global emotional state" of the character by viewing her or his face. The point/object shot is the "focuser" because it identifies what the character is viewing, or the object of the character's emotion.

The point/glance shot identifies emotion only in a broad sense, because without knowledge of the cause of the character's emotion, my understanding of her experience can only be approximate.[4] For example, a point/glance shot of Jeff (James Stewart) in *Rear Window* (1954) alerts me to his increasing fear, but the point/object shot focuses my understanding of the emotion by showing that Lisa (Grace Kelly) is in the murderer's apartment across the way, and that the murderer is about to enter the apartment. Thus we come to understand that Jeff's fear is not fear for himself, or an objectless dread, but rather fear that Lisa will be discovered and harmed. Point-of-view editing, then, communicates information about emotion in an efficient and powerful way.

Important though it may be, the point-of-view structure is not *necessary* for the powerful communication of emotion in movies. The object of a character's emotion can be communicated in other ways. Think, for example, of the musical motif that signals the presence of the shark in *Jaws* (1975). Moreover, and more important for this chapter, even given a lone closeup of a character's face the spectator can often comprehend the relevant emotion because we recognize that particular facial expressions signify identifiable emotional experiences.

To account for the successful communication of emotion via the face, we should note the psychological literature on cross-cultural uniformity in facial expressions. Paul Ekman, a chief proponent of the claim for universal facial expressions, claims the existence of pancultural facial expressions for five or six basic emotions. As Ekman writes, there "seems little basis for disputing the evidence that for at least five emotion categories there are facial behaviors specific to each emotion and that these relationships are invariant across cultures."[5]

Ekman, C. E. Izard, and S. S. Tomkins all hold to some variation of the "efference hypothesis," the proposal that the universal recognition of facial expression implies an underlying innate emotion "program" for each of a number of primary emotions.[6] These emotion programs are thought to include automatic neural "messages" to the facial musculature that—without "override" in accordance with social display conventions—produce the emotional facial expression. This in part accounts for the universal recognition of basic emotions on characters' faces whether a film is screened in Japan, France, or Brazil.[7]

None of these studies rules out cultural variation in emotional expression and recognition, but rather they find a core of pancultural similarities for the expression and recognition of basic emotions. Central to Ekman's claims, for example, is his contention that universal tendencies in facial expression are tempered by display rules, social conventions governing the appropriateness of emotional expression on the human face. These rules for the display of emotion are based on many factors, including social context, social status, and gender. In addition, while facial expressions are universal for central or basic emotions such as fear and sadness, the expressions for shame, envy, and other less basic emotions are more culturally variable.[8]

The *communication* of information about emotion, however important, is just part of the story. Viewing the human face can move beyond communication to *elicit* an emotional response in the viewer. That the face both communicates information about and elicits emotion is true both in our everyday lives and in our film-viewing experience. The represented face elicits emotion by various means, including the processes of "emotional contagion" as induced by "affective mimicry" and "facial feedback."

Emotional contagion is the phenomenon of "catching" others' emotions or affective states. It occurs in many ways and in diverse contexts. When our friends laugh and smile while telling us a story, we often laugh and smile in response, even if we fail to see the humor in the story itself. Their laughter is contagious. As most teachers know, when one student conspicuously yawns in the classroom, others are sure to follow. A cheering crowd at a sports match can elevate our level of excitement, while a room full of downtrodden people saps our energy and casts a pall on the occasion. We often recognize that when viewing films or plays, enthusiastic audience responses often build on each other, while an unresponsive audience can make the film or play seem dull and lifeless. Béla Belázs recognized the importance of contagion for the cinema in his emphasis on nonverbal expression. As he writes, "If we look at and understand each other's faces and gestures, we not only understand, we also learn to feel each other's emotions."[9] Although we sometimes resist the affective tenor of those around us, we have a tendency to "catch" others' moods and emotions.[10]

Contagion may result from variables other than viewing faces, such as seeing another's body posture or hearing crowd laughter. Nonetheless, the human face occupies a central place in eliciting emotion. An essential piece of the psychological puzzle here is *affective mimicry*. Elaine Hatfield et al. argue that humans have a "pervasive tendency automatically to mimic and synchronize expressions, vocalizations, postures, and movements with those of another person."[11] We are consciously aware only of a small portion of our tendencies in this respect. Since our minds are "modular" and capable of parallel processing, we can monitor another's emotions while doing other things, for example, carrying on a conversation or following a narrative. But more significantly, we not only monitor emotions, but often mimic the facial expressions of those with whom we interact.

We also sometimes mimic the facial expressions of people we see on film and video. In one experiment among many that produced similar results, researchers secretly videotaped students as they viewed a three-minute videotaped interview in which a man told either a happy or a sad story. Researchers then asked judges to rate the facial expressions of the students on videotape. As might be expected, subjects' faces mirrored those of the storyteller. They had happier faces when viewing the happy tale and sad faces when viewing the sad one.[12]

So far this is intuitively unsurprising. The next hypothesis, however, is far less intuitive. Today most theorists agree that our subjective emotions are influenced by *facial feedback,* such that the one who mimics a facial expression actually catches the emotions of the one mimicked. According to the *facial feedback hypothesis,* our facial expressions provide us with proprioceptive feedback which at most determines and at the least influences our emotional experience. For example, when I mimic a sad protagonist on film by making a sad face, this contributes to my subjective feeling of sadness. If I mimic a fearful face, it may actually make me fearful or increase my feeling of suspense.

A strong version of the hypothesis contends that facial feedback alone is sufficient to create emotional experience, or that feedback from facial expressions are actually constitutive of emotional experiences.[13] The weakest version of the hypothesis asserts that facial feedback influences emotional experience under some conditions, but is not sufficient to cause an emotion. Nico Frijda, for example, argues that facial feedback "is not the major determinant of emotional experience, and cannot be a sufficient condition for it." Moreover, Frijda claims, facial feedback contributes to emotional experience if and only if it complements other emotion processes already occurring.[14]

It is not my purpose to adjudicate between strong and weak versions of the facial feedback hypothesis. My argument depends on our accepting only the weak version of the hypothesis for film, the claim that facial feedback contributes to emotional experience if and only if it complements other emotion processes. Thus I demonstrate below the strategies used by filmmakers in tandem with the face to elicit empathic response. If it turns out that the strong version is in fact correct, this of course strengthens my argument.

Upon further consideration, the frequent and consistent use of extended closeups of emoting faces on film provides more evidence for the feedback hypothesis. Closeups of protagonists' emotional faces are often presented for much longer than is necessary for the mere communication of emotion, or for the cogitation necessary to comprehend the character's situation. In such cases, their purpose must be to promote spectator empathy through facial feedback and emotional contagion.

Spectator Empathy

Our orientation toward film or literary characters has vaguely been called *identification,* but a better term is *character engagement.*[15] *Identification* is misleading because it implies a losing of the self in the other, whereby our identity as a separate individual momentarily becomes lost or weakened as we identify with a character on the screen. While such a relationship is certainly possible, it is not the only way to engage with characters, and probably not normative for most spectators. As others have argued, we engage with characters from the perspective of a separate self, or from the "outside."[16] *Engagement* is broader and more neutral, better able to embody the wide variety of experiences that characterize our orientation toward characters, ranging from adulation to active dislike, from affective mimicry to revulsion. *Engagement* allows for empathy and antipathy, sympathy and indifference, and certainly implies no melding of minds or identities.[17]

Within the numerous possible varieties of character engagement, where does empathy lie? There is much disagreement about just what empathy is.[18] Let me begin by saying what empathy is not. First, empathy is not a single emotion. Nearly all definitions of empathy stipulate that to empathize with another requires sharing her or his emotional experience, at least in part. When we empathize with a joyful friend, we feel joy or happiness, but when we empathize with a sad friend, we feel sadness. To return to the scene from *Yankee Doodle Dandy*, empathy for Cohan involves a mixture of compassion, admiration, and perhaps pity. So rather than a single emotion, empathy may incorporate varied sorts of emotional experiences.[19]

Empathy consists of a capacity or disposition to know, to feel, and to respond congruently to what another is feeling, and the process of doing so. I may lack the capacity for empathy if I am distracted by my own problems and continually fail to notice what those around me are feeling. If I do notice and understand, but consistently fail to respond congruently, then perhaps I am indifferent or hostile, and/or my capacity for empathy is weak.

Returning to the *Yankee Doodle Dandy* example, when we empathize with Cohan at least two processes occur, both characteristic of empathy in general. First, we undertake a kind of mental simulation by which I imagine and dwell on his condition. We do not necessarily imagine being Cohan, but imagine what Cohan must be thinking and feeling. We imagine his pride in his accomplishments and his patriotic fervor as he joins the marching, singing crowd. After being referred to as an oldtimer, perhaps he experiences a touch of self-pity and regret that he has been largely forgotten by the public, and that he is nearing the end of his life (his parents and wife all are deceased).

Second, to experience empathy I must have emotions *congruent* to those I imagine Cohan is feeling. To respond "congruently" to another's emotions is to respond in a way that evinces commonality or solidarity with the person's goals or desires. If I scowl or laugh derisively when Cohan begins to sing "Over There," this is an expression of indifference or hostility. On the other hand, when I respond with compassion, admiration, or adulation, I am expressing solidarity in that I share Cohan's orientation toward his experience, and perhaps even some similar feelings. Neither empathy nor the affective congruence on which empathy depends require that I experience the *same* emotions I imagine Cohan does. Congruent emotions are sufficient for empathy.

Some scholars draw a sharp distinction between sympathetic and empathetic responses to film characters. Alex Neill writes that while sympathy and empathy are both "other-focused" emotional responses, sympathy requires that, for example, I fear *for* you, while empathy allows me also to fear *with* you. Neill claims that in sympathy my response need not reflect what the other is feeling. I may feel pity or fear for you irrespective of what you feel.

James Cagney as Broadway producer George M. Cohan
in *Yankee Doodle Dandy* (1942).

In principle, I can sympathize with another without feeling anything at all. On the other hand, to empathize with another, Neill claims, "is to experience the emotion(s) that he experiences."[20]

The distinction between empathy and sympathy, however, is far less clear than this. When Jacques falls off his bicycle, I may empathize with him without sharing his emotions. I may feel compassion for him, for example, but he may feel only anger at the pedestrian who caused the accident. I take my response to be empathetic, even though my emotional experience is far different than his. Moreover, I may empathize with Cohan at the end of *Yankee Doodle Dandy* by feeling admiration and compassion for him, even though he does not feel admiration or compassion for himself (perhaps he feels pride and self-pity). As I mentioned above, empathy requires congruent emotion, but not wholly shared emotions.

If empathy is defined as shared feeling, and sympathy as concern with no shared feeling, then it will be difficult to determine where empathy ends and sympathy begins. Arguably, I can never share exactly the same feelings as a person with whom I empathize. Vicarious experience can be similar to our own, but it is far less intense. This seems especially true of my empathy for film characters, since at some level I must realize that the characters are fictional. But putting aside for the moment the problem of sharing feelings with a fictional character, one still wants to ask, "Which of a character's feelings must I share for me to feel empathy?" On the other hand, to say that sympathy ends when we share feelings with another seems too restrictive. In either case, the distinction between sympathy and empathy is not clearly made.

The fact that empathy as shared feeling and sympathy as concern shade into each other might cause no conceptual trouble. After all, red shades into orange, but few of us would deny that red and orange are separate colors. Empathy and sympathy, however, have no central examples, like red and orange, that are clearly differentiated. Take sympathy, for example. It is questionable that sympathy should be defined as concern that demands no congruent or shared feelings. Alex Neill's distinction between empathy and sympathy does not correspond with dictionary definitions, which typically appeal to "shared feeling" to define the word "sympathy." Moreover, in ordinary usage, the appeal to shared feeling cannot adequately distinguish empathy from sympathy. Both may involve a shared moral and affective stance toward another's situation, and neither requires an identity of feeling between observer and observed.

For the purposes of this chapter it is better to maintain a loose definition of empathy because empathy is neither a simple process nor one clearly understood. Empathy may involve several varied feelings that evolve and shade into each other. Empathy incorporates both cognitive and physiological, voluntary and involuntary processes. It involves both imagining the situation of a character from the outside and, perhaps in a few cases, imagining being a character. Most important, it is dependent on a temporal process of narration, together with the stream of evaluations and inferences cued by the narration.

The Face in the Scene of Empathy

The most common use of the human face in film is to give information about characters' reactions. However, scenes of empathy go beyond this. At the end of *Stella Dallas* (1937), for example, the camera lingers on Stella's face as she views the wedding of her estranged daughter. Even after we have understood the implications of the situation, we continually return to Stella's face. To use Carroll's terminology, the range and focus of Stella's emotions have been sufficiently communicated, yet her face remains on screen. As I argued above, the depicted face not only *communicates* information about emotion, but also *elicits* an emotional response.

I have already made the distinction between eliciting emotional response in the viewer and communicating information to the viewer about a character's emotion. We must also distinguish between *elicitors* and *conditioners* of affective response. Emotional contagion in film is dependent not merely on the characteristics of the film—*elicitors* of response—but also on *conditioners* of response such as viewing context and individual differences.[21] One of the most powerful affective experiences in my moviegoing life occurred at a sold-out screening of the horrific *Alien* (1979). The audience members were extremely responsive; the palpable fear and suspense in the theater became contagious due to their frequent murmurs and sighs. Their shouts and screams made the film's shocks and surprises all the more powerful. Contagion doesn't move only from character to spectator, but between spectators.[22] This is one form of the conditioning of affective response—viewing context.

Individual differences also condition response. Persons clearly have varied capacities for both understanding and reacting to others' emotional states. Some are able to read others' emotions more accurately and quickly than others. Some are more prone to mimic others' emotions, while others are more likely to react emotionally to others. For example, gender may play a significant role in empathic experience. Some psychological research shows that in Western culture, at least, women are both more expressive of various emotions and surpass males in recognizing and interpreting others' emotional states based on nonverbal expression.[23] This suggests that females tend to have a superior capacity for empathy in Western culture.

Conditioners such as viewing context and individual differences play a key role in film empathy, but they raise complex issues that could occupy entire research programs and are clearly beyond the scope of this chapter. My major concern here will be with elicitors—characteristics of the film that elicit response—rather than conditioners. This assumes a spectator who has become engrossed in the film and is having the affective response intended by the film's makers. Throughout what comes below I will be referring to this implied spectator. However, I do not wish to deny or condemn alternative kinds of responses.

Eliciting empathy via the represented face is not a simple matter. The human face can serve as a stimulus for emotion, but such a function is not automatic or unproblematic. As mentioned above, the weak version of the efference hypothesis holds that facial feedback contributes to emotional experience if and only if it complements emotion processes already occurring. Moreover, the face itself is a complex signifier of emotion. In many circumstances, the face constantly changes and shifts expression, a clear result of the transient nature of both thought and emotion. This can make faces difficult to interpret. To complicate matters, the face is used for much else than to convey emotions. Among its other central functions are the giving of conversational signals and the hiding of emotions. Given the intuitive plausibility of these considerations, filmmakers employ particular strategies to maximize the probability that the represented face will elicit an empathetic emotional response.

Attention

Attention must be focused on the character's facial expression to elicit contagion. This can be accomplished in many ways, from the use of the closeup, to shallow focus, to point-of-view structures. Scenes of empathy often incorporate progressively closer shots as a stylistic means of focusing our attention on the character's interior life. At the end of *Stella Dallas,* we cut from a medium long shot to a medium shot to a medium closeup to a full head shot of Stella as the intended emotional contagion increases. In the last shot of *Stella Dallas,* Stella walks toward the camera, and as her stride picks up, she nears the camera, so that we may focus on her face. The camera moves in to express and encourage progressive interiority, and to focus our attention squarely on Stella's facial expression.

Duration

The duration of the shot (or scene) must be sufficient to allow for the response it is intended to elicit. Many closeups and other shots of the face are too short in duration to provide for such a response, and are designed only to communicate emotion information. Shots within scenes of empathy are often of much longer duration.

Average shot lengths in mainstream films have been steadily decreasing since the 1960s. By 1981, the average shot length for motion pictures was roughly 10 seconds. (For some action pictures, shot length is much shorter, for example *Die Hard II* [3.1 seconds], *The Crow* [2.7 seconds], and *The Fugitive* [3.9 seconds].)[24] It has been estimated that today's average film contains roughly 1,200 shots. If we take the 1,200 shots figure, and consider two hours to be the average length of a feature, then the average shot length would be about six seconds.[25]

Contrast this with the length of shots used in scenes of empathy. For example, in *The Piano* (1993), Ada (Holly Hunter) comes to her new island home but must leave her piano, her chief means of expression, behind on the beach. As a group of men leads her deep into the jungle, they reach a vantage point from which Ada views the abandoned piano. Here we get a 21-second closeup of Ada's sorrowful face. Later in the film, after the piano is sold against Ada's will, we are shown a similar closeup, this time 33 seconds in duration.

The discussion of mere shot length, however, is not sufficient to understand the durational elements of scenes of empathy. Characteristic of such scenes are point-of-view structures that alternate between point/glance shots and the point/object shots. The duration of the entire point-of-view structure becomes the relevant variable here. At the end of *Stella Dallas,* none of the shots are as long as those mentioned in *The Piano.* In fact, the climactic closeup—a full head shot of Stella—is but 15 seconds long. However, the entire scene, during which we continually return to Stella's face from point/object shots of her daughter's wedding, is over two minutes in duration. For another example, in the famous scene that closes *City Lights,* in which the formerly blind Flower Vendor recognizes her benefactor as the Little Tramp, the film alternates for over one minute between closeups of the two faces as they express a range of emotions. At the end of *Blade Runner,* Roy Batty (Rutger Hauer) relates his cherished memories to Deckard (Harrison Ford), then bows his head and expires. Here we get almost one minute of a closeup of Batty, punctuated by brief point/glance shots of Deckard.

Empathy is a process that occurs in time, and emotions take time to catch. Therefore, the faces are either left on the screen for sufficient duration, or else we continually return to them within the point-of-view structure. Emotions also have a residual effect. Once they are caught, they are not quickly overcome. This in part accounts for the placement of scenes of compassionate empathy at the end of many films, where an emotional response can serve as a release, and where it will not interfere with the comprehension of succeeding narrative developments.

Allegiance

Allegiance to the character whose face is presented in part determines the degree of contagion and empathy. As psychologists note, we are more likely to catch the emotions of those with whom we construe our relationship as one of relatedness and/or likeness rather than independence and uniqueness.[26] Moreover, we are more likely to respond with emotional contagion to those we like. If we have no allegiance for a film character, or if we exercise an active antipathy, then the likelihood of our responding empathetically is diminished. Even if we respond somewhat involuntarily to the human face, if it is the face of one to whom we are indifferent, we are more likely to distance ourselves, let our attention wander, or intentionally counteract the affective prompt.

Narrative Context

Narrative context is probably the most complex and significant elicitor of empathic response. If empathy is in part a cognitive process, the narrative must lay the proper foundation for empathy to occur. Insufficient or inappropriate narrative development will counteract or even contradict our tendency toward emotional contagion and mimicry.

As persons skilled (to lesser or greater degrees) in social discourse, we implicitly recognize that the faces of those around us are used for diverse purposes. In public situations, the face is as likely to be used to hide emotions or to facilitate conversation as it is to reveal genuine interior states. In scenes of empathy, however, the face expresses the interiority of the character. For this reason, such scenes place characters in situations in which their facial expressions will not be understood as misleading.

One means of doing this is to make the situation private or, in other words, to put the emoting character in a situation where she or he believes no one is observing. In such situations, social display rules are irrelevant and the face becomes an accurate sign of emotion. In the scenes from *The Piano* mentioned above, there are no characters other than Ada in the immediate vicinity, and none to view her private expressions of sorrow. In the scenes of empathy in both *Yankee Doodle Dandy* and *Stella Dallas,* the characters are placed in manifestly public settings, but go unnoticed by other characters in the fictional world. In *Blade Runner,* Roy Batty knows that Deckard is watching his emotion display. However, since Batty's death is impending, the context does not call for hiding his emotions or altering his facial expression. On the contrary, his speech here is a kind of confession, a heartfelt expression of his cherished memories and his deepest regrets. In all of these cases, the filmmakers create a context in which we may interpret the face as an accurate sign of inner experience.

Whether a facial expression is a public or private display is one sense in which narrative context is important. In another sense, narrative context must justify the spectator's empathy in moral terms. We do not extend our empathy easily or without conditions, and are wary of attempts to elicit unearned or misplaced emotion, or what is called sentimentality.[27] A paradigmatic case of sentimentality occurs in *Mr. Holland's Opus* (1995). Glenn Holland (Richard Dreyfuss) is an ambitious musician and composer for whom economic necessity requires that he take a job as a high school teacher. Holland had been obsessed with his career and was a lousy parent to his deaf son. However, he comes to realize that he has been a neglectful parent and decides to make amends. His penance comes in the form of an improbable and impromptu solo performance at a public concert, during which he sings John Lennon's "Beautiful Boy (Darling Boy)" to his deaf son in the audience.

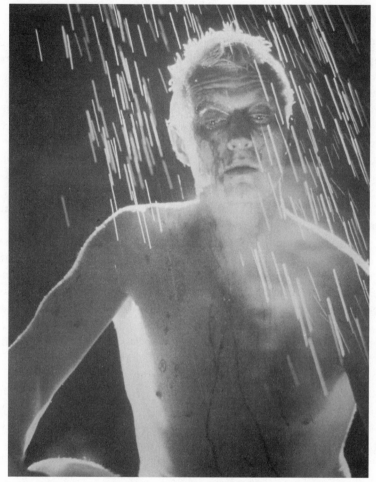

Rutger Hauer as the "replicant" Roy Batty, giving his dying soliloquy.
From Ridley Scott's *Blade Runner* (1982).

But why should the spectator so easily accept this sudden change of heart, given that, aside from this impromptu performance, we have seen little evidence of Holland's improved parenting? And why should the audience at the concert be interested, given that even those who know Holland personally are unlikely to be aware of the miserable relationship between him and his son? (This ignores the question of the propriety of a mediocre singer surprising an audience with a vocal solo.) The intended empathy here is unearned and improbable, and therefore sentimental.

To avoid sentimentality and to sufficiently justify the spectator's empathy, scenes of empathy must be put in moral context that assumes a good deal of information about the character in question. For this reason, scenes of empathy often occur at the film's end, after such a context has been developed. Our response to Stella at the end of *Stella Dallas* comes only after a full exposition of her character and situation. However, scenes of empathy may also occur within the body of the narrative, as in many of Frank Capra's films. In *Mr. Smith Goes to Washington* (1939), for example, the scene of empathy occurs at the Lincoln Memorial where Jefferson Smith (James Stewart) mourns his loss of ideals and the corrupt state of the world. After some words of encouragement from his secretary (Jean Arthur), however, he decides to carry on the fight anyway, leading to the upbeat ending we expect from Capra.

To contextualize empathy, films often attempt to elicit an empathetic response only after a protagonist has undergone some kind of trial or sacrifice, has neared the end of her or his life, or in some cases, has actually died. As we have seen, the empathy scene in *Yankee Doodle Dandy* occurs near the end of Cohan's life. The empathy scene in *Stella Dallas* occurs after Stella has sacrificed her relationship with her daughter for the daughter's benefit. The scene in *Blade Runner* occurs after Batty has saved Deckard's life and approaches his own death. In many films, our response to the scene of empathy may hinge on whether we believe the character deserves our empathy. In *The Piano*, our response to the scenes of empathy depends on whether we believe Ada is justified in her experience of deep sorrow when faced with the loss of her piano. To take another example, if we believe Jefferson Smith in *Mr. Smith Goes to Washington* to have been hopelessly naive from the beginning, we may not empathize with his despair when he recognizes the corruption in the federal government.

Scenes of empathy are often used sparingly, and the most powerful instances are reserved for a kind of emotional and cognitive summation of the ideological project of the film. In *Yankee Doodle Dandy*, the use of the face is meant to solidify the rhetorical position of the film by reinforcing empathy for an exemplary man. If the spectator is suspicious of the values he represents—patriotic fervor, for example—then the empathetic response to Cohan's face may be tempered by a resistance to the fervor Cohan so clearly embraces. Empathy, like other emotional responses, is fully integrated in the film's moral and ideological project.[28]

Affective Congruence

Empathic response also depends on *affective congruence* between narrative context, character engagement, various uses of film style and technique, and the psychological impressions and responses they generate. In *Art and Illusion*, E. H. Gombrich writes of synesthesia, which he defines as "the splashing over of impressions from one sense modality to another."[29] For example, various sounds can suggest visual impressions, and the sounds of some words seem to fit their conventional meaning, such as "flicker," "blinking," and "scintillating." Various uses of sight and sound have correspondences in which artists have long been interested. Such correspondences extend beyond cross-modal sensory experience to the realm of affect and emotion. For example, research suggests that audiences tend to relate various stylistic features, such as the wavy or jagged lines of a drawing, with affects such as calmness or nervousness.[30]

Such discussions of affective congruence have clear potential for film studies because film is such a hybrid art, mixing compositional elements such as line, mass, and color, sounds such as music, patterns of speech, and noise, together with apparent movement, rhythms, and cadences, and in addition perceptually realistic representations of persons and environments. No doubt affective and synesthetic correspondences have complex origins in natural, cultural, and personally idiosyncratic factors. But we need not fully understand the causes of affective congruence to recognize its usefulness in eliciting powerful affective responses. Thus, for example, the pattern of editing in the Odessa Steps sequence of *Battleship Potemkin* (1925) works in congruence with the events depicted and other stylistic features to elicit suspense and excitement.

In this volume, Jeff Smith is particularly concerned with the affective congruence of music in his "Movie Music as Moving Music: Emotion, Cognition, and the Film Score." There he argues that affective congruence occurs when the affective meaning of film music and other film elements match or are fitting. Most significantly for my purposes, Smith argues that when the affective meaning of other elements of a film are pronounced, the use of fitting music heightens that affective meaning, giving it a charge stronger than either the music or the other elements alone.

Of course, this kind of congruence has marked significance for scenes of empathy. If the filmmaker's goal is to increase the probability that the spectator will experience emotional contagion, then cross-modal congruence is an obvious strategy. In fact, most scenes of empathy *do* incorporate music as an essential element to elicit response. In the *Yankee Doodle Dandy* scene, of course, we hear a rousing rendition of "Over There," intended to strengthen our admiration of Cohan for his talent and patriotic dedication. During the scene of empathy that ends *Stella Dallas,* a plaintive melody played by stringed instruments expresses the combination of happiness and sorrow Stella is imagined to feel. Evocative music is also used in the relevant scenes from *Blade Runner* and *The Piano.* The conventional scene of empathy uses music for affective congruence and to encourage emotional contagion. And since affective mimicry and emotional contagion likely occur only when married to other emotion-eliciting processes, we can see why music and other stylistic elements are typically used in scenes of empathy.

Conclusion

As I have argued, the represented face plays an important role in eliciting spectator empathy for film characters. Emotional contagion is an involuntary phenomenon. Yet empathy itself is not involuntary, or at least not wholly so. Facial mimicry and emotional contagion are merely parts of a more complex process. If we accept a weak version of the efference hypothesis, then facial mimicry would occur, and would affect spectator response, only when used in tandem with other congruent and mutually reinforcing factors. For this reason I have written of the scene of empathy as a combination of techniques and strategies.

This description of the conventional scene of empathy, however, leaves many questions for further study. We could explore the conventional use of the human face in various genres or in the work of particular directors. Moreover, I have written of the use of the face to elicit empathy, but closeups of the human face have other functions. What of closeups that lack the contextual factors I described above? Might some films play on the involuntary processes of emotional contagion, but discourage contagion through various distancing strategies? We might also examine in greater detail the rhetorical, ideological, and aesthetic uses of the represented face. These issues deserve further study in an investigation of the represented face on film.

NOTES

Introduction

1. W. K. Wimsatt and Monroe Beardsley, "The Affective Fallacy," in *Critical Theory Since Plato*, ed. Hazard Adams (New York: Harcourt Brace Jovanovich, 1971), 1027.

2. T. S. Eliot, *Hamlet* (1919).

3. T. S. Eliot, "Tradition and the Individual Talent" (1919), in *Twentieth-Century Literary Criticism*, ed. David Lodge (London: Longman, 1972), 76.

4. George Dickie and Richard J. Sclafani, eds., *Aesthetics: A Critical Anthology* (New York: St. Martin's Press, 1977), 755–815.

5. Clive Bell, "Art as Significant Form: The Aesthetic Hypothesis," in ibid., 44.

6. Ibid., 46.

7. William Lyons, *Emotion* (Cambridge: Cambridge University Press, 1980), 100–104.

8. Colin Radford, "How Can We Be Moved by the Fate of Anna Karenina?" *Proceedings of the Aristotelian Society*, Supp. vol. 49 (1975): 67–70.

9. Roger Scruton, *Art and Imagination: A Study in the Philosophy of Mind* (London: Methuen, 1974).

10. Kendall Walton, *Mimesis as Make-Believe: On the Foundations of the Representational Arts* (Cambridge: Harvard University Press, 1990).

11. Gregory Currie, *Image and Mind: Film, Philosophy, and Cognitive Science* (Cambridge: Cambridge University Press, 1995), 144–45.

12. Hans Kreitler and Shulamith Kreitler, *Psychology of the Arts* (Durham, N.C.: Duke University Press, 1972).

13. William James, "What Is an Emotion?" *Mind* 9 (1884): 188–205.

14. Pamela K. Adelmann and R. B. Zajonc, "Facial Efference and the Experience of Emotion," in *Annual Review of Psychology* 40, ed. M. R. Rosenzweig and L. W. Porter (1989): 249–80; Paul Ekman, Robert W. Levenson, and Wallace V. Friesen, "Autonomic Nervous System Activity Distinguishes among Emotions," *Science* 221, no. 4616 (1983): 1208–10; Carroll E. Izard, "Facial Expressions and the Regulation of Emotions," *Journal of Personality and Social Psychology* 58 (1990): 487–98.

15. Walter Cannon, "The James-Lange Theory of Emotions: A Critical Examination and an Alternative Theory," *American Journal of Psychology* 39 (1927): 106–24; Walter Cannon, "Again the James-Lange and Thalamic Theories of Emotion," *Psychological Review* 38 (1931): 281–95.

16. Joseph LeDoux, *The Emotional Brain: The Mysterious Underpinnings of Emotional Life* (New York: Simon and Schuster, 1996); Jaak Panksepp, "The Anatomy of Emotions," in *Emotion: Theory, Research and Experience,* vol. 3, ed. Robert Plutchik and Henry Kellerman (New York: Academic Press, 1986), 91–124.

17. Magda B. Arnold, *Emotion and Personality* (New York: Columbia University Press, 1960); Stanley Schachter and Jerome E. Singer, "Cognitive, Social, and Physiological Determinants of Emotional State," *Psychological Review* 69 (1962): 379–99.

18. Richard S. Lazarus, *Emotion and Adaptation* (New York: Oxford University Press, 1991), 192.

19. Nico Frijda, *The Emotions* (Cambridge: Cambridge University Press, 1986).

20. James R. Averill, "A Constructivist View of Emotion," in *Emotion: Theory, Research, and Experience,* vol. 1, ed. Robert Plutchik and Henry Kellerman (New York: Academic Press, 1980), 305–39.

21. Catherine A. Lutz, *Unnatural Emotions: Everyday Sentiments on a Micronesian Atoll and Their Challenge to Western Theory* (Chicago: University of Chicago Press, 1988).

22. Silvan S. Tomkins, *Affect, Imagery, and Consciousness:* vol. 1, *The Positive Affects* (New York: Springer, 1962); vol. 2, *The Negative Affects* (New York: Springer, 1963). Also see Frijda, *The Emotions.*

23. Christian Metz, *The Imaginary Signifier: Psychoanalysis and the Cinema,* trans. Celia Britton, Annwyl Williams, Ben Brewster, and Alfred Guzzetti (Bloomington: Indiana University Press, 1980); Laura Mulvey, "Visual Pleasure and Narrative Cinema," in *Movies and Methods,* ed. Bill Nichols (Berkeley: University of California Press, 1985), 2:303–15.

24. Claire Johnston, ed., "Notes on Women's Cinema," BFI pamphlet, 1973; Mary Ann Doane, *The Desire to Desire: The Woman's Film of the 1940s* (Bloomington: Indiana University Press, 1987); Gaylyn Studlar, *In the Realm of Pleasure: Von Sternberg, Dietrich, and the Masochistic Aesthetic* (Urbana: University of Illinois Press, 1988); Linda Williams, *Hard Core: Power, Pleasure, and the Frenzy of the Visible* (Berkeley: University of California Press, 1989).

25. E. Ann Kaplan, "The Case of the Missing Mother: Maternal Issues in Vidor's *Stella Dallas,*" *Camera Obscura* 20–21 (May–Sept. 1989): 198.

26. Linda Williams, "Something Else Besides a Mother: *Stella Dallas* and the Maternal Melodrama," in *Issues in Feminist Film Criticism,* ed. Patricia Erens (Bloomington: Indiana University Press, 1991), 137–62.

27. Patrice Petro, *Joyless Streets: Women and Melodramatic Representation in Weimar Germany* (Princeton: Princeton University Press, 1989); Miriam Hansen, *Babel and Babylon: Spectatorship in American Silent Film* (Cambridge: Harvard University Press, 1991).

28. Otto Fenichel, "The Ego and the Affects," *Psychoanalytic Review* 28 (1941): 47–60; David Rapaport, "On the Psychoanalytic Theory of Affects," in *Psychoanalytic Psychiatry and Psychology, Clinical and Theoretical Papers,* ed. Robert P. Knight and Cyrus R. Friedman (New York: International Universities Press, 1954),

274–310; Stuart Hampshire, "Notions of the Unconscious Mind," in *States of Mind,* ed. Jonathan Miller (New York: Pantheon, 1983), 110–15.

29. Jerome C. Wakefield, "Freud and the Intentionality of Affect," *Psychoanalytic Psychology* 9, no. 1 (1992): 2.

30. Jerome C. Wakefield, "Why Emotions Can't Be Unconscious: An Exploration of Freud's Essentialism," *Psychoanalysis and Contemporary Thought* 14, no. 1 (1991): 63.

31. Hugo Munsterberg, *The Film: A Psychological Study* (New York: Dover Publications, 1970), 48, 53.

32. V. F. Perkins, *Film as Film: Understanding and Judging Movies* (Middlesex: Penguin Books, 1972), 134–57.

33. Edward Branigan, *Point of View in the Cinema* (Berlin: Mouton, 1984); David Bordwell, *Narration in the Fiction Film* (Madison: University of Wisconsin Press, 1985); Noël Carroll, *Mystifying Movies: Fads and Fallacies in Contemporary Film Theory* (New York: Columbia University Press, 1988); David Bordwell, *Making Meaning: Inference and Rhetoric in the Interpretation of the Cinema* (Cambridge: Harvard University Press, 1989).

34. David Bordwell and Noël Carroll, eds., *Post-Theory: Reconstructing Film Studies* (Madison: University of Wisconsin Press, 1996). See also Joseph D. Anderson, *The Reality of Illusion: An Ecological Approach to Cognitive Film Theory* (Carbondale: Southern Illinois University Press, 1996); David Bordwell, "A Case for Cognitivism," *Iris* 9 (1989): 11–40; Edward Branigan, *Narrative Comprehension and Film* (New York: Routledge, 1992); Noël Carroll, *The Philosophy of Horror, or Paradoxes of the Heart* (New York: Routledge, 1990); Noël Carroll, *Theorizing the Moving Image* (Cambridge: Cambridge University Press, 1996); Paul Messaris, *Visual "Literacy": Image, Mind, and Reality* (Boulder, Colo.: Westview Press, 1994).

35. Murray Smith, *Engaging Characters: Fiction, Emotion, and the Cinema* (Oxford: Clarendon Press, 1995); Ed S. Tan, *Emotion and the Structure of Narrative Film: Film as an Emotion Machine,* trans. Barbara Fasting (Mahwah, N.J.: Erlbaum, 1996); Torben Kragh Grodal, *Moving Pictures: A New Theory of Film Genres, Feelings, and Cognition* (Oxford: Clarendon Press, 1997).

36. Carroll, *Mystifying Movies,* 227.

Chapter 1. Film, Emotion and Genre

1. By only alluding to cognitively impenetrable affects here, I do not want to suggest that other states—such as pleasure and desire—do not warrant study. I consider those to be topics for future research. I have even attempted some preliminary work on desire in my book *A Philosophy of Mass Art* (Oxford: Clarendon, 1998).

2. When I say that ordinary language treats these examples as paradigmatic, what I have in mind is that, when asked, competent language users will tend to offer phenomena like these—especially fear, anger, sadness and love—as central instances of emotional states.

3. Ed S. Tan, *Emotion and the Structure of Narrative Film: Film as an Emotion Machine,* trans. Barbara Fasting (Mahwah, N.J.: Erlbaum, 1996).

4. William James, "What Is an Emotion?" in *Mind* 9 (1884): 188–205.

5. Robert Solomon, "The Jamesian Theory of Emotion in Anthropology," in *Culture Theory: Essays on Mind. Self and Emotion*, ed. Richard A. Shweder and Robert A. LeVine (Cambridge: Cambridge University Press, 1984), 214.

6. Though the case that follows is made up, it is not entirely fanciful, since experiments like it have been run. A classic example in the literature is Stanley Schachter and Jerome E. Singer, "Cognitive, Social, and Physiological Determinants of State," excerpted in *What Is An Emotion?*, ed. Cheshire Calhoun and Robert C. Solomon (Oxford: Oxford University Press, 1984), 173–83.

7. Here it might be argued that there are some emotional states, like free-floating depression, that do not take objects. Rather than deny that there are such states, I prefer to take advantage of the distinction I drew earlier between affects broadly construed and paradigmatic emotional states. Perhaps free-floating depression is just not a core case of the emotions proper. Maybe it is an affective state brought about by chemical imbalances in the body.

8. Some garden-variety emotions may also include—in addition to cognitions and bodily feelings—desires as a typical or even a necessary component.

9. In this, I will restrict myself to the case of viewing narrative fiction films rather than to abstract and/or nonnarrative films. I have made this methodological decision not only because it makes the job easier, but because I think that we will be in a better position to understand the operation of the emotions in the latter when we understand it in relation to the former. Unfortunately, in this paper, I only have space to deal with the case of the fictional narrative.

I will also not be considering the role of music in engendering movie emotion in this paper. However, I have made a stab at that topic in Noël Carroll, "Notes on Movie Music," in my *Theorizing the Moving Image* (Cambridge: Cambridge University Press, 1996).

10. With respect to the arguments in this paper, see also Noël Carroll, "Art, Nature and Emotion," in *The Emotions and Art*, ed. Mette Hjort and Sue Laver (Oxford: Oxford University Press, 1997); and my *Philosophy of Mass Art*, esp. chap. 4.

11. I address the use of point-of-view editing to prefocus audience attention emotively in my "Toward a Theory of Point-of-View Editing: Communication, Emotion and the Movies," in *Theorizing the Moving Image*.

12. I talk of what is "generally" or "very frequently" the case in fiction films here because sometimes a character or a scene in a film may be emotively marked in an initially ambiguous way. This is a *standard* deviation from the norm whose existence I would not wish to deny. However, above I am talking about the norm in order to illustrate what I mean by talking about the emotive prefocusing of scenes, sequences and characters. Moreover, even where the filmic phenomena are ambiguously marked, that too is generally (barring cases of ineptitude) a function of the filmmakers' design and prefocusing activity.

13. The notion of dysphoric and euphoric emotion here comes from Keith Oatley, *Best-Laid Schemes* (Cambridge: Cambridge University Press, 1992), 107–9, 174–77.

14. This section has been inspired by an important article by Flo Leibowitz. See

her "Apt Feelings, or Why 'Women's Films' Aren't Trivial," in *Post-Theory: Reconstructing Film Studies*, ed. David Bordwell and Noël Carroll (Madison: University of Wisconsin Press, 1996).

15. The account of horror derives from Noël Carroll, *The Philosophy of Horror, or Paradoxes of the Heart* (New York: Routledge, 1990). See also Noël Carroll, "Horror and Humor," in *Philosophy and Literature* (forthcoming).

16. See David Pole, "Disgust and Other Forms of Aversion," in his *Aesthetics, Form and Emotion*, ed. George Roberts (New York: St. Martin's Press, 1983).

17. For further discussions of suspense, see Noël Carroll, "Toward a Theory of Film Suspense," in *Theorizing the Moving Image* (Cambridge: Cambridge University Press, 1996); and Noël Carroll, "The Paradox of Suspense," in *Suspense: Conceptualizations, Theoretical Analyses, and Empirical Explorations*, ed. Peter Vorderer, Hans J. Wulff, and Mike Friedrichsen (Hilldale, N.J.: Erlbaum, 1996).

Chapter 2. Sentiment in Film Viewing

1. G. W. Hohmann, "Some Effects of Spinal Cord Lesions on Experienced Emotional Feelings," in *Psychophysiology* 3 (1966): 143–56.

2. R. F. Brissenden, *Virtue in Distress: Studies in the Novel of Sentiment from Richardson to Sade* (London: Macmillan, 1974). Also see Annemieke Meijer, "The Pure Language of the Heart: Sentimentalism in the Netherlands, 1775–1800," Ph.D. diss., Utrecht University, 1995.

3. Robert Lang, *American Film Melodrama* (Princeton: Princeton University Press, 1989).

4. Thomas Schatz, *Hollywood Genres: Formulas, Filmmaking and the Studio System* (Philadelphia: Temple University Press, 1981), 222.

5. Murray Smith, *Engaging Characters* (Oxford: Clarendon Press, 1995).

6. Steven Neale, "Melo Talk: On the Meaning and Use of the Term 'Melodrama' in the American Trade Press," *The Velvet Light Trap* 32 (1993): 66–89.

7. Elly Konijn, *Acteurs Spelen Emoties* (Amsterdam: Boom, 1994).

8. Carl Plantinga, "Affect, Cognition and the Power of Movies," *Postscript* 13, no. 1 (Fall 1993): 10–29.

9. Ed Tan, "Film-Induced Affect as a Witness Emotion," *Poetics* 23 (1995): 7–32; Ed Tan, *Emotion and the Structure of Narrative Film: Film as an Emotion Machine*, trans. Barbara Fasting (Mahwah, N.J.: Erlbaum, 1996).

10. Nico H. Frijda, *The Emotions* (Cambridge: Cambridge University Press, 1986).

11. For a more detailed discussion of the various emotions and their joint temporal structure, see Tan, *Emotion and the Structure of Narrative Film*.

12. Frijda, *The Emotions*, 53.

13. Helmuth Plessner, *Lachen und Weinen* (Bern: Francke, 1941).

14. J. S. Efran and T. J. Spangler, "Why Grown-ups Cry: A Two-Factor Theory and Evidence from 'The Miracle Worker,'" *Motivation and Emotion* 3 (1979): 63–71.

15. Tan, "Film-Induced Affect," and *Emotion and the Structure of Narrative Film*. See also Ed Tan and Gijsbert Diteweg, "Suspense, Predictive Inference and Emotion in Film Viewing," in *Suspense: Conceptualizations, Theoretical Analyses*,

and Empirical Explorations, ed. Peter Vorderer, Hans J. Wulff, and Mike Friedrichsen (Mahwah, N.J.: Erlbaum, 1996), 149–88.

16. David Bordwell, *Narration in the Fiction Film* (Madison: University of Wisconsin Press, 1985).

17. Harry H. Harlow, "On the Meaning of Love," *American Psychologist* 13
(1958): 673–85; Harry H. Harlow and Robert R. Zimmerman, "Affectional Response in the Infant Monkey," *Science* 130 (1959): 412–32.

18. John Bowlby, *Attachment* (London: Hogarth Press and the Institute of Psychoanalysis, 1969); Bowlby, *Separation: Anxiety and Grief* (London: Hogarth Press
and the Institute of Psychoanalysis, 1973); Bowlby, *Loss, Sadness, and Depression*
(London: Hogarth Press and the Institute of Psychoanalysis, 1980).

19. Bowlby, *Loss, Sadness, and Depression,* 41.

20. Nico H. Frijda, "De Wetten van het Gevoel," in *De Psychologie Heeft Zin,* ed.
Nico H. Frijda (Amsterdam: Prometheus, 1993), 129.

21. See, e.g., W. K. Lombardo, G. A. Cretser, B. Lombardo, S. L. Mathis, "For
Cryin' Out Loud—There Is a Sex Difference," *Sex Roles* 9 (1983): 987–95.

22. Lothar Mikos, "Souvenir-écran and Scenic Comprehension: Understanding Film as a Biographical Drama of the Spectator," *Iris* 19 (Autumn 1995): 17.

23. Frijda, *The Emotions,* 225, 352.

24. E.g., Torben Kragh Grodal, *Moving Pictures: A New Theory of Film Genres,
Feelings, and Cognition* (Oxford: Clarendon Press, 1997).

25. Noël Carroll, *The Philosophy of Horror, or Paradoxes of the Heart* (New York:
Routledge, 1990); Eric de Kuyper, *Filmische Hartstochten (Filmic Passions)* (Weesp,
The Netherlands: Wereldvenster, 1984).

26. Dolf Zillmann, "The Psychology of Suspense in Dramatic Exposition," in
Suspense, ed. Vorderer, Wulff, and Friedrichsen, 199–232.

27. See John Ellis, *Visible Fictions* (London: Routledge, 1982); Richard Maltby
and Ian Craven, *Hollywood Cinema* (Oxford: Blackwell, 1995), chap. 7.

28. Paul Comisky and Jennings Bryant, "Factors Involved in Generating Suspense," *Human Communication Research* 9 (1982): 49–58.

29. de Kuyper, *Filmische Hartstochten.*

30. This kind of feeling has been described in the aesthetic literature as part of
"the sublime." Late eighteenth-century aestheticians such as Burke and Kant
described the sublime as that which overwhelms the beholder at first and then
affords for mastery of his or her unsettling feelings. In nature the abyss or steep
mountain are examples of the sublime.

31. Sigmund Freud, *The Future of an Illusion,* standard ed., vol. 21 (1927; London: Hogarth Press, 1953).

Chapter 3. The Sublime in Cinema

Note: I am grateful to Peg Brand, Alan Richardson, and the volume editors for
useful criticisms of earlier drafts. My colleague Anne Jacobson not only offered
helpful comments but introduced me to a whole new literature of cognitive science on the emotions. I also thank the other participants at a colloquium on Philosophy and Film at the University of Colorado where an earlier version was read

(Luc Bovens, Ted Cohen, Timothy Gould, Marian Keane, and Thomas Wartenberg).

1. Immanuel Kant, *The Critique of Judgement,* trans. James Creed Meredith (Oxford: Clarendon Press, 1969), 104/256. This and subsequent references are to this translation; pagination refers first to this version and then to the German edition.

2. I can mention here two other treatments of the sublime in film: "The Street Angel and the Badman: *The Good Woman of Bangkok*" *Photofile* 35 (1991): 12–15, in which Adrian Martin uses the notion of the sublime in an analysis of Dennis O'Rourke's avant-garde documentary, *The Good Woman of Bangkok.* (I am grateful to Philip Robertson for drawing this article to my attention and sending me a copy of it from Hong Kong.) Also Rob Wilson, "Cyborg America: Policing the Social Sublime in *Robocop* and *Robocop 2,*" in *The Administration of Aesthetics: Censorship, Political Criticism, and the Public Sphere,* ed. Richard Burt (Minneapolis: University of Minnesota Press, 1994), 289–306.

3. See Jacques Derrida, *The Truth in Painting,* trans. Geoff Bennington and Ian McLeod (Chicago: University of Chicago Press, 1987), esp. 14–147, "The Parergon"; Jean-Francois Lyotard, *Lessons on the Analytic of the Sublime (Kant's Critique of Judgment, sections 23–29),* trans. Elizabeth Rottenberg (Stanford, Calif.: Stanford University Press, 1994); Slavoj Zizek, *The Sublime Object of Ideology* (London: Verso, 1989).

4. The term is used by Paul Crowther in *The Kantian Sublime: From Morality to Art* (Oxford: Clarendon Press, 1989), 155.

5. See Samuel H. Monk's explication of Burke in *The Sublime: A Study of Critical Theories in Eighteenth–Century England* (New York: Modern Language Association, 1935), 96–97.

6. In this chapter, I will not be considering how work by cognitivist philosophers, such as Gregory Currie, *Image and Mind: Film, Philosophy, and Cognitive Science* (Cambridge: Cambridge University Press, 1995); or Noël Carroll, *The Philosophy of Horror, or Paradoxes of the Heart* (New York: Routledge, 1990), and *A Philosophy of Mass Art* (Oxford: Clarendon, 1998), would bear on the topic of the sublime.

7. See Roland Barthes, "The Face of Garbo," from *Mythologies;* reprinted in *Film Theory and Criticism,* ed. Gerald Mast, Marshall Cohen, and Leo Braudy (New York: Oxford University Press, 1992), 628–31.

8. One suggestion I have heard is that the sublime is simply the condition of cinema itself when films are viewed as they were meant to be, in a movie theater (Marty Fairbairn, H-Film Electronic Discussion List, December 14, 1995).

9. On this issue, see Derrida, *Truth in Painting,* 125–26, 140–43; and Lyotard, *Peregrinations: Law, Form, and Event* (New York: Columbia University Press, 1988), 40–43.

10. Here I am indebted to Jerrold Levinson's "Messages in Art," in *Art and Its Messages: Meaning, Morality, and Society,* ed. Stephen Davies (University Park: Penn State University Press, 1995), 70–83.

11. The subject occupies pages 90–204 of the Meredith translation. My account

is indebted to various sources, including Crowther; Timothy Gould, "Intensity and Its Audiences: Toward a Feminist Perspective on the Kantian Sublime," in *Feminism and Tradition in Aesthetics,* ed. Peggy Zeglin Brand and Carolyn Korsmeyer (University Park: Penn State University Press, 1995), 66–87; Paul Guyer, *Kant and the Experience of Freedom* (Cambridge: Cambridge University Press, 1993); and John H. Zammito, *The Genesis of Kant's "Critique of Judgment"* (Chicago: University of Chicago Press, 1992).

12. "Two things fill the mind with ever new and increasing admiration and awe, the oftener and more steadily we reflect on them: the starry heavens above me and the moral law within me"; Kant, *Critique of Practical Reason,* trans. Lewis White Beck (New York: Liberal Arts Press, 1956), 166.

13. I owe this comparison to Marian Keane.

14. My point here is similar to that made by Peter Lamarque in "Tragedy and Moral Value," in *Art and Its Messages,* ed. Davies, 59–69. However, Lamarque does not invoke the notion of rupture or reflexive artistic features of a work in the way I do.

15. The film shows its black and Indian characters, and perhaps the women as well, as victims of the European (males) plans.

16. Ed S. Tan, *Emotion and the Structure of Narrative Film: Film as an Emotion Machine,* trans. Barbara Fasting (Mahwah, N.J.: Erlbaum, 1996).

17. Thus his focus is on what he calls witness emotion episodes (58). For an overview of the issues about whether film is an illusion, see Joseph Anderson and Barbara Anderson, "The Case for an Ecological Metatheory," in *Post-Theory,* ed. Bordwell and Carroll, 347–67. For Tan's discussion of this, see *Emotion and the Structure of Narrative Film,* 227–32, 236–48. For an opposing view, see Gregory Currie, *Image and Mind: Film, Philosophy, and Cognitive Science* (Cambridge: Cambridge University Press, 1995), 19–47.

18. Tan, *Emotion and the Structure of Narrative Film,* 230–32; the reference is to Carroll, *The Philosophy of Horror, or Paradoxes of the Heart* (New York: Routledge, 1990), 74.

19. He discusses valences of emotion in relation to plot in terms of balance and its disturbance or restoration (59–60), and treats empathy and sympathy in some detail (190–93), arguing that film sympathy is felt at less cost than it requires in the real world and is positive for viewers because it leads them to have a more favorable opinion of themselves (192).

20. On this page he also develops the admittedly grisly metaphor of the viewer as a head without a body.

21. Tan comments, "Other aspects of the artefact, such as acting, may strike almost any viewer" (65).

22. Tan does seem to recognize this when he writes that "in a general sense, it may be that the more intense the emotion, the greater the likelihood the viewer will realize this is a special experience and be aware of what he or she is seeing is indeed an artefact" (65).

23. See the articles by Joseph LeDoux and Jeffrey A. Gray in *The Nature of Emo-*

tion: Fundamental Questions, ed. Paul Ekman and Richard J. Davidson (New York: Oxford University Press, 1994).

24. See Antonio Damasio, *Descartes' Error: Emotion, Reason, and the Human Brain* (New York: Putnam, 1994).

25. Joseph LeDoux, *The Emotional Brain: The Mysterious Underpinnings of Emotional Life* (New York: Simon and Schuster, 1996).

26. Ibid., 19.

27. They are low-level reflexive responses; blue-ribbon grade-A emotions; and systems for higher sentiments (p. 23). See Jaak Panksepp, "Basic Emotions Ramify Widely in the Brain, Yielding Many Concepts That Cannot Be Distinguished Unambiguously . . . Yet," in *The Nature of Emotions: Fundamental Questions*, 86–88.

28. See Jeffrey Gray, "Three Fundamental Emotion Systems," in *Nature of Emotion*, ed. Ekman and Davidson, 243–47; each system itself has three levels, behavioral, neural, and cognitive or computational (245).

29. See Joseph LeDoux, "Cognitive-Emotional Interactions in the Brain," 216–23; and Carroll E. Izard, "Cognition Is One of Four Types of Emotion-Activating Systems," 203–7, in *Nature of Emotion*.

30. See LeDoux, *Emotional Brain*.

31. Damasio, *Descartes' Error*, 125–26.

32. An example of an attempt to begin using cognitive science in a way that recognizes these gaps is Ellen Spolsky's *Gaps in Nature: Literary Interpretation and the Modular Mind* (Albany: State University of New York Press, 1993).

33. Damasio criticizes standard views about the differentiation of lower from higher brain structures; see *Descartes' Error*, 128.

34. See, e.g., Mark Johnson, *Moral Imagination: Implications of Cognitive Science for Ethics* (Chicago: University of Chicago Press, 1993).

Chapter 4. The Emotional Basis of Film Comedy

1. Paul E. McGhee, *Humor: Its Origin and Development* (San Francisco: W. H. Freeman, 1979), 6.

2. John Morreal, "Humor and Emotion," in *The Philosophy of Humor*, ed. Morreal (Albany: State University of New York Press, 1987), 212–24.

3. Henri Bergson, "Laughter: An Essay on the Meaning of the Comic," in *Comedy*, ed. Wylie Sypher (Garden City, New York: Doubleday, 1956).

4. This is essentially the Darwinian view of emotions. It supposes, first, that we have emotions because they evolved and, second, that they evolved because they confer upon individuals of biological species an adaptive advantage, *by inclining them to act appropriately in situations that have important consequences for their well-being.* See Charles Darwin, *The Expression of Emotions in Man and Animals* (1872; Chicago: University of Chicago Press, 1965). This conception of emotions is still one of the most influential. For example, it is the foundation of R. Plutchik's *Emotions: A Psychoevolutionary Synthesis* (New York: Harper and Row, 1980), and N. H. Frijda's *The Emotions* (Cambridge: Cambridge University Press, 1986).

5. Christian Metz, *The Imaginary Signifier: Psychoanalysis and the Cinema*,

trans. Celia Britton, Annwyl Williams, Ben Brewster, and Alfred Guzzetti (Bloomington: Indiana University Press, 1982).

6. Noël Carroll, *Mystifying Movies: Fads and Fallacies in Contemporary Film Theory* (New York: Columbia University Press, 1988), 180.

7. David Bordwell, *Narration in the Fiction Film* (Madison: University of Wisconsin Press, 1985).

8. Ibid., 39–40.

9. Bordwell never puts this contention quite so baldly, but it is the key to David Bordwell, Janet Staiger, and Kristin Thompson's, *The Classical Hollywood Cinema* (New York: Columbia University Press, 1985). Bordwell and his colleagues make the case, in that book, that there exists a powerful predilection among paying audiences for this kind of story-centered problem solving that shaped the classical Hollywood cinema. For a detailed explication of this line of argument in *The Classical Hollywood Cinema,* see Dirk Eitzen, "Evolution, Functionalism, and the Study of American Cinema," *The Velvet Light Trap,* no. 28 (Fall 1991): 73–85.

10. Dirk Eitzen, "Comedy and Classicism," in *Film Theory and Philosophy,* ed. Richard Allen and Murray Smith (New York: Oxford University Press, 1997), 394–411, develops this argument more extensively and cites some of the many film scholars who have come to similar conclusions.

11. Psychoanalytic theorists have written a great deal about the *desire* attached to movies, but that is something different. When we speak of emotional impulses, we are talking not about libidinal urges, but about conscious gratifications. We like comedy because it makes us laugh. We like melodrama because it makes us cry. We like sex and violence because they arouse and excite us. And so on. Regardless of the source of these feelings, it is their manifestations in awareness that prompt us to go to movies. And these manifestations are a topic that psychoanalytically oriented film theorists have scarcely broached.

12. Ed. S. Tan, *Emotion and the Structure of Narrative Film,* trans. Barbara Fasting (Mahwah, N.J.: Erlbaum, 1996).

13. See Smith's *Engaging Characters* (Oxford: Clarendon, 1995).

14. For brief reviews, see Patricia Keith-Spiegel, "Early Conceptions of Humor," in *The Psychology of Humor,* ed. Jeffrey H. Goldstein and Paul E. McGhee (New York: Academic Press, 1972), 3–39, and Morreal, ed., *Philosophy of Humor.*

15. See Jeffrey H. Goldstein, "Cross Cultural Research: Humour Here and There"; Thomas R. Shultz, "A Cross-Cultural Study of the Structure of Humour"; and Patricia J. Castell and Jeffrey H. Goldstein, "Social Occasions for Joking," all in *It's a Funny Thing, Humour,* ed. A. J. Chapman and H. C. Foot (Oxford: Pergamon Press, 1977), as well as Mahadev L. Apte, *Humor and Laughter* (Ithaca, N.Y.: Cornell University Press, 1985).

16. R. A. Spitz and K. M. Wolf, "The Smiling Response," *Genetic Psychology Monographs* 34 (1946): 57–125.

17. F. L. Goodenough, "Expressions of Emotion in a Blind-Deaf Child," *Journal of Abnormal and Social Psychology* 27 (1932): 328–33.

18. J.A.R.A.M. Van Hooff, "A Comparative Approach to the Phylogeny of

Laughter and Smiling," in *Non-Verbal Communication,* ed. R. A. Hinde (Cambridge: Cambridge University Press, 1972), 209–37.

19. M. Kenderdine, "Laughter in the Preschool Child," *Child Development* 2 (1931): 228–30. For a review of other similar studies, see A. J. Chapman, "Humor and Laughter in Social Interaction and Some Implications for Humor Research," in *Handbook of Humor Research,* ed. P. E. McGhee and J. H. Goldstein (New York: Springer, 1983), 1:135–57.

20. Sigmund Freud, *Der Witz und seine Beziehung zum Unbewussten,* standard ed., vol. 8. (London: Hogarth Press, 1962).

21. See, for example, A. Radcliffe-Brown, "On Joking Relationships" and "A Further Note on Joking Relationships," in *Structure and Function in Primitive Society* (London: Cohen and West, 1952).

22. See, for example, A. J. Chapman, "Funniness of Jokes, Canned Laughter, and Recall Performance," *Sociometry* 36 (1973): 569–78; A. J. Chapman, "Humor and Laughter"; and A. J. Fridlund, "Sociality of Solitary Smiling," *Journal of Personality and Social Psychology* 60 (1991): 220–40.

23. M. K. Rothbart, "Laughter in Young Children," *Psychological Bulletin* 80 (1973): 247–56; L. A. Sroufe and J. P. Wunsch, "The Development of Laughter in the First Years of Life," *Child Development* 43 (1972): 1326–44.

24. Van Hooff, "Phylogeny of Laughter and Smiling."

25. Studies of humor among older children and adults have resulted in many other robust findings. There is almost always an element of surprise in humor. There is almost always an element of cognitive challenge as well: some incongruity that needs to be resolved. Amusement is accompanied by faster heart rate and respiration, increased galvanic skin response, and other symptoms of arousal. On the other hand, amused laughter is associated with a sudden decline in arousal; amused smiling, with a relaxed state (as opposed to a state of concentration). Any perceived challenge to our comfort, identity, or sense of security lessens our amusement. Accordingly, sympathizing or identifying with the object of a joke tends to diminish its impact. Conversely, hostility toward the object of a joke tends to augment its impact. Any element of social unacceptability tends to increase the impact of humor, if it is not perceived as a personal challenge. And there are many others. The empirical literature on humor is regrettably nowhere neatly digested, but it is best summarized in McGhee's *Humor* and in the collected essays in *It's a Funny Thing* and *Handbook of Humor Research,* all cited above.

26. There is some debate about whether resolution is necessary or whether mere incongruity suffices. For instance, one group of studies dedicated to demonstrating the latter proposition shows that people asked to gauge the weight of a series of objects laugh when they reach one of surprisingly different weight from all the previous ones. The original study is reported in G. Nerhardt, "Humor and Inclination to Laugh: Emotional Reactions to Stimuli of Different Divergence from a Range of Expectancy," *Scandinavian Journal of Psychology* 11 (1970): 185–95. It is not necessary to take up this debate here beyond pointing out that there is, in fact, a resolution of sorts in such experiments: the subject is forced to revise his or her expectations to encompass the discrepant stimulus.

27. It is of course conceivable that there is no functional explanation for either humans' taste for sugar or their sense of humor. Some of the hereditary features of organisms are vestiges of eons-old adaptations that serve no ongoing purpose. Others are the purely coincidental by-product of valuable adaptations, which themselves have no function. Still, even though it is *conceivable* that our taste for sugar has no functional explanation, given its profound dietary consequences, that is unlikely in the extreme. The same is true of our sense of humor. All of the studies cited above on the profound social and psychological consequences of laughter and smiling provide very strong evidence that our sense of humor is no evolutionary accident.

28. Darwin, *The Expression of Emotions in Man and Animals.*

29. Frijda, *The Emotions,* 52.

30. Seeing characters squirm in dangerous, painful, or embarrassing situations does not always result in humor, of course. Sometimes it results in suspense or unease. Why is this? The simplest answer is that humor involves what Gregory Bateson calls a play frame. Humor requires that we suppose that no genuine harm is intended by behaviors or situations which might otherwise appear harmful or challenging. This can happen in movies when we construe either a *character* as playful (as in the case of Sally's fake orgasm in *When Harry Met Sally*) or a *depiction* as playful (as in the example cited earlier from *Shawshank Redemption*). Bateson discusses play frames in "A Theory of Play and Fantasy," in *Steps to an Ecology of Mind* (San Francisco: Chandler Publishing, 1972).

31. Incidentally, nonfiction films do not ordinarily afford us this level of safety. That is why we may feel somewhat uneasy about laughing at the well-meaning but shamefully shallow beauty queen in *Roger and Me,* for example.

32. This is the main conclusion Antonio Damasio draws from his work with emotion-impaired patients: as the experience of emotion declines in his patients, so does their power of problem-solving, even though their memory, attention, intelligence, and language skills are unimpaired. See his *Descartes' Error: Emotion, Reason, and the Human Brain* (New York: Putnam, 1994).

Chapter 5. Local Emotions, Global Moods, and Film Structure

1. In particular, see a special issue of *Post Script* 13, no. 1 (Fall 1993) and the work of Noël Carroll, including "Toward a Theory of Film Suspense," *Persistence of Vision* 1 (Summer 1984): 65–89; "The Power of Movies," *Daedalus* 114, no. 4 (Fall 1985): 79–103; *The Philosophy of Horror, or Paradoxes of the Heart* (New York: Routledge, 1990); and "Toward a Theory of Point-of-View Editing: Communication, Emotion, and the Movies," *Poetics Today* 14, no. 1 (Spring 1993): 122–41.

2. Murray Smith, *Engaging Characters: Fiction, Emotion, and the Cinema* (Oxford: Clarendon Press, 1995); Ed S. Tan, *Emotion and the Structure of Narrative Film: Film as an Emotion Machine,* trans. Barbara Fasting (Mahwah, N.J.: Erlbaum, 1996); Torben Kragh Grodal, *Moving Pictures: A New Theory of Film Genres, Feelings, and Cognition* (Oxford: Clarendon Press, 1997).

3. Tan, *Emotion and the Structure of Narrative Film,* 43–47.

4. In discussions of emotion in general within psychology and philosophy, the

emotion most commonly referred to is fear. Fear satisfies all the characteristics of the emotion prototype. It is clearly object-oriented, has a clear goal (the removal of the fearful object from one's presence), and provides a strong action tendency (to fight or flee). Perhaps fear, then, is the central example that best exhibits the emotion prototype to psychologists and philosophers, much as a robin is arguably the central exemplar of the category "bird" in American society.

5. David Bordwell, *Narration in the Fiction Film* (Madison: University of Wisconsin Press, 1985).

6. Tan argues that interest is the primary emotion that helps the spectator make narrative and emotional sense out of a film. Our interest is organized by themes, which are cognitive scenarios guiding our expectations concerning character actions, motivations, and possible narrative outcomes. Common themes include betrayal, self-sacrifice, and deceit. The script for these themes is composed of smaller plot units which are the major plot landmarks, such as successes, losses, malicious acts, and so on. Understanding the organization of these plot units into themes is central to understanding a film's emotional appeals.

7. Grodal posits a model of narrational flow which governs the normal processing of film images and narrative information. This viewer's processing usually progresses in a downstream manner from simpler to more complex processes, beginning with the encounter with the images themselves. At the higher levels, viewers appraise actions and organize them into narrational schemes, such as characters, motivations, and goals. Through identification and empathy we ally ourselves with characters in pursuit of goals, and the resulting emotional experience (the modal quality) often depends on how those character goals are achieved or blocked. For instance, if the narration focuses on a goal-driven character who has active control of the fictional world, then we experience a mode of affect which Grodal calls tense. Blocking those goals leads to a modality he calls saturation, in which tension accumulates because it cannot be transformed into an action/motor tendency. Characters can be blocked by diegetic means or by external forces (e.g., an avant-garde filmmaker choosing to repeat a character's action over and over, not letting us gain the satisfaction of having that action completed). By whatever means, the blocking and achieving of character goals is central to the modal qualities Grodal enumerates.

8. Noël Carroll, *Mystifying Movies: Fads and Fallacies in Contemporary Film Theory* (New York: Columbia University Press, 1988), 213–25.

9. Richard S. Lazarus, James R. Averill, and E. M. Opton Jr., "Toward a Cognitive Theory of Emotions," in *Feelings and Emotions,* ed. Magda B. Arnold (New York: Academic Press, 1970).

10. The best one-volume summary of this large body of research concerning the various emotional subsystems is *Handbook of Emotions,* ed. Michael Lewis and Jeannette M. Haviland (New York: Guilford Press, 1993). In particular, see Joseph E. LeDoux, "Emotional Networks in the Brain," 109–18; John T. Cacioppo, David J. Klein, Gary G. Berntson, and Elaine Hatfield, "The Psychophysiology of Emotion," 119–43; Richard J. Davidson, "The Neuropsychology of Emotion and Affective Style," 143–54; Jeffery Pittam and Klaus R. Scherer, "Vocal Expression and

Communication of Emotion," 185–98; and Linda A. Camras, Elizabeth A. Holland, and Mary Jill Patterson, "Facial Expression," 199–208.

11. This model is similar to the ones found in Leonard Berkowitz, "On the Formation and Regulation of Anger and Aggression: A Cognitive-neoassociationistic Analysis," *American Psychologist* 45, no. 4 (April 1990): 494–503; Gordon Bower and Paul R. Cohen, "Emotional Influences in Memory and Thinking: Data and Theory," in *Affect and Cognition*, ed. Margaret Sydnor Clark and Susan T. Fiske (Hillsdale, N.J.: Erlbaum, 1982), 291–331; Peter J. Lang, "A Bio-informational Theory of Emotional Imagery," *Psychophysiology* 16, no. 6 (1979): 495–512; and Howard Leventhal, "A Perceptual-motor Theory of Emotion," in *Advances in Experimental Social Psychology*, ed. Leonard Berkowitz (New York: Academic Press, 1984), 17:117–82.

12. Walter Cannon discusses examples of the "as if" phenomenon in Marañon's work of the 1920s. See Cannon, "The James-Lange Theory of Emotions: A Critical Examination and an Alternative Theory," *American Journal of Psychology* 39 (1927): 113.

13. For more detail on the limbic system, see Joseph LeDoux, *The Emotional Brain: The Mysterious Underpinnings of Emotional Life* (New York: Simon and Schuster, 1996).

14. For clarity's sake I use the term *script* to denote the cognitive core of a particular emotion and *prototype* to refer to the common characteristics of emotions in general. There is one basic emotion prototype, involving action tendencies, goal orientation, object orientation, and so on. There are different scripts for different emotions. The script for jealousy, for instance, involves loving someone and suspecting that someone else may be gaining your lover's affection. The emotion prototype provides a central organizing principle for the scripts for particular emotions.

15. Paul Ekman, "An Argument for Basic Emotions," *Cognition and Emotion* 6, no. 3/4 (1992): 169–200; Paul Ekman, "Expression and the Nature of Emotion," in *Approaches to Emotion*, ed. Klaus R. Scherer and Paul Ekman (Hillsdale, N.J.: Erlbaum, 1984), 319–43.

16. Pio Ricci-Bitti and Klaus R. Scherer, "Interrelations between Antecedents, Reactions, and Coping Responses," in *Experiencing Emotion: A Cross-Cultural Study*, ed. Klaus R. Scherer, Harald G. Wallbott, and Angela B. Summerfield (Cambridge: Cambridge University Press, 1986), 129–41.

17. Richard J. Davidson and Andrew J. Tomarken, "Laterality and Emotion: An Electrophysiological Approach," in *Handbook of Neuropsychology*, ed. Francois Boller and Jordan Grafman (Amsterdam: Elsevier, 1989), 3:419–41; John M. Gottman and Robert W. Levenson, "Assessing the Role of Emotion in Marriage," *Behavioral Assessment* 8, no. 1 (1986): 31–48.

18. Elisha Y. Babad and Harald G. Wallbott, "The Effects of Social Factors on Emotional Reactions," in *Experiencing Emotion*, ed. Scherer, Wallbott, and Summerfield, 154–72.

19. Nico H. Frijda, "Moods, Emotion Episodes, and Emotions," in *Handbook of Emotions*, ed. Lewis and Haviland, 381–403. The largest body of psychological

research on mood examines how mood affects memory tasks. For a summary of this research, see Gordon H. Bower, "Mood and Memory," *American Psychologist* 36, no. 2 (February 1981): 129–48.

20. Kristin Thompson, *Breaking the Glass Armor: Neoformalist Film Analysis* (Princeton: Princeton University Press, 1988), 3. I share Thompson's concern that preconceived methods tend toward predetermined outcomes, which narrow the analysis and create cookie-cutter criticism. The challenge in formulating an approach is to choose assumptions that do not prejudice the approach toward one particular cinematic narrational paradigm.

21. A stinger is a loud musical burst.

22. Emotional narrative cues can be said to be goal-oriented if they provide information crucial to a character's goal pursuit. Non-goal-oriented cues do not provide information vital to goal achievement; they exist for other purposes, such as the cueing of an appropriate emotional orientation. Non-goal-oriented cues could be excised from a film without significant impact on whether or not a character achieves a goal. Their excision, however, might significantly alter the pattern of emotional cueing.

23. David Ansen, "Highland Fling," *Newsweek,* February 28, 1983, 79; *Variety,* February 16, 1983; Pauline Kael, *New Yorker,* March 21, 1983, 115–18; Stanley Kauffmann, "Highland Fling, French Flummery," *New Republic,* March 21, 1983, 24; James M. Wall, "Local Hero," *Century Christian,* June 22–29, 1983, 622; Richard Schickel, "Scotch Broth," *Time,* February 21, 1983, 80; Janet Maslin, "Oily Fairyland," *New York Times,* February 17, 1983, 25; Vincent Canby, "Vitality and Variety Buoy New Movies from Britain," *New York Times,* March 6, 1983, sec. 2, 17.

Chapter 6. Emotions, Cognitions, and Narrative Patterns in Film

1. See my *Moving Pictures: A New Theory of Film Genres, Feelings, and Cognition* (Oxford: Clarendon, 1997), and "Romanticism, Postmodernism, and Irrationalism," in *Post-modernism and the Visual Media,* Skevens special issue (Copenhagen: Department of Film and Media Studies, 1992).

2. See, e.g., Grodal, *Moving Pictures; Post-Theory: Reconstructing Film Studies,* ed. David Bordwell and Noël Carroll (Madison: University of Wisconsin Press, 1996); Ed Tan, *Emotion and the Structure of Narrative Film: Film as an Emotion Machine,* trans. Barbara Fasting (Mahwah, N.J.: Erlbaum, 1996); Noël Carroll, *Mystifying Movies: Fads and Fallacies in Contemporary Film Theory* (New York: Columbia University Press, 1988).

3. Susan T. Fiske and Shelley E. Taylor, *Social Cognition,* 2nd ed. (New York: McGraw-Hill, 1991), 247–57.

4. For an overview, see Nico H. Frijda, *The Emotions* (Cambridge: Cambridge University Press, 1986).

5. See, e.g., Douglas G. Mook, *Motivation: The Organization of Action* (New York: Norton, 1987), 200–207.

6. Carroll E. Izard, *The Psychology of Emotions* (New York: Plenum Press, 1991).

7. D. G. Dutton and A. P. Aron, "Some Evidence for Heightened Sexual Attraction under Conditions of High Anxiety," *Journal of Personality and Social Psychol-*

ogy 30, no. 4 (1974): 310–17; on the relabeling of arousal see P. W. Hoon, J. P. Wincze, and E. R. Hoon, "A Test of Reciprocal Inhibition: Are Anxiety and Sexual Arousal in Women Mutually Inhibitory?," *Journal of Abnormal Psychology* 86 (1977): 65–74.

8. George Lakoff, *Women, Fire, and Dangerous Things: What Categories Reveal about the Human Mind* (Chicago: University of Chicago Press, 1987), and his "The Contemporary Theory of Metaphor," in *Metaphor and Thought,* ed. Andrew Ortony, 2d ed. (Cambridge: Cambridge University Press, 1993).

9. Rudolph Arnheim, *Art and Visual Perception: A Psychology of the Creative Eye* (Berkeley: University of California Press, 1974), 343–403; and A. Michotte, *Causalité, permanence et réalité phénomenales* (Louvain: Publications Universitaires, 1962), and *The Perception of Causality* (London: Methuen, 1963).

10. Edward Twitchell Hall, *The Hidden Dimension* (New York: Doubleday, 1966).

11. Antonio R. Damasio and Hanna Damasio, "Brain and Language," in *Mind and Brain: Readings from Scientific American* (New York: Freeman, 1993), 54–65.

12. For an overview of mimicry, see Murray Smith, *Engaging Characters: Fiction, Emotion, and the Cinema* (Oxford: Clarendon Press, 1995), 98–102. On empathy see Dolf Zillman, "Empathy: Affect from Bearing Witness to the Emotions of Others," in *Responding to the Screen: Reception and Reaction Processes,* ed. Jennings Bryant and Dolf Zillman (Hillsdale, N.J.: Erlbaum, 1991), 135–67.

13. Noël Carroll, *Theorizing the Moving Image* (Cambridge: Cambridge University Press, 1996), 127–28.

14. On "identification," or what Murray Smith calls "character engagement," see Smith, *Engaging Characters.*

15. Izard, *Psychology of Emotions.*

16. David Marr, *Vision: A Computational Investigation Into the Human Representation and Processing of Visual Information* (San Francisco: Freeman, 1982); Semir Zeki, *A Vision of the Brain* (London: Blackwell Science, 1993); and Grodal, *Moving Pictures.*

17. For an introduction to brain architecture, see Bryan Kolb and Ian O. Wishaw, *Fundamentals of Human Neuropsychology* (New York: Freeman, 1990).

18. Grodal, *Moving Pictures.*

19. Edward Branigan, *Narrative Comprehension and Film* (New York: Routledge, 1992).

20. Tom Gunning, "An Aesthetic of Astonishment: Early Film and the (In)Credulous Spectator," in *Viewing Positions: Ways of Seeing Film,* ed. Linda Williams (New Brunswick, N.J.: Rutgers University Press, 1994); Sergei Eisenstein, *Film Form,* trans. and ed. Jay Leyda (New York: Harcourt Brace Jovanovich, 1949), 45–63.

21. Frijda, *The Emotions,* 71.

22. Ibid., 59–60.

23. Branigan, *Narrative Comprehension in Film.*

24. William F. Brewer, "The Nature of Narrative Suspense and the Problem of Rereading," in *Suspense: Conceptualizations, Theoretical Analyses, and Empirical*

Explorations, ed. Peter Vorderer, Hans J. Wulff, and Mike Friedrichson (Hillsdale, N.J.: Erlbaum, 1996).

25. See Tan, *Emotion and the Structure of Narrative Film.*

26. Ray Jackendoff, *Consciousness and the Computational Mind* (Cambridge: MIT Press, 1987); Grodal, *Moving Pictures.*

27. Grodal, *Moving Pictures,* 165.

28. Christian Metz, *The Imaginary Signifier* (Bloomington: Indiana University Press, 1982), 189.

29. David Bordwell, *Narration in the Fiction Film* (Madison: University of Wisconsin Press, 1985), 39.

30. Jackendoff, *Consciousness and the Computational Mind;* Grodal, *Moving Pictures.*

31. Frijda, *The Emotions,* 213–14.

32. For a more comprehensive analysis, see my *Moving Pictures.*

Chapter 7. Movie Music as Moving Music

1. There are, of course, narrative and thematic reasons for using Beethoven in this scene, but the only motivation given within the diegesis is that the music acts to heighten the experimental subject's emotional responses. My point here is simply that it is very difficult to claim that the "Ode to Joy" of Beethoven's Ninth is appropriate to or expressive of the atrocities depicted onscreen.

2. Claudia Gorbman, *Unheard Melodies: Narrative Film Music* (Bloomington: University of Indiana Press, 1987).

3. I am thinking here of work by Leonard Meyer, Eugene Narmour, John Sloboda, Fred Lerdahl and Ray Jackendoff, and Peter Kivy.

4. See my article, "Unheard Melodies?: A Critique of Psychoanalytic Theories of Film Music," in *Post-Theory: Reconstructing Film Studies,* ed. David Bordwell and Noël Carroll (Madison: University of Wisconsin Press, 1996), 230–47.

5. See, e.g., Gorbman's *Unheard Melodies,* 79–82; Caryl Flinn's *Strains of Utopia: Gender, Nostalgia, and Hollywood Film Music* (Princeton: Princeton University Press, 1992); Kathryn Kalinak's *Settling the Score: Music in the Classical Hollywood Film* (Madison: University of Wisconsin Press, 1992), 86–88; George Burt, *The Art of Film Music* (Boston: Northeastern University Press, 1994), 10–11; and William Darby and Jack Du Bois's *American Film Music: Major Composers, Techniques, Trends, 1915–1990* (Jefferson, N.C.: McFarland and Company, 1991).

6. Murray Smith, *Engaging Characters: Fiction, Emotion, and the Cinema* (Oxford: Clarendon Press, 1995), 2–3.

7. Samuel L. Chell, "Music and Emotion in the Classical Hollywood Film: The Case of *The Best Years of Our Lives,*" *Film Criticism* 8, no. 2 (Winter 1984): 27–38.

8. Ibid., 34–35.

9. For a discussion of this problem, see Smith, *Engaging Characters,* 54–63, 74–81; Noël Carroll, *The Philosophy of Horror, or Paradoxes of the Heart* (New York: Routledge, 1990), 95–96; and Kendall Walton, "Fearing Fictions," *Journal of Philosophy* 75, no. 1 (January 1978): 5–27.

10. See Langer's *Philosophy in a New Key: A Study in the Symbolism of Reason, Rite, and Art,* 3rd ed. (Cambridge: Harvard University Press, 1957), 204–45.

11. See Raffman's *Language, Music, and Mind* (Cambridge: MIT Press, 1993), 37–62.

12. See Hanslick's *The Beautiful in Music,* trans. Gustav Cohen (Indianapolis: Bobbs-Merrill, 1957); and Stravinsky's *The Poetics of Music* (Cambridge: Harvard University Press, 1942).

13. For a discussion of art and intentionality, see Peter Kivy, *Sound Sentiment: An Essay on the Musical Emotions* (Philadelphia: Temple University Press, 1989), 101–8; Smith, *Engaging Characters,* 59–63; Alan Tormey, *The Concept of Expression: A Study in Philosophical Psychology and Aesthetics* (Princeton: Princeton University Press, 1971); and Patricia Greenspan, *Emotions and Reasons: An Inquiry into Emotional Justification* (New York: Routledge, 1988).

14. See Kivy, *Sound Sentiment,* 102–8.

15. See Kivy's *Sound Sentiment* and *Music Alone: Philosophical Reflections on the Purely Musical Experience* (Ithaca, N.Y.: Cornell University Press, 1990). For responses to Kivy's work, see Anthony Newcomb, "Sound and Feeling," *Critical Inquiry* 10 (1984); Malcolm Budd, *Music and Emotions* (London: Routledge and Kegan Paul, 1985), and "Music and the Communication of Emotion," *Journal of Aesthetics and Art Criticism* 47, no. 2 (Spring 1989): 129–38; Peter Mew, "The Expression of Emotion in Music," *British Journal of Aesthetics* 25, no. 1 (Winter 1985): 33–42; Daniel A. Putnam, "Why Instrumental Music Has No Shame," *British Journal of Aesthetics* 27, no. 1 (Winter 1987): 55–61; Jenefer Robinson, "The Expression and Arousal of Emotion in Music," *Journal of Aesthetics and Art Criticism* 52, no. 1 (Winter 1994): 13–22; and Francis Sparshott, "Music and Feeling," *Journal of Aesthetics and Art Criticism* 52, no. 1 (Winter 1994): 23–35.

16. Kivy, *Sound Sentiment,* 12–26.

17. Ibid., 71–111.

18. Kivy does, however, give some indications of his thinking about this subject. In a discussion of emotion in literary and pictorial representation, Kivy admits that he is aroused to anger by the cruelty of Simon Legree when he reads *Uncle Tom's Cabin* and by the outrage of Nazi air raids depicted in Picasso's *Guernica.* Presumably this anger also translates to cinematic treatments of similar subjects. Kivy also acknowledges, however, that there is considerable debate about how fictions are capable of sparking such full-blooded emotional responses.

19. Gorbman, *Unheard Melodies,* 190.

20. See Radford's "Emotions and Music: A Reply to the Cognitivists," *Journal of Aesthetics and Art Criticism* 47, no. 1 (Winter 1989): 69–76; and "Muddy Waters," *Journal of Aesthetics and Art Criticism* 49, no. 1 (Summer 1991): 242–52. For Kivy's response to Radford, see "Auditor's Emotions: Contention, Concession, and Compromise," *Journal of Aesthetics and Art Criticism* 51, no. 1 (Winter 1993): 1–12.

21. The reasons for this difference are extremely complex and are generally outside the scope of this essay. Why the tendency to arouse emotions is strong in some listeners and weak in others is a subject of future inquiry and is bound to stir considerable debate. It is worth pointing out, however, that some reasons are evi-

dent in the examples theorists choose to support their case. To some extent, this difference can be traced to differences in the type of music that is listened to, differences in the auditors' musical backgrounds, differences in the associations they bring to certain pieces of music, differences in the context of the listening situation, and differences in the moods the listeners bring to the listening situation.

22. See Smith, *Engaging Characters*, 59–63; Greenspan, *Emotions and Reasons*; and Ronald de Sousa, *The Rationality of Emotion* (Cambridge: MIT Press, 1987).

23. Noël Carroll, *Mystifying Movies: Fads and Fallacies in Contemporary Film Theory* (New York: Columbia University Press, 1988), 213–25.

24. See Joseph Anderson, *The Reality of Illusion: An Ecological Approach to Cognitive Film Theory* (Carbondale: Southern Illinois University Press, 1996), 86–89.

25. Fred Karlin and Rayburn Wright, *On the Track: A Guide to Contemporary Film Scoring* (New York: Schirmer Books, 1990), 140.

26. Ibid., 128.

27. Smith, *Engaging Characters*, 5–8.

28. I should stress here that by highlighting the cognitive reception of musical affect, I do not mean to argue that audience members would not share or feel Sarah's sense of violation. Indeed, an individual spectator's emotional response can in fact be congruent with that of a character. Rather, I am simply suggesting that if Fiedel's music has effectively communicated Sarah's emotional anguish to the audience, then the music has served this particular dramatic function.

29. Kalinak, *Settling the Score*, 87.

30. Besides the experiments conducted on the relations between film music and emotion, others have investigated the relationship between film music and memory, film music and awareness, and film music and narrative closure. Still other experiments have explored spectators' ability to match scenes with cues composed to accompany them and the influence that scores in certain film genres have on spectators' understanding of narrative developments and inferences about narrative outcomes. See, e.g., Annabel J. Cohen, "Understanding Musical Soundtracks," *Empirical Studies of the Arts* 8, no. 2 (1990): 111–24; Marilyn Boltz, Matthew Schulkind, and Suzanne Kantra, "Effects of Background Music on the Remembering of Filmed Events," *Memory and Cognition* 19, no. 6 (1991): 593–606; William Forde Thompson, Frank A. Russo, and Don Sinclair, "Effects of Underscoring on the Perception of Closure in Filmed Events," *Psychomusicology* 13 (1994): 9–27; Scott D. Lipscomb and Roger A. Kendall, "Perceptual Judgement of the Relationship Between Musical and Visual Components in Film," *Psychomusicology* 13 (1994): 60–98; and Claudia Bullerjahn and Markus Güldenring, "An Empirical Investigation of Effects of Film Music Using Qualitative Content Analysis," *Psychomusicology* 13 (1994): 99–118.

31. For an overview of this research, see John A. Sloboda, "Empirical Studies of Emotional Response to Music," in *Cognitive Bases of Musical Communication*, ed. Mari Ries Jones and Susan Halleran (Washington D.C.: American Psychological Association, 1992), 33–46.

32. Sandra K. Marshall and Annabel J. Cohen, "Effects of Musical Soundtracks

on Attitudes toward Animated Geometric Figures," *Music Perception* 6, no. 1 (Fall 1988): 95–113.

33. Annabel J. Cohen, "Effects of Music on the Interpretation of Dynamic Visual Displays," in Annabel J. Cohen (chair), "Symposium on Recent Developments in Music Cognition: Processing of Internal and External Structure," *Canadian Psychology* 30 (1989): 343.

34. See Cohen, "Understanding Musical Soundtracks," 115.

35. Annabel J. Cohen, "Associationism and Musical Soundtrack Phenomena," *Contemporary Music Review* 9 (1993): 163–78.

36. George Sirius and Eric F. Clarke, "The Perception of Audiovisual Relationships: A Preliminary Study," *Psychomusicology* 13 (1994): 119–32.

37. The authors are careful to point out that the simplicity and lack of narrative context in the visual components of the study may have been an important factor in their failure to elicit semantic meanings consistent with true audiovisual percepts.

38. Boltz, Schulkind, and Kantra, "Effects of Background Music," esp. 600–602.

39. For other viewers, however, the arousal of emotions may not reach the same level of intensity. Rather than being deeply affected, they may simply recognize the emotional states that are communicated to them through the combination of music and narrative. In this latter instance, viewers simply comprehend the emotional qualities of the scene by making judgments about the character's actions and motivations. In other words, viewers in these circumstances understand Merrick's sense of regret and resignation, but are not moved by it.

40. Cohen, "Associationism and Musical Soundtrack Phenomena," 173.

41. Philip Tagg, "An Anthropology of TV Music?," paper presented at the annual meeting of the Sonneck Society for American Music, Madison, 1995.

42. There is some evidence, however, to suggest that all musical affect is localized. In an experiment conducted by Barbara Tillman and Emmanuel Bigand, subjects were asked to rate the expressiveness of piano pieces by Bach, Mozart, and Schönberg on 29 semantic scales. In an interesting twist, however, only half the subjects heard the pieces in their original order. The other half heard inverted versions of the pieces, which had been chunked into short segments that were approximately six seconds in length and reordered. Although for both groups there was a strong association between music and expressiveness, this did not seem to be affected by the ordering of the pieces' smaller segments. Since the chunking of the piece destroyed its large-scale structure, the researchers were led to conclude that formal structure had little effect on the overall impression of musical expressiveness. The results have obvious pertinence for film music since they suggest that affective meaning can be communicated in cues as brief as six seconds and that the score's large-scale structure may have little impact on the viewer's recognition of the music's emotional expressiveness. This is especially significant, I think, since it suggests that while the essentially fragmentary nature of a film score may affect its musical coherence, it has little effect on its emotional expressiveness. See Barbara Tillman and Emmanuel Bigand, "Does Formal Structure Affect Perception of Musical Expressiveness?" *Psychology of Music* 24 (1996): 3–17.

Tillman and Bigand, however, confine themselves to issues of musical structure and do not address the relationship between expressiveness and narrative context. This would seem important for an investigation of film music since it is commonly thought that the development of a set of associations across a narrative text has some effect on the music's expressiveness. In *Breakfast at Tiffany's,* e.g., the theme "Moon River" seems to have more affective meanings at the end of the film than it does at the beginning insofar as it has accumulated a set of specific associations with the narrative.

43. Sloboda, "Empirical Studies of Emotional Response to Music," 33–39.

44. See Bernstein's "The Aesthetics of Film Music: A Highly Personal View," *Film Music Notebook* 4, no. 1 (1978).

45. Simon Frith, "Mood Music: An Inquiry into Narrative Film Music," *Screen* 25, no. 3 (1984): 83.

46. The latter element is often thought to be a key reason why spectators go out and purchase soundtrack albums. For more on this, see my *The Sounds of Commerce: Marketing Popular Film Music* (New York: Columbia University Press, 1998).

47. Quoted in Fred Karlin, *Listening to Movies: The Film Lover's Guide to Film Music* (New York: Schirmer Books, 1994), 14.

Chapter 8. Time and Timing

1. David Bordwell captures this idea in *Narration in the Fiction Film* (Madison: University of Wisconsin Press, 1985), 74. He claims that it is impossible to alter a film's discourse-time or time of presentation, yet it is possible if one has the film on videotape. Nevertheless, having the ability to alter the discourse-time of a film does not keep it from having a canonical discourse-time.

2. Seymour Chatman, "What Novels Can Do That Films Can't (and Vice Versa)," in *Film Theory and Criticism: Introductory Readings,* 4th ed., ed. Gerald Mast, Marshall Cohen, and Leo Braudy (New York: Oxford University Press, 1974), 404.

3. Alexander Sesonske, "Time and Tense in Cinema," *Journal of Aesthetics and Art Criticism* (Summer 1980): 419–26.

4. Susan Feagin, *Reading with Feeling: The Aesthetics of Appreciation* (Ithaca, N.Y.: Cornell University Press, 1996). See esp. chap. 1.

5. I have been told of people who have seen *Independence Day* and who antecedently believed that there are aliens who visit the earth via what we call UFOs. They are not amused because they take the movie seriously and its playful parody is lost.

6. David Bordwell amply describes and illustrates the three possible durational relationships (equality, expansion, contraction) between what he calls projection time and fabula time in *Narration in the Fiction Film,* chap. 6.

7. Leonard Klady, "Jim Jarmusch," *American Film* 12, no. 1 (October 1986): 47.

8. Brooks Adams, "Report from New York: Turtle Derby," *Art in America* 85, no. 6 (June 1997): 35.

9. *American Heritage Dictionary of the English Language,* ed. William Morris (Boston: American Heritage Publishing and Houghton Mifflin, 1969), 1141.

10. "Home and Away," interview with Peter Keogh, *Sight and Sound* 2 (August 1992): 9.

11. For a noncognitive account of the startle response, see Jenefer Robinson, "Startle," *Journal of Philosophy* 92 (1995): 53–74.

Chapter 9. Narrative Desire

Work on this essay was supported by the Australian Research Council and by the Research School of Social Sciences, Australian National University. I am grateful to a number of people, including Henry Fitzgerald, Richard Holton, Chandran Kukathas, Rae Langton, Roy Perret and Michael Smith, for valuable discussion when a previous version which was read to the Philosophy Society, Research School of Social Sciences, ANU. Carl Plantinga, Ian Ravenscroft, and Greg Smith read an earlier version and made suggestions, many of which I have tried to accommodate.

1. See Richard Maltby, "A Brief Romantic Interlude: Dick and Jane Go to 3½ Seconds of the Classical Hollywood Cinema," in *Post-Theory: Reconstructing Film Studies,* ed. David Bordwell and Noël Carroll (Madison: University of Wisconsin Press, 1996), 434–59.

2. See, e.g., Rae Langton, "Sexual Solipsism," *Philosophical Topics* 23 (1995): 149–87, and his "Love and Solipsism," in *Love Analysed,* ed. Roger Lamb (Boulder, Colo.: Westview Press, 1997).

3. This essay continues the project of "The Moral Psychology of Fiction," *Australasian Journal of Philosophy* 73 (1995): 250–59, and "Realism of Character and the Value of Fiction," in *Ethics and Aesthetics,* ed. Jerrold Levinson (Cambridge: Cambridge University Press, 1998).

4. See my "The Paradox of Caring: Fiction and the Philosophy of Mind," in *Emotion and the Arts,* ed. Mette Hjort and Sue Laver (Oxford: Oxford University Press, 1997). Later I shall give a simple and intuitive test for whether a desire is real or imaginary.

5. So, for example, certain works of fiction encourage the imagining that this very narrative is the product of one of the characters. I will ignore complications of this kind.

6. "Startle" refers to the specifically reflex reaction caused by, say, hearing a loud noise. The duration of the response is about half a second, and involves certain characteristic facial and bodily movements, as well as changes in the autonomic nervous system. It is involuntary, people are often unaware of engaging in it, and the reaction does not depend on the stimulus being unexpected. It is common to humans and a number of other species. There is some uncertainty as to whether startle should be thought of as a primitive version/ancestor of fear or of surprise, or of both. See Jenefer Robinson, "Startle," *Journal of Philosophy* 92 (1995): 53–74.

7. See Thomas Nagel, "What Is It Like to Be a Bat?," in his *Mortal Questions* (Cambridge: Cambridge University Press, 1979).

8. See, e.g., Paul Ekman et al., "Autonomous Nervous System Activity Distin-

guishes among the Emotions," *Science* 221 (1983): 1208–10. Schachter and Singer's well-known experiments that indicate that subjects' identification of their emotions is context dependent is best seen as showing that feelings are not uniquely paired with emotions rather than, as Schachter and Singer claim, that the very identity of an emotion depends on how it is labeled by the subject (S. Schachter and J. Singer, "Cognitive, Social, and Physiological Determinants of Emotional State," *Psychological Review* 69 [1965]: 379–99).

9. See, e.g., Robert Stalnaker, *Inquiry* (Cambridge: MIT Press, 1984).

10. "I was many years ago so shocked by Cordelia's death, that I know not whether I ever endured to read again the last scenes of the play till I undertook to revise them as an editor." Quoted in A. D. Nuttall, *Why Does Tragedy Give Pleasure?* (Oxford: Clarendon Press, 1996), 101.

11. Carroll, *Mystifying Movies: Fads and Fallacies in Contemporary Film Theory* (New York: Columbia University Press, 1988).

12. Richard Gerrig and Deborah Prentice, "Notes on Audience Response," in *Post-Theory: Reconstructing Film Studies,* 388–403.

13. Ibid., 392.

14. Paul Harris, "Fictional Absorption: Implications for Culture," in *Intersubjective Communication and Emotion in Ontogeny,* ed. S. Braten (Hillsdale, N.J.: Erlbaum, 1997).

15. D. G. Morrow, S. Greenspan, and G. Bower, "Accessibility and Situation Models in Narrative Comprehension," *Journal of Memory and Language* 26 (1987): 165–87.

16. A. Glenberg, M. Meyer, and K. Lindem, "Mental Models Contribute to Foregrounding during Text Comprehension," *Journal of Memory and Language* 26 (1987): 69–83.

17. J. B. Black, T. J. Turner, and G. H. Bower, "Point of View in Narrative Comprehension, Memory and Production," *Journal of Verbal Learning and Verbal Behavior* 18 (1979): 187–98.

18. I try to provide a more comprehensive treatment in "Getting a Life: Narrative and the Concept of Time," in *The Argument of Time,* ed. Jeremy Butterfield, British Academy Centennial Essays (forthcoming).

19. I don't think it is in general the case that the desire for knowledge be of the form that *I* know this, though this will indeed be one very common form; you might have a narrative desire based on what you wish your descendants to know.

20. See Frank Jackson, "Epiphenomenal Qualia," *Philosophical Quarterly* 32 (1982): 127–36.

21. See Gregory Currie and Ian Ravenscroft, "Mental Simulation and Motor Imagery," *Philosophy of Science* 64 (1997): 161–80, for discussion and references.

22. See my "Mental Imagery as the Simulation of Vision," *Mind and Language* 10 (1995): 25–44.

23. Kendall Walton, *Mimesis as Make-Believe* (Cambridge: Harvard University Press, 1990).

Chapter 10. Identification and Emotion in Narrative Film

Note: I would like to thank the editors of this volume and Alex Neill for their helpful comments on this paper. A shorter version of the paper was read at the Society for Cinema Studies Conference at Ottawa in 1997, and I am grateful to the participants on that occasion for discussion of the paper.

1. Jean-Louis Baudry, "Ideological Effects of the Basic Cinematographic Apparatus" in *Film Theory and Criticism,* 4th ed., ed. Gerald Mast, Marshall Cohen, and Leo Braudy (New York: Oxford University Press, 1992), 311.

2. For a discussion and critique of these claims, see Noël Carroll, *Mystifying Movies: Fads and Fallacies in Contemporary Film Theory* (New York: Columbia University Press, 1988); and also see my "On Cinema and Perversion," *Film and Philosophy* 1 (1994): 3–17.

3. Noël Carroll, *The Philosophy of Horror, or Paradoxes of the Heart* (London: Routledge, 1990), 96.

4. Gregory Currie, *Image and Mind: Film, Philosophy, and Cognitive Science* (Cambridge: Cambridge University Press, 1995), 174–76.

5. Murray Smith, *Engaging Characters: Fiction, Emotion, and the Cinema* (Oxford: Oxford University Press, 1995). Sometimes, as on p. 73, he seems to think of the idea of engagement as an analysis of the notion of identification; more generally, as on p. 93, he presents it as a replacement for that of identification.

6. Carroll, *Philosophy of Horror,* 89. I am not accusing Carroll of embracing the fallacious argument I attack in this paragraph.

7. See also ibid., 63–68, for a critique of illusionistic and suspension of disbelief theories of emotional responses to fictions.

8. Richard Wollheim, *The Thread of Life* (Cambridge: Harvard University Press, 1984), 75.

9. Ibid., 75–76.

10. This root idea of understanding another by imagining oneself in her place (the idea of *verstehen* as a mode of cognition of others) should be distinguished from the notion of simulation as employed in simulation theory. The latter construes the more basic notion of *verstehen* in computational terms. For an application of simulation theory to cinema, see Currie, *Image and Mind.* For some objections to this use of simulation theory, see my "Imagination, Interpretation, and Film," *Philosophical Studies* 89 (1998): 331–41.

11. Currie, *Image and Mind,* 174–6.

12. Smith, *Engaging Characters,* 157.

13. Kendall Walton, *Mimesis as Make-Believe: On the Foundations of the Representational Arts* (Cambridge: Harvard University Press, 1990), 174–83.

14. This has been urged by Smith in *Engaging Characters,* e.g., 222.

15. See Alex Neill, "Empathy and (Film) Fiction," in *Post-Theory: Reconstructing Film Studies,* ed. David Bordwell and Noël Carroll (Madison: University of Wisconsin Press, 1996).

16. For a convincing defense of the claim that such emotions are possible, see Richard Moran, "The Expression of Feeling in Imagination," *Philosophical Review* 103 (1994): 75–106.

17. See Neill, "Empathy and (Film) Fiction," for an illuminating discussion of the differences between empathy and sympathy.

18. Carroll, *Philosophy of Horror*, 90–92.

19. What Carroll says does not in any case support his position: "If the correspondences are only partial, why call the phenomenon *identification* at all? If two people are rooting for the same athlete at a sporting event, it would not appear appropriate to say that they are identifying with each other. They may be unaware of each other's existence" (Carroll, *Philosophy of Horror*, 92). But even if the spectators had exactly the same emotional states, they would still not be identifying with each other. Rather, empathic identification requires one to feel what another is feeling, *because* one recognizes that he is feeling it. This is why the spectators are not identifying with each other, not because of the fact that they are not sharing all their emotional states.

20. Carroll also objects that the swimmer's fear is based on a belief that she is in danger, whereas my empathic fear is based only on imagining that I am in danger. But this does not show that the fear is not shared, since as he has himself argued, the object of fear is a thought-content, whether or not it is asserted, and the thought contents are the same in both cases. (For his "Thought Theory" of emotional response, see Carroll, *Philosophy of Horror*, 79–88.)

21. This shot also doubles as a reaction shot of Starling: for the significance of reaction shots, see below.

22. This is what Murray Smith terms allegiance with a character: see Smith, *Engaging Characters*, esp. chap. 5. He holds that the notion of identification cannot distinguish allegiance from other senses in which we are engaged with a character: but as we have seen, the notion of identification can in fact be refined so as to recognize this case.

23. For a fine discussion of this phenomenon, and of Truffaut's thoughts thereon, see Smith, 156–61.

24. For a discussion of *The Crying Game* to which I am indebted, see Matthew Kieran, "Art, Imagination, and the Cultivation of Morals," *Journal of Aesthetics and Art Criticism* 54 (1996): 337–51, at 338.

25. This construal of the film is argued for by George Wilson in his *Narration in Light: Studies in Cinematic Point of View* (Baltimore: Johns Hopkins University Press, 1986), chap. 6.

Chapter 11. Gangsters, Cannibals, Aesthetes, or Apparently Perverse Allegiances

Note: Thanks to Carl Plantinga and Greg Smith for comments on earlier versions of this essay. I would also like to acknowledge audiences at the University of London (American Studies Seminar) and the University of Kent (Philosophy Society), and my students, in particular Rob Daniel, Angela Groth, and Ruth Merskey.

1. Though I will not repeat his arguments, I should note that Berys Gaut has argued compellingly against the various theorists who treat the cinema as *inherently*—in its very technology and social conditions—perverse. See Berys Gaut, "On Cinema and Perversion," *Film and Philosophy* 1 (1994): 3–17.

2. *Random House College Dictionary,* rev. ed (New York: Random House, 1975), 992. The strength of the "deflection" is of course variable, as is evident in the use of the word "perverse" to describe everything from obstinacy and contrariness to masochism and perjury. What all of these cases share, however, is the idea of willful, deliberate action which flies in the face of an accepted norm or practice. Thus, while recognizing this range of possibilities, I do not wish to separate "contrariness" from more extreme instances of normative deviation.

3. Timo Airaksinen, *The Philosophy of the Marquis de Sade* (London: Routledge, 1995).

4. Evolutionary biology might seem like an unlikely ally in my argument here against the moralism in the language of "perversion," in so far as such biology is often presumed to be relentlessly and narrowly concerned with discovering the adaptive purposes of the features of a species—that is, the role of these features in promoting fitness for survival in a given environment. But this is a mistaken or at least myopic view of the kinds of arguments advanced by evolutionary biologists: consider Stephen Jay Gould's arguments for biological potentiality, as opposed to the biological determinism associated with E. O. Wilson's sociobiology, and in general the emphasis Gould places on the diversity and creativity of biological species at both the cultural and evolutionary levels. See, for example, Stephen Jay Gould, "Biological Potentiality versus Biological Determinism," in *Ever Since Darwin* (Harmondsworth: Pelican, 1980). Recently Gould has criticized what he calls "Darwinian Fundamentalism," the view that the mechanism of adaptation alone can account for all of evolution. "Darwinian Fundamentalism," *New York Review of Books,* June 12, 1997, 34–37.

5. Stephen Jay Gould and Elizabeth S. Vrda, "Exaptation—A Missing Term in the Science of Form," *Paleobiology* 8, no. 1 (1982): 4–15.

6. "Paraphilia" is the term used by sexologist John Money to draw the moralistic poison out of what are commonly, and legally, termed "perversions." John Money, *Gay, Straight, and In-Between: The Sexology of Erotic Orientation* (New York: Oxford University Press, 1988), 7, 216.

7. Paul R. Abramson and Steven D. Pinkerton, *With Pleasure: Thoughts on the Nature of Human Sexuality* (New York: Oxford University Press, 1995), 28.

8. Both examples inspired here by Thomas Nagel's essay "Sexual Perversion," which can be found in Thomas Nagel, *Mortal Questions* (New York: Cambridge University Press, 1979). Airaksinen does not regard first-order perversity as authentic perversity, but rather (Aristotelian) "brutishness," in which the agent acts immorally but without an understanding of his action, and/or without volition (Airaksinen, *Marquis de Sade,* 28). For Nagel, on the other hand, first-order perversity seems much more important than second-order perversity.

9. The first sense of "perverse" provided by the *Random House College Dictionary* is "willfully determined not to do what is expected or desired; contrary"; one sense of "pervert" is given as "to misconstrue or misinterpret, esp. deliberately" (992).

10. Murray Smith, *Engaging Characters: Fiction, Emotion, and the Cinema*

(Oxford: Clarendon Press, 1995). Chap. 3 provides an overview; chaps. 5 and 6 provide detailed accounts of alignment and allegiance.

11. Berys Gaut, review of *Engaging Characters, British Journal of Aesthetics* 37, no. 1 (Jan. 1997): 97.

12. Rob Daniel, unpublished student essay, 40–41.

13. Edgar Allen Poe, "The Imp of the Perverse," in *Poetry and Tales* (New York: Library of America, 1984), 829. See also Abramson and Pinkerton, *With Pleasure*, 54. Similarly, David Cronenberg has commented, "There is a vicarious thrill involved in seeing the forbidden": *Cronenberg on Cronenberg*, rev. ed., ed. Chris Rodley (London: Faber and Faber, 1996), 50.

14. I underplay these possibilities in *Engaging Characters,* but I do so for a reason: once we accept the possibility of perverse allegiance, it becomes much more difficult to prise apart alignment and allegiance, because every alignment can be said to produce allegiance, whether "normal" or "perverse." Films like *Naked* and *Maniac,* however, establish that there is a third possibility: that we can be aligned with a character with whom we have no positive allegiance, normal or perverse, but only a negative allegiance—an antagonism. We should not close off the possibility of, nor deny the existence of, film narratives which deliberately ask us to follow and witness the actions of a character we simply find wholly undesirable and deplorable.

15. Among the most influential are Laura Mulvey, "Visual Pleasure and Narrative Cinema" *Screen* 16, no. 3 (Autumn 1975): 6–18, reprinted in *Visual and Other Pleasures* (London: Macmillan, 1989); Gaylyn Studlar, *In the Realm of Pleasure: Von Sternberg, Dietrich, and the Masochistic Aesthetic* (Urbana: University of Illinois Press, 1988); and Carol Clover, *Men, Women, and Chainsaws: Gender in the Modern Horror Film* (London: BFI, 1992).

16. By this definition, Stanley Kubrick's *A Clockwork Orange* (1971), for example, does not solicit perverse allegiance, for the film asks us to sympathize with Alex not because he rapes and murders—acts that are represented in a suitably horrific fashion—but rather because of the violence, humiliation, and degradation that are subsequently inflicted upon him by the state.

17. I draw this example from the discussion of Wolfenstein and Leites in Richard Maltby and Ian Craven, *Hollywood Cinema: An Introduction* (Oxford: Blackwell, 1995), 44.

18. Martha Wolfenstein and Nathan Leites, *The Movies: A Psychological Study* (Glencoe, Ill.: Free Press, 1950); quoted in ibid., 44.

19. Deborah Knight, "Aristotelians on *Speed,*" in *Film Theory and Philosophy,* ed. Richard Allen and Murray Smith (Oxford: Clarendon Press, 1997), 361.

20. Wolfenstein and Leites, *The Movies,* 300.

21. For a more detailed discussion of "imagining from the inside," or what is commonly called empathy, see Murray Smith, "Imagining from the Inside," in *Film Theory and Philosophy,* ed. Allen and Smith.

22. It is important to stress here that the emotions we experience in response to fictions are real emotions, in spite of the fact that we know the object of these emotions to be fictional. For discussions of this apparent paradox, see Smith,

Engaging Characters, 54–58; and Noël Carroll, *The Philosophy of Horror, or Paradoxes of the Heart* (New York: Routledge, 1990), chap. 2.

23. Wolfenstein and Leites's study is psychoanalytic in character, and not given very much attention or credence these days, so I had better say a word or two on both these matters, which might appear to be difficult given my nonpsychoanalytic framework. On this point, I believe that that part of their argument which I have extracted is independent of a commitment to psychoanalysis (of any variety). Concepts such as fantasy and wish-fulfillment may have a psychoanalytic coloring—precisely because of the domination of this tradition in certain domains of study—but severed from the more distinctive psychoanalytic concepts of repression and the unconscious, they are widely used folk psychological concepts that may be legitimately developed in nonpsychoanalytic psychologies as much as in psychoanalytic ones. The independence of what we might call the "imaginative slumming it" argument from a psychoanalytic framework is also supported by the presence of a very similar argument in Rick Altman's (nonpsychoanalytic) writings on the psychological dynamics and satisfactions of genre films, discussed in the text below.

24. Rick Altman, "Cinema and Genre," in *The Oxford History of World Cinema,* ed. Geoffrey Nowell-Smith (Oxford: Oxford University Press, 1996), 279, 280.

25. Carroll, *Philosophy of Horror,* chap. 1.

26. See also the remarks on John McNaughton's *Henry: Portrait of a Serial Killer* (1990) in Smith, *Engaging Characters,* 194.

27. See the discussion of the character "alloy" in ibid., 209.

28. Cynthia Freeland suggests that the manner in which *Silence of the Lambs* "encourages the audience to sympathize with brilliant serial killer Hannibal Lecter" is likely to provoke audiences into self-consciousness concerning their attitudes toward horror representations: "Realist Horror," in *Philosophy and Film,* ed. Cynthia Freeland and Thomas Wartenberg (New York: Routledge, 1995), 139.

29. Oscar Wilde, quoted in Richard Ellmann, *Oscar Wilde* (London: Hamish Hamilton, 1987), 214.

30. Jonas Mekas, "On the Baudelairean Cinema," *Village Voice,* May 2, 1963; reprinted in Jonas Mekas, *Movie Journal: The Rise of a New American Cinema, 1959–1971* (New York: Collier Books, 1972), 85.

31. Susan Sontag, "Jack Smith's *Flaming Creatures,*" in *Against Interpretation* (New York: Dell, 1969), 234.

32. H. L. Mencken, introduction to Oscar Wilde, *A House of Pomegranates,* quoted in Karl Beckson, *Oscar Wilde: The Critical Heritage* (London: Routledge and Kegan Paul, 1970), 382.

33. Wilde, quoted in Ellmann, *Oscar Wilde,* 310.

34. Noël Carroll has made this claim for *Entr'acte* (1924), a Dada film whose lineage can be traced back to Aestheticism and Decadence. Noël Carroll, "*Entr'acte,* Dada, and Paris," *Millenium Film Journal* 1, no. 1 (Winter 1977–78): 5–11.

35. Arthur Danto, "Robert Mapplethorpe," in *Encounters and Reflections: Art in the Historical Present* (New York: Noonday Press, 1991), 212.

36. Ibid., 213, 216. On the distinctions among amoral acts, immoral acts,

amoralism, and immoralism relevant to my argument, see Tony Skillen, "Confession and Collusion: Gide's *The Immoralist*," unpublished manuscript.

37. Mekas, "On the Baudelairean Cinema," 85–86.

38. Jonas Mekas, "On *Blonde Cobra* and *Flaming Creatures*," *Village Voice*, October 24, 1963; reprinted in Mekas, *Movie Journal*, 102.

39. Ellmann, *Oscar Wilde*, 218.

40. In this film, the potentially disturbing nature of many of the bizarre and perverse sexual routines indulged in by characters is largely neutralized by the sheer wackiness of their endeavors, and the overtly ritualized nature of many of them. For example, a middle-aged man and an older woman live opposite each other, and "conspire" with each other's sadistic fantasies—but in the form of stuffed dummies rather than as persons. This doesn't entirely blunt the sinister quality of their fantasies, especially given the surreal ending in which the old woman appears to have died from wounds that would have been inflicted on her had she actually been present during the acting out of the man's fantasy with a dummy; but it is still quite unlike, say, reading Sade or Bataille.

41. John Money makes a vital but often overlooked point on this matter: "All [paraphilias] may afflict either homosexuals or heterosexuals, with no special affinity for either . . . The gay movement, because of its focus on the struggle for gay political rights, has not properly differentiated gay rights from paraphilic rights; nor has it recognized the potential hazards of the more dangerous paraphilias either to gay individuals or to the political reputation of the movement. Conversely, the enemies of the gay movement also have not differentiated gay rights from paraphilic rights, and have equated being homosexual as the first stage of a degenerative descent into paraphilia . . . There is no substantiating evidence for this heresy. It is based on total ignorance of paraphilia in general, and of the high degree of specificity of each paraphilia in particular." Money, *Gay, Straight, and In-Between*, 181.

42. The gimp/rape scene is, however, depicted in such a way that ironic detachment is balanced against the menace of the actions.

43. Noël Carroll, "Moderate Moralism," *British Journal of Aesthetics* 36, no. 3 (July 1996): 230–31.

44. For the benefit of American readers, I should point out that the adjective "Whitehouseian" is derived not from past or present incumbents of the White House, but from Mary Whitehouse, president of the National Viewers and Listeners Association in Britain, scourge of the permissive society.

45. Quoted in *Cronenberg on Cronenberg*, ed. Rodley, 50; see also 66 and 198.

46. Robert Solomon, review of Noël Carroll, *The Philosophy of Horror*, *Philosophy and Literature* 16 (1992): 173.

47. This seems to be Cronenberg's paraphrase of the review by Robert Fulford, quoted in *Cronenberg on Cronenberg*, ed. Rodley, 51.

48. Clover, *Men, Women, and Chainsaws*, 76.

49. Angela Groth, unpublished student essay, 6.

50. Quoted in *Cronenberg on Cronenberg*, ed. Rodley, 82; see also 151; note also

the similarity in this respect with *Crash*, 194: "Where are the sympathetic characters?," and 201.

51. Colin Radford, *Driving to California: An Unconventional Introduction to Philosophy* (Edinburgh: Edinburgh University Press, 1996), 138–39.

Chapter 12. The Scene of Empathy and the Human Face on Film

1. Stephen Prince, "The Discourse of Pictures: Iconicity and Film Studies," *Film Quarterly* 47, no. 1 (Fall 1993): 16–28.

2. Béla Bélazs, *Theory of the Film: Character and Growth of a New Art* (1952; New York: Dover Publications, 1970), 42.

3. Noël Carroll, "Toward a Theory of Point-of-View Editing: Communication, Emotion, and the Movies," in Carroll, *Theorizing the Moving Image* (Cambridge: Cambridge University Press, 1996), 125–38.

4. Ibid., 130–32.

5. Paul Ekman, ed., *Emotion in the Human Face*, 2nd ed. (Cambridge: Cambridge University Press, 1982), 142.

6. S. S. Tomkins, *Affect, Imagery, and Consciousness* (New York: Springer, 1962); C. E. Izard, *The Face of Emotion* (New York: Appleton-Century-Crofts, 1971); C. E. Izard, *Human Emotions* (New York: Plenum Press, 1977).

7. Charles Eidsvik argues that the universal understanding of basic facial expressions *in film* is the result of the pervasive influence of Hollywood, and that Hollywood has in fact established a more-or-less universal language of filmic facial expression. "Reading Faces: Cognitive and Cultural Problems," unpublished paper, Symposium on Cognitive Science and the Future of Film Studies, April 1997, University of Kansas. Moreover, Eidsvik assumes that this "language" relates only tangentially to real-world facial expressions. However, such a view would need to account for the means by which Hollywood established itself initially. How did early spectators understand facial expressions before Hollywood established such a "language"? Clearly, if early audiences did not comprehend the facial expressions of actors, then it would be difficult to account for the popularity of the films. On the other hand, if early audiences did comprehend facial expression, how can we account for such recognition? This early recognition would seem to imply the universality of such expressions rather than a language of expression peculiar to film. My own view is that the facial expressions of actors in film have their roots in real-world facial expressions. Even the exaggerated faces of Jim Carrey have their basis in the facial arrays characteristic of emotion expression in extra-filmic situations.

8. One researcher who differs with Ekman et al. is Alan J. Fridlund, who argues that facial expressions are a means of social communication rather than expressions of inner emotions. In many cases, he argues, the face hides emotions rather than expresses them. In my opinion, however, Fridlund overstates his case. His argument that facial expressions are used to communicate socially is well taken, but does not compromise Ekman and others' claims that the face can and does mirror inner emotions. Whether the face reveals emotions, hides emotion, or is used to communicate in complex social interractions depends on context. It is

interesting to note that in many scenes of empathy, the facial expression of the major character is private, in that no other characters in the film's diegesis are viewing it. In such cases, social communication and display rules are irrelevant, and the face becomes primarily an expressor of inner feeling.

9. Bélazs, *Theory of the Film*, 44.

10. For a thorough exploration of the phenomenon of emotional contagion see Elaine Hatfield, John T. Cacioppo, and Richard L. Rapson, *Emotional Contagion* (Cambridge: Cambridge University Press, 1994).

11. Ibid., 48.

12. C. K. Hsee, E. Hatfield, J. G. Carlson, and C. Chemtob, "The Effect of Power on Susceptibility to Emotional Contagion," *Cognition and Emotion* 4 (1990): 327–40.

13. Tomkins, *Affect, Imagery, and Consciousness;* Izard, *Face of Emotion.*

14. Nico H. Frijda, *The Emotions* (Cambridge: Cambridge University Press, 1986), 236.

15. This is the term used by Murray Smith in his *Engaging Characters: Fiction, Emotion, and the Cinema* (Oxford: Clarendon Press, 1995). I argue for the use of the term "identification" in "Affect, Cognition, and the Power of Movies," *Post Script*, 13, no. 1 (Fall 1993): 10–29. I now agree with Smith and others that "identification" is too confusing to be useful.

16. See Noël Carroll, *The Philosophy of Horror, or Paradoxes of the Heart* (New York: Routledge, 1990), 88–96; Gregory Currie, *Image and Mind: Film, Philosophy, and Cognitive Science* (Cambridge: Cambridge University Press, 1995), 164–97.

17. In this volume, Berys Gaut attempts to rehabilitate the term "identification." While Gaut's stipulative definition of identification is certainly an improvement over general usage, the term as used in ordinary language still is vague. Gaut's definition of "identification" is no doubt useful, but general usage of the term may nonetheless encourage widespread confusion. Thus I believe an effective strategy is to develop more precise terminology.

18. For an overview of various theories of empathy, see Dolf Zillman, "Empathy: Affect From Bearing Witness to the Emotions of Others," in *Responding to the Screen: Reception and Reaction Processes,* ed. Jennings Bryant and Dolf Zillman (Hillsdale, N.J.: Erlbaum, 1991), 135–41.

19. Richard S. Lazarus, *Emotion and Adaptation* (New York: Oxford University Press, 1991), 287–89.

20. See Alex Neill, "Empathy and (Film) Fiction," in *Post-Theory: Reconstructing Film Studies,* ed. David Bordwell and Noël Carroll (Madison: University of Wisconsin Press, 1996), 175–77.

21. Susan Feagin uses these terms in her *Reading with Feeling: The Aesthetics of Appreciation* (Ithaca, N.Y.: Cornell University Press, 1996), 25–31.

22. On the other hand, of course, certain kinds of crowd behavior—catcalls or incessant talking, for example—can weaken affective response.

23. See Carolyn Saarni, "Socialization of Emotion" (435–46), and Leslie R. Brody and Judith A. Hall, "Gender and Emotion" (447–60), both in *Handbook of*

Emotions, ed. Michael Lewis and Jeannette M. Haviland (New York: Guilford Press, 1993).

24. These figures are taken from Noël Carroll's "Film, Attention, and Communication," *The Great Ideas Today*, ed. Mortimer Jerome Adler (Chicago: Encyclopedia Brittanica, 1996), 22. Carroll obtained his statistics from Barry Salt's *Film Style and Technology: History and Analysis* (London: Starword Press, 1992), 263, 283, and from conversations with David Bordwell.

25. See John Hora, "Cinematographers Publicly Oppose HDTV Standard: The American Society of Cinematographers' Viewpoint," and Robert Primes, "ASC Message to Japan," *Widescreen Review* 4, no. 6 (Nov./Dec. 1995): 98 and 22. Carroll, in "Film, Attention, and Communication," uses these sources to show that the current average length of shots is about the same as for 1981. However, the statistics, if accurate, in fact show that average shot length has lowered from 10 seconds to 6 seconds since 1981.

26. Hatfield et al., *Emotional Contagion*, 148.

27. For a more extensive discussion of sentimentality, see my "Emotion and Ideological Film Criticism," in *Film Theory and Philosophy*, ed. Richard Allen and Murray Smith (New York: Oxford University Press, 1997).

28. My point is *not* that empathy is inherently mystifying. See ibid.

29. E. H. Gombrich, *Art and Illusion* (Princeton: Princeton University Press, 1972), 366–67.

30. For an illuminating discussion of "fittingness," see Nicholas Wolterstorff, *Art in Action* (Grand Rapids: Eerdmans, 1980), 96–121.

SELECT BIBLIOGRAPHY

Film and Emotion

Affron, Charles. *Cinema and Sentiment*. Chicago: University of Chicago Press, 1982.

Braudy, Leo. *The World in a Frame*. Garden City, N.Y.: Anchor, 1976.

Bryant, Jennings, and Dolf Zillman, eds. *Responding to the Screen: Reception and Reaction Processes*. Hillsdale, N.J.: Erlbaum, 1991.

Carroll, Noël. *The Philosophy of Horror, or Paradoxes of the Heart*. New York: Routledge, 1990.

———. "Toward a Theory of Film Suspense." *Persistence of Vision* 1 (Summer 1984): 65–89.

———. "Toward a Theory of Point-of-View Editing: Communication, Emotion, and the Movies." *Poetics Today* 14, no. 1 (Spring 1993): 122–41.

Currie, Gregory. *Image and Mind: Film, Philosophy, and Cognitive Science*. Cambridge: Cambridge University Press, 1995.

Durgnat, Raymond. *Films and Feelings*. London: Faber, 1967.

Gaut, Berys. "On Cinema and Perversion." *Film and Philosophy* 1 (1994): 3–17.

Gerrig, Richard J., and Deborah Prentice. "Notes on Audience Response." In *Post-Theory*, ed. Bordwell and Carroll.

Grodal, Torben Kragh. *Moving Pictures: A New Theory of Film Genres, Feelings, and Cognition*. Oxford: Clarendon Press, 1997.

Gunning, Tom. "An Aesthetic of Astonishment: Early Film and the (In-)credulous Spectator." In *Viewing Positions: Ways of Seeing Film*, ed. Linda Williams. New Brunswick, N.J.: Rutgers University Press, 1994.

Leibowitz, Flo. "Apt Feelings, or Why 'Women's Films' Aren't Trivial." In *Post-Theory*, ed. Bordwell and Carroll.

Munsterberg, Hugo. *The Film: A Psychological Study*. New York: Dover, 1970.

Neill, Alex. "Empathy and (Film) Fiction." In *Post-Theory*, ed. Bordwell and Carroll.

Perkins, V. F. *Film as Film: Understanding and Judging Movies*. Harmondsworth: Penguin Books, 1973.

Plantinga, Carl. "Affect, Cognition, and the Power of Movies." *Post Script* 13, no. 1 (Fall 1993): 10–29.

———. "Movie Pleasures and the Spectator's Experience: Toward a Cognitive Approach." *Philosophy and Film* 2, no. 2 (1995): 3–19.

———. "Notes on Spectator Emotion and Ideological Film Criticism." In *Film The-*

ory and Philosophy, ed. Richard Allen and Murray Smith. Oxford: Oxford University Press, 1997.

——. "Spectacles of Death: Clint Eastwood and Violence in *Unforgiven.*" *Cinema Journal* 37, no. 2 (Winter 1998): 65–83.

Smith, Murray. *Engaging Characters: Fiction, Emotion, and the Cinema.* Oxford: Clarendon Press, 1995.

——. "Film Spectatorship and the Institution of Fiction." *Journal of Aesthetics and Art Criticism* 53, no. 2 (Spring 1995): 113–28.

——. "The Logic and Legacy of Brechtianism." In *Post-Theory,* ed. Bordwell and Carroll.

Tan, Ed S. *Emotion and the Structure of Narrative Film: Film as an Emotion Machine.* Translated by Barbara Fasting. Mahwah, N.J.: Erlbaum, 1996.

——. "Film-Induced Affect as a Witness Emotion." *Poetics* 23 (1995): 7–32.

Tan, Ed S., and Gijsbert Diteweg. "Suspense, Predictive Inference, and Emotion in Film Viewing." In *Suspense: Conceptualizations, Theoretical Analyses, and Empirical Explorations,* ed. Peter Vorderer, Hans J. Wulff, and Mike Friedrichsen, 71–91. Mahwah, N.J.: Erlbaum, 1996.

Truffaut, Francois. *Hitchcock,* Rev. ed. New York. Simon and Schuster, 1983.

Wolfenstein, Martha, and Nathan Leites. *The Movies: A Psychological Study.* New York: Atheneum, 1970.

Film and Cognition

Anderson, Joseph. *The Reality of Illusion: An Ecological Approach to Cognitive Film Theory.* Carbondale: Southern Illinois University Press, 1996.

Bordwell, David. "A Case for Cognitivism." *Iris* 9 (Spring 1989): 11–40.

——. *Narration in the Fiction Film.* Madison: University of Wisconsin Press, 1985.

Bordwell, David, and Noël Carroll, eds. *Post-Theory: Reconstructing Film Studies.* Madison: University of Wisconsin Press, 1996.

Branigan, Edward. *Narrative Comprehension and Film.* New York: Routledge, 1992.

Carroll, Noël. *Mystifying Movies: Fads and Fallacies in Contemporary Film Theory.* New York: Columbia University Press, 1988.

——. *Theorizing the Moving Image.* Cambridge: Cambridge University Press, 1996.

Messaris, Paul. *Visual "Literacy": Image, Mind, and Reality.* Boulder, Colo.: Westview Press, 1994.

Peterson, James. *Dreams of Chaos, Visions of Order: Understanding the American Avant-Garde Cinema.* Detroit: Wayne State University Press, 1994.

Plantinga, Carl. *Rhetoric and Representation in Nonfiction Film.* Cambridge: Cambridge University Press, 1997.

Pudovkin, V.I. *Film Technique and Film Acting.* Translated by Ivor Montagu. New York: Grove Press, 1960.

The Other Arts and Emotion

Aristotle. *The Poetics.* In *Aristotle's Theory of Poetry and Fine Art,* 4th ed. Translated by S. H. Burcher. New York: Dover Publications, 1955.

Beardsley, Monroe C. *Aesthetics from Classical Greece to the Present*. University of Alabama Press, 1966.

Belfiore, Elizabeth S. *Tragic Pleasures: Aristotle on Plot and Emotion*. Princeton: Princeton University Press, 1992.

Boruah, Bijoy H. *Fiction and Emotion: A Study in Aesthetics and the Philosophy of Mind*. Oxford: Clarendon Press, 1988.

Chapman, A. J., and H. C. Foot, eds. *It's a Funny Thing, Humour*. Oxford: Pergamon Press, 1977.

Currie, Gregory. *The Nature of Fiction*. Cambridge: Cambridge University Press, 1990.

Dissanayake, Ellen. *Homo Aestheticus: Where Art Comes From and Why*. New York: Free Press, 1992.

Feagin, Susan. *Reading with Feeling: The Aesthetics of Appreciation*. Ithaca, N.Y.: Cornell University Press, 1996.

Goldstein, Jeffrey H., and Paul E. McGhee, ed. *The Psychology of Humor*. New York: Academic Press, 1972.

Kivy, Peter. *Music Alone: Philosophical Reflections on the Purely Musical Experience*. Ithaca, N.Y.: Cornell University Press, 1990.

———. *Sound Sentiment: An Essay on the Musical Emotions*. Philadelphia: Temple University Press, 1989.

Kreitler, Hans, and Shulamith Kreitler. *Psychology of the Arts*. Durham, N.C.: Duke University Press, 1972.

Lamarque, Peter. "How Can We Fear and Pity Fictions?" *British Journal of Aesthetics* 21, no. 4 (Autumn 1981): 291–304.

Langer, Susanne. *Feeling and Form: A Theory of Art*. New York: Scribner's, 1953.

Lipps, T. "Empathy and Aesthetic Pleasure." In *Aesthetic Theories: Studies in the Philosophy of Art*, ed. Karl Aschenbrenner and Arnold Isenberg. Englewood Cliffs, N.J.: Prentice-Hall, 1965.

Mauron, Charles. *Aesthetics and Psychology*. Translated by Roger Fry and Katherine John. Port Washington, N.Y.: Kennikat Press, 1970.

Novitz, David. *Knowledge, Fiction, and Imagination*. Philadelphia: Temple University Press, 1987.

Nussbaum, Martha C. *Love's Knowledge: Essays on Philosophy and Literature*. New York: Oxford University Press, 1990.

Radford, Colin. "How Can We Be Moved by the Fate of Anna Karenina?" *Proceedings of the Aristotelian Society*, Supp. vol. 49 (1975): 67–70.

Robinson, Jenefer. "The Expression and Arousal of Emotion in Music." In *Aesthetics: A Reader in the Philosophy of the Arts*, ed. David Goldblatt and Lee B. Brown. Upper Saddle River, N.J.: Prentice-Hall, 1997.

Rorty, Amélie Oksenberg. "The Psychology of Aristotelian Tragedy." *Midwest Studies in Philosophy* 41 (1991): 53–72.

Scruton, Roger. *Art and Imagination: A Study in the Philosophy of Mind*. London: Methuen, 1974.

Sloboda, John A. "Empirical Studies of Emotional Response to Music." In *Cogni-*

tive Bases of Musical Communication, ed. Mari Ries Jones and Susan Halleran. Washington, D.C.: American Psychological Association, 1992.

Walton, Kendall. *Mimesis as Make-Believe: On the Foundations of the Representational Arts.* Cambridge: Harvard University Press, 1990.

Wollheim, Richard. "Imagination and Identification." In *On Art and the Mind.* Cambridge: Harvard University Press, 1974.

———. *The Thread of Life.* Cambridge: Harvard University Press, 1984.

Emotion (General)

Armon-Jones, Claire. *Varieties of Affect.* Toronto: University of Toronto Press, 1991.

Averill, J. R. *Anger and Aggression: An Essay on Emotion.* New York: Springer, 1982.

Buck, Ross. *The Communication of Emotion.* New York: Guilford Press, 1984.

Cornelius, Randolph R. *The Science of Emotion: Research and Tradition in the Psychology of Emotions.* Upper Saddle River, N.J.: Prentice-Hall, 1996.

Crawford, June, Susan Kippax, Jenny Onyx, Una Gault, and Pam Benton. *Emotion and Gender: Constructing Meaning from Memory.* London: Sage, 1992.

Damasio, Antonio. *Descartes' Error: Emotion, Reason, and the Human Brain.* New York: Putnam, 1994.

Darwin, Charles. *The Expression of Emotions in Man and Animals.* New York: Philosophical Library, 1955.

De Sousa, Ronald. *The Rationality of Emotion.* Cambridge: MIT Press, 1987.

Ekman, Paul, ed. *Emotion in the Human Face,* 2nd ed. Cambridge: Cambridge University Press, 1982.

———. *The Face of Man: Expressions of Universal Emotions in a New Guinea Village.* New York: Garland Press, 1980.

Ekman, Paul, and Richard J. Davidson, eds. *The Nature of Emotion: Fundamental Questions.* New York: Oxford University Press, 1994.

Fiedler, Klaus and Joseph Forgas, eds. *Affect, Cognition, and Social Behavior: New Evidence and Integrative Attempts.* Toronto: C. J. Hogrefe, 1988.

Frijda, Nico H. "Appraisal and Beyond: The Issue of Cognitive Determinants of Emotion." [Special issue] *Cognition and Emotion* 7 (1993): 357–87.

———. *The Emotions.* Cambridge: Cambridge University Press, 1986.

Gordon, Robert M. *The Structure of the Emotions: Investigations in Cognitive Philosophy.* New York: Cambridge University Press, 1987.

Greenspan, Patricia S. *Emotions and Reasons: An Inquiry into Emotional Justification.* New York: Routledge, 1988.

Harris, Paul L. *Children and Emotion: The Development of Psychological Understanding.* Oxford: Basil Blackwell, 1989.

Hatfield, Elaine, John T. Cacioppo, and Richard L. Rapson. *Emotional Contagion.* Cambridge: Cambridge University Press, 1994.

Hochschild, Arlie Russell. *The Managed Heart: Commercialization of Human Feeling.* Berkeley: University of California Press, 1983.

Izard, Carroll E. *The Face of Emotion.* New York: Appleton-Century-Crofts, 1971.

———. *The Psychology of Emotions.* New York: Plenum Press, 1991.

Kavanaugh, Robert D., Betty Zimmerberg, and Steven Fein. *Emotion: Interdisciplinary Perspectives*. Mahwah, N.J.: Erlbaum, 1996.

Kemper, Theodore D. *A Social Interactional Theory of Emotions*. New York: John Wiley and Sons, 1978.

Kitayama, Shinobu, and Hazel Rose Markus. *Emotion and Culture: Empirical Studies of Mutual Influence*. Washington, D.C.: American Psychological Association, 1994.

Lazarus, Richard S. *Emotion and Adaptation*. New York: Oxford University Press, 1991.

LeDoux, Joseph. *The Emotional Brain: The Mysterious Underpinnings of Emotional Life*. New York: Simon and Schuster, 1996.

Lutz, Catherine A. *Unnatural Emotions: Everyday Sentiments on a Micronesian Atoll and Their Challenge to Western Theory*. Chicago: University of Chicago Press, 1988.

Lyons, William. *Emotion*. Cambridge: Cambridge University Press, 1980.

Oatley, Keith. *Best-Laid Schemes: The Psychology of Emotion*. Cambridge: Cambridge University Press, 1992.

Ortony, Andrew, Gerald L. Clore, and Allan Collins. *The Cognitive Structure of Emotion*. Cambridge: Cambridge University Press, 1988.

Robinson, Jenefer. "Startle." *Journal of Philosophy* 92 (1995): 53–74.

Sartre, Jean-Paul. *The Emotions: Outline of a Theory*. Translated by Bernard Frechtman. New York: Philosophical Library, 1948.

Scherer, Klaus R., and Paul Ekman, eds. *Approaches to Emotion*. Hillsdale, N.J.: Erlbaum, 1984.

Scherer, Klaus, Harald G. Wallbott, and Angela B. Summerfield. *Experiencing Emotion: A Cross-cultural Study*. Cambridge: Cambridge University Press, 1986.

Solomon, Robert C. *The Passions: The Myth and Nature of Human Emotion*. Garden City, N.Y.: Anchor Press, 1976.

Stearns, Carol Zisowitz, and Peter N. Stearns. *Anger: The Struggle for Emotional Control in America's History*. Chicago: University of Chicago Press, 1986.

Stearns, Peter N. *Jealousy: The Evolution of an Emotion in American History*. New York: New York University Press, 1989.

Stein, Nancy L., Bennett Leventhal, and Tom Trabasso. *Psychological and Biological Approaches to Emotion*. Hillsdale, N.J.: Erlbaum, 1990.

Strongman, K. T. *The Psychology of Emotion: Theories of Emotion in Perspective*, 4th ed. Chichester: John Wiley and Sons, 1996.

Wegman, Cornelis. *Psychoanalysis and Cognitive Psychology*. London: Academic Press, 1985.

Zajonc, R. B. "Emotion and Facial Efference: A Theory Reclaimed." *Science* 228 (April 1985): 15–21.

CONTRIBUTORS

NOËL CARROLL is Monroe C. Beardsley Professor of the Philosophy of Art at the University of Wisconsin-Madison. His latest book is *A Philosophy of Mass Art* (Oxford: Oxford University Press, 1998).

GREGORY CURRIE is Head of the School of Arts and Professor of Philosophy at Flinders University in Adelaide, Australia. Among his books is *Image and Mind: Film, Philosophy, and Cognitive Science* (Cambridge: Cambridge University Press, 1995).

DIRK EITZEN is an assistant professor of film studies at Franklin and Marshall College. His essays have appeared in *Iris, Post Script, Cinema Journal, Film History,* and elsewhere. He is currently working on a book on historical documentaries. Eitzen is also an award-winning documentary filmmaker.

SUSAN FEAGIN is Associate Professor of Philosophy at the University of Missouri–Kansas City. She is the author of *Reading with Feeling: The Aesthetics of Appreciation* (Ithaca, N.Y.: Cornell University Press, 1996) and has published many articles on aesthetics.

CYNTHIA FREELAND is Associate Professor of Philosophy and Director of Womens Studies at the University of Houston. She has published several essays on aesthetics and film, and is the coeditor of *Film and Philosophy* (New York: Routlege, 1995).

NICO H. FRIJDA is Emeritus Professor of Experimental and Theoretical Psychology at the University of Amsterdam. Author of *The Emotions* (Cambridge: Cambridge University Press, 1986), his major field of interest over the last 15 years is the psychology of emotion.

BERYS GAUT, who teaches at the University of St. Andrews, Scotland, earned his doctorate in philosophy from Princeton University. He has published articles on general aesthetics, film, ethics, and political philosophy in journals such as the *Journal of Aesthetics and Art Criticism, British Journal of Aes-*

thetics, Film and Philosophy, Philosophical Papers, and *Forum for Modern Language Studies.*

TORBEN GRODAL is Professor of Film Studies at the University of Copenhagen. Among his books is *Moving Pictures: A New Theory of Film Genres, Feelings, and Cognition* (Oxford: Clarendon Press, 1997).

CARL PLANTINGA is Associate Professor of Film at Hollins University. He is the author of *Rhetoric and Representation in Nonfiction Film* (Cambridge: Cambridge University Press, 1997), and has published on film and psychology, nonfiction film, and film theory.

GREG M. SMITH is Assistant Professor of Communication Studies at Carlow College in Pittsburgh. His work has appeared in *Cinema Journal, Journal of Film and Video,* and other publications. He completed his Ph.D. in film studies at the University of Wisconsin–Madison with a dissertation on emotion and film narrative. His anthology, *On a Silver Platter: CD-ROMs and the Promises of a New Technology,* is forthcoming from New York University Press.

JEFF SMITH teaches film at New York University. He has published articles in *Cinema Journal, The Velvet Light Trap,* and in *Post-Theory: Reconstructing Film Studies.* He completed his Ph.D. in film studies at the University of Wisconsin–Madison with a dissertation on Hollywood film music of the 1960s. He is the author of *The Sounds of Commerce: Marketing Popular Film Music* (New York: Columbia University Press, 1998).

MURRAY SMITH is Lecturer in Film Studies at the University of Kent at Canterbury (U.K.). He is author of *Engaging Characters: Fiction, Emotion, and the Cinema* (Oxford: Clarendon Press, 1995), and coeditor (with Richard Allen) of *Film Theory and Philosophy* (Oxford University Press, 1997).

ED S. H. TAN teaches film and television studies at the Free University in Amsterdam and is author of *Emotion and the Structure of Narrative Film* (Hillsdale, N.J.: Erlbaum, 1995).

INDEX

Library of Congress Cataloging-in-Publication Data

Passionate views : film cognition and emotion / edited by Carl Plantinga and Greg M.
Smith
    p. cm.
    Includes bibliographical references and index.
    ISBN 0-8018-6010-5 (alk. paper). — ISBN 0-8018-6011-3 (pbk. : alk. paper)
    1. Motion picture audiences—Psychology.   2. Motion pictures—Psychological
aspects.   I. Plantinga, Carl R.   II. Smith, Greg M., 1962–   .
PN1995.9.A8P47   1999
791.43'01'9—dc21   98-43308   CIP